Studies in the History of Medieval Religion
VOLUME XXXVII

WAR AND THE MAKING OF MEDIEVAL MONASTIC CULTURE

Studies in the History of Medieval Religion

ISSN 0955–2480

Founding Editor
Christopher Harper-Bill

Series Editor
Frances Andrews

Previously published titles in the series
are listed at the back of this volume

WAR AND THE MAKING OF MEDIEVAL MONASTIC CULTURE

KATHERINE ALLEN SMITH

THE BOYDELL PRESS

© Katherine Allen Smith 2011

All Rights Reserved. Except as permitted under current legislation no part of this work may be photocopied, stored in a retrieval system, published, performed in public, adapted, broadcast, transmitted, recorded or reproduced in any form or by any means, without the prior permission of the copyright owner

The right of Katherine Allen Smith to be identified as the author of this work has been asserted in accordance with sections 77 and 78 of the Copyright, Designs and Patents Act 1988

First published 2011
The Boydell Press, Woodbridge
Reprinted in paperback 2013

ISBN 978 1 84383 616 2 hardback
ISBN 978 1 84383 867 8 paperback

Transferred to digital printing

The Boydell Press is an imprint of Boydell & Brewer Ltd
PO Box 9, Woodbridge, Suffolk IP12 3DF, UK
and of Boydell & Brewer Inc.
668 Mt Hope Avenue, Rochester, NY 14620–2731, USA
website: www.boydellandbrewer.com

The publisher has no responsibility for the continued existence or accuracy of URLs for external or third-party internet websites referred to in this book, and does not guarantee that any content on such websites is, or will remain, accurate or appropriate.

A CIP catalogue record for this book is available from the British Library

This publication is printed on acid-free paper

Contents

Acknowledgments		vii
List of Abbreviations		ix
Introduction		1
1	Encountering War in the Scriptures and Liturgy	9
2	Monks and Warriors: Negotiating Boundaries	39
3	Spiritual Warfare: The History of an Idea to c.1200	71
4	Martial Imagery in Monastic Texts	112
5	Warriors as Spiritual Exemplars	156
Conclusion		197
Appendix: *The Loricati*, c.1050–1250		201
Bibliography		203
Index		229

Dedicated to the memory of
Mary Martin McLaughlin (1919–2006)
beloved teacher and friend

Acknowledgments

Looking back from the end of my first decade of teaching, I can appreciate how lucky I have been to find excellent teachers at every stage of my training. Though neither is a teacher by trade, my parents have fostered my interest in the past for as long as I can remember. Ben Kohl and Karen Robertson introduced me to the joys of research and set me on the path to becoming a medievalist during my sophomore year of college. As a graduate student, I was fortunate to have the chance to study paleography with and serve as teaching assistant to the awe-inspiring Robert Raymo, and am sorry he did not live to see the publication of this book. The steady encouragement of Jill Claster, a former teacher who has become a dear friend, helped me over the hurdles of qualifying exams, dissertation defense, job-hunting, and pedagogical challenges. For the past decade my husband Michael has helped me translate Middle English, work through conceptual and technical problems, and always given in to my pleas of 'just one more church' on our travels.

Two mentors taught me to listen to the voices of the past with a sympathetic ear. Although this study did not begin as a dissertation, it is no less indebted to the mentorship of my graduate advisor, Penny Johnson, whose influence has strongly shaped my approach to scholarship and teaching. My decade-long friendship with the late Mary Martin McLaughlin, whom I first met while working on my undergraduate thesis on medieval nuns, meant more to me than I can say. Her well-loved books have kept me company throughout these past three years of writing, and I hope she would not mind my offering this book to her in return.

Many scholars served as sounding-boards and shared their expertise with me, often taking time away from their own research to do so. Scott Wells read the entire manuscript and offered invaluable suggestions for improvement. Conversations with Susan Wade helped me think through various aspects of monastic identity. I am grateful to the following colleagues who offered advice and encouragement and shared their unpublished work: Greta Austin, Karen Cheatham, Michael Curley, Denise Despres, Sandy Evans, Kriszta Kotsis, Matt Kuefler, Jennifer Thibodeaux, Tony Perron, Jane Tibbets Schulenburg, and David Tinsley. The anonymous reader for Boydell & Brewer offered detailed and insightful feedback. Any errors of fact or judgment that remain are entirely my own responsibility.

Finally, thanks are due to my colleagues and students at the University of Puget Sound, my academic home of the past five years. I count myself lucky to have supportive and congenial colleagues in the History Department and across the university, along with students who, to my delight, seem to take it for granted that the distant past is fascinating and worth studying. Humanities librarian Peggy Burge helped me navigate the Northwest Consortium, and the staff of the Collins Library Interlibrary Loan Office cheerfully tracked down many obscure titles. I also wish to thank the University for awarding me a Mellon Junior Sabbatical Fellowship, which, along with a grant from the Graves Foundation, allowed me to bring this project to completion.

An earlier version of the last subsection of Chapter 5 was previously published as 'Saints in Shining Armor: Martial Asceticism and Masculine Models of Sanctity, ca. 1050–1250' in *Speculum: A Journal of Medieval Studies* 83, no. 3 (July 2008): 572–602. I gratefully acknowledge the permission of the journal's editors to reprint this material.

Abbreviations

AASS	*Acta sanctorum quotquot toto orbe coluntur*. Ed. J. Bollandus et al. 68 vols. Antwerp, 1643–1894
BHL	*Bibliotheca hagiographica latina antiquae et mediae aetatis*. 2 vols. Subsidia hagiographica 6. Brussels, 1898–1901. *Supplement*, Subsidia Hagiographica 70. Brussels, 1986
CCSL	Corpus christianorum, series latina. Turnhout, 1947–
CF	Cistercian Fathers Series. Kalamazoo, MI, 1970–
CS	Cistercian Studies Series. Kalamazoo, MI, 1969–
FC	Fathers of the Church Series. Washington, D.C., 1947–
Mansi	*Sacrorum conciliorum nova et amplissima collectio*. Ed. Giovanni Domenico Mansi and Philippe Labbé. 31 vols. Florence, 1759–98; repr. Graz: Akademische Druck- und Verlagsanstalt, 1960–1
MGH SS	*MGH Scriptores in folio et quarto*. Ed. G.H. Pertz et al. Hanover and Leipzig, 1826–
MGH SS RerMerov	*MGH Scriptorum Rerum Merovingicarum*. Ed. Bruno Krusch et al. 7 vols. Hanover, 1885–1920
PL	*Patrologia cursus completus: series latina*. Ed. J.-P. Migne. 221 vols. Paris, 1841–64
RB	*RB 1980: The Rule of Benedict in Latin and English with Notes*. Ed. and trans. Timothy Fry et al. Collegeville, MN, 1981
RHC Occ	*Recueil des Historiens des Croisades, Historiens occidentaux*. Ed. Académie des Inscriptions et Belles Lettres. 5 vols. Paris, 1841–1906
SBO	*Sancti Bernardi Opera*. Ed. Jean Leclercq, H.-M. Rochais, and C.H. Talbot. 8 vols. Rome, 1957–77
SC	Sources chrétiennes. Paris, 1943–

Introduction

Among the sculpted capitals of the Romanesque church of Notre-Dame in Beaugency (dép. Loiret) modern visitors may notice a pair of human figures engaged in a curious and striking scene of combat. In the midst of a forest of columns topped with acanthus leaves and vines in which few human faces are visible, at precisely the point where the nave meets the choir, a fight to the death has just ended. The unlikely victor, an unarmed, unarmored young man, stands to the left, his slingshot still dangling from his right hand, a stone he will not now need gripped in his left. His opponent, whose huge size would prevent him from standing upright within the capital even if he should miraculously recover, is frozen in the act of falling to the ground, felled by a single fatal blow from the young man's sling. This is, of course, David and Goliath.

While the medieval sculptor included a number of details found in the biblical narrative (1 Sam. 17), he also followed contemporary convention in representing Goliath as a knight; with his conical helmet, mailed hauberk, and kite-shaped shield, the fallen giant is accoutered for battle in the latest twelfth-century style.[1] Like its iconography, the capital's meaning can be interpreted in light of both the biblical text upon which it is based and the social and spiritual world of its makers. In the Hebrew Bible, the lesson to be learned from David's victory over Goliath is announced by the young hero himself: 'You come to me with a sword, and with a spear, and with a shield,' he taunts the Philistine warrior, 'but I come to you in the name of the Lord of hosts, the God of the armies of Israel, which you have defied.' 'The Lord saves not with sword and spear,' the text continues, 'for it is His battle, and He will deliver you into our hands' (1 Sam. 17:45, 47). Medieval monastic exegetes saw in these passages a timeless warning about the dangers of pride and an exhortation to humility, but also a promise that the Church would triumph over its arrogant and violent enemies in their own day. In such a reading, David's triumph became the victory of virtue over vice, the spirit over the flesh, the holy man over the devil. If Goliath was a bad knight, David was a good monk.

Today a parish church, when the church of Notre-Dame was built in the 1140s to serve the Augustinian canons of Beaugency it stood (as it does now) in the shadow of the great donjon of the powerful lords of Beaugency, its western façade just a stone's throw from the fortress' towering stone walls.[2] Maintaining

---

[1] For more examples, see J.J.G. Alexander, 'Ideological Representation of Military Combat in Anglo-Norman Art,' *Anglo-Norman Studies* 15 (1992), 1–24.

[2] The donjon has been dated by dendrochronology to the first third of the eleventh century. At the time the church of Notre-Dame was built, such close proximity of castles and religious communities was hardly unusual, as shown by Jane Martindale, 'Monasteries and Castles: The Priories of St-Florent de Saumur in England after 1066,' in *England*

good relations with the local castellans was imperative for the canons, as their community was enclosed by the castle's (no longer extant) outer curtain wall.[3] The canons had replaced an earlier monastic community about which little is known, apart from the fact that its members feuded with the lords of Beaugency in the late 1070s, after the seigneur Lancelin II built over part of the monks' cemetery without permission.[4] Although the dispute had been resolved by 1081, there may have been lingering ill will, as these religious were dispossessed at the instigation of Lancelin's son Ralph, who refounded the house as an Augustinian community soon after his return from the First Crusade.[5] Though they greatly benefited from the generosity of Ralph and his heirs, the canons lived, literally, in the shadow of the castle of Beaugency and depended upon its masters for protection – a reality underscored by Ralph himself when he laid his sword-belt upon the church's altar to signify his guardianship of the community.[6]

Given this historical background, it is tempting to see in the David and Goliath capital an allegory of the relationship between the two powers, the local noble house and the religious community. Positioned at the boundary between the canons' choir and the public areas of the church where they could be easily seen by both clergy and lay worshippers, the sculpted figures broadcast a message about the proper relationship between the chapter of Notre-Dame and the lords of Beaugency, and, in a larger sense, that between those who relied on their own strength and those who trusted in divine support. Indeed, it is hard to escape the conclusion that the canons selected the capital's location and subject matter with the aim of preaching to the Goliaths of the twelfth century.

But the purpose of this study is not to speculate about how such a message might have been received by those outside the monastic community, but rather to discover what it reveals about how those within it defined their own purpose. A medieval canon of Beaugency would have been as likely to read the David and Goliath capital as emblematic of the ongoing spiritual battle within himself as he was to interpret it in light of clerical–knightly conflicts staged in the wider world. For monastic thinkers in the Central Middle Ages (c.950–1200), war was not simply a worldly evil but a path to self-knowledge and even a way of imitating Christ; encountered at every turn in the texts and rituals that shaped

---

in the Eleventh Century: Proceedings of the 1990 Harlaxton Symposium, ed. Carola Hicks (Stamford, 1992), 135–56.

[3] For a discussion of the church's construction and relations between the chapter and the seigneurial house at this time, see Eliane Vergnolle, 'La collégiale Notre-Dame de Beaugency: les campagnes romanes,' Bulletin monumental 165 (2007), 71–90, 131–3.

[4] The building in question was a church, Saint-Sépulchre, which Lancelin had given into the keeping of the powerful Benedictine abbey of La Trinité, Vendôme. A charter of 1081 detailing this dispute is preserved in the cartulary of La Trinité; Cartulaire de l'abbaye cardinale de la Trinité de Vendôme, 5 vols, ed. Charles Métais (Paris, 1893–1904), 2: 3–7 (no. 301).

[5] Ralph's role in the reform of the house is discussed in light of the charter evidence by G. Vignat, Cartulaire de l'abbaye de Notre-Dame de Beaugency, Mémoires de la Société archéologique et historique de l'Orléanais 16 (Orléans, 1887), xlviii–xlix. The foundation charter of the abbey is ibid., 130–3 (no. 113).

[6] Cartulaire de Beaugency, ed. Vignat, 135 (no. 115).

life in the monastery, war was among the most useful tools in the monk's meditative arsenal, and its language and symbolism were intimately woven into his identity. The Goliaths of the twelfth century were not just violent laymen, but the vices that raged within the souls of the cloistered, formidable enemies who could only be subdued by the inner warrior, the David, of each embattled monk. But David and Goliath were just the tip of the rhetorical iceberg; monastic writers employed a wide range of military analogies to describe every stage of their spiritual development and all of the activities central to their calling, and to create a specialized martial language which they used mainly in speaking or writing to one another. Surveying the works of the most prominent – and most intensively studied – writers of this period, it is difficult to find individuals who did *not* use such language. But despite (or, perhaps, because of) the frequency with which martial imagery crops up in monastic texts, this material has received little attention from modern scholars, who have tended to dismiss it as formulaic or ignore it altogether.

This imagery deserves closer study, because it has much to tell us about how professed religious saw themselves, as well as how they negotiated their relationship with the world outside the monastery. An exploration of how monastic writers used the language of war to describe their calling sheds new light on several relationships which have long been of interest to scholars of medieval Europe: the medieval Christian rapport with the past, as described in the Scriptures and patristic texts; the ties between the monastery and secular society, particularly the world of the warrior aristocracy (from which most members of religious orders were recruited in this period); and the role of the Church in defining the moral parameters of warfare and the emerging ideal of Christian knighthood. In this sense, this is a study of the frequent, often surprising, intersections between the secular and the sacred, or 'the intimate links between the martial and the spiritual' which, as Abigail Wheatley has asserted, 'have often been obscured by modern historical perspectives.'[7]

It is a basic premise of this study that medieval religious did not live, indeed, could not live, exclusively in the realm of the sacred, wholly isolated from the secular world and its concerns. While recent scholarship has revealed the ways in which the institutional Church influenced the spirituality of arms-bearers,[8] the other side of this relationship, namely the penetration of the outside world into the spiritual life of the cloister, has hitherto attracted much less attention. If arms-bearers' relationships with religious institutions shaped their personal conceptions of sin, penance, and salvation, these contacts left their imprint on

---

[7] Abigail Wheatley, *The Idea of the Castle in Medieval England* (York, 2004), 89.
[8] A number of recent studies have emphasized the ongoing dialogue between clerical and lay spirituality in medieval Europe: for example, Sarah Hamilton, *The Practice of Penance, 900–1050* (Woodbridge, 2001), and William J. Purkis, *Crusading Spirituality in the Holy Land and Iberia, c.1095–c.1187* (Woodbridge, 2008). The extent to which relations with monastic communities shaped the piety of arms-bearers has been demonstrated particularly convincingly by Marcus Bull in his *Knightly Piety and the Lay Response to the First Crusade: The Limousin and Gascony, c.970–c.1130* (Oxford, 1993).

those living within the monastery as well. While it has been established that religious communities were deeply concerned with the promotion of peace and settlement of disputes,[9] war was arguably as powerful an agent as peace in the making of monastic culture.

As the case of the canons of Beaugency illustrates, medieval monastic communities depended on the generosity and goodwill of those who lived by the sword, and accordingly needed to be mindful of the spiritual concerns of arms-bearers. But members of religious houses were also attentive to the martial concerns of lay patrons to a degree not generally recognized; monastic sources unapologetically attest that monks took an interest in the construction (and demolition) of castles, read manuals of military strategy, chronicled contemporary battles in bloody detail, and kept up with the latest technological developments in weaponry, armor, and siege machines. Above all, war provided a treasure trove of conceptual tools that could be used to gain a better understanding of the monastic ideal, and of the Christian condition more generally. A medieval Christian who abandoned the world for the cloister would have soon found that their new life was as deeply informed by warfare, albeit of a better, spiritual sort, as was the existence of any worldly knight. To argue that monks defined themselves solely in opposition to warriors is an oversimplification that overlooks what is, to my mind, one of the most fascinating aspects of monastic spirituality; monks *were* warriors, whose success in spiritual battle required the possession of many of the same virtues embraced by contemporary knights (e.g., loyalty, bravery, and physical endurance), but also the rejection of vices associated with the latter group – anger, vanity, and above all, pride.

A few words about the scope of the study are in order. First, while some of my examples concern communities of religious women or female solitaries, this is primarily a study of writings by, for, and about men: monks, regular canons, hermits, and, to a lesser extent, bishops (many of whom came from monastic backgrounds). This emphasis on men should not be taken to imply that religious women had no interest in war, conceptually or otherwise; some nuns, canonesses, and female recluses described their spiritual vocation in martial terms, and were sometimes described by male contemporaries as spiritual warriors. But I have chosen to focus primarily on male religious because during the Central Middle Ages war was literally brought home to monastic men in ways it was not for their female counterparts. From the eleventh century onwards changing patterns of recruitment to men's religious communities brought adult warriors into the cloister in large and unprecedented numbers, forcing monastic men to think in new, not necessarily polarizing, ways about the identities of the knight

---

[9] As discussed in Chapter 2, the figures of the peaceful cleric and the violent lay warrior are commonplaces of ecclesiastical rhetoric in this period, though in reality some warrior elites supported and promoted peace and monastic communities were often embroiled in violent disputes involving armed force. For the rhetoric of war and peace in this period, see Constance Brittain Bouchard, *'Every Valley Shall Be Exalted': The Discourse of Opposites in Twelfth-Century Thought* (Ithaca, NY, 2005), chapter 4.

and the monk.¹⁰ While contemporary nuns were necessarily obliged to negotiate relationships with lay arms-bearers, as a group they were not confronted with the problem of integrating former warriors into their communities; nor could individual nuns have had the personal experience of military training and combat that a significant number of monks undoubtedly possessed by c.1100. Thus, in the chapters that follow, I have tried to offer answers to the question of why military matters and metaphors appealed so strongly to religious men, and have, for the most part, left the equally interesting and important question of how war shaped the experiences and identities of their female counterparts for future scholars to pursue.

Geographically speaking, the bulk of the evidence considered in the following chapters comes from northern France and England, with occasional detours to Italy, Languedoc, and the Empire. In recognition of the powerful influence of patristic and Carolingian writers on later authors, this book takes a long view of warfare in monastic texts, but its main focus is on the eleventh and twelfth centuries, a period in which the identities of the monk and the lay warrior were in a state of flux. These conceptual fluctuations can be linked to some of the major spiritual and political developments of this era: transformations of the monastic ideal by reformers and founders of new orders; the rethinking of the role of warrior elites in the economy of salvation; church leaders' attempts to regulate the waging of war within Christendom; and the rise of the crusading movement. In their efforts to make the identities of 'those who fought' and 'those who prayed' sharply distinct, reformers inadvertently opened up a grey area between monks and knights, inhabited by hybrid figures who straddled both identities: lay crusaders and members of the new military orders whose armed combat was understood to have physical *and* spiritual dimensions; warriors-turned-monks who were venerated as saints; and holy ascetics who donned real armor to battle the devil and his minions. Some monastic writers viewed these denizens of the grey area between the 'orders' as monstrous, while others held them up to their fellow religious as spiritual exemplars. Above all, in their struggles to fit these newcomers into their vision of the world's spiritual hierarchy, monastic homilists and hagiographers reaffirmed the longstanding identification of monasticism with the highest form of combat.

This study opens with two chapters devoted to the textual and experiential sources of the military imagery found in medieval monastic texts. Chapter 1 explores the significance of war in the Scriptures and the complex exegetical and liturgical traditions that grew up around them during the first millennium. The Hebrew Bible's narratives of ancient military campaigns and the Pauline concept of the spiritual warrior exercised a particularly strong influence on later monastic exegetes, so that medieval monks came to see themselves as heirs to both the warriors of ancient Israel and the Pauline soldier who fought the forces of evil with spiritual arms. Chapter 2 examines how the culture of lay arms-bearers intersected with that of the cloister through patronage, conver-

---

10 These changing recruitment practices are discussed in detail in Chapter 2.

sion, and conflict during the Central Middle Ages. Particular attention is paid to changing patterns of monastic recruitment, which brought large numbers of repentant warriors into monasteries beginning in the eleventh century, and to the practical and conceptual challenges this shift presented for the religious communities these men joined (and for converts themselves). Taken together, these first two chapters foreground a major theme of this book, namely that the study of sacred texts equipped monastic writers with hermeneutic tools with which to 'read' the world around them, even as lived experience simultaneously informed the textual products of the cloister.

Chapter 3 surveys the history of spiritual warfare and the related concept of the *miles Christi* ('soldier of Christ') in the Christian tradition from Late Antiquity through the twelfth century, showing how membership in the *militia Christi* ('soldiery of Christ')[11] became central to monastic self-definition in the early Middle Ages, and noting the subsequent expansion of this spiritual army to include pious knights, crusaders, and members of the military orders, in particular the Templars. Tracing this discourse of spiritual warfare from its earliest origins through the era of the early Crusades clarifies the importance of the *miles Christi* ideal in shaping the identities of martyrs, desert ascetics, monks, and finally lay participants in the holy wars of the medieval Church, and situates these groups within a single, millennium-long spiritual genealogy.

The last two chapters explore the various uses of warfare and warriors in the rich Latin homiletic and hagiographical traditions of the eleventh and twelfth centuries. Monastic writers' uses of martial rhetoric is the subject of Chapter 4, which identifies common allegories – including single combat, pitched battles, and siege imagery – in letters and sermons written for consumption in the cloister, and links these to ongoing debates about the monastic ideal, as well as to contemporary developments in the military sphere which monks followed with fervent interest. This survey shows that writers from all the major religious orders spoke the language of war with a confidence that belied their official status as men of peace, and developed a distinctive form of meditation intended to cultivate practitioners' monastic virtues through the constant practice of spiritual battle.

Finally, Chapter 5 affirms that warriors could serve as spiritual exemplars for members of religious communities, reversing the traditional spiritual hierarchy of the medieval Church in which clerics were meant to instruct lay arms-bearers in matters of faith. While monks promoted the cults of ancient military martyrs, during the eleventh and twelfth centuries two new types of warrior-saints rose to prominence in monastic hagiography. The first of these was the pious arms-bearer who, after years of worldly military service (often including crusading), heeded a call to join the army of Christ by taking monastic vows; the second was the *loricatus*, an ascetic who engaged in spiritual battle wearing actual armor, either his own or that of a knightly patron. The *vitae* of these holy

---

[11] This phrase is used in several ways by medieval authors; it may also refer to the 'warfare of Christ,' the spiritual combat waged by *milites Christi* against evil forces.

warriors acknowledged the new reality of knightly conversion as a driving force in monastic culture, even as they reaffirmed the monk's ancient claim to the title of *miles Christi*.

Modern narratives of medieval monastic history have generally omitted discussions of war, as a subject properly left to military historians and scholars of the lay aristocracy.[12] The central argument of this study, that monastic identity was negotiated through constant confrontations (both real and imagined) with war and warriors, adds to a growing body of scholarship undermining one of the central divisions historians have long emphasized in their reconstruction of the medieval past: the ideological separation of peace-loving religious communities from bloodthirsty knights, of 'those who prayed' from 'those who fought.' The recognition of spiritual warfare as a major force in the creation of monastic culture, and an important conceptual tool for negotiating the Church's relationship with secular arms-bearers, promises to help us better understand the relationship between the cloister and the world, and ultimately religion and violence, in an era which saw the rise of Christian knighthood and new forms of Church-sanctioned holy war.

---

[12] Introductory surveys of medieval monasticism have tended to omit considerations of religious communities' involvement in warfare, and to overlook the significance of the *miles Christi* ideal within monastic spirituality. Representative of this approach are the otherwise excellent studies of Christopher Brooke, *The Age of the Cloister* (Mahwah, NJ, 2003); and Clifford H. Lawrence, *Medieval Monasticism: Forms of Religious Life in Western Europe in the Middle Ages* (New York, 1984). There have, of course, been numerous studies of the relationship between violence and the medieval Church more generally, most of which have focused on the reforming papacy and its role in promoting holy war. Foundational works are Carl Erdmann, *The Origin of the Idea of Crusade* (first pub. in 1935 as *Die Enstehung des Kreuzzugsgedankens*), trans. Marshall W. Baldwin and Walter Goffart (Princeton, 1977); P. Alphandéry, *La Chrétienté et l'idée de la croisade* (Paris, 1954); and Étienne Delaruelle, *L'Idée de la croisade au Moyen Age* (Turin, 1980). Important more recent studies include: H.E.J. Cowdrey, *The Crusades and Latin Monasticism, 11th–12th Centuries* (Aldershot, 1999); and the essays collected in *The Peace of God: Social Violence and Religious Response in France Around 1000*, ed. Thomas F. Head and Richard Landes (Ithaca, NY, 1992).

1

Encountering War in the Scriptures and Liturgy

Warfare seeped into monastic life through the sacred texts that formed the basis of monks' daily reading, chanted prayers, and private meditation. Those who sought escape from a violent world in the peaceful confines of the cloister were constantly confronted by images of battle. The Bible, above all, was a treasure trove of military history and martial imagery; indeed, its very words could surround the speaker with impenetrable armor, or become potent weapons with the power to curse and even kill.[1] Beginning in the earliest Christian centuries, generations of exegetes built up a thick carapace of interpretation around every mention of war, historical and allegorical, in the Old and New Testaments. This exegetical project, begun by patristic theologians and subsequently taken up by early medieval monks, tackled the historical wars of the ancient Israelites head-on, transforming them through an interpretive sleight of hand into prefigurations of the spiritual struggles of Christ and the apostles, and later martyrs and ascetics. The Gospels and Pauline Epistles supplied Christian writers with the concept of the 'soldier of Christ,' or *miles Christi*, as well as a symbolic vocabulary to describe his entirely spiritual form of warfare. By the Central Middle Ages, monastic understanding of Pauline spiritual combat had come to be mediated by a rich commentary tradition which encouraged the monk's self-identification with the *miles Christi* ideal. Along with the interactions between living warriors and monks considered in the next chapter, this body of scriptural and exegetical texts was the most important ingredient in the creation of a distinctly monastic ideal of spiritual combat.

While acknowledging the possibility that all Christians could take part in the battle for salvation, commentators from the patristic age onwards particularly associated spiritual combat with celibate ascetics and members of monastic communities. The status of the monk as an elite spiritual warrior was reinforced through the liturgical texts and rituals that lay at the heart of medieval monastic experience. In their daily singing of the Psalms, above all, monastic liturgists were confronted with violent descriptions of glorious victories and agonizing defeats. As heirs of a rich exegetical tradition emphasizing the Psalter's allegorical and mystical meanings, they were able to discern in these prayers lessons in

---

1   For examples, see Lester K. Little, *Benedictine Maledictions: Monastic Cursing in Romanesque France* (Ithaca, NY, 1993), 89, 188–90.

combat intended for the edification of *milites Christi* like themselves. Monastic self-identification with the tradition of spiritual warfare was reaffirmed daily in the celebration of the Divine Office, when members of religious communities equipped themselves with the '*arma Dei*' (Eph. 6:11) and waged battle against invisible evil spirits on behalf of themselves and their lay patrons. Though banned from bearing weapons and participating in actual warfare, monks' unquestioned prowess in liturgical combat gave them power over the evil forces that threatened all Christians and reinforced their self-perception as the defenders of Christendom.

Making sense of war in the Hebrew Bible

Saint Benedict's *Rule* recommended as bedtime reading for monks a selection from Cassian's *Conferences* or the *Lives of the Fathers*, 'or at any rate something else that will benefit the hearers, but not the Heptateuch or the Books of Kings, because it will not be good for those of weak understanding to hear these writings at that hour; they should be read at other times.'[2] What was there in these books of the Bible that the venerable abbot feared would keep weak-minded brothers awake into the wee hours? In a word, war. Epic battles and bloody conquests comprise much of the action in the historical books of the Hebrew Bible and, of those Benedict mentions here, the last two books of the Heptateuch (Joshua and Judges) and the books of Kings are particularly full of military action.[3] Nonetheless, these stories were an unavoidable part of sacred history and as such were to be read and contemplated, mined for lessons and metaphors, and celebrated in the Divine Office.

Over the course of the first millennium exegetical traditions were developed which helped monastic readers approach these ancient conflicts in the proper spirit. Benedict had by no means been the first to express these sorts of concerns; as early as the second century a sect called the Marcionites had called for the Old Testament to be excised from the biblical canon, citing (among other reasons) its frequent depictions of bloodshed, vengeance, and cruelty as proof that the Hebrew 'God of Hosts' was fundamentally distinct from the benevolent Christian God.[4] The Marcionites' attack on the canon forced early Christian writers to clarify their views on the warfare of the Old Testament. The theologian Origen (d.254) led the way, arguing for a non-literal, 'spiritual' interpreta-

---

[2] RB 42.3–4, p. 243. Nearly a century earlier, the Gothic bishop Wulfila had expressed similar concerns about the violence in Kings having an undesirable effect on the bellicose Goths; see D.H. Green, *The Millstätter Exodus: A Crusading Epic* (Cambridge, 1966), 209.

[3] A useful overview is Susan Niditch, *War in the Hebrew Bible: A Study of the Ethics of Violence* (New York, 1993).

[4] Harry Y. Gamble, 'Marcion and the "Canon",' in *The Cambridge History of Christianity, Vol. 1: Origins to Constantine*, ed. Margaret M. Mitchell and Frances M. Young (Cambridge, 2006), 487–528. For a closer look at Marcion's *Antitheses* (known to historians only through Tertullian's systematic rebuttal), see Adolf Harnack, *Marcion: The Gospel of the Alien God*, trans. John E. Steely and Lyle D. Bierma (Durham, NC, 1990).

tion of the wars of the Hebrews, in which the campaigns of the kings of Israel became prefigurations of the spiritual battles fought by Christ and the apostles.[5] 'If those carnal wars had not symbolized spiritual wars,' Origen wrote, 'I do not think that the books of the histories of the Jews would ever have been translated by the apostles to be read in the churches by the disciples of Christ, who came to teach peace.'[6] Gerard Caspary has written that Origen 'both rejects and intensifies the wars of the Old Testament'; while insisting, on the one hand, that Christians were morally obligated to condemn the Israelites' wars of conquest, he viewed the Incarnation as ushering in a new and unprecedented age of conflict which would be fought entirely on a spiritual plane.[7] As Henri de Lubac has shown, Origen's interpretation of warfare in the Hebrew Bible exerted a strong influence on monastic exegetes throughout the Middle Ages.[8] Despite the pall cast over his teachings in Late Antiquity, Latin translations of Origen's scriptural commentaries and homilies (made by Rufinus and Jerome, and sometimes attributed to the latter) continued to be widely available in monastic libraries, and directly inspired some of the greatest minds of the twelfth-century Renaissance.[9]

Origen's reading of war in the Scriptures was in keeping with his identification of four hierarchical 'senses' of Scripture: the historical (or literal), allegorical (or spiritual), tropological (or moral), and anagogical (or prophetic) meanings. Later monastic readers similarly sought to identify multiple levels of meaning, and to follow Augustine's injunction to look beyond what he termed the Bible's 'bodily images' – its historical narratives and anecdotes about worldly experiences – to the spiritual meaning concealed within.[10] The most influential early monastic writers adopted and expanded upon this view, developing a method of reading in which every word of the Scriptures was to be studied and savored. Cassian encouraged monks to practice spiritual reading of the Scriptures as a refuge from the 'turbulent thoughts' that assailed the minds of even the most

---

5   Adolf Harnack, *Militia Christi: die christliche Religion und der Soldatenstand in den ersten drei Jahrhunderten* (Tübingen, 1905), 46–8.
6   'Nisi bella ista carnalia figuram bellorum spiritualium gererent, nunquam, opinor, Iudaicarum historiarum libri discipulis Christi, qui venit pacem docere, legendi in ecclesiis fuissent ab apostolis traditi ....' Cited by Harnack, *Militia Christi*, 102.
7   Gerard E. Caspary, *Politics and Exegesis: Origen and the Two Swords* (Berkeley, CA, 1979), 18f.
8   Henri de Lubac, *Medieval Exegesis: The Four Senses of Scripture*, trans. Mark Sebanc (Grand Rapids, MI, 1998), 170 and 384n.; idem, *Histoire et esprit: l'intelligence de l'Écriture d'après Origène* (Paris, 1950), 186–90. For the articulation of the four- or three-fold senses of scripture by Ambrose, Augustine, and Jerome, see Robert E. McNally, *The Bible in the Early Middle Ages* (Westminster, MD, 1986), chapter 9.
9   Jean Leclercq, 'Origène au XIIe siècle,' *Irénikon* 24 (1951), 425–39.
10 Useful introductions to these exegetical principles are: Paul M. Blowers, 'Interpreting Scripture,' in *The Cambridge History of Christianity, Vol. 2: Constantine to c.600*, ed. Augustine Casiday and Frederick W. Norris (Cambridge, 2007), 618–36; Gillian R. Evans, *The Language and Logic of the Bible: The Earlier Middle Ages* (Cambridge, 1984), 1–5; de Lubac, *Medieval Exegesis*, chapter 1; and Beryl Smalley, *The Study of the Bible in the Middle Ages* (Notre Dame, IN, 1964), 8–26.

pious,[11] while Benedict's *Rule* integrated *lectio divina* into the monastic routine.[12] Benedict pointed to the moral as well as spiritual value of this sort of reading, insisting that every word of Scriptures, correctly (i.e., spiritually) interpreted, could aid in the cultivation of virtue.[13]

Working according to the principles of this exegetical tradition, patristic thinkers transformed the prophets and kings of the Hebrew Scriptures into exemplars of Christian virtues, and their medieval successors went a step further, making them over into honorary *milites Christi*. Military leaders like Moses, Joshua, and David were natural choices for ecclesiastical writers seeking virtuous archetypes with which to inspire lay warriors, and as spiritual warriors they became acceptable exemplars for monks as well. It is significant that Ambrose, in his *De Officiis*, recommended as a behavioral model for clerics the warrior David, as well as Abraham, Moses, Elisha, and Job.[14] Augustine had taught that the wars of Moses, Joshua, and their successors prefigured the Church's struggles against pagans and heretics in his own day, and Carolingian writers living in a new Christian empire surrounded by enemies of the faith adopted similar rhetoric.[15] But whereas Augustine had approved the participation of Christians in Roman military campaigns, and taught that a war carried out under the aegis of legitimate authority and with the right intentions could even be viewed as an act of love, later Carolingian writers living in an age of invasion and civil war were less willing to excuse the violence of laymen. The ninth-century abbot Hrabanus Maurus' identification of clerical *milites*, rather than contemporary warriors, as the true heirs of the warriors of the Old Testament is indicative of shifting ecclesiastical sentiments.[16]

Next to the warrior-king David, Job was the most celebrated spiritual warrior of the Old Testament.[17] This role was suggested in part by the proclamation of Job 7:1 that 'A man's life upon the earth is a warfare (*militia*),' and acceptance of Job as a model for monks may reflect the centrality of the concept of *militia* within the eremitic and especially the coenobitic ideals.[18] In his *Life of Antony*,

---

[11] Cassian, *Collationes*, 1.18, ed. and trans. Eugène Pichery as *Conférences*, 3 vols, SC 42, 54, 64 (Paris, 1955–9), 1: 99; *Conferences*, trans. Colm Luibheid (New York, 1985), 52. There are strong similarities here to the exegetical methods of Gregory the Great, though the extent of Gregory's familiarity with Cassian's work remains unclear; see Gillian R. Evans, 'Exegesis,' in *The Thought of Gregory the Great* (Cambridge, 1986), 80–95.

[12] RB 48.10–14, pp. 69–70.

[13] RB 73.2–6, p. 95.

[14] Ambrose, *De officiis*, 1.25.117–42; 1.36.179–204; 1.43.219–30, ed. Ivor J. Davidson (Oxford, 2001), 184–200, 220–36, 242–50.

[15] Frederick H. Russell, *The Just War in the Middle Ages* (Cambridge, 1975), 16–26; Janet L. Nelson, 'Violence in the Carolingian World and the Ritualization of Ninth-Century Warfare,' in *Violence and Society in the Early Medieval West*, ed. Guy Halsall (Woodbridge, 1998), 90–107 (at 91–2).

[16] Russell, *Just War*, 30–1.

[17] As described in Chapter 4 below, David's combat with Goliath became an influential model for the monk's battle against temptation and evil spirits.

[18] Cf. Job 10:17 and 14:14. For the history of exegesis of Job which emphasized the significance of *militia*, see Réginald Grégoire, 'Esegesi biblica e "*militia Christi*",' in *Militia Christi e*

for example, Athanasius took Job's sufferings as a model for the holy man's spiritual struggle.[19] Gregory the Great's hugely influential *Moralia in Job* read Job as a spiritual warrior battling the devil, and offered his forbearance as an example of how the righteous might use the virtue of patience as a weapon. Gregory, like many of his contemporaries, subscribed to the idea that clerics, and especially monks, were the heirs to this sort of warfare, and his *Moralia* became a major vehicle for the transmission of this idea to future generations.[20] Later exegetes identified Job's afflictions with the ascetic battle against temptation that was the particular province of monks and hermits, and even retroactively equipped him with the spiritual weapons and armor described in the Epistles.[21] As Odo of Cluny (d.942) wrote in his *Moralium in Job*, the *militia* of Job 7:1 was composed of those chosen few (*homines electi*), that is, monks, who had 'liberated themselves from the slavery of the worldly way of life.'[22] Bernard of Clairvaux, in the first of his eighty-six sermons on the Song of Songs, expressed this parallel even more explicitly when he wrote that the proclamation of Job 7:1 was fulfilled in the life of the monk, with its 'daily trials and combats arising from the flesh, the world and the devil.'[23]

In the Central Middle Ages, ecclesiastical thinkers continued the process of transforming the Israelites into *milites spirituales* and even *milites Christi*, whose

---

crociata nei secoli XI-XIII: Atti della undecima Settimana internazionale di studio, Mendola, 28 agosto–1 settembre 1989 (Milan, 1992), 21–45 (esp. 28–31 and 36–9). While *militia* could also denote 'service' of a non-military sort, Grégoire makes clear that medieval exegetes read this passage as a reference to Job's spiritual warfare. See Chapter 3 for a discussion of the concept of *militia* in early medieval monastic rules and hagiography.

[19] On spiritual warfare in the *Vita Antonii*, see Chapter 3. David Brakke has emphasized the importance of Job as a monastic exemplar for Athanasius in his *Demons and the Making of the Monk: Spiritual Combat in Early Christianity* (Cambridge, MA, 2006), 30.

[20] *Moralia in Job*, 32.11.14, 33.14.28, ed. Marcus Adriaen, 3 vols, CCSL 143–143B (Turnhout, 1979–85), 3: 1639–40, 1697–8. For this reading, see Carole Straw, *Gregory the Great: Perfection in Imperfection* (Berkeley, CA, 1988), 61–3; and Claude Dagens, *Saint Grégoire le Grand: culture et expérience chrétienne* (Paris, 1977), 100, 107, 187f.

[21] See, for example, the Carolingian abbot Paschasius Radbertus' *Expositio in evangelium Matthaei libri XII*, lib.3, CCCM 56, ed. Beda Paulus (Turnhout, 1984), 235–6; and the twelfth-century abbot and bishop Bruno of Asti's *Expositio in Job commentarius*, c.7, PL 164: 577.

[22] Odo of Cluny, *Epitome Moralium in Job libri XXXV*, 16.25, PL 133: 311–12: 'Cui tamen militiae electorum hominum numerus jungitur, qui per sublime mentis desiderium a terrenae conversationis servitute liberantur, de quibus per Paulum dicitur: "Nemo militans Deo, implicat se negotiis saecularibus (2 Tim. 2:4)".' Even without the scriptural reference (which would have called to medieval readers' minds the immediately preceding verse: 'labora sicut bonus miles Christi Iesu'), Odo's wording seems to refer to the monastic ideal.

[23] Bernard of Clairvaux, *Sermones super Cantica*, Sermon 1.9, in SBO 1: 6–7: 'Sed et in quotidianis exercitiis et bellis, quae nulla hora pie in Christo viventibus desunt a carne, a mundo, a diabolo, sicut militiam esse vitam hominis super terram incessanter experimini in vobismetipsis, quotidiana necesse est cantica pro assecutis victoriis innovari.' Trans. Kilian Walsh, *Bernard of Clairvaux on the Song of Songs 1*, CF 4 (Kalamazoo, MI, 1971), 5–6. For the Cistercian engagement with images of spiritual battle related to the Book of Job, see Conrad Rudolph, *Violence and Daily Life Reading, Art, and Polemics in the Cîteaux Moralia in Job* (Princeton, 1997), chapter 4.

divinely sanctioned campaigns against the Amalekites, Canaanites, and others they linked not only to the spiritual combat of the Christian life but also to evolving concepts of just war.[24] By the end of the first millennium, Anglo-Saxon churchmen were likening their rulers' struggles with pagan Norse invaders to the wars of ancient Israel against unbelieving tribes.[25] Discussions of just war by eleventh- and twelfth-century canonists and homilists also made ample use of Old Testament precedents.[26] On the eve of a Christian attack on the Muslim city of Mahdia in 1087, for instance, Bishop Benedict of Modena addressed members of the Norman–Italian force as worthy successors to the Israelites, urging them to emulate Joshua, David, and Judah Maccabee as they marched into battle.[27]

Considered from an exegetical perspective, the spiritualization of Old Testament warfare paved the way for a new understanding of the arms-bearer as holy warrior, physically struggling against unbelief even while he was inwardly engaged in spiritual warfare. In twelfth-century monastic chronicles of the First Crusade, history and scriptural exegesis merged, so that the expedition to Jerusalem became the fulfillment of Old Testament prophecies and the crusaders the heirs of ancient Israelite warriors.[28] In Guibert of Nogent's *Gesta Dei per Francos*, Pope Urban II tells would-be crusaders at Clermont, 'If the Maccabees once deserved the highest praise for piety because they fought for their rituals and their temple, then you too, O soldiers of Christ, deserve such praise, for taking up arms to defend the freedom of your country.'[29] In Fulcher of Chartres' account of the same speech, Urban again references Old Testament warfare: 'Under Jesus Christ, our Leader, may you struggle for your Jerusalem, in Christian battle line, most invincible line, even more successfully than did the sons of Jacob of old.'[30] For Robert of Reims, the members of the crusading army were present-day Israelites and their spiritual leader, the papal legate Adhemar of Le Puy, a second Moses, while a particularly fearsome Turkish warrior was Goliath reborn.[31] Just

---

[24] M.-D. Chenu, *Nature, Man and Society in the Twelfth Century: Essays on New Theological Perspectives in the Latin West*, ed. and trans. Jerome Taylor and Lester Little (Chicago, MI, 1968), 158.

[25] *A Pre-Conquest English Prayer Book*, ed. B.J. Muir, Henry Bradshaw Society 103 (Woodbridge, 1988), 21 and 29–30 (nos. 6 and 11); discussed by Jean Flori in *La guerre sainte: La formation de l'idée de croisade dans l'Occident chrétien* (Paris, 2001), 137.

[26] Russell, *Just War*, 68–73.

[27] H.E.J. Cowdrey, 'The Mahdia Campaign of 1087,' *English Historical Review* 92 (1977), 1–29 (at 25).

[28] Additional illusions to spiritual warfare in crusading chronicles are discussed in Chapter 3.

[29] *Gesta Dei per Francos*, 2.1, ed. R.B.C. Huygens, CCCM 127A (Turnhout, 1996), 112–13; trans. Robert Levine as *The Deeds of God through the Franks* (Woodbridge, 1997), 43. For similar comparisons between the crusaders and Maccabees, see the verse history of Gilo of Paris, *Historia vie Hierosolimitane*, ed. and trans. C.W. Grocock and J.E. Siberry (Oxford, 1997), 160–1; and Raymond of Aguilers, *Historia Francorum qui ceperunt Iherusalem*, c.6, RHC Occ. 3: 245; trans. John Hugh Hill and Laurita L. Hill (Philadelphia, PA, 1968), 35.

[30] *Fulcherius Carnotensis Historia Hierosolymitana*, 1.3.7, ed. Heinrich Hagenmeyer (Heidelberg, 1913), 136–7; trans. August C. Krey in *The First Crusade: The Accounts of Eye-Witnesses and Participants* (Gloucester, MA, 1958), 35.

[31] Robert of Reims, *Historia Iherosolimitana*, 1.4 (Adhemar/Moses), 2.16 (Israelites), 4.8 (Israelites), 4.20 (Goliath), and 6.12 (Israelites), in RHC Occ. 3: 731, 747, 779, 786–7;

as God had rewarded the Israelites' faith with victories and punished their sins with defeats, churchmen saw divine intervention as equally responsible for the crusaders' conquests of Antioch and Jerusalem and the reverses suffered after the failure of the crusade of 1101.[32] According to Raymond of Aguilers, a clerical chronicler and participant in the First Crusade, it was the God of the Israelites, 'strong and mighty in battle' (Ps. 23:8), who awarded the crusading army victory at Antioch in 1098.[33] But whereas Moses and his successors had 'fought carnal wars only to fill their bellies,' as Guibert of Nogent explained, the crusaders were more truly spiritual warriors in the sense that they fought to glorify God rather than themselves, and in so doing 'marked modern times with a display of divine power such as has never occurred in history.'[34]

As the exegetical transformation of Old Testament warriors into *milites Christi* continued during the eleventh and twelfth centuries, then, the kings and warriors of Israel became closely associated with the emerging ideals of Christian knighthood. The abbot Andreas of Strumi claimed in his *Vita Arialdi* (written c.1075) that Erlembald, the pious knight who led the Milanese Pataria, had considered converting to the monastic life until he was told by the holy deacon Arialdo that 'his merit with God would be greater if he were to remain a knight and fight on behalf of the Church, as Mathathias and his sons had formerly done.'[35] The monastic chronicler Orderic Vitalis (d.1142) reported that Gerald of Avranches, a chaplain at the court of Earl Hugh of Chester, preached sermons to the earl's men in which he combined 'tales of the combat of holy knights drawn from the Old Testament' with accounts of the exploits of Christian warrior-saints from the distant and not-so-distant past.[36] The association between contemporary *milites Christi* and ancient Israelite warriors may have been created in the minds of arms-bearers thanks to the preaching of men like Gerald as well as the composition of vernacular epics dramatizing Old Testament events. In one such work, the Millstätter Exodus, composed in the early twelfth century by an anonymous German cleric, the Israelites appear as pious Christian crusaders and their Egyptian enemies display all the qualities associated by twelfth-century churchmen with wicked knights: arrogance, vanity, lust for glory, and indifference to God's will.[37] But these texts attest, above all, to their clerical authors' fascination with

---

trans. Carol Sweetenham as *Robert the Monk's History of the First Crusade* (Burlington, VT, 2005), 83, 98, 125, 133, and 155.

32 Jonathan Riley-Smith, *The First Crusade and the Idea of Crusading* (Philadelphia, PA, 1991), 125 and 133.
33 *Historia Francorum*, c.5, ed. and trans. Hill and Hill, 40.
34 Quoted in Riley-Smith, *Idea of Crusading*, 141.
35 Andreas of Strumi, *Vita S. Arialdi*, c.15, MGH SS 30/ 2: 1047–75. The biblical reference is to 1 Macc. 2.
36 Orderic Vitalis, *The Ecclesiastical History*, 6 vols, ed. and trans. Marjorie Chibnall (Oxford, 1968–80), 3: 216–17: 'et de ueteri testamento nouisque Christianorum gestis imitanda sanctorum militum tirocinia ubertim coaceruabat.' Gerald goes on to name Saints Demetrius, George, Theodore, Sebastian, Maurice and the Theban Legion, along with the Carolingian warrior-turned-monk William of Gellone. For the cults of these and other warrior-saints in the medieval West, see Chapter 5.
37 Green, *Crusading Epic*, 97–9 and 104–5.

the historical wars of the Hebrew Bible, as well as their belief that exegesis could not only help them understand past conflicts but also help resolve the ethical questions surrounding contemporary warfare.

Making sense of war in the New Testament

Compared to the books of the Hebrew Bible, at first glance those of the New Testament seem hardly to mention war at all, except as the evil opposite of the peaceful state in which Christians should live with one another as well as with their enemies.[38] But startling, sometimes perplexing references to discord and bloodshed punctuate the New Testament.[39] While Christ warned Peter that 'all who take the sword shall perish by the sword (Matt. 26:52),' earlier in the same Gospel He enigmatically declared, 'Do not think that I came to bring peace upon the earth: I came not to bring peace, but the sword (Matt. 10:34).' Christ predicted the siege and bloody conquest of Jerusalem (Luke 19:41–44), and alluded to the coming end of the world as a series of violent, terrifying events (Matt. 24: 6, 40–41). The Book of Revelation predicted that the last days would be given over to a great war between the followers of the Lamb and the Beast in which mercy would be shown to none. Like their modern counterparts, medieval Christians puzzled over how to interpret such violent imagery in light of the Gospels' overarching message of peace.[40]

The evangelists cast soldiers as violent adversaries: Roman soldiers arrested Christ (Matt. 27:27; Luke 7:8), mocked and tortured him (Luke 23:36; John 19:1–2). But they also hint at the possible redemption of warriors, as when John the Baptist preached to the soldiers (Luke 3:14) and Christ praised the faith of the centurion (Matt. 8; Luke 7:1–10). The Gospels and Acts also describe acts of violence committed by Christ and his followers, among them the scourging of the money-changers in the Temple (Mark 11:15; John 2:14–15), Peter's attack on the priest's servant (John 18:10), and the blinding of Saul on the road to Damascus (Acts 9). An important exegetical precedent was set when Saint Augustine glossed these incidents as acts of love, akin to parents' correction of wayward children. Building on this interpretation, later apologists for the crusading movement would even argue that holy wars against Muslims were

---

[38] As in Matt. 5:39, Mark 9:4, and John 14:27. For convenient summaries of the themes of war and peace in the New Testament, upon which the following discussion draws, see Raymond Hobbs, 'The Language of Warfare in the New Testament,' in *Modelling Early Christianity: Social-Scientific Studies of the New Testament in its Context*, ed. Philip F. Esler (London and New York, 1995), 259–62; and Joseph F. Kelly, *The World of the Early Christians: Message of the Fathers of the Church* (Collegeville, MN, 1997), 160–2.

[39] On violent and martial imagery in the New Testament, see John Helgeland, *Christians and the Military: The Early Experience* (Philadelphia, PA, 1985), 10–20.

[40] For Carolingian exegetes' attempts sought to resolve the seeming contradiction between these two passages from the Gospel, see Mary Alberi, '"The Sword Which You Hold in Your Hand": Alcuin's Exegesis of the Two Swords and the Lay *Miles Christi*,' in *The Study of the Bible in the Carolingian Era*, ed. Celia Chazelle and Burton Van Name Edwards, Medieval Church Studies 3 (Turnhout, 2003), 117–31.

similarly waged out of love, not for non-Christian adversaries but rather for fellow Christians in the East.[41]

The patristic era also saw the development of the *Christus victor* motif, as clerical writers portrayed Christ as a triumphant warrior, the commander of celestial armies and the hero who vanquished death and the devil in the 'combat' of the crucifixion.[42] The opening stanza of the still-popular hymn *Pange lingua*, written by the sixth-century bishop Venantius Fortunatus, expresses this latter concept well: 'Sing of the glorious battle in which the sacrificed redeemer of the world conquered, and of his noble triumph on the cross.'[43] In the hands of Carolingian exegetes such as Paschasius Radbertus, Christ's temptation in the desert (Matt. 4:1–10) became a martial confrontation with the devil.[44] Scholars once held that such military imagery reflected missionaries' attempts to accommodate Christian notions of sacrifice and salvation to a pagan Germanic warrior ethic, but this thesis has increasingly been called into question.[45] While the *Christus victor* topos may well have appealed to bellicose Frankish and Saxon elites, it nonetheless had strong roots in the early Christian culture of the Roman Empire.

The same Late Antique exegetes who sought to transform the historical wars of the Hebrew Bible into spiritual struggles also allegorized the spiritual struggles of Christ, the apostles, and martyrs as combats. Origen described Saints Peter and Paul in martial terms that would be at home in later *Christus victor* poems like the *Heliand* or the *Dream of the Rood*. In his *Homilies on Numbers*, he likened the apostles' missionary efforts to the military exploits of Joshua, the great Hebrew warrior who was Moses' heir. Like Joshua, Peter and Paul were great war-heroes, Origen wrote:

> who fought so many battles, destroyed so many barbaric nations, cut down so many enemies, gained so much booty and so many triumphs, who come back with hands bloody from the killing of their enemies, whose feet are red from the blood and who washed their hands in the blood of sinners. For they killed in the morning all the sinners of this earth and exterminated their image from the city of God, for they killed and vanquished various nations of demons.[46]

---

[41] Jonathan Riley-Smith, 'Crusading as an Act of Love,' *History* 65 (1980), 177–92; repr. in *The Crusades: The Essential Readings*, ed. Thomas F. Madden (London, 2002), 32–50 (at 43–4). For a more recent assessment of Augustine's influence on later notions of just war, see Robert L. Holmes, 'St. Augustine and the Just War Theory,' in *The Augustinian Tradition*, ed. Gareth B. Matthews (Berkeley, CA, 1999), 323–44.

[42] Jean Leclercq, '"Militare Deo" dans la tradition patristique et monastique,' in *Militia Christi et crociata nei secoli XI–XIII. Atti della undecima settimana internazionale di studio*, 3–18 (at 8).

[43] *Analecta Hymnica Medii Aevi*, 55 vols, ed. Clemens Blume and Guido Maria Dreves (Leipzig, 1886–1922), 50: 70 (no. 66): 'Pange, lingua, gloriosi proelium certaminis / et super crucis trophaeo dic triumphum nobilem, / qualiter redemptor orbis immolatus vicerit.'

[44] Grégoire, 'Esegesi biblica e "Militia Christi",' 35.

[45] See the succinct remarks and bibliography in Rachel Fulton, *From Judgment to Passion: Devotion to Christ and the Virgin Mary, 800–1200* (New York, 2002), 29–31.

[46] Cited and trans. Horst Richter, '*Militia Dei*: A Central Concept for the Religious Ideas of the Early Crusades and the German *Rolandslied*,' in *Journeys Toward God: Pilgrimage*

At the very least, modern readers might find such a description of preaching and conversion somewhat odd, but the key to its meaning lies in Origen's exegetical theory: the Hebrew warriors of the Old Testament were typologically bound to the apostles and Christ himself, the heroes of the New Testament, and like them were to be understood as warriors only in allegorical or spiritual terms. Origen employed vivid martial rhetoric in order to convey his heroes' otherwise indescribable spiritual strength, their power over the forces of evil, their triumph over unbelief and death. In speaking of Paul's martyrdom in his *Dialogues*, Gregory the Great employed a similar rhetorical strategy: 'God's fearless warrior refused to be held back inside the walls [of Damascus] and sought the open field of battle.'[47] Here, as in many of the *passiones* of the martyrs, the language of war is used to transform what might otherwise seem to be a passive act – the submission of oneself to torture and death – into a dramatic martial confrontation.[48]

It was only natural for Christian writers to transform Paul into a warrior, since it was he who had supplied them with a symbolic vocabulary of spiritual combat.[49] For Paul the righteous life entailed endless struggles against interior weakness and external temptations, in which sin must be outrun, outflanked, and outfought. The Epistles consistently describe inner struggle in physical terms, applying military and athletic metaphors separately or in combination (as in 2 Tim. 4:7), and link these to the ascetic mortification of the flesh (1 Cor. 9:23–27). The Christian is a competitor in a race that can have only one victor (Phil. 2:16, 3:14; 1 Cor. 9:23–27) and in which salvation is the prize to be won. But above all the Christian is a warrior, in the language of the Vulgate a *miles Christi* (2 Tim. 2:3) encased in impenetrable spiritual armor, who fights 'the good fight of faith (1 Tim. 6:12).' The Epistles repeatedly allude to the arms and armor of the Christian warrior: they are made of light, the better to fight the works of darkness (Rom. 13:12); forged not from carnal matter but out of the power of God (1 Cor. 10:4); and mimic the equipment of contemporary Roman soldiers in their basic components if not their purpose (Eph. 6:11–17). Like members of a cohort, Christians are commanded to support their fellow-soldiers (*commilitones* in Phil. 2:25 and Philem. 2) whose sole loyalty is to their commander, Christ (2 Tim. 2:4).

---

and Crusade, ed. Barbara N. Sargent-Baur (Kalamazoo, MI, 1992), 107–126 (at 113–14). The Latin text reads: 'qui tamen pugnaverunt, tot gentes barbaras deleverunt, tot hostes prostraverunt, tanta spolia, tot triumphos ceperunt, qui cruentis manibus de caede hostium redeunt, quorum pes tinctus est in sanguine et manus suas laverunt in sanguine peccatorum. Interfecerunt quippe in matutinis omnes peccatores terrae, et imaginem eorum exterminaverunt de civitate Domini. Vicerunt quippe et peremerunt diversas daemonum gentes....' Origen, *Homiliae in Numeros*, in *Opera Omnia*, 25 vols, ed. C.H.E. Lommatzsch (Berlin, 1831–48), 10: 318–19.

[47] *Dialogues*, 2.3, 3 vols, ed. Adalbert de Vogüé and trans. Paul Antin, SC 251, 260, 265 (Paris, 1978–79), 2: 148–9: 'Fortis etenim praeliator Dei teneri intra claustra noluit, certaminis campum quaesiuit'; trans. Odo J. Zimmerman as *Gregory the Great: Dialogues*, FC 39 (Washington D.C., 1959), 65.

[48] On martial rhetoric in the passions of the martyrs, see Chapter 3.

[49] As Helgeland (*Christians and the Military*, 16) observes, none of the military metaphors in the New Testament is attributed to Jesus.

Modern scholars have shown that the Epistles' descriptions of inner struggle, as well as the military and athletic imagery in which these are cloaked, derive from Stoic philosophy, especially the work of Seneca and Philo, as well as the Hebrew Bible.[50] But they also reflect the specific concerns of the primitive Christian community, a community rooted in the values of the first-century Mediterranean world. Raymond Hobbs has argued that the Epistles' military metaphors, and their emphasis on the importance of honor, obedience to authority, and willingness to sacrifice oneself for a worthy cause, were carefully selected to construct a model of the virtuous Christian that referenced familiar heroic types – the champion athlete and the loyal soldier – admired by Roman Christians. The Christian was to be an athlete in the sense that he maintained perfect control over his body, and a soldier in the sense that his commitment to his chosen cause and community was absolute; he signaled his loyalty unto death by taking a solemn vow (the *sacramentum* of baptism, which borrowed the traditional Roman term for a military oath) and proudly displayed his battle scars as proof of his steadfastness.[51]

Patristic exegesis of the Epistles, as well as early Christian hagiography, expanded upon the Pauline theory of spiritual warfare and assured its role in the construction of a Christian (and particularly a clerical) identity in the medieval West.[52] In one of the earliest exegetical works to address the theme of spiritual warfare, Origen's commentary on Ephesians (which in turn directly inspired Jerome's work on the same text), we can see the model *miles Christi* taking shape.[53] Here the battleground of the spiritual warrior is this world in the present day, his main opponent the devil. Though the discussion is loaded with realistic martial details – the soldier of Christ takes his position in the front line of battle, wearing the breastplate specially forged for him by God, and crouches behind a shield buffeted by the enemy's flaming arrows – Origen and Jerome were clearly eager to impress the allegorical meaning of the passage on their readers.[54] Paul had begun the task of supplying symbolic values for each piece of the spiritual

---

[50] Victor C. Pfitzner, *Paul and the Agon Motif: Traditional Athletic Imagery in the Pauline Literature* (Leiden, 1967), esp. chapters 7 and 8. Antecedents in the Hebrew Bible include Isa. 59:17, 1 Macc. 3:3, and Wisd. 5:17–23. For non-biblical literary references in Paul, see Hobbs, 'Language of Warfare,' 263–4.

[51] Hobbs ('Language of Warfare,' 260–8) suggests such rhetoric may have appealed most directly to Christian men, since the role of the soldier (like that of the athlete) was traditionally masculine in Classical Antiquity.

[52] Useful overviews of patristic exegesis of the Epistles are Alexander Souter, *The Earliest Latin Commentaries on the Epistles of St. Paul* (Oxford, 1927); and Maurice Wiles, *The Divine Apostle: The Interpretation of St Paul's Epistles in the Early Church* (Cambridge, 1967). For a comprehensive list of early medieval commentaries on the Epistles, see McNally, *Bible in the Early Middle Ages*, 109–16.

[53] For a discussion of Jerome's dependence upon Origen, whose exegetical works are in many cases known only through Jerome, see the introduction to *The Commentaries of Origen and Jerome on St Paul's Epistle to the Ephesians*, ed. and trans. Ronald E. Heine (Oxford, 2002); and Margaret A. Schatkin, 'The Influence of Origen upon St. Jerome's Commentary on Galatians,' *Vigiliae Christianae* 24 (1970), 49–58.

[54] The relevant passages are in *Commentaries of Origen and Jerome*, ed. Heine, 261–8.

warrior's equipment, linking his breastplate to justice, his girdle to truth, his shield to faith, and his sword to the Spirit, and Origen and Jerome erected their more extended discussion of Christian virtue on this framework. Supplied with the armor of God, the virtuous man must 'be able to stand in the faith of the gospel and not fall in persecution'; his loins girded with truth, the *miles Christi* guards his chastity at all costs, a pursuit in which he is aided by the breastplate of truth, so he will not 'fall in desire or in regard to the passions.'[55] This association between spiritual warfare and chastity, which is not present in Ephesians 6 but builds on the concept of struggle against the flesh found throughout the Epistles, paved the way for spiritual warfare to become the particular province of a celibate elite within the Church.

While Augustine never composed a continuous commentary on the Epistles, his exegetical writings on Paul were available to later medieval readers via the excerpts from his sermons, tracts, and letters compiled by Eugippius, Bede, Hrabanus Maurus, and Florus of Lyon.[56] Much of the material on spiritual warfare in these *florilegia* comes from Augustine's tremendously influential *Enarrationes in Psalmos*, a work in which he drew a clear parallel between the imagery of divine warfare in the Psalms and the Christian agon of the Epistles.[57] But Augustine also examined the theme in sermons and treatises such as his *De agone Christiano*, an anti-Donatist treatise in which the Epistles' martial lessons become the basis for what Augustine called 'a rule of faith and precepts for right living.'[58] Written not for a clerical elite but for simple believers, the *De agone* nonetheless contains many precepts which later contributed to the making of a distinctly clerical ideal of spiritual warfare: the righteous Christian must conquer 'the inordinate love for things temporal,' subjugate his body, and renounce 'sinful pleasures.'[59] By the end of the patristic age there had emerged a clear image of the *miles Christi* as a master of self-control, ideally vowed to chastity, who renounced worldly wealth and rank in the expectation of heavenly rewards.[60] While these qualities all have their basis in the Epistles, in the context of Late Antique Christianity such a model was closely identified with two groups: the martyrs, who by the mid fourth century had passed into legend, and their spiritual heirs, monks.[61]

---

[55] *Commentaries of Origen and Jerome*, ed. Heine, 262–4.

[56] See the introduction to Bede's *Excerpts from the Works of Saint Augustine on the Letters of the Blessed Apostle Paul*, trans. David Hurst, CS 183 (Kalamazoo, MI, 1999), 8–10; and P.-I. Fransen, 'D'Eugippius à Bède le Vénérable: à propos de leurs florilèges Augustiniens,' *Revue Bénédictine* 97 (1987), 187–94.

[57] See, for example, the material excerpted by Bede from the *Enarrationes* on Ps. 30, 34, and 77; *Excerpts from the Works of Saint Augustine*, trans. Hurst, 249–50.

[58] For the *De agone Christiano*, see N. Joseph Torchia, '*De agone Christiano*,' in *Augustine Through the Ages: An Encyclopedia*, ed. Allan Fitzgerald and John C. Cavadini (Grand Rapids, MI, 1999), 15–16.

[59] *De agone Christiano*, c. 2 and 6, PL 40: 291–2, 294; trans. Robert P. Russell in *Saint Augustine: Christian Instruction…*, FC 2 (Washington D.C., 1947), 317 and 321–2.

[60] Leclercq, '"Militare Deo".'

[61] Edward E. Malone, *The Monk and the Martyr: The Monk as Successor of the Martyr* (Washington D.C., 1950).

Later monastic commentators on Paul relied heavily on the interpretations of Origen, Jerome, and Augustine.[62] Insofar as we can speak of a distinctive monastic genre of exegesis up to the twelfth century, it is characterized by a reverence for patristic texts that elevates them almost to the level of Scripture.[63] To borrow Gilbert Dahan's evocative metaphor, many monastic exegetes conceived of their work less as unique creative expressions than as contributions to a longstanding collective enterprise, as stones added to a single great building begun by the Fathers and continually under construction since then.[64]

Working in the midst of the Carolingian exegetical renaissance, the ninth-century monk and archbishop Hrabanus Maurus composed continuous commentaries on all of the Epistles that synthesized and added to this patristic tradition.[65] Hrabanus followed the earlier exegetical tendency to merge Paul's spiritual athlete and soldier into a single ideal.[66] Observing the combination of military and athletic language in 1 Corinthians 9:25–27, he offered the following memorable image: the race Paul speaks of is to be run in the stadium of each Christian's heart, where God, 'the resident arbiter and superintendent of the games (*agonotheta*), continually awaits our fight (*pugna*) and our race (*cursus*).'[67] Himself an imperial vassal of the feuding Carolingian dynasty, Hrabanus spoke of Christ as the strong emperor of a unified spiritual army: 'just as an emperor rules his kingdom with the aid of warriors (*milites*), so the Savior defends the profession and discipline of the one God.'[68] But no matter how vividly Hrabanus described these spiritual combats or competitions, he continued to affirm their allegorical nature. The spiritual warfare of which the apostle wrote consisted of eternal vigilance against the snares of the devil, while to be a *miles Christi* was

---

[62] For the importance of these authors to later exegetes, see the introduction to William of Saint-Thierry, *Exposition on the Epistle to the Romans*, CF 27, ed. John D. Anderson and trans. John Baptist Hasbrouck (Kalamazoo, MI, 1980); and the introduction to *Expositiones Pauli Epistolarum ad Romanos, Galathas et Ephesios e codice Sancti Michaelis in periculo Maris* (Avranches, Bibl. mun. 79), ed. Gérard de Martel (Turnhout, 1995).

[63] Christopher de Hamel, 'Commentaries on the Bible,' in his *The Book: A History of the Bible* (London, 2001), 92–113.

[64] Dahan (*L'Exégèse chrétienne de la Bible en Occident médiéval, XIIe–XIVe siècle*, 82) defines monastic exegesis as a genre with the following characteristics: a tendency to 'anthologize' earlier, especially patristic, works; a distinct tropology, linked to the values and customs of monastic life; and a close engagement with the disciplines of the *trivium*, especially grammar and rhetoric.

[65] For an introduction to Carolingian exegesis and a catalogue of known exegetical works from the period, see Pierre Riché, 'Instruments de travail et méthodes de l'exégète à l'époque carolingienne,' in *Le Moyen Âge et la Bible*, ed. Pierre Riché and Guy Lobrichon, Bible de tous les temps 4 (Paris, 1984), 147–161.

[66] Hrabanus Maurus, *Enarrationum In Epistolas Beati Pauli*, PL 112: 9–834; for examples, see the conflation of *agon* and *certamen* at col. 630 (commenting on 1 Tim. 6:12) and that of *miles* and *athleta* at col. 632 (commenting on 2 Tim. 2:5).

[67] Hrabanus Maurus, *Enarrationum*, PL 112: 86. Compare with the similar imagery of one of Saint Augustine's sermons discussed below in Chapter 3 (at n.12).

[68] Hrabanus Maurus, *Enarrationum*, PL 112: 216 (commenting on 2 Cor. 10:4).

to 'hasten to do everything that is hard and strenuous in the contemplation of piety.'[69]

For later exegetes the ideal Pauline spiritual warrior was not necessarily a monk, but the patristic association of the *miles Christi* with ascetic virtue persisted in the minds of clerical writers. Commenting on the agon motif from 1 Corinthians, the Italian bishop Atto of Vercelli (d.960) described the Christian warrior-athlete as a manly hero, a chaste disciplinarian of the flesh: 'he does not fight like a boy (*pueriliter*), for boys when they fight are accustomed merely to beat the air.' Recognizing his own body as his most formidable opponent, he trained for the fight by fasting like a wrestler (*luctator*) before a big bout, and by girding his loins with lead plates (*laminas plumbeas*) – perhaps following Cassian's famous advice to monks in his *Institutes*.[70] Speaking of the injunction to the *miles Christi* to abstain from worldly entanglements (2 Tim. 2:3–4), Atto suggested such advice seemed particularly intended for churchmen, the true heirs to the apostle's spiritual warfare.[71]

Eleventh- and twelfth-century exegetes added new layers of symbolic imagery to earlier interpretations of the Pauline *miles Christi*. The renewed concern with heresy and conversion found in much clerical writing after c.1050, for instance, manifests itself in exegetical readings of spiritual warfare. Bruno of Chartreuse (d.1101) glossed the *arma militiae nostrae* of 2 Corinthians 10:4 as weapons endowed with the power to destroy 'the most stubborn heresies and philosophical arguments,' as well as bring infidels under Christ's yoke.[72] The *Commentary on Romans* by William of Saint-Thierry, whose martial imagery was rooted not only in the patristic tradition but also in descriptions of spiritual warfare by contemporary Cistercian writers, likewise embodied sin as a wicked king who rules with the support of an army of heresies 'always ready for battle, besieging the stronghold of the virtues (*castra virtutum*).'[73] Another Benedictine, Hervé of Déols (d.1150), envisioned the race of 1 Corinthians 9:24–26 as a competition between Jews, heretics, and Christian spiritual athletes for the prize of salvation.[74]

But if the enemies of the *miles Christi* changed over time, the ideal of the soldier of Christ remained closely tied to traditional clerical, and particularly monastic, virtues. Paul's exhortations echoed in the minds of later generations

---

[69] Hrabanus Maurus, *Enarrationum*, PL 112: 466–7 (commenting on 2 Cor. 10:3–4) and col. 642 (commenting on 2 Tim. 2:3): 'militem te Christi estimans omne quod durum est et laboriosum contemplatione pietatis ferre depropera....' On Hrabanus as an exegete, see Philippe Le Maître, 'Les méthodes exégétiques de Raban Maur,' in *Haut Moyen-Age: culture, éducation et societé*, ed. Michel Sot (La Garenne Colombes, 1990), 343–52.

[70] Atto of Vercelii, *Expositio Epistolarum Beati Pauli*, PL 134: 372. Cassian's reference to lead plates is found in his *Institutes*, 6.7.2, ed. and trans. Jean-Claude Guy as *Institutions cénobitiques*, SC 109 (Paris, 1965), 270–2.

[71] Atto of Vercelii, *Expositio*, PL 134: 690.

[72] Bruno of Chartreuse, *Expositio in Epistolas Sancti Pauli*, PL 153: 262.

[73] William of Saint-Thierry, *Expositio in Romanos*, 6.12, PL 180: 607; trans. Hasbrouck, *Commentary*, 119.

[74] Hervé of Déols, *Commentaria in Epistolas divi Pauli*, PL 181: 905.

of monastic writers who, even more so than patristic exegetes, envisioned themselves fighting alongside him as part of an elite corps of spiritual warriors. The apostle's own asceticism was glossed as a great contest with the devil, and his missionary campaigns as a series of glorious conquests. Odo of Cluny described the apostle as 'a soldier of God's encampments.'[75] For Peter Damian (d.1072), Paul was a beloved 'spiritual drillmaster,' while Guy de Pin (d.1136), fifth prior of La Grande Chartreuse, dubbed the apostle the supplier of 'invincible weapons' from the vast celestial armory.[76] All those living under monastic discipline practiced a version of the warfare articulated in the Epistles, not only when they imitated Paul's asceticism but when they meditated on sacred texts. This was nowhere more evident than in the monastic celebration of the Divine Office, in which monks relived the victories of countless earlier generations of *milites Christi*.

War and the Divine Office

Monastic liturgies offered frequent opportunities for extended meditation on the Bible's history and symbolism, since scriptural language appeared throughout the liturgical hours in the form of Gospel readings and Psalms, as well as prayers and hymns which incorporated biblical texts. In light of recent work by historical musicologists, who have read liturgical compositions and performances as expressions of monastic identity, it seems clear that daily performance of the Divine Office helped shape monastic self-definition, including identification with the role of *miles Christi*.[77] Any effort to reconstruct how monastic performers would have understood representations of warfare in the Bible must begin with the Psalms, the wellspring of the liturgy in all religious houses. In monasteries following the Benedictine *Rule* to the letter, forty psalms were sung each day, but some houses developed traditions incorporating over one hundred, and at Cluny by the eleventh century the monks made time for one hundred and seventy psalms daily.[78] Centuries earlier, some monasteries had even aspired to

---

[75] Odo called Paul a 'miles castrorum Dei' (perhaps referring to the *castra Dei* of Gen. 32:2) in *Collationum libri tres*, 3.9, PL 133: 597.

[76] For Peter Damian's reference to Paul as the 'instructor sacrae militiae,' see Letter 10, ed. Kurt Reindel in *Die Briefe des Petrus Damiani*, 4 vols (Munich, 1983–93), 1: 135. The letter to Pope Innocent II attributed to Guy de Pin is included in *The Chronicle of the Abbey of Morigny, France, c. 1100–1150*, trans. Richard Cusimano (New York, 2003), 116–17.

[77] For examples of this approach, see Susan Boynton, *Shaping a Monastic Identity: Liturgy and History at the Imperial Abbey of Farfa, 1000–1125* (Ithaca, NY, 2006); eadem, 'Performative Exegesis in the Fleury *Interfectio puerorum*,' *Viator* 29 (1998), 39–64; and C. Clifford Flanigan, Kathleen Ashley and Pamela Sheingorn, 'Liturgy as Social Performance: Expanding the Definitions,' in *The Liturgy of the Medieval Church*, ed. Thomas J. Heffernan and E. Ann Matter (Kalamazoo, MI, 2001), 674–714.

[78] Barbara H. Rosenwein, 'Feudal War and Monastic Peace: Cluniac Liturgy as Ritual Aggression,' *Viator* 2 (1971), 127–57 (at 132). On the Psalms in the liturgy more generally, see John Harper, *The Forms and Orders of the Western Liturgy from the Tenth through the Eighteenth Century* (Oxford, 1991), 67–72.

the practice of 'day and night psalmody,' accomplished by dividing the monks into shifts.[79] The perceived power of such perpetual prayer is also reflected in hagiographers' frequent claims that holy monks and hermits habitually prayed the Psalter many times through without stopping.[80]

In his *Rule* Saint Augustine had expressed his hope, in a passage often quoted by later authors, that 'When you pray to God in Psalms and hymns, the words you speak should be alive in your hearts.'[81] Augustine's sentiment reflected the custom that the Psalter must be memorized by newly professed monks, so that the words would come unbidden to their minds, and – rather than merely reciting them by rote – each phrase would eventually call up complex associations, engaging the mind and heart on multiple levels.[82] The better acquainted individuals were with the Scriptures and their exegetical traditions, the greater the number of connections they could make, and the longer they practiced psalmody the closer they came to unlocking the hidden mystical meaning of the words. In his *Conferences* Cassian explained that the monk, after countless repetitions, 'penetrates so deeply into the thinking of the Psalms that he sings them not as though they had been composed by the prophet but as if he himself had written them, as if this were his own private prayer uttered amidst the deepest compunction of heart.'[83]

Throughout the Psalms, God is invoked in the twin roles of protector of the chosen people and destroyer of their enemies. Many passages in the Psalms hearken back to the wars of the Israelites described in the Heptateuch, and describe God's power and the struggles of his people in explicitly martial terms. He is the 'God of armies,'[84] 'mighty in battle,'[85] a just judge who in his anger brings low the impious and destroys the enemies of his people. The God of the Psalms is unmistakably a warrior; armed with a sword, shield, and bow, and riding in a chariot surrounded by an innumerable host, he teaches the faithful to fight and emboldens them to march fearlessly into battle against their enemies.[86] The chosen people can expect divine support on the field of battle, but only

---

[79] Barbara H. Rosenwein, 'Perennial Prayer at Agaune,' in *Monks and Nuns, Saints and Outcasts*, ed. Sharon Farmer and Barbara H. Rosenwein (Ithaca, NY, 2000), 37–56.

[80] Joseph Dyer, 'The Psalms in Monastic Prayer,' in *The Place of the Psalms in the Intellectual Culture of the Middle Ages*, ed. Nancy van Deusen (Albany, NY, 1999), 59–89 (at 59–60).

[81] See the text and translation by George Lawless, *Augustine of Hippo and His Monastic Rule* (Oxford, 1987), 84–5. The Latin text reads: 'Psalmis et hymnis cum orates deum, hoc uersetur in corde quod profertur in uoce.' For the place of this sentiment in the history of monastic approaches to the Psalms, see Dyer, 'The Psalms in Monastic Prayer,' 62–3.

[82] I am paraphrasing Dyer ('Monastic Prayer,' 67). See also the following: Jacques Dubois, 'Comment les moines du Moyen Âge chantaient et goutaient les Saintes Écritures,' in *Le Moyen Âge et la Bible*, ed. Riché and Lobrichon, 261–98; and Jean Leclercq, *The Love of Learning and Desire for God: A Study of Monastic Culture*, trans. Catharine Misrahi (New York, 1982), 75–7.

[83] Cassian, *Collationes* 10.11, ed. Pichery, 2: 92; trans. Luibheid, *Conferences*, 137.

[84] As in Ps. 23:10, 45:8,12, 79:5, 8, 20, and 88:9.

[85] Ps. 23:8: 'quis est iste rex gloriae Dominus fortis et potens Dominus fortis in proelio ....'

[86] For example, Ps. 7:13, 17:15, 34:2–3, 44:4–6, and 67:18.

those who put their faith in God rather than in their own strength may hope for victory in war.⁸⁷

But these one hundred and fifty poems recording the struggles of the Israelites were identified as prophetic, rather than historical, texts; their true meaning, exegetes believed, could only be uncovered through a typological reading that sought in the words of the Hebrew Bible proof of the truth of Christianity and prophecies of specific New Testament events.⁸⁸ Already by the end of the sixth century, a rich commentary tradition had developed which would shape later allegorical readings of the Psalms.⁸⁹ The most influential among the early exegetes, Augustine and Cassiodorus (who was heavily influenced by Augustine),⁹⁰ both sought to 'Christianize' the Psalms, and accomplished this in part by emphasizing the prayers' spiritual meaning at the expense of their historical significance. Late Antique Christians who viewed themselves as the new chosen people spiritualized, or stripped away altogether, the material trappings of war from the bellicose God of the Psalms.

Augustine, who elsewhere formulated the concept of the *bello deo auctore*, the temporal war sanctioned by divine authority, developed in his *Enarrationes in Psalmos* allegorical readings for every weapon in the Hebrew God's arsenal. Commenting on the violent imagery of Psalm 7:13–14, in which the unconverted are threatened with God's sword and bow,⁹¹ for example, Augustine concluded that the bow represented the Scriptures, its arrows the apostles, and the sword Christ.⁹² Cassiodorus' *Expositio Psalmorum* built on Augustine's exegetical foundation, similarly emphasizing non-literal, spiritual meanings of the psalmist's many descriptions of warfare and weaponry.⁹³ Both writers reshaped the martial imagery of the Psalms to fit the mold of Pauline spiritual warfare. Augustine

---

87 See Ps. 17:33–5, 19:8, 26:3, 34:1–3, 36, 43, 45:8–12, and 88.
88 Blowers, 'Interpreting Scripture,' 620–1; G. Lampe, 'The Exposition and Exegesis of Scripture, I: To Gregory the Great,' in *Cambridge History of the Bible*, 3 vols, ed. Peter R. Ackroyd et al. (Cambridge, 1963), 2: 155–83.
89 For the medieval commentary tradition, see Dyer, 'Monastic Prayer,' 68–72, and Marie-Josèphe Rondeau, *Les commentaires patristiques du Psautier (IIIᵉ–Vᵉ siècles)*, Orientalia Christiana Analecta 219 (Rome, 1982). For a comprehensive list of early medieval commentaries on the Psalms, see McNally, *Bible in the Early Middle Ages*, 100–1; and for a guide to individual authors' interpretations of each psalm, Claude Jean-Nesmy, *La tradition médite le psautier chrétien*, 2 vols (Paris, 1973–4).
90 The texts are Augustine, *Enarrationes in Psalmos*, ed. E. Dekkers, CCSL 38–40 (Turnhout, 1956); and Cassiodorus, *Expositio Psalmorum*, in *Opera*, 3 vols, ed. M. Adriaen, CCSL 97–8 (Turnhout, 1958). All translations are taken from Augustine, *Expositions of the Psalms*, 6 vols, trans. Maria Boulding (Park, NY, 2000–4); and Cassiodorus, *Explanation of the Psalms*, 3 vols, trans. P.G. Walsh (New York, 1990–1).
91 Ps. 7:13–14 reads: 'Except you will be converted, he will brandish his sword; he hath bent his bow, and made it ready. And in it he hath prepared the instruments of death, he hath made ready his arrows for them that burn.'
92 *Enarrationes in Psalmos*, 7.13–14, ed. E. Dekkers, 1: 45–6; trans. Boulding, 1: 124–5. For other allegorical readings of armor and weaponry, see *Enarrationes*, 34(1).1–2 and 44.4, ed. Dekkers, 1: 300–1, 496–7; trans. Boulding, 2: 46–7, 289–90.
93 *Expositio Psalmorum*, 7.13–15, 34.3, 43.7, 44.6, M. Adriaen, 1: 85–6, 157, 305–6, 394, 406–7; trans. Walsh, 1: 106, 182, 337, 431, 444.

explained, for instance, that God's 'shield and spear' (Ps. 34:2) were none other than the souls of the righteous, who were in turn equipped by God with 'glorious weapons that have never known defeat, invisible and splendid; but spiritual and invisible arms, of course, since it is invisible enemies that we have to fight.'[94] Just as the victories of the Israelites over their enemies were mirrored in Christ's struggle and triumph over death and the devil, so did the spiritual warfare of each believer mirror God's own warfare. Christians fought in the spirit through prayer and good works, and won victories over invisible enemies not by relying on their own strength but by humbly acknowledging their weakness and putting their trust in God.[95]

It would be difficult to overestimate the influence of these patristic commentaries on later exegesis, and indeed on monastic spirituality. Augustine's *Enarrationes* was, during the ninth through twelfth centuries, among the works most frequently copied in monastic scriptoria, sometimes even referred to by copyists as the *Psalterium secundum Augustinum*, a title that implicitly elevated Augustine from the level of commentator to that of original author.[96] Cassiodorus' *Expositio* was similarly widely available to monastic liturgists and exegetes throughout the early Middle Ages.[97] Augustine and Cassiodorus' glosses were often copied into Psalter manuscripts in whole or in part, with the exegetical texts interspersed with or framing the scriptural text.[98] Illuminated Psalters often present 'visual commentaries' that attest to the artists' familiarity with patristic exegesis of the text.[99] Christopher de Hamel reminds us that many monks would have known the words of Augustine's commentary almost as well as those of the Psalter itself, and that the act of reading such an exegetical text, not unlike the act of reading or chanting the Psalms, 'was itself a spiritual exercise, interspersed with prayer and private meditation.'[100]

The lasting influence of the Augustinian–Cassiodorian tradition may be seen in the numerous Psalm commentaries produced in the Carolingian period. Writing at the great monastery of Fulda, the Benedictine monk Walafrid Strabo (d.849) repeated the patristic view that the warfare described in the Psalms was to be understood allegorically as God's victory over the devil, and typologically

---

[94] *Enarrationes in Psalmos*, 34(1).1–2, ed. Dekkers, 1: 300–1; trans. Boulding, 2: 46–7.
[95] See both writers' comments on Ps. 143:1 ('Blessed be the Lord my God, who teaches my hands to fight, and my fingers to war'): Augustine, *Enarrationes*, 143.1–5, ed. Dekkers, 3: 2072–6; trans. Boulding, 6: 360–4; Cassiodorus, *Expositio*, 143, ed. M. Adriaen, 2: 1281–9; trans. Walsh, 3: 413–14.
[96] As Christopher de Hamel (*History of the Bible*, 98) observes, 'It is as if Augustine actually wrote the Psalter' for the copyist who gave the *Enarrationes* this title.
[97] Margaret T. Gibson, 'Carolingian Glossed Psalters,' in *The Early Medieval Bible: Its Production, Decoration, and Use*, ed. Richard Gameson (Cambridge, 1994), 78–100 (at 96–7).
[98] Gibson, 'Carolingian Glossed Psalters,' 96–100.
[99] Koert van der Horst, 'The Utrecht Bible: Picturing the Psalms of David,' in *The Utrecht Psalter in Medieval Art*, ed. Koert van der Horst, William Noel and Wilhelmina C.M. Wüstefeld (Tuurdijk, 1996), 22–84 (at 55 and 71–2).
[100] de Hamel, *History of the Bible*, 103–4 (quoting 103).

as a prediction of the Incarnation and the Last Judgment.[101] In the slightly later *Enarrationum in Psalmos* of another Benedictine, Remigius of Auxerre (d.908), the warfare of the Psalms merged with the spiritual combat of Paul as well as the spiritualized wars of the Hebrews. In many instances, Remigius used the language of the Epistles to gloss the martial images of the Psalms: so Psalm 61 is said to define the true *miles Christi* as he who puts his whole trust in God and encourages others to do the same, thereby 'inviting them to the race (*cursum*)'; and the psalmist's descriptions of God as a warrior summon to mind the spiritual armor of Ephesians 6.[102] Commenting on the trials of the Hebrews, Remigius repeatedly quoted 2 Timothy 2:5 ('no one is crowned who has not lawfully fought'), noting that the time when the meek will be rewarded still lies in the future; meanwhile, 'the persecutor will not neglect his duties, and so he must be fought.'[103] That Remigius used Paul's words so unconsciously in this context indicates that by the eve of the tenth century the tradition of reading the spiritual warfare of the Epistles back onto the Hebrew Bible was so firmly entrenched in the Christian exegetical tradition as to require no explanation.

After the flowering of Carolingian exegesis, the tenth and early eleventh centuries saw the composition of relatively few original scriptural commentaries, though monks continued, of course, to study the Scriptures and their commentary tradition.[104] During the exegetical revival that drew vitality from the reforms of the later eleventh and twelfth centuries, monastic authors (like their patristic predecessors) focused more exegetical attention on the books of the Old Testament, including the Psalms, than on the New Testament.[105] Insisting on the fundamental unity of Scripture, this new generation of exegetes tended to follow patristic interpretations of warfare in the Psalms closely. For instance, Bruno of Chartreuse's association of 'the Lord mighty in battle' (Ps. 28:3 and elsewhere) with the resurrected Christ, triumphant over death, is directly based on Augustine's reading of the same passage.[106] But other connections Bruno makes, such as the glossing of the sword of God (Ps. 44:4) as the spiritual sword of Ephesians 6:17, reflect the later exegetical assimilation of the historical warfare of the Psalms to the spiritual combat of the Epistles.[107] Similar connections abound in

---

101 See, for example, his glosses on Ps. 7:7, 13–4 and 9:4–7; Walafrid Strabo, *Expositio in viginti primos psalmos*, PL 114: 764–6 and 769.
102 Remigius of Auxerre, *Enarrationum in psalmos liber unus*, PL 131: 453, 234, and 319.
103 Remigius of Auxerre, *Enarrationum*, PL 131: 158, 334, and 447.
104 Fulton, *Judgment to Passion*, 315–17.
105 Jean Leclercq, 'Écrits monastiques sur la Bible aux XIe-XIIIe siècles,' *Mediaeval Studies* 15 (1953), 95–106 (at 95); and idem, 'The Exposition and Exegesis of Scripture: From Gregory the Great to Saint Bernard,' in *The Cambridge History of the Bible*, ed. Ackroyd, 2: 183–97 (esp. 190–2).
106 Bruno of Chartreuse, *Expositio in Psalmos*, PL 152: 731; compare with Augustine's *Enarrationes in Psalmos*, 23.8; trans. Boulding, 1: 247.
107 Bruno of Chartreuse, *Expositio in Psalmos*, PL 152: 827. Bruno of Asti makes the same connection to Eph. 6:17 in his *Expositio in Psalmos*, PL 164: 718.

other contemporary Psalm commentaries, such as that by Bruno of Asti, and in sermons, such as those of Hildebert of Lavardin (d.1133).[108]

It should come as no surprise that for monks who collectively sang selections from the Psalms daily, and recited the Psalter alone as a meditative or penitential exercise, its language naturally became part of the vocabulary they used to describe their calling, express their feelings and analyze their experiences.[109] Like the military campaigns of the Heptateuch or the spiritual warfare of the Epistles, the Psalter's martial imagery readily sprang to the lips of monks in times of crisis, as evidenced by its appearance in clamors, liturgical rites in which religious communities beseeched God and the saints for help against worldly enemies. Adopting the language of the Hebrew poet crying out for divine protection, monks called down heavenly vengeance on the local castellans, bishops, or even predatory religious houses whom they cast in the guise of the ancient enemies of Israel.[110] As we will see in the following chapters, monastic writers identified themselves with the spiritual warriors of the Hebrew Bible, especially David, to whom the Psalms were attributed, as strongly as they did the Pauline *miles Christi*, and used his prayers as potent weapons in their daily combats.

Liturgical warfare

If martial imagery was thoroughly embedded in the scriptural texts of the Divine Office, liturgical actions mediated monastic communities' relationship to war and warriors, and the perception of liturgical prayer as a particularly potent form of spiritual warfare strongly shaped monastic spirituality.[111] The earliest leaders of the Church had inherited from pagan antiquity a conviction that prayers and related rituals helped ensure success in battle, and it became accepted practice for ecclesiastics to pray for the victory of Christian rulers allied to the Church, on the understanding that the pious victors would in turn commit themselves to

---

[108] Bruno of Asti, *Expositio*, PL 164: 763 (on Ps. 20); 932 (on Ps. 64); 1024 (on Ps. 83); 1041 (on Ps. 88); 1058 (on Ps. 91); 1079 (on Ps. 100); 1173 (on Ps. 123). Hildebert of Lavardin's *De militia christiana*, which is written in the form of a sermon, links the spiritual arms of Ephesians with specific passages from the Psalms; see *Sermones de diversis*, c.27, PL 171: 867–71.

[109] On the more general medieval concern with the language of liturgical prayer, see Éric Palazzo, *Liturgie et société au moyen âge* (Paris, 2002), 29–35. Paul F. Gehl has also argued that the continual repetition of the Psalms strongly influenced the style of monastic composition; see his 'Mystic Language Models in Monastic Educational Psychology,' *Journal of Medieval and Renaissance Studies* 14 (1982), 219–43 (esp. 225–7).

[110] Little, *Benedictine Maledictions*, 62–4.

[111] On war and the liturgy, see Christopher J. Holdsworth, 'An Airier Aristocracy: The Saints at War,' *Transactions of the Royal Historical Society* 6th ser., 6 (1996), 103–22; Michael McCormick, 'The Liturgy of War in the Early Middle Ages: Crisis, Litanies, and the Carolingian Monarchy,' *Viator* 15 (1984), 1–23; idem, 'The Liturgy of War from Antiquity to the Crusades,' in *The Sword of the Lord: Military Chaplains from the First to the Twenty-First Century*, ed. Doris L. Bergen (Notre Dame, 2004), 45–67; and Rosenwein, 'Liturgy as Ritual Aggression.'

the promotion of peace.¹¹² Liturgical prayer, as performed by well-trained experts, was a potent weapon. The malediction of a holy man or woman was believed to have an immediate, physical impact on its unfortunate object, as illustrated by a story from Gregory the Great's *Dialogues*, a work that remained a favorite of later generations of monastics. A holy hermit named Florentius rashly cursed four monks who had poisoned his pet bear, Gregory remembered, but when the men were struck with leprosy Florentius was overcome with guilt and wept for the rest of his life over what he had done. God had worked this terrible miracle, Gregory explained, so that Florentius 'would never again presume to hurl the javelin of malediction (*iaculum maledictionis*), no matter how great his grief.'[113]

Lay patrons who shared this view went to great lengths to guarantee that liturgical weapons were wielded *for* rather than against them. In the early Middle Ages it was not unheard of for monks to offer up prayers for a patron's victory on the battlefield itself. Bede shows the seriousness with which such petitions were regarded in his account of the Battle of Chester (c.616), at which the Northumbrian ruler Æthelfrith found that his heretical Welsh opponents had brought along monks from the abbey of Bangor to pray for the destruction of Æthelfrith's army. Catching sight of the holy men, the king cried out, 'If then they cry to their God against us, in truth, though they do not bear arms, yet they fight against us, because they oppose us by their prayers,' and ordered his warriors to cut down the monks before attacking the Welsh army.[114] In the Carolingian era, rulers retained the view that prayers were powerful 'arms of faith,' most efficacious when deployed simultaneously by as many subjects as possible, and the emperor Charlemagne made it clear that he regarded any monastery's refusal to pray for royal victories as nothing short of treason.[115] Charlemagne's reign, which has been identified as a watershed moment for the liturgy of war, saw the evolution of what Michael McCormick has termed 'combat-related rituals' – elaborate pre-battle liturgical processions and prayers intended to boost morale and ensure the victories upon which royal prestige was based.[116] These prayers for victory, which combined martially inflected selections from the Psalms with texts derived from Late Antique sources, portrayed the Frankish rulers as leaders of God's chosen people, the heirs of Moses, Joshua, and David, and their enemies, who were likened to the Egyptians and the Amalekites, as 'infidel barbarians.'[117]

---

[112] Michael McCormick, *Eternal Victory: Triumphal Rulership in Late Antiquity, Byzantium, and the Early Medieval West* (Cambridge, 1986); Erdmann, *Idea of Crusade*, 28–9.

[113] Gregory the Great, *Dialogues*, 3.15, ed. and trans. de Vogüé, 2: 320–1. Cited by Little, *Benedictine Maledictions*, 89.

[114] *Ecclesiastical History of the English People*, 2.2, trans. Leo Sherley-Price and R.E. Latham (Harmondsworth, 1990), 107.

[115] McCormick, 'Liturgy of War in the Early Middle Ages,' 4–5 (quoting a letter from Charlemagne to Pope Hadrian I). See also David S. Bachrach, *Religion and the Conduct of War, c. 300–1215* (Woodbridge, 2003), chapter 2; and Nelson, 'Ninth-Century Warfare.'

[116] Michael McCormick, 'Liturgy of War from Antiquity to the Crusades,' 49–51; idem, *Eternal Victory: Triumphal Rulership*, 369f.

[117] The irony of substituting the texts' original '*Romani regni*' for '*Francorum regni*,' given that the latter had been among the original enemies whose defeat the prayers were intended

Annotations to liturgical calendars suggest that great victories were commemorated with liturgical celebrations in Carolingian Francia; Charles the Bald, for instance, granted property to the abbey of Saint-Denis on the understanding that its monks would celebrate the anniversary of Charles' defeat of his half-brother and rival Louis the German in 859.[118]

Although large-scale organized prayer networks lasted only as long as the Carolingian Empire itself, the liturgies of war developed under Charlemagne did not simply disappear in the upheavals that followed his death; rather, older prayers and ceremonials were adapted to changing political realities. Local lords and bishops replaced Carolingian emperors as the beneficiaries of victory-giving prayers, and new enemies – Vikings, Muslims, and Magyars – replaced the Saxons and Avars.[119] Like earlier war-prayers, these formulae incorporated martial imagery from the Hebrew Bible, linking the past and present victories of *Deus victor* and positioning medieval warriors within a long genealogy of holy conquerors stretching back to the kings of ancient Israel.[120] Since warriors and clerics alike held that the sinfulness of society was a root cause of the invasions, and viewed the power of the saints as a potent defensive weapon, the intercessory prayers of monastic communities were often credited with protecting Christian armies from defeat by pagans.[121]

Hagiographers boasted of the power of monastic prayer and the defensive abilities of individual saints in miracle collections. The attribution of military victories to the intercession and even participation of saints, a common feature of later crusading chronicles, proliferated during the invasions of the ninth and tenth centuries.[122] Even as celebrated a champion of humility as Benedict of Nursia was not above appearing on the battlefield, as we hear in a ninth-century miracle from the Orléanais abbey of Fleury. When Fleury's monks fled an impending Viking attack on their abbey, a local lord routed the would-be raiders with the assistance of Benedict, who, as the warrior later reported, 'held the reins of my horse in his left hand and, holding a staff in his right, sent many of the enemy falling to their death.'[123] Similarly, after the monastery of Saint-

to ensure, seems to have been lost on early medieval liturgists. See, for examples, McCormick, *Eternal Victory*, 344–9; and Pierre Riché, 'La Bible et la vie politique dans le haut Moyen Age,' in *Le Moyen Age et la Bible*, ed. Riché and Lobrichon, 385–400.

[118] McCormick, *Eternal Victory*, 361–2.
[119] Michael McCormick, 'Liturgie et guerre des Carolingiens à la première croisade,' in *Militia Christi et crociata*, 222–3; and idem, *Eternal Victory*, 349–50.
[120] McCormick, 'Liturgie et guerre,' 226–7.
[121] Bachrach, *Religion and the Conduct of War*, 61–5.
[122] See Bernard S. Bachrach, 'The Combat Sculptures at Fulk Nerra's "Battle Abbey" (c. 1005–1012),' *Haskins Society Journal* 3 (1991), 63–80 (here 74). Bachrach notes that in the ninth century a burg in the Touraine (later called Nouy) was known as '*burgum Sancti Martini Belli*' in recognition of the saint's role in defeating a party of Norsemen at that spot. Christopher Holdsworth ('An Airier Aristocracy,' 117) cites an appearance by Saint Paulinus at Nola during the city's siege by the Goths as the earliest case in the West of a saint appearing during a battle.
[123] Citation and translation from Thomas Head, *Hagiography and the Cult of Saints: The Diocese of Orléans, 800–1200*, Cambridge Studies in Medieval Life and Thought 4th ser.,

Germain-des-Prés was sacked during a Viking raid on Paris, a monk of the abbey beheld the holy bishop Germanus 'in helmet and hauberk, and weary as though just coming from the field of battle,' where he had engaged the blasphemers who had attacked his community.[124]

Monasteries continued to serve as focal points for liturgies of war in the tenth and eleventh centuries, as strong ties of patronage and intercession came to bind families of arms-bearers to individual houses. Monastic liturgists developed programs of prayer which could simultaneously promote their houses' interests and those of lay *potentes* for whom success in war was naturally a major concern. By c.1000, lay patrons more often sought monastic support on the eves of important campaigns against rival Christian lords than pagan invaders, and were becoming as concerned with purging themselves of the sin of killing fellow Christians as with assuring themselves of divine support in battle. Religious institutions had in turn become less concerned to defend themselves against pagan invaders than against the predations of local Christian warlords, and monastic liturgists emphasized their power to bless and protect lay defenders while damning their enemies and depriving them of saintly protection.[125] Clerics compared the rich variety of anathema and excommunication formulae at their disposal to the arsenals of weapons available to lay warriors, and most lay elites threatened with such powerful arms were inclined to take them seriously.[126] While monastic communities lacked the power of excommunication reserved for the episcopate, they were by no means helpless in this regard – curses and clamors allowed them to call down the wrath of their saints on violators of their rights and property.[127]

---

14 (Cambridge, 1990), 53. For the Latin text by the monk Adelarius, see *Les miracles de Saint Benoît écrits par les Adrevald, Aimon, André, Raoul Tortaire et Hugues de Sainte Marie, moines de Fleury*, 1.41, ed. Eugène de Certain (Paris, 1858), 83–9. A later tale from the Fleury collection (*ibid*., 5.15, pp. 212–13) recounted by the monk Andrew in the 1040s describes Benedict as a 'battle leader (*certaminis primicerium*).'

[124] *Translatio S. Germani Parisiensis anno 846*, c.29, ed. Carolus de Smedt, *Analecta Bollandiana* 2 (1883), 69–98 (at 90–1).

[125] Thomas Head, 'The Judgment of God: Andrew of Fleury's Account of the Peace League of Bourges,' in *The Peace of God*, ed. Head and Landes, 219–238 (and for further references 237, n.56). Power relations between monks and local lay lords were dramatized by rituals, including liturgical ones, and much of the aggression between religious communities and their enemies (many of whom were once and future allies) was in turn highly ritualized. See Barbara H. Rosenwein, *To Be the Neighbor of Saint Peter: The Social Meaning of Cluny's Property, 909–1049* (Ithaca, NY, 1989); and Barbara H. Rosenwein, Thomas Head and Sharon Farmer, 'Monks and Their Enemies: A Comparative Approach,' *Speculum* 66 (1991), 764–96.

[126] As argued by Jeffrey Alan Bowman, *Shifting Landmarks: Property, Proof, and Dispute in Catalonia Around the Year 1000* (Ithaca, NY, 2004), 69–80; and Daniel F. Callahan, 'The Cult of the Saints in Aquitaine,' in *The Peace of God*, ed. Head and Landes, 165–83 (esp. 172–8). Canon 20 of the First Lateran Council (held in 1123) employed a common turn of phrase when it threatened those who would attack or despoil monks or clerics with the 'sword of anathema (*gladio anathematis*)'; see *Conciliorum Oecumenicorum Decreta*, 3rd ed., ed. G. Alberigo et al. (Bologna, 1973), 194.

[127] Patrick J. Geary, 'Humiliation of Saints,' in *Living with the Dead in the Middle Ages* (Ithaca, NY, 1994), 95–115 (here 96–7).

Monks performed liturgies of war simultaneously as clerical intercessors and warriors of the spirit; indeed, their perception of themselves as *milites Christi* powerfully shaped their experience of such rites. But even the daily performance of the Divine Office was a potent form of spiritual warfare. The genealogy of this self-perception was patristic; Augustine had famously persuaded Boniface, the Roman governor of Africa, not to abandon his post for a monastery on the grounds that worldly military service and spiritual military service in the cloister were not diametrically opposed but rather complementary, and indeed quite similar, occupations. Augustine wrote:

> Those who abandon all the affairs of this age and then serve the Lord in fully continent chastity certainly have a higher place before him. Still, the apostle says that, 'Each one has his own proper gift from God: one this way and another that (1 Cor. 7:8).' Thus others fight for you against invisible enemies by praying (*orando pugnant*); you work for them against visible barbarians by fighting (*pugnando*).[128]

The concept of liturgical warfare continued to inform perceptions of the monastic ideal in the Central Middle Ages. At the abbey of Agaune in the Rhône Valley, a community dedicated to Saint Maurice and the soldier-martyrs of the Theban Legion, monks were divided into seven liturgical 'squadrons,' or *turmae*, who prayed (and thus symbolically fought) in shifts.[129] The twelfth-century Cistercian Thomas of Perseigne later wrote that monks waged war (*bellum committere*) with prayer in church, and recovered from their battle wounds in chapter and through manual labor.[130] Seeking to explain the presence of monks in William I's invading army in 1066, both the monastic chronicler Orderic Vitalis and the Norman priest William of Poitiers (himself a former knight) offered identical explanations: the duke had brought them so that they might 'fight with their prayers' alongside his soldiers at Hastings.[131] As a cleric, the crusading chronicler Raymond of Aguilers may well have had such imagery in mind when he reversed it, and twice likened the Christian battle lines of the First Crusade to liturgical processions.[132]

Some of the most extended martial allegories of the liturgy appear in clerical treatises meant to instruct readers in the proper performance and symbolic significance of the Divine Office.[133] The Carolingian liturgist Amalarius of Metz (d.c.850) depicted the Church's never-ending cycle of prayer as a battle for

---

[128] Augustine, Letter 189.5, *Epistolae*, PL 33: 855. For commentary, see Helgeland, *Christians and the Military*, 77.
[129] Rosenwein, 'Perennial Prayer,' 52–4.
[130] Thomas of Perseigne, *Cantica canticorum*, PL 206: 254.
[131] Cited by Bachrach, *Religion and the Conduct of War*, 84 and n.105–6; see William of Poitiers, *Gesta Guillelmi*, ed. R.H.C. Davis and Marjorie Chibnall (Oxford, 1998), 124; and Orderic Vitalis, *Ecclesiastical History*, ed. Chibnall, 2: 172.
[132] Riley-Smith, *Idea of Crusading*, 84.
[133] As observed by Michael Evans, 'An Illustrated Fragment of Peraldus' *Summa* of Vice: Harleian MS 3244,' *Journal of the Warburg and Courtauld Institutes* 45 (1982), 14–68 (at 17 and n.22); and Chenu, *Nature, Man, and Society*, 152 and n.14, who provides some of the references discussed here.

which Christians trained by keeping their bodies and minds free of sin.[134] But if all believers could potentially fight with their prayers, the leading roles in battle were reserved for clerics and especially priestly celebrants of the mass, whom Amalarius described as warriors (*agonothetae* or *pugnatores*) whose duty it was to supply weaker combatants with the arms of virtue and the armor of sacramental benediction.[135] This figure of the priestly warrior was more fully developed by a number of clerical liturgists in the twelfth and early thirteenth centuries. Writing in c.1162, John Beleth likened the vestments of priestly warriors (*pugiles*) to suits of spiritual armor, which combined elements from Ephesians 6 with contemporary equipment: his sandals are greaves (*ocreae*), his amice a helmet (*galea*), his alb a breastplate or hauberk (*lorica*), his girdle a bow (*arcus*), and undergirdle a quiver (*pharetra*). He has for a spear his stole, for a shield his chasuble, and for a sword his service-book. And at the moment the priest reads from the Gospel, he runs through the devil with the sword of the Word.[136] The exegetical reading of the mass formulated by another liturgist, the Italian bishop Sicard of Cremona (d.1215), freighted the ceremony with multiple levels of allegorical meaning (*figurantes*): first, it recalled the great victories Israel had won over its enemies with divine support; second, it was an expression of the fight all Christians carry on 'against principles and powers' (Eph. 6:12). The priest was advised to 'hold in his mind (*habere in mentem*)' these levels of meaning while performing the sacrament that commemorated the spiritual struggles of countless generations.[137]

In his *Gemma animae* the priest and monk Honorius Augustodunensis (d.c.1151) developed what is arguably the most elaborate symbolic interpretation of liturgical warfare from this period.[138] Honorius described a fully 'armed' liturgical procession entering the church in battle formation as follows:

> For the procession of the priest and clergy and people is like the advancing of a ruler and his army (*exercitus*) to war. With albs underneath and copes above, or dressed in other sacred garments, these men are like knights girded for battle with hauberks (*milites pugnaturi subtus loricis*) underneath and shields above.... When we bear before us the cross and banner, it is as though the imperial standard is carried by the standard bearers, while the cantors follow in succession like two

---

134 Amalarius of Metz, *De ecclesiasticis officiis libri quatuor*, 1.1, 1.7 and 4.3, PL 105: 996, 1003 and 1171.
135 Amalarius of Metz, *De ecclesiasticis officiis*, 3.37, PL 105: 1156–7: 'Sacerdos noster, ut prudens agonotheta et pugnator, quantum in majore periculo videt milites fore, tantum munit eos amplius sua benedictione. Arma nostra contra diabolum, sunt humilitas et caeterae virtutes. Vult sacerdos noster, ut nostris armis vestiti simus: propterea jubet per ministrum ut humiliemus capita nostra Deo, et ita tandem infundit super milites protectionem benedictionis suae.'
136 John Beleth, *Summa de ecclesiasticis officiis*, c.32–3, ed. Herbert Douteil, CCCM 41A (Turnhout, 1976), 61–4. In c.33, John explicitly quotes Eph. 6:12 to the effect that priests fight evil spirits rather than earthly enemies. The *lorica*, sandals ('foot-coverings' in Eph. 6:15), shield, and helmet are all Pauline elements.
137 Sicard of Cremona, *Mitrale, seu de officiis ecclesiasticis summa*, PL 213: 144; cf. cols. 60 and 263.
138 Honorius Augustodunensis, *Gemma animae*, c.72–82, PL 172: 566–70.

approaching armies. Between them walk the masters and precentors, like the commanders of an army urging them on to war, and the priors follow like the captains of an army arranging the host.[139]

The signal for the battle to commence was given when the clerics began chanting their prayers, and immediately fiery demons attacked, only to be repelled with the shield of faith and the sword of the Word, the spiritual weapons of Ephesians 6.[140] In the midst of this melee, the priest was called out to single combat (*duellum*) with the devil, recreating through his liturgical actions the temptation of Christ and David's confrontation with Goliath.[141] Like John Beleth, Honorius equipped his priestly warrior with explicitly Pauline arms and armor,[142] and his reading of the mass as a battle was clearly informed by traditional exegesis of the Epistles, which, as we have seen, customarily drew parallels between the apostle's spiritual combat and the historical wars of the Hebrew Bible. Like priests, monks were conditioned to view their liturgical duties in militaristic terms. Peter Damian, for instance, employed martial rhetoric very similar to that used by contemporary liturgists to describe the experience of the Divine Office. He scolded Hugh, the Cluniac bishop of Besançon, for allowing monks and clerics to sit in the cathedral during the mass and offices, on the grounds that

> when we pray, we fight in a battle line (*acies*) against the assaults of a vicious foe, so that the enemy must either feebly yield to us the victory, or exult over us who have fallen in the cause of the Lord. When these enemies see our bodies growing faint as we sit there exhausted, they are at once sure of gaining the victory because our spirit has collapsed....[143]

The physical posture of prayer not only signaled the monk's refusal to make any concessions to human weakness, but hinted at his identity as a soldier, fighting with the weapons of prayer among his brothers-in-arms. A monastic procession making its way to church for the night-office put Damian in mind of an army on

---

[139] Honorius Augustodunensis, *Gemma animae*, c.72, PL 172: 566: 'Pontificis namque et cleri, populique processio, est quasi imperatoris, et cujusdam exercitus ad bello progressio. Hi cum subtus albis, et desuper cappis, vel aliis solemnibus vestibus induuntur, quasi milites pugnaturi subtus loricis, desuper clypeis muniuntur.... Quasi imperiale signum et vexilla a signiferis anteferuntur, cum ante nos crux et vexilla geruntur. Quasi duo exercitus sequuntur, dum hinc inde ordinatim cantantes gradiuntur. Inter quos vadunt magistri et praecentores, quasi cohortium ductores ac belli incitatores. Sequuntur priores, quasi exercitus duces atque agminum ordinatores.'

[140] Honorius Augustodunensis, *Gemma animae*, c.75, PL 172: 567.

[141] Honorius Augustodunensis, *Gemma animae*, c.78–80, PL 172: 568–9.

[142] Honorius Augustodunensis (*Gemma animae*, c.82, PL 172: 570), who wrote at least a decade earlier, was likely the source for Beleth's enumeration of spiritual arms.

[143] Peter Damian, Letter 111, ed. Reindel, *Briefe*, 3: 251–2: 'et cum oramus, tunc velut in acie contra malignorum hostium temptamenta confligimus, ut nobis omnino necesse sit aut superantibus enerviter cedere, aut corruentibus in Domino plausibiliter insultare. Qui cum corpora nostra marcida sessione contemplantur ebescere, de ruina quoque interioris hominis ilico sperant se victoriam optinere.' Trans. Blum, *Letters*, 4: 251.

the march, to be admired for the discipline of its organization and perfect coordination of its movements. As he wrote to a fellow monastic superior,

> And truly how beautiful is the appearance of the army (*militia*), especially at the night hours, when the brothers form a wedge, aroused as if by the clamor of the trumpets, and inspired to make ready for the divine contest (*certamen*), they go out in unison as if hurrying forward in a well-ordered battle line (*acies*). Although the wing of boys goes in front, the youth follows just like a squadron of soldiers, whereas last, following upon the footsteps [of the rest], are the old men, namely, the strength of the battle (*robur ... belii*), who guard the rear of the whole army lest anyone fall or the hidden enemy assail it.[144]

While strict order and obedience were required for the monastic community to carry out its liturgical responsibilities properly, camaraderie within the ranks was, to Peter's mind, equally important. As in war, seasoned veterans (the monastic *seniores*) were entrusted with the training and encouragement of new recruits (oblates or newly professed monks), who were especially vulnerable to the enemy's weapons.

For their part, lay donors who patronized religious communities implicitly acknowledged that monks possessed greater prowess than they on the spiritual battlefield. As Barbara Rosenwein has written of the liturgy of Cluny in this period, '[i]ntercession was a weapon with which to fight the devil, to thwart his progress in his great war with God, and to help God win his rights over the souls of men.'[145] The martial associations of liturgical prayer meant that a monastery need not be raised up on a battlefield or within the precincts of a castle to be a war memorial;[146] by virtue of their association with spiritual warfare, *all* religious houses were monuments to the eternal battle Christians waged against sin with the weapons of prayer and penance. As we shall see in Chapter 4, monastic writers often described the cloister as an impregnable fortress, perpetually under siege by demonic forces, its towers defended by legions of spiritual warriors. That patrons and monks alike viewed their calling in these terms is evidenced by the martial language of foundation charters, such as that issued to the monks of the New Minster at Winchester by the Anglo-Saxon king Edgar in 966:

> The abbot is armed with spiritual weapons and supported by a troop of monks anointed with the dew of heavenly graces. They fight together in the strength of Christ with the sword of the spirit against the aery wiles of the devils. They

---

[144] Peter Damian, Letter 153, ed. Reindel, *Briefe*, 4: 49: 'Et re vera quam pulchra militiae species, praecipue nocturnes horis, cum fratres quasi tubarum clangoribus excitati cuneum faciunt, et tanquam directa acie properantes, attoniti ad procinctum divini certaminis concorditer gradiuntur. Cum videlicet puerorum ala precedit, iuvenum vero tanquam manipulorum turma subsequitur, postrema autem legentes vestigia senes, belli scilicet robur, ne subsidat aliquis, ne vel hostis furtivus immergat, totius exercitus terga custodiunt.' Trans. Blum and Irven M. Resnick, *Letters*, 6: 52.
[145] Rosenwein, 'Feudal War and Monastic Peace,' 145.
[146] For examples of such foundations, see Chapter 2.

defend the king and the clergy of the realm from the onslaughts of their invisible enemies.[147]

Here the customary social roles of monks and patron are reversed; rather than promising the new community protection from worldly enemies, Edgar himself receives assurances that the monks of Winchester will defend him against the demonic forces that invisibly threaten his kingdom. In the logic of the charter, the very function of monks is to wage war, and on the spiritual battlefield even kings are reduced to the status of bystanders.

If a king could entrust the spiritual defense of his lands to monastic garrisons, noble patrons with sufficient resources enlisted troops of monks to fight for their souls. Orderic Vitalis made this point through a speech he attributed to his father, the clerk Odelerius. According to Orderic, Odelerius urged his noble patron, the powerful earl of Shrewsbury Roger Montgomery, to endow a house of Benedictine monks who would battle the devil for their patron's soul:

> Consider now what duties are performed in monasteries obedient to a rule by those trained in the service of God. Countless benefits are obtained there every day, and Christ's garrisons (*castrenses Christi*) struggle manfully against the devil. Assuredly the harder the struggle of the spiritual warrior (*agonotheta*) the more glorious will be his victory, and the more precious his trophies in the courts of heaven. ... And so, great and noble earl, I faithfully admonish you to found a monastery while you may in your country, which you have acquired and not inherited, as a citadel of God (*monachile castrum*) against Satan, where the cowled champions (*cucullati pugiles*) may engage in ceaseless combat against Behemoth for your soul.[148]

The community envisioned here was duly founded as Shrewsbury Abbey, and Orderic's younger brother Benedict, as well as Odelerius himself, ultimately joined the ranks of its monastic warriors.[149] This *monachile castrum*, built in the 1080s in the shadow of Roger Montgomery's great stone castle, was not so much a refuge of peace as a different type of fortress, one defended not by Norman knights but by reform-minded Benedictine monks.[150] From the chronicler's perspective, Roger Montgomery's sins could best be atoned for not through the

---

[147] Quoted in R.W. Southern, *Western Society and the Church in the Middle Ages* (Harmondsworth, 1970), 224–5. With characteristic acuity, Southern observed that lay patrons like Edgar eagerly donated land to monastic foundations because they 'believed that their temporal and eternal welfare equally depended on the warfare of the monks.'

[148] Orderic Vitalis, *Ecclesiastical History*, ed. Chibnall, 3: 144–7. Orderic's use of the word *agonotheta* here, which Chibnall translates as 'spiritual warriors,' is particularly interesting, since medieval writers used the term for lay warriors as well; one eleventh-century dictionary defined it as '*preliator uel praemii auctor*.' As Marco Mostert notes, *agonotheta* and *agonista* were sometimes used interchangeably, though the latter 'had a moral and ecclesiological flavor.' See *The Political Theory of Abbo of Fleury* (Hilversum, 1987), 100n.

[149] As described by Orderic, *Ecclesiastical History*, 5.14, ed. Chibnall, 3: 148–9.

[150] For background on the post-Conquest history of Shewsbury and the foundation of its abbey, see Marjorie Chibnall, *The World of Orderic Vitalis: Norman Monks and Norman Knights* (Oxford, 1984), 4–13.

promotion of peace but by further acts of war, albeit war of a better, spiritual sort. While Orderic undeniably wrote for a monastic audience, and Odelerius' speech bears the hallmarks of contemporary eulogies on the monastic life,[151] it nonetheless suggests that churchmen might have encouraged lay patrons to see the intercessory function of monks in martial terms, as indeed monks did themselves.

Conclusion

Many of the activities most evocative of the peace of the medieval cloister – private lectio, biblical study and exegesis, liturgical prayer – brought war to the forefront of the monastic experience. Theological and exegetical conventions shaped the reception of war in sacred texts, so that the military history of the Hebrew Bible and the Epistles' theory of spiritual combat came to depend upon one another, interpretively speaking; the campaigns of Israel foreshadowed the spiritual struggles of Christ and the apostles, and this typology enabled readers to neutralize the real violence described in the historical books of the Old Testament. For monastic exegetes, spiritual (or spiritualized) war became central to the historical and allegorical narratives of Christianity. In the words of the twelfth-century canon Hugh of Saint-Victor,

> the Incarnate Word is our King, who came into this world to war with the devil; and all the saints who lived before His coming are soldiers, as it were, going before their King, and those who have come after and are still to come, even to the end of the world, are soldiers following their King.[152]

Read through the lens of Pauline spiritual warfare and its patristic elaborations, ancient Hebrew warriors became worthy models for monks to emulate, not in spite of their martial prowess but because of it. Christ and the apostles were also venerated as spiritual warriors, not because of a Germanic tendency to recast Christian virtue in a militaristic mold but because generations of deeply Roman patristic interpreters had unambiguously suggested this interpretation. In the performance of the Divine Office, arguably *the* defining activity of coenobitic life in the Central Middle Ages, monastic performers sought the aid of the Psalms' 'Lord of Hosts' as they fought against invisible enemies for their own souls and those of fellow Christians. What is more, medieval arms-bearers were encouraged to view religious communities as strongholds of prayer, in which monastic combatants battled tirelessly for their own souls and those of their worldly protectors.

We must remember, finally, that biblical accounts of battles fought, cities sacked, and whole peoples put to the sword were not 'just stories' to medieval monastic readers. Jean Leclercq's concept of 'biblical imagination' is useful for

---

[151] As observed by Chibnall, ed., *Ecclesiastical History*, 3: 143n.
[152] Hugh of Saint-Victor, *De sacramentis christianae fidei*, Prologue, c.2, PL 176: 183; trans. Roy J. Deferrari as *On the Sacraments of the Christian Faith* (Cambidge, MA, 1951), 3–4.

understanding how members of medieval religious communities were trained 'to picture, to "make present," to see all the details provided by the texts [of the Bible]: the colors and dimensions of things, the clothing, bearing, and actions of the people, the complex environment in which they move[d].'[153] When individual monks 'saw' the sacred wars of the biblical past with their inner eyes during *lectio* or prayer, they could not help but see them as contemporary artists depicted them, that is, fought by armies of very contemporary-looking knights equipped with up-to-date arms, armor, and siege-machines.[154] Monastic illuminators often adorned Psalters with scenes of spiritual struggle acted out by figures who could pass for secular warriors, to reinforce the lesson that these texts described *milites Christi* fighting demons or vices.[155] In this way, monastic exegetes effected a conflation of the heroic past of the Hebrew Bible and the present, no less bellicose, world of their own experience. Through a process akin to what scholars of religion have termed the 'reactualization of sacred events,' monks learned to step into this timeless heroic world merely by reading – indeed, the primacy of the Scriptures within monastic culture meant that they could hardly avoid stepping into it at every turn.[156] Within this meditative space, as warriors of the spirit, monks relived ancient battles and confronted their own weaknesses in new combats. But if the battles of Scripture could be brought to life through exegesis and liturgical performance, we shall see in the next chapter that encounters with living warriors were equally important in helping monks negotiate their relationship to the warfare described in their sacred texts.

---

[153] Leclercq, *Love of Learning*, 75.
[154] C. Griffith Mann, 'Picturing the Bible in the Thirteenth Century,' in *The Book of Kings: Art, War, and the Morgan Library's Medieval Picture Bible*, ed. William Noel and Daniel Weiss (London, 2002), 39–59; for the representation of spiritual combatants as contemporary *milites*, see Alexander, 'Ideological Representation of Military Combat'; and Rudolph, *Violence and Daily Life*, chapter 4.
[155] For this imagery in relation to monastic spirituality, see Kathleen M. Openshaw, 'Weapons in the Daily Battle: Images of the Conquest of Evil in the Early Medieval Psalter,' *Art Bulletin* 75 (1993), 18–38.
[156] For discussion of reactualization in connection with religious rites and festivals, see Mircea Eliade, *The Sacred and the Profane*, trans. Willard Trask (New York, 1968), 106–7.

2

Monks and Warriors: Negotiating Boundaries

'It is good for a man to know his established order,' wrote the twelfth-century canon Philip of Harvengt, 'and its limit or boundary, lest he impudently presume to go beyond its fixed boundaries, or weakly shrink from them.'[1] Philip's sentiment reflects the deeply felt concern with the definition of orders (*ordines*) and the reinforcement of boundaries between them that runs through much of the writing of eleventh- and twelfth-century churchmen. This interest did not consistently reflect a real or imagined tripartite system of 'those who prayed, fought, and worked'; throughout this period, various schema were current which divided society into anywhere from two to seven groups according to a variety of criteria including vocation, birth, gender, religion, and marital status.[2] Nevertheless, one division all theorists recognized as fundamental was that between the clergy and laity, who were distinguished by their respective spiritual statures, social functions, and legal jurisdictions. Many writers further insisted on the existence of a monastic *ordo*, usually judged to be superior to the secular clergy, from whom monks and nuns were distinguished by their enclosure, poverty, stability, dress, and diet.[3] In reality, of course, there was no monolithic monastic 'order' in the Central Middle Ages, a period which saw the proliferation of new religious orders as well as the emergence of hybrid groups within the Church whose exact status remained unclear. Neither members of the monastic *ordo* in the traditional sense, nor truly part of the laity, members of the military orders, lay brothers and sisters, and wandering hermits all defied categorization, to the consternation of clerical theorists.[4]

---

[1] Philip of Harvengt, *De institutione clericorum*, 4.86, in PL 203: 781; trans. based on Giles Constable, 'The Orders of Society,' in his *Three Studies in Medieval Religious and Social Thought* (Cambridge, 1998), 263.

[2] The classic study of the tripartite model of *oratores*, *bellatores*, and *laboratores* is Georges Duby, *The Three Orders: Feudal Society Imagined*, trans. Arthur Goldhammer (Chicago, MI, 1980). For historiographical discussions and critiques of these views of the long-term dominance of the tripartite system in France and elsewhere, see Constable, 'Orders of Society,' 285–8; and Elizabeth A.R. Brown, 'George Duby and the Three Orders,' *Viator* 17 (1986), 51–64. For Carolingian concerns with *ordo*, see E. Ortigues, 'Haymon d'Auxerre, théoricien des trois ordres,' in *L'Ecole carolingienne d'Auxerre de Murethach à Rémi, 830–908*, ed. Dominique Iogna-Prat, C. Jeudy, and Guy Lobrichon (Paris, 1991),181–227.

[3] For many examples, see Constable, 'Orders of Society,' 285–92, 303–4.

[4] A problem discussed by Giles Constable, 'The Place of the Crusader in Medieval Society,' *Viator* 29 (1998), 377–403.

If traditional parameters of monastic identity were in flux during this period, so too were understandings of the social roles and spiritual standing of lay arms-bearers. Between the late tenth and late twelfth centuries, men who made their living from warfare gained recognition as a distinct *ordo* (of *bellatores* or *pugnatores*) which in reality comprised a number of sub-groups ranging from landless foot soldiers (*pedites*) to highly trained mounted fighters or knights (*equites* or more commonly *milites*), castellans who dominated local areas, and counts and dukes whose power could rival that of kings. In c.1000, only those members of the upper strata of warriors were considered 'noble,' but two centuries later knights, castellans, and territorial lords had merged into a single social group of *nobiles* with its own code of conduct, rituals, and acknowledged obligations to members of the clergy and non-noble dependents, as well as to fellow nobles.[5] Warriors' values and codes of conduct developed within a broader Christian cultural framework, and on an individual level were shaped by direct contacts with members of the regular and secular clergy who sought to impress on them the duties entailed in the emerging ideal of Christian knighthood. Clerics thus played a key role in the theoretical definition of a new *ordo* of warriors.[6] But tenth- and eleventh-century ecclesiastical reformers also depended to a large degree on the support of the warrior aristocracy, who extended patronage and protection to 'reformed' prelates and founded monastic communities affiliated with the new orders.[7] The monastic *ordo* and the emerging warrior class thus came to be bound together by complex ties of interdependence, complementarity, and opposition.

Warfare and related activities played a key role in the theorization of both the monastic and warrior *ordines* from the tenth century onwards, as social and spiritual distinctions between those who bore arms and those who renounced them were felt to be increasingly important. In a process that has been amply documented by historians of ecclesiastical reform, clerics were distanced from the laity through the renunciation of particular behaviors coded as polluting and damaging to the power and purity of the church. Paramount among these renunciations was sex (and, for priests, marriage), and strict adherence to vows of celibacy became a hallmark of the 'reformed' clergy. Anxious about the buying and selling of Christ's patrimony, reformers likewise attacked simony, and warned of

---

[5] For a concise explanation of this complex process, see Constance Brittain Bouchard, *Strong of Body, Brave and Noble: Chivalry and Society in Medieval France* (Ithaca, NY, 1998), chapter 1.

[6] Perhaps the most convincing case for the influence of clerical values on arms-bearers is made by Bull, *Knightly Piety*. But see Matthew Strickland, *War and Chivalry: The Conduct and Perception of War in England and Normandy, 1066–1217* (Cambridge, 1996), 97, for the contention that warriors 'stood to gain little temporal profit from adherence to the moral dictates of the Church,' and so embraced them selectively and ignored them when they stood to lose by them.

[7] John Howe, 'The Nobility's Reform of the Medieval Church,' *American Historical Review* 93 (1988), 317–39; Constance Brittain Bouchard, *Sword, Miter, and Cloister: Nobility and the Church in Burgundy, 980–1198* (Ithaca, NY, 1987).

the moral contagion of wealth in general.[8] While clerical celibacy and simony have received a great deal of scholarly attention, another issue widely addressed by reformers and conveners of church councils in this period, the bearing of arms and shedding of blood, has often been overlooked. In the words of Richard Kaeuper, eleventh-century reformers 'pressed forward an effort to disarm the clergy as a complement to directing the armed might of knighthood.'[9] The clerical creation of a new Christian knighthood, an *ordo* that monopolized the bearing of arms in defense of Christendom, in turn prompted a rethinking of traditional clerical responsibilities and identities.

This chapter will evaluate some of the ways in which clerics, especially members of monastic orders, sought to set themselves apart from (and above) arms-bearers in the late tenth through twelfth centuries. Rather than exclusively emphasizing how professed religious defined themselves in opposition to lay warriors, the discussions below focus on two types of transformation, the conversion of individual warriors to the monastic life and the monastic colonization of battle sites, which reveal fault lines in the boundaries between the two groups. As shown in the previous chapter, the Scriptures, exegetical traditions, and liturgical performance supplied monastic writers with a theory and vocabulary of spiritual warfare, but encounters with lay warriors – who might be enemies, patrons, kinsmen, or converts – shaped monks' understanding of temporal warfare. Churchmen often railed against the wickedness of earthly military service (hence the favorite medieval Latin pun, '*militia, id est, malitia*') but they also found in the world of the *bellatores* a rich fund of metaphors which proved useful not only for thinking through their relationship with lay arms-bearers but for expressing fundamental truths about themselves.

---

[8] There is an immense literature on the so-called Gregorian Reform. Gerd Tellenbach, *Church, State, and Christian Society at the Time of the Investiture Contest*, trans. R.F. Bennett (Oxford, 1940; repr. Toronto, 1991), remains a fundamental work. For more recent assessments and updated bibliography, see I.S. Robinson, *The Papacy, 1073–1198: Continuity and Innovation* (Cambridge, 1990); and Maureen C. Miller, *Power and the Holy in the Age of the Investiture Conflict: A Brief History with Documents* (Boston, 2005). On the enforcement of clerical celibacy and its impact on clerical self-definition, see the essays in *Medieval Purity and Piety: Essays on Medieval Clerical Celibacy and Religious Reform*, ed. Michael Frassetto, Garland Medieval Casebooks 19 (New York, 1998); Dyan Elliott, 'The Priest's Wife: Female Erasure and the Gregorian Reform,' in *Medieval Religion: New Approaches*, ed. Constance Hoffman Berman (New York, 2005), 123–55; Jo Ann McNamara, 'The *Herrenfrage*: The Restructuring of the Gender System, 1050–1150,' in *Medieval Masculinities: Regarding Men in the Middle Ages*, ed. Clare A. Lees, Medieval Cultures 7 (Minneapolis, 1994), 3–29; Maureen Miller, 'Masculinity, Reform, and Clerical Culture: Narratives of Episcopal Holiness in the Gregorian Era,' *Church History* 72 (2003), 25–52; and eadem, 'Why the Bishop of Florence Had to Get Married,' *Speculum* 81 (2006), 1055–91.
[9] Richard W. Kaeuper, *Chivalry and Violence* (Oxford, 1999), 66.

Men of war and men of peace?

The clerical reformers of the tenth and eleventh centuries who promoted a new role for lay warriors as defenders of the Church were equally insistent that members of their own *ordo* should leave arms-bearing and bloodshed to worldly 'professionals.' This was nothing less than a divine mandate, as God and the saints themselves were held to be strong supporters of this ideal ordering of society.[10] This view was affirmed by the eleventh-century monastic chronicler Ralph Glaber, who related a remarkable story told to him by Hervé, the treasurer of Saint-Martin in Tours, who had received a warning from the saintly patron of his house regarding the martial sins committed by earlier generations of the abbey's monks. One day while Hervé was at prayer in the monks' church, Saint Martin appeared to him and 'in gentle tones' delivered this message:

> You can be assured that I intercede specially with the Lord for those who serve him zealously in this church. [But] certain of these have become more involved than is proper in the business of this world, and while serving the arms of war (*armis ... militaribus famulantes*) they have fallen victim to them in battle (*trucidati in prelio deciderunt*). I do not wish to conceal from you that it was only with difficulty that I won from the clemency of Christ that, snatched from the servants of the shadows, they should dwell in places of refreshment and delight.[11]

Hervé was a particularly fitting recipient of this vision, being himself, as the chronicler tells us, of noble birth and 'related by blood to some of the most ferocious men of this age.'[12] As a nobleman, a monk, and a man of peace, Hervé was also an ideal spokesman for the saint's message: members of religious communities who bore arms and fought, in defiance of their sacred vows, risked not only their lives but their very salvation. Saint Martin's own history, which was perhaps better known to medieval Christians than that of any saint, also made him an appropriate messenger. The son of a Roman tribune, Martin had joined the army as a young man but suffered a crisis of conscience over the conflict between his profession and his faith. Martin's famous conclusion, reported by Sulpicius Severus, that 'I am a soldier of Christ: I am not allowed to fight' could be just as appropriately applied to eleventh-century monks as Late Antique soldiers.[13] But by the time Ralph Glaber wrote, Martin had come to represent not only the

---

[10] M.-D. Chenu (*Nature, Man, and Society*, 225) emphasized that the concept of *ordo* implied division according to a divine plan.
[11] *Historiarum Libri Quinque*, 3.4.15, in Rodulfus Glaber, *Opera*, ed. Neithard Bulst, trans. John France and Paul Reynolds (Oxford, 1989), 118–21.
[12] *Historiarum Libri Quinque*, 3.4.14, ed. Bulst, 112–13.
[13] Sulpicius Severus, *Vita S. Martini*, 4.3, in *Vie de Saint Martin: Introduction, texte, traduction, et commentaire*, 3 vols, ed. J. Fontaine, SC 133–5 (Paris, 1967–9), 1: 260: 'Christi ego miles sum: pugnare mihi non licet.' For importance of Martin as a model for monks, see Chapter 3.

monk as *miles Christi* but the emerging ideal of Christian knighthood, and was thus an arbiter *par excellence* of both spiritual and temporal warfare.[14]

Martin's message was hardly new in the early eleventh century; prohibitions against monks (and priests) bearing weapons and participating in warfare dated back to the early centuries of the Church's history.[15] In fact, since monks had traditionally been expected to remain chaste, renounce private wealth, and avoid bloodshed, some scholars have seen in the reform movements of the Central Middle Ages a desire to 'monasticize' the clergy as a whole. But more recent studies by Maureen Miller and others have posited that reformers were less concerned with erasing the distinctions between monastic and secular clergy than with emphasizing those between clerical men and laymen. In order to win their competition with secular elites over the exercise of authority in the world, ecclesiastical leaders formulated a new model of the 'reformed' cleric as a man who willingly rejected what Miller identifies as 'most of the outward markers of lay masculinity,' in the form of women, arms, and control of resources.[16]

In Hervé's day this process was still in its early stages, and the sense of urgency that accompanied these bans was fairly new. A frequent complaint of tenth- and eleventh-century monastic reformers was that the behavior of clerics was indistinguishable from that of laymen: monks and priests (the latter often being married) were charged with unchastity and accused of neglecting their tonsure and dressing in a way that made them indistinguishable from laymen. That many clerics bore arms, whether for protection, sport, or warfare, was another commonly voiced complaint.[17] Indeed, the presence of arms (and, more to the point, men skilled in their use) in many religious houses made the business of monastic reform positively dangerous. When the saintly abbot Odo of Cluny and his supporters arrived to reform the abbey of Fleury in the 930s, the monks of that house violently resisted what they understood to be a threat to their independence. John of Salerno relates in his *Vita Sancti Odonis* that, hearing of the reformers' approach,

> some [of the monks], arming themselves with swords, went up onto the roof of the building, as though to hurl stones and missiles on their enemies from the sky. Others took up shields and swords to guard the door of the monastery, saying they would die before they allowed these men to come in, or would receive an abbot of another community.[18]

---

14 For the transformations of Martin up to the tenth century, see Barbara H. Rosenwein, 'St. Odo's St. Martin: The Uses of a Model,' *Journal of Medieval History* 4 (1978), 317–31.
15 For prohibitions against clerics serving in the military, except as chaplains, see Bachrach, *Religion and the Conduct of War*, 59 and n.116.
16 Miller, 'Narratives of Episcopal Holiness,' 27.
17 See, for example, Gregory VII's proclamation against monks and clerks who bore arms and committed homicide; in *The Epistolae Vagantes of Pope Gregory VII*, ed. and trans. H.E.J. Cowdrey (Oxford, 1972), 152–3 (Appendix A).
18 John of Salerno, *Vita S. Odonis*, 3.8, PL 133: 81; trans. Gerard Sitwell in *St. Odo of Cluny: Being the Life of St. Odo of Cluny by John of Salerno and Life of St. Gerald of Aurillac by St. Odo* (London, 1958), 80.

Less than a century later, Abbo, the superior of the now-reformed abbey of Fleury, was killed by a lance-wielding monk while trying to break up a brawl at the priory of La Réole, a dependent house notorious for spiritual laxity. Having died in the cause of reform, his biographer Aimo declared, Abbo was a martyr, whose holiness was proclaimed by the miracles that immediately proliferated at his tomb.[19]

Even if one is inclined to view the unchaste, violent cleric as a straw man invented by reformers, there is no denying the conceptual importance of this anti-model within ecclesiastical rhetoric. Beginning in the tenth century, church leaders stepped up efforts to distance all churchmen, including monks, from temporal warfare and its material trappings. Amy G. Remensnyder has shown that, far from being solely concerned with restraining the violence of laymen, conveners of peace councils held in the late tenth and eleventh centuries sought to preserve the ritual purity of churchmen's bodies by prohibiting their contact with blood, weaponry, and the bodies of the opposite sex. Like their fellows who married or committed simony, clerics who bore arms were anathematized as impure disrupters of the church's ideal peaceful state. While the contemporary reconceptualization of Christian knighthood rendered bloodshed by lay warriors acceptable and even praiseworthy under certain circumstances, a monk or priest who armed himself 'like a warrior (*ut miles*)'– even to defend ecclesiastical property – rendered himself unfit to touch liturgical objects or administer the sacraments.[20]

The language of the peace councils is particularly interesting here. The sources frequently refer to the masses of peasants and townspeople who attended such gatherings as the 'unarmed mob (*inermis vulgus*).'[21] These crowds were the natural allies of the peace movement's clerical promoters, who were similarly expected to be unarmed. Bishops and abbots did sometimes arm themselves and lead makeshift mob-armies against belligerent local lords, even though they risked being reviled by reformed peers for acting like arms-bearers instead of relying on the power of God and his saints. Clerics who bore 'secular weapons (*arma saecularia*)' were denied the protections canon law extended to their unarmed fellows who trusted in spiritual arms.[22] Within the ideal order that had

---

[19] Aimo of Fleury, an eyewitness to the events at La Réole, composed his *Vita et martyrio S. Abbonis abbatis Floriaci* soon after Abbo's death in 1004. For the account of Abbo's death, see c.20, PL 139: 410–11. A later, less detailed account of the events is given by Ralph Glaber, *Historia libri quinque*, 3.3.11, ed. Bulst, 112–13. For a discussion of Abbo as a martyr to reform, see Head, *Hagiography and the Cult of Saints*, 253–4.

[20] Amy G. Remensnyder, 'Pollution, Purity, and Peace: An Aspect of Social Reform between the Late Tenth Century and 1076,' in *The Peace of God*, ed. Head and Landes, 280–307; and Kathleen G. Cushing, *Reform and the Papacy in the Eleventh Century: Spirituality and Social Change* (Manchester, 2005), chapter 6 (esp. 125–8).

[21] For the importance of this unarmed populace to the success of individual peace meetings, see Richard Landes, 'Popular Participation in the Peace of God,' and Thomas F. Head, 'The Judgment of God: Andrew of Fleury on the Peace League of Bourges,' both in *The Peace of God*, eds. Head and Landes, 184–218 and 219–38. This is also a central theme of R.I. Moore, *The First European Revolution, c. 975–1215* (Oxford, 2000).

[22] Remensnyder, 'Pollution, Purity, and Peace,' 286–7. The councils often specified '*arma*

emerged by the late eleventh century, clerics were simultaneously classed with other 'helpless' social groups – peasants, townspeople, and women of all classes – who laid claim to warriors' protection, and with the most powerful, by reason of their privileged access to the *virtus* of saints.

The main targets of such legislation were the upper clergy, abbots and bishops who were usually the scions of aristocratic families and often lived in a manner barely distinguishable from that of lay lords, serving in royal and imperial armies and engaging in private wars with lay *potentes* and even fellow prelates.[23] In the Carolingian Empire capitularies had mandated that the upper clergy personally take part in imperial campaigns, and few of their number had objected to this duty on principle. By Friedrich Prinz's count, at least ten bishops were killed in combat between 886 and 908 alone.[24] Fighting bishops remained a feature of medieval society throughout the reform movements of the next two centuries. During the civil-war-torn reign of the German emperor Henry IV (r.1050–1106) prelates fought on both the imperial and papal sides, those in the latter group boasting that their suffering in battle constituted a form of martyrdom.[25] The German episcopate's bloodthirsty reputation had become something of a joke by the 1220s, when Caesarius of Heisterbach reported a Parisian clerk to have exclaimed, 'I can believe a great deal, but there is one thing I can never believe, namely that any bishop in Germany can ever be saved!'[26] French and English rulers relied to a lesser extent on troops raised by ecclesiastical vassals, which is not to say that these regions lacked fighting prelates.[27] Nor was bishops' involve-

---

militiaria' or '*arma saecularia*,' suggesting weapons were seen as by their very nature 'knightly' or 'secular,' and perhaps underscoring the distinction between arms of this type and *arma spiritualia*. For examples, see Mansi, 19: 271–2 (Puy), and 830 (Narbonne).

[23] For a close reading of a feud between one monastery, Saint-Victor of Marseilles, and a group of local knights in the late eleventh century, see Patrick Geary, 'Vivre en conflit dans une France sans état: Typologie des méchanismes de règlement des conflits, 1050–1200,' *Annales ESC* 41 (1986), 1107–33.

[24] Friedrich Prinz, *Klerus und Krieg im früheren Mittelalter. Untersuchgen zur Rolle der Kirche beim Aufbau der Königsherrschaft*, Monographien zur Geschichte des Mittelalters 2 (Stuttgart, 1971), 81–7.

[25] Karl Leyser, 'Warfare in the Western European Middle Ages: The Moral Debate,' in *Communications and Power in Medieval Europe: The Gregorian Revolution and Beyond*, ed. Timothy Reuter (London, 1994), 189–203 (here 196).

[26] Caesarius added, somewhat humorlessly, that while the military obligations of his country's prelates might sometimes distract them from spiritual responsibilities, nevertheless a number of them had in the past been recognized as saints. See *Dialogus miraculorum*, 2.27, 2 vols, ed. Joseph Strange (Cologne, 1851), 1: 99; trans. H. von E. Scott and C.C. Swinton Bland as *The Dialogue on Miracles*, 2 vols (New York, 1929), 1: 110–11. In most cases bishops participated only indirectly in military campaigns, supervising the raising of troops whom they did not personally accompany on campaign. See Timothy Reuter, 'Episcopi cum sua militia: The Prelate as Warrior in the Early Staufer Era,' in *Warriors and Churchmen in the High Middle Ages: Essays Presented to Karl Leyser* (London, 1992), 79–93.

[27] Reuter, 'Prelate as Warrior,' 80–1 and 84–8. Odo of Bayeux, the half-brother of William I of England, is one famous Anglo-Norman example; the monastic chronicler Orderic Vitalis said of another eleventh-century warrior-bishop, Geoffrey of Coutances, that he was more fit 'to instruct knights in hauberks to fight than clerks in vestments to sing.' See *Ecclesiastical History*, ed. Chibnall, 2: 266. Another prelate, Hugh of Noyers, bishop of

ment in warfare necessarily evidence that they were 'unreformed'; as formal or informal supporters of the peace movement, the episcopate might be called on to employ military force in their role as champions of the unarmed in rural and urban contexts, or to restrain predatory nobles from attacking church property.[28] And clerical chroniclers lauded the role played by Adhemar of Monteil, papal legate and bishop of Le Puy, as simultaneously a spiritual and military leader of the First Crusade.[29]

But the lower clergy – priests, monks, and canons – had been expected to abstain from carrying weapons, hunting, and above all, participation in warfare since Late Antiquity. Beginning in the fifth century, church councils had upheld the lower clergy's exemption from military service, and these rulings continued to be cited by canonists throughout the Central Middle Ages.[30] Although exceptions were made for priests who accompanied troops as chaplains and relic-bearers, Carolingian capitularies reiterated earlier bans on the lower clergy's participation in war, and forbade them to bear arms for any reason.[31] Despite frequent repetition of these injunctions, cases of priests, monks, lay brothers, and even nuns accused of bearing weapons and shedding blood remained quite common in later centuries.[32] For example, numerous monks took part in the Battle of Hastings (1066), and their presence on the battlefield was noted over a century later at Gisors (1198).[33] Councils of the tenth and eleventh centuries consistently included monks and nuns as well as priests in their bans on clerical

Auxerre (d.1206), was said to have enjoyed reading the Roman military strategist Vegetius and discussing his ideas with knights. See Philippe Contamine, *War in the Middle Ages*, trans. Michael Jones (London, 1984), 211.

[28] On the complex relationship of European bishops to contemporary reform movements, see *The Bishop Reformed: Studies of Episcopal Power and Culture in the Central Middle Ages*, ed. John S. Ott and Anna Trumbore Jones (Burlington, VT, 2007). The essays by John S. Ott ('Both Mary and Martha') and Valerie Ramseyer ('Pastoral Care as Military Action') both discuss instances of the use of force by bishops.

[29] There is no doubt that Adhemar served as a commander and personally participated in battles during the expedition; in fact, even after his death at Antioch numerous crusaders reported that he appeared in spirit to take part in the final assault on Jerusalem. See James A. Brundage, 'Adhemar of Puy: The Bishop and His Critics,' *Speculum* 34 (1959), 201–12.

[30] For a detailed survey of prohibitions in medieval canon law, see Ferminio Poggiaspalla, 'La chiesa e la partecipazione dei chierici alla guerra nella legislazione conciliare fino allo Decretali di Gregorio IX,' *Ephemerides iuris canonici* 15 (1959), 140–53.

[31] On Carolingian military chaplains, see Bachrach, *Religion of War*, 39 and 45–7. See, for example, the prohibition on clerical arms-bearing in *Capitularia*, c.321, PL 97: 723.

[32] For fighting priests, see Patricia H. Cullum, 'Clergy, Masculinity and Transgression in Late Medieval England,' in *Masculinity in Medieval Europe*, ed. D.M. Hadley (New York, 1999), 178–96; Jennifer D. Thibodeaux, 'Man of the Church, or Man of the Village? Gender and the Parish Clergy in Medieval Normandy,' *Gender and History* 18 (2006), 380–99; and Kent G. Hare, 'Clerics, War, and Weapons in Anglo-Saxon England,' in *The Final Argument: The Imprint of Violence on Society in Medieval and Early Modern Europe*, ed. Donald J. Kagay and L.J. Andrew Villalon (Woodbridge, 1998), 3–12. On incidents of violence in monasteries (mostly after 1200), see Jane Sayers, 'Violence in the Medieval Cloister,' *Journal of Ecclesiastical History* 41 (1990), 533–42.

[33] For Hastings, see below, n.55; for Gisors, see G.B. Flahiff, 'Deus non vult: A Critic of the Third Crusade,' *Mediaeval Studies* 9 (1947), 162–88 (at 177 and n.65).

arms-bearing and direct participation in war.[34] The degree of specificity found in the Council of Charroux's pronouncement of anathema against 'any priest, deacon, or other member of the clergy bearing arms, that is, a shield, sword, hauberk, or helmet,' suggests the high level of anxiety about physical contact with military equipment that prevailed in reforming circles by the late tenth century.[35] The conveners of the council could have been thinking of contemporary men like Gimon of Conques, a warrior-turned-monk who entered the abbey of Sainte-Foy, Conques, without leaving behind either his 'fierce and manly heart' or his martial equipage, which included 'a cuirass, a helmet, a lance, a sword, and all kinds of instruments of war.'[36]

Reformers railed against men of Gimon's persuasion who violated the sanctity of the cloister and infected their brethren with their violent tendencies. In the eleventh century Peter Damian complained that abbots were to be found in military encampments, where one 'will often see cowled heads scattered among the pressing crowd of helmeted men in armor, present under the guise of negotiating peace.' Worse, such men profaned their monasteries by using them as storehouses for their knightly equipment, 'while priestly attire used in the service of the holy altar is often found to be moth-eaten.'[37] Like many reformers, Peter contrasted the world, which rewarded brute strength and cruelty, with the monastery or hermitage, where peace-loving men could take refuge.[38] When this sanctuary was invaded by lay warriors, or even worse, by monks playing the part of warriors, monastic chroniclers were loud in their denunciations. Incidents of bloody civil strife at the English abbeys of Glastonbury (1083) and Cerne (1145) were particularly shocking to contemporaries because they so flagrantly violated right order.[39] One of the most notorious incidents was the 'schism' at Cluny in the 1120s, caused when a former abbot, Pons, invaded the cloister with a band of 'knights and foot-soldiers hired with sacred gold' and drove his rival Peter the Venerable into exile with his supporters.[40] As Peter remembered years later,

---

[34] See the following examples from eleventh-century church councils, in Mansi, 19: 483 (Toulouges), 830 (Narbonne), and 1073 (Vic).
[35] Mansi, 19: 90.
[36] *Liber miraculorum Sancte Fidis*, 1.26, ed. Luca Robertini (Spoleto, 1994), 128; trans. Pamela Sheingorn as *The Book of Sainte Foy* (Philadelphia, PA, 1995), 93–4. For a discussion of Gimon in the context of Bernard of Anger's eleventh-century miracles, see Kathleen Ashley and Pamela Sheingorn, *Writing Faith: Text, Sign, and History in the Miracles of Sainte Foy* (Chicago, MI, 1999), 36–7.
[37] Peter Damian, Letter 105.5, ed. Reindel, *Briefe*, 3: 160–1; trans. Blum, *Letters*, 4:164–5.
[38] Peter Damian, Letter 87.5, ed. Reindel, *Briefe*, 2: 508; trans. Blum, *Letters*, 3: 302.
[39] For these incidents, see David Hiley, 'Thurstan of Caen and Plainchant at Glastonbury: Musicological Reflections on the Norman Conquest,' *Proceedings of the British Academy* 72 (1986), 57–90; and Gilbert Foliot, *The Charters and Letters of Gilbert Foliot*, ed. A. Morey and C.N.L. Brooke (Cambridge, 1967), 76–9, 82–3, 85–94, 97–9 (nos. 38–41, 46, 49–57, 62–4).
[40] On these events, which have been subject to a number of interpretations, see most recently Joachim Wollasch, 'Das Schisma des Abtes Pontius von Cluny,' *Francia* 23 (1996), 31–52. Peter's own account is in *De miraculis*, 2.12, ed. Denise Bouthillier, CCCM 83 (Turnholt, 1988), 117–20 (quoting 120).

Pons 'abstained from no kind of warfare, nor from theft of property, nor from the slaughter of men.'[41] In short, the renegade abbot's behavior was a transgression against his *ordo*. By his own account, Peter refused to repay violence with violence: as he later remembered in a letter to Bernard of Clairvaux, 'When countless numbers [of men] turned aside and committed crimes never before heard of in the monastic order (*ordine monastico*), they never felt my sword, never its sharp point, never my spear, and scarcely did they ever hear a harsh word from my mouth.'[42] To be a monk was, for Peter, to be a man of peace, who might wield only the spiritual sword, namely the word of God (Eph. 6:17).[43] As Peter's contemporary Honorius Augustodunensis declared, no man who bore arms could rightly be called a monk.[44] Similar sentiments were expressed by critics of monks who defied papal orders by becoming crusaders, thus flouting their vows of obedience and stability as well as 'apostasizing' from their order by assuming the guise of warriors.[45] The monk Bernard *Grossus* remembered, years later, that after Pope Urban II called for the First Crusade at Clermont in 1095, 'not only abbots and monks but even hermits deserted their monasteries and went off to Jerusalem.'[46] Fifty years on, the appeal of crusading for professed religious had evidently not waned, as Bernard of Clairvaux lamented that monks and lay-brothers of his order were rushing off to join the armies of the Second Crusade.[47] Approached about the possibility of personally leading an expedition to the East, Bernard, for whom the monastic ideal was synonymous with *spiritual*

---

[41] *De miraculis*, 2.12, ed. Bouthillier, 120. For discussion of these passages in light of Peter's attitude toward violence and right order, see Gregory A. Smith, '*Sine rege, sine principe*: Peter the Venerable on Violence in Twelfth-Century Burgundy,' *Speculum* 77 (2002), 1–33 (at 16).

[42] Peter the Venerable, Letter 192, in *The Letters of Peter the Venerable*, 2 vols (Cambridge, MA, 1967), ed. Giles Constable, 1: 446; trans. in Smith, 'Peter the Venerable on Violence,' 17–18.

[43] In this letter, Peter uses the story of Pons to introduce a discussion of the 'two swords' theory of secular and ecclesiastical authority; see Letter 192, in *Letters*, ed. Constable, 1: 446, and for commentary, 2: 228–9.

[44] Honorius Augustodunensis, *Summa gloria*, c.1 and 9, MGH Libelli de lite 3: 69; cited by Constable, 'Orders,' 302 and n.212.

[45] For overviews of the problem, see Elizabeth Siberry, *Criticism of Crusading, 1095–1274*. (Oxford, 1985), 39f.; James Brundage, 'A Transformed Angel (X 3.31.18): The Problem of the Crusading Monk,' in *Studies in Medieval Cistercian History presented to Jeremiah F. O'Sullivan*, ed. M. Basil Pennington, CS 13 (Spenser, MA, 1971), 55–62; idem, 'Crusades, Clerics, and Violence: Reflections on a Canonical Theme,' in *The Experience of Crusading, Vol. 1: Western Approaches*, ed. Marcus Bull and Norman Housley (Cambridge, 2003), 147–56; and Purkis, *Crusading Spirituality*, 12–16. It is significant that Urban II reiterated prohibitions against clerics bearing arms at the Council of Clermont in 1095, the same council at which he called for the First Crusade; see *The Councils of Urban II, Vol. 1: Decreta Claromontensia*, ed. Robert Somerville (Amsterdam, 1972), 74, 113, 143.

[46] Geoffrey Grossus, *Vita b. Bernardi fundatoris congregationis de Tironio*, c.16, PL 172: 1378.

[47] Bernard of Clairvaux, Letter 544, in SBO 8: 511–12.

warfare, recoiled in horror: 'Who am I to arrange armies in battle order, to lead forth armed men? I could think of nothing more remote from my calling.'[48]

As warfare became an increasingly important marker of boundaries between worldly power and spiritual authority, men of the sword and men of God, debates swirled over definitions of just war and church leaders edged closer to definitive rulings on when and against whom war could be waged by Christians.[49] Even the most active clerical promoters of peace fell short of advocating an end to *all* war; as they saw it, wars were ordained (or at least permitted) by God, and strife was a natural feature of celestial as well as earthly society.[50] The Scriptures, after all, described the fall of Satan and the rebel angels as the result of their military defeat by the archangel Michael and his cohort (Rev. 12: 7–9), and predicted that the minions of the Beast would arrive in the form of an army of monstrous mounted warriors to herald the approaching end of the world (Rev. 9:7–10). Visions of the afterlife frequently included descriptions of angels and demons doing battle for the souls of dead Christians.[51] Writing at the height of the peace movement, Fulbert of Chartres (d.1028) wistfully expressed his hope that all wars would cease, and all spears and swords be beaten into scythes and ploughshares (fulfilling the prophecy of Isa. 2:4), but also composed a special prayer to be said by warriors going into battle who wished to fight well.[52] Fulbert's outlook was characteristic of an ecclesiastical approach to arms-bearers that, in the words of Richard Kaeuper, 'constantly mix[ed] praise and denunciation to produce a society in which the Church could live, and an armed force with which the Church could work.' Warriors, in turn, were offered a choice: they could devote themselves to *militia*, piously serving God and His representatives; or they could give vent to their evil impulses in *malitia*, evildoing, and be damned.[53]

Although, as we saw in Chapter 1, the early medieval Church had sometimes given its blessing to the wars of Christian kings, in Fulbert's day many churchmen continued to doubt whether secular warfare could be anything other than *malitia*. In the earliest Christian centuries most theologians had interpreted the Gospels' message of peace and love as a prohibition against Christians serving in the military, and many patristic writers who wrote vividly about spiritual combat had been, strictly speaking, pacifists.[54] Even after the Church's

---

[48] Bernard of Clairvaux, Letter 256.4, in *SBO* 8: 164–5; trans. Bruno Scott James, *The Letters of St. Bernard of Clairvaux* (Chicago, MI, 1953), 472 (no. 399).
[49] James A. Brundage, 'Holy War and the Medieval Lawyers,' repr. in *The Crusades, Holy War, and Canon Law* (Ashgate, 1991), 99–140; Russell, *Just War*, chapters 2–3.
[50] Kaeuper, *Chivalry and Violence*, 63; Strickland, *War and Chivalry*, 71; James A. Brundage, 'The Limits of War-Making Power: The Contribution of Medieval Canonists,' repr. in *The Crusades, Holy War, and Canon Law*, 69–85 (at 73).
[51] Little, *Benedictine Maledictions*, 191.
[52] *The Letters and Poems of Fulbert of Chartres*, ed. and trans. Frederick Behrends (Oxford, 1976), 248 and 149 (nos. 135 and 149).
[53] Kaeuper, *Chivalry and Violence*, 64.
[54] Augustine of Hippo was, of course, an important exception in this regard. A large body of literature exists on the early Christian debate over military service; Harnack, *Militia Christi*, is still a fundamental work, though it should be read in conjunction with more recent studies such as Helgeland, *Christians and the Military*; Louis J. Swift, *The Early*

leadership had reconciled itself to welcoming soldiers into the fold, and the first steps had been taken in the creation of a theory of just war, most early medieval churchmen continued to regard soldiers as evildoers and denounce warfare as a reprehensible activity that stained participants not only with blood but, far worse, with sin. The killing of another Christian in single combat or battle, regardless of the circumstances, carried a heavy penance in canon law, and even warriors who killed pagans were subject to spiritual penalties if they killed for plunder.[55] Despite the fact that William of Normandy had secured papal approval for his invasion of England in 1066, penances were meted out to all who fought with him at Hastings (including monks and clerics) according to the numbers of men they had killed or wounded.[56] The dominant clerical attitude up to the eleventh century was, in the words of one anonymous penitentialist, that warriors followed a calling 'which cannot be carried out without some doing of evil.'[57] Hints of a model of Christian knighthood were to be found already in the tenth and early eleventh centuries, when greater emphasis came to be placed on intentionality in the judgment of sins, including participation in warfare. But the watershed in the transformation of the Church's attitude towards war and warriors occurred in the second half of the eleventh century.[58]

Already by c.1000 there had emerged a model of the just Christian warrior as protector of the poor and weak and defender of the Church's interests. While most churchmen continued to see the violence of military life as fundamentally incompatible with Christian virtues, others sought to define a new ideal, a secular *potens* who fought only to protect the poor and weak and used legitimate force to defend the interests of the Church. Already in the tenth century Abbo of Fleury had articulated an ideal of just lay warriors (*agonistae*) who 'fight most sagaciously the adversaries of the holy Church of God.'[59] In the course

Fathers on War and Military Service (Wilmington, 1983); and M. Whitby, 'Deus Nobiscum: Christianity, Warfare, and Morale in Late Antiquity,' in *Modus Operandi: Essays in Honour of Geoffrey Rickman*, ed. M. Austin, J. Harries and C. Smith (London, 1998), 191–208.

[55] Karl Leyser, 'Early Medieval Canon Law and the Beginnings of Knighthood,' in *Communications and Power in Medieval Europe, 1: The Carolingian and Ottonian Centuries*, ed. Timothy Reuter (London, 1994), 51–71; H.E.J. Cowdrey, 'Bishop Ermenfried of Sion and the Penitential Ordinance Following the Battle of Hastings,' *Journal of Ecclesiastical History* 20 (1969), 225–42.

[56] Cowdrey, 'Bishop Ermenfried,' 242.

[57] Interestingly, the author classifies both the soldier and the merchant as followers of professions that necessitate an '*admixtio mali*.' See *De vera ac falsa poenitentia ad Christum devotam*, c.15, PL 40: 113–30 (at col. 1125). This is a pseudo-Augustinian work of the eleventh century.

[58] More generally, see Erdmann, *Idea of Crusade*; Flori, *Guerre sainte*; Ernst-Dieter Hehl, 'War, Peace, and the Christian Order,' in *The New Cambridge Medieval History, IV: c.1024–c.1198*, ed. David Luscombe and Jonathan Riley-Smith (Cambridge, 2004),185–228; and Christopher Holdsworth, 'Ideals and Reality: Some Attempts to Control and Defuse War in the Twelfth Century,' in *The Church and War: Papers Read at the 21st Summer Meeting and the 22nd Winter Meeting of the Ecclesiastical History Society*, ed. W.J. Sheils, Studies in Church History 20 (Oxford, 1983), 59–78.

[59] Abbo's use of the term *agonista* is perhaps inspired by 2 Tim. 2:5. Quoted in Mostert, *Abbo of Fleury*, 93–4.

of the next century, reform-minded popes carved out new roles for warriors, first as defenders of the papacy against its enemies, and later as holy warriors commissioned to extend the boundaries of Christendom. These men were no doers of *malitia*, but faithful members of Christ's *militia*, who marched into battle with solemnly blessed weapons and under the holy war banners of the saints, confident that a place had been reserved for them in heaven.[60] The creation of these new roles, as monastic contemporaries realized, granted arms-bearers an unprecedented degree of autonomy in matters of salvation. Just as importantly, warriors no longer needed to become men of peace (i.e., monks) in order to live Christian, even holy, lives, provided they adhered to the rules of war laid down by the Church. As the Benedictine abbot Guibert of Nogent (d.1124) famously wrote of the early crusading movement,

> God ordained holy wars in our time, so that the knightly order (*ordo equestris*) and the erring mob (*vulgus oberrans*), who, like their ancient pagan models, were engaged in mutual slaughter, might find a new way of earning salvation. Thus, without having chosen (as is customary) a monastic life, without any religious commitment, they were compelled to give up this world; free to continue their customary pursuits, nevertheless they earned some measure of God's grace by their own efforts.[61]

But even while the emerging model of Christian knighthood opened up new paths to salvation for men reluctant to give up the profession of war, many warriors continued to adhere to the traditional belief that heaven was best sought in the cloister. As we saw in the previous chapter, monks actively encouraged the laity to view monasteries as citadels of faith, where the bloodstained souls of worldly warriors could be washed clean through purifying spiritual combat. Accommodating the ever-larger numbers of penitent warriors who sought entrance into the religious life after c.1000 presented practical and conceptual challenges for religious houses. In the abstract, the presence of knightly converts spurred monks to think hard about the theoretical relationship between the lay warrior (the *miles saecularis*) and the *miles Christi*, a subject we will take up in Chapters 4 and 5. More practically, it proved difficult for many former men of war to make the transition to monastic life, and impossible for them to avoid bringing their new brethren into close contact with the bellicose world from which they had come.

---

[60] On this process and evolving models of spiritual warfare, see Chapter 3. See also Erdmann, *Idea of Crusade*, 35–56 and 74–7; Jean Flori, 'Mort et martyre des guerriers vers 1100: L'exemple de la Première Croisade,' *Cahiers de civilisation médiévale* 34 (1991), 121–39.

[61] Guibert of Nogent, *Gesta Dei per Francos*, 1.1, ed. Huygens, 87: 'instituit in nostro tempore prelia sancta deus, ut ordo equestris et vulgus oberrans, qui vetustae paganitatis exemplo in mutuas versabantur cedes, novum repperirent salutis promerendae genus, ut nec funditus, electa, uti fieri asolet, monastica conversatione seu religiosa qualibet professione, seculum relinquere cogerentur, sed sub consueta licentia et habitu ex suo ipsorum officio dei aliquatenus gratiam consequerentur.' Trans. Levine, *Deeds of God*, 28.

The conversion of warriors to monastic life

One of the strongest links between war and monastic culture was literally embodied by the presence within many communities of men who had lived as *bellatores* before entering the religious life.[62] Warriors might enter a monastery under a variety of circumstances: they might suddenly develop (or have always secretly harbored) an aversion to bloodshed; they might make a battlefield vow to devote themselves to God; or they might receive wounds that rendered them unable to fulfill their military and social obligations. These men could not have entirely forgotten their experiences of war, though they may well have come to view them in a different light. Nor, even as they gradually learned to think and act like monks, did they necessarily cut themselves off from friends and kin who remained in the world. With the proliferation of new orders such as the Carthusians, Premonstratensians, and Cistercians, who rejected the practice of child oblation yet continued to draw most of their numbers from the families of warrior elites, such adult converts were a substantial and ever-growing component of the monastic population from the eleventh century onwards.[63] This marked a radical departure from the practice of child oblation, which had provided the majority of recruits to monasteries before 1000, and which had been predicated on the belief that the prayers of those raised from childhood in the cloister would be purer and more pleasing to God.[64] But with the decline of oblation in the eleventh and twelfth centuries, many men who had spent their youths training to fight not only made successful transitions into the religious life but rose to positions of influence within their communities and even gained reputations for holiness. That they were able to do so was as much because of as in spite of their bellicose pasts.[65]

The circumstances under which warriors entered monastic life varied widely, as attested by the charters, chronicles, and works of hagiography that preserve their stories, but one constant among many of these conversion scenarios is war. As Philip of Navarre declared in the thirteenth century, 'When knights and other military men are at war and get into danger they have more fear of the Lord, and are in greater fear of death, than when they are banqueting at home or living in a land at peace.'[66] Charters, chronicles, and *vitae* are filled with stories of warriors-turned-monks which seem to bear out Philip's observation. Young

---

[62] Of course, large numbers of those who took monastic vows also did so as child oblates or as enfeebled or dying postulants who joined houses *ad succurrendum*. For an overview of monastic recruitment from warrior families in this period, see Bouchard, *Strong of Body*, chapter 5; and on entrance *ad succurrendum* more specifically, see Jean Leclercq, 'La vêture ad succurrendum,' *Studia Anselmiana* 3rd ser., 37 (1955), 158–68.

[63] Joseph H. Lynch, *Simoniacal Entry into Religious Life from 1000 to 1260* (Columbus, OH, 1976), chapters 1 and 2; Charles de Miramon, 'Embracer l'état monastique à l'âge adulte (1050–1200): Étude sur la conversion tardive,' *Annales HSS* 56/4 (1999), 825–49.

[64] A detailed study of the concept and practice of oblation is Mayke de Jong, *In Samuel's Image: Child Oblation in the Early Medieval West* (Leiden, 1996).

[65] On the figure of the converted warrior in monastic hagiography, see Chapter 5.

[66] Quoted in Alexander Murray, *Reason and Society in the Middle Ages* (Oxford, 1978), 376;

men whose early experiences of war were especially terrifying might seek to escape the years of fighting that lay ahead by the expedient of monastic profession. Such was the case with the young German nobleman Everard, the younger brother of the count of Berg, whose decision to join the Cistercians of Morimond took shape while he rode home after a particularly bloody engagement in which several hundred men had been killed.[67] Practical considerations lay behind the conversions of some warriors to the monastic life, though the spiritual benefits to be gained from this step cannot have been lost on even the most pragmatic converts. Taking the habit might even be a last resort for a nobleman hoping to avoid being brought to justice for dishonorable or criminal behavior.[68] Some men were driven to seek shelter in the cloister after receiving a serious wound that effectively ended their fighting days.[69] The Norman nobleman William Giroie, who joined the Benedictines of Bec after being blinded and castrated by his own lord, may have felt he had no choice but to become a monk.[70]

Others viewed the religious profession as an alternative to going on crusade, as both options required some of the same sacrifices and, it seems, were believed (at least by some laymen) to confer comparable spiritual benefits. Recent scholarship has emphasized the quasi-monastic nature of crusading as presented in chronicles of the First Crusade, and William Purkis has convincingly argued that contemporaries viewed crusading as a novel form of *imitatio Christi*, one that directly challenged the monastic model.[71] Lay arms-bearers may have viewed crusading and monastic conversion as points along a single spiritual continuum. We know that one noble leader of the 1101 Crusade, Count William of Nevers, decided to join the Carthusians rather than take part in the Second Crusade.[72] Odo Arpinus, the former viscount of Bourges, was another veteran of the 1101 expedition who renounced warfare upon his return home. Odo left the world to enter the abbey of Cluny on the advice of Pope Pascal II, who advised him that he risked losing the spiritual benefits he had accrued by his suffering in the East if he returned to the 'muddy road' of worldly life, where he would soon be mired

---

see Philip of Navarre, *Les quatres ages de l'homme*, c.76, ed. Marcel de Fréville (Paris, 1888), 44.

[67] On Everard, see Herbert Grundmann, 'Adelsbekehrungen im Hochmittelalter: *Conversi und Nutriti* im Kloster,' in Joseph Fleckenstein and Karl Schmid, ed., *Adel und Kirche: Gerd Tellenbach zum 65. Geburtstag dargebracht von Freunden un Schulern* (Frieburg, 1968), 341–2.

[68] See, for example, the case of Hugh of Crécy described in *The Chronicle of Morigny*, trans. Cusimano, 50–1; Caesarius of Heisterbach tells a similar story of the conversion of a nobleman facing a death sentence in *Dialogus miraculorum*, 1.31, trans. Scott and Bland, 1: 38–9.

[69] See the examples of such converts in Bull, *Knightly Piety*, 126–7; and Amy Livingstone, 'Brother Monk: Monks and Their Family in the Chartrain, 1000–1200AD,' in *Medieval Monks and Their World: Ideas and Realities*, ed. David Blanks, Michael Frassetto and Amy Livingstone (Leiden, 2006), 93–115.

[70] Orderic Vitalis, *Ecclesiastical History*, ed. Chibnall, 2: 15.

[71] This is a central argument of Purkis, *Crusading Spirituality*.

[72] William's (presumably advanced) age may well have played a role in his decision not to return to the East. For this and other examples, see Siberry, *Criticism of Crusading*, 37.

in sin once again.⁷³ Understanding that some laymen wavered between going East and embracing the religious life, monastic writers took pains to emphasize the spiritual superiority of the latter option.⁷⁴ Caesarius of Heisterbach, for instance, recounted an *exemplum* about a canon of Liège who was moved by Saint Bernard's preaching of the Second Crusade to take the cross, 'not indeed of that overseas expedition, but of the Order, judging it better for his soul's health to imprint the enduring cross forever upon his heart than to sew the short-lived sign upon his garment for a season.'⁷⁵

If many returning crusaders became monks, at least some warriors came to regret that they had not taken the cross before retiring to the cloister. In the *Vision of Gunthelm*, a text attributed to Peter the Venerable that circulated widely in the twelfth and thirteenth centuries, a strapping young English *miles* guilty of many sins decided to go on crusade 'so that he might make atonement to Christ by scattering His enemies with his famous strength,' but was persuaded by a well-meaning abbot to join the Cistercians instead. The religious life was, the abbot explained, far superior to any worldly endeavor, including crusading: 'if it pleased him to visit Jerusalem, he should approach [the heavenly Jerusalem] of which he would not be some [earthly] citizen, whose vision [of the earthly Jerusalem] in this life would be of no assistance to his salvation.'⁷⁶ When, as a novice, Gunthelm continued to dream of taking the cross, and finally decided to abandon the monastery, a demon attacked the young man in his cell, leaving him near death. Gunthelm's soul was subsequently escorted through Hell and Heaven by Saint Benedict and the archangel Raphael, who convinced him, before returning him to his body, that he would achieve salvation only by persevering in the religious life. This *visio* seems to reflect the very real appeal the crusading movement held not only for knights but for monks, an appeal which is only beginning to be recognized.⁷⁷

The penalties for apostasy were serious, and many laymen reluctant to take irreversible religious vows chose instead to join the *societas* or *confraternitas* of a particular house. This could entail a formal ceremony in which the new *confrater*

---

73 Orderic Vitalis narrates the story of Odo's conversion in his *Ecclesiastical History*, ed. and trans. Chibnall, 5: 350–3 (here 352). On Odo's eventful career before and after his entrance into religious life, see Giles Constable, 'The Three Lives of Odo Arpinus: Viscount of Bourges, Crusader, Monk of Cluny,' in *Religion, Text, and Society in Medieval Spain and Northern Europe: Essays in Honor of J.N. Hillgarth*, ed. Thomas E. Burman, Mark D. Meyerson, and Leah Shopkow (Toronto, 2002), 183–99.

74 Siberry, *Criticism of Crusading*, 35–41.

75 Caesarius of Heisterbach, *Dialogus miraculorum*, 1.6, ed. and trans. Scott and Bland, 1: 12–15 (quoting 13). Siberry (*Criticism of Crusading*, 36) suggests this was probably Archdeacon Philip of Liège. Compare Caesarius' story of a nobleman named Henry who was moved to join Clairvaux by Bernard's preaching of the Crusade, and whose baser-born servant was advised by Bernard to content himself with going East (*Dialogus*, 1.16, ed. Strange, 1: 23–5).

76 See the edition of the *Visio Gunthelmi* by Giles Constable, 'The Vision of Gunthelm and Other Visions Attributed to Peter the Venerable,' *Revue Bénédictine* 66 (1956), 92–114 (here 106).

77 The most thorough consideration to date is Purkis, *Crusading Spirituality*, chapter 1.

offered a donation and the monks confirmed his new standing, which entitled him to inclusion in the community's prayers as well as eventual burial in its cemetery. Arms-bearers often cemented such bonds of confraternity just before a major battle.[78] The relatives of a warrior killed in battle might seek to obtain such quasi-monastic status for him posthumously, as did the kin of Geoffrey *Festucam*, who donated a parcel of the dead man's land to the canons of Angers in 1095 on the understanding that they would bury Geoffrey in the cathedral and add his name to their martyrology.[79] But if confraternity conferred spiritual benefits on laymen, such relationships also threatened to entangle monastic communities in distinctly secular negotiations. Such proved to be the case for the abbey of Montiérender in the eleventh century, when its monks received an urgent appeal from a *miles* and *confrater* named Hugh, who had been wounded in battle and taken prisoner. Hugh successfully petitioned the monks to ransom him 'out of fraternity' so that he might become a monk at Montiérender.[80]

Although much work remains to be done on the relationships between monastic men and women and their families, there is ample evidence that bonds of kinship influenced many converts' decisions to enter particular communities, and that these bonds were unlikely to be neatly severed at the moment of profession. It was common for an aristocratic family to patronize a single monastery over many decades, with members donating property, presenting children as oblates, converting as adults or entering the house *ad succurrendum* in every generation.[81] Unsurprisingly, families also sought to appoint relatives to positions of influence in the communities they patronized.[82] Young men were often given as oblates to communities where a brother, uncle, or male cousin was already

---

[78] For such relationships, see Megan McLaughlin, *Consorting with Saints: Prayer for the Dead in Early Medieval France* (Ithaca, 1994), 168f. On the related phenomenon of *donati*, laypeople who entered into bonds of confraternity with particular houses, becoming 'semi-religious,' neither fully monastic nor fully lay, see Charles de Miramon, *Les 'Donnés' au moyen âge: Une forme de vie religieuse laïque (v.1180-v.1500)* (Paris, 1999).

[79] McLaughlin, *Consorting with Saints*, 168. For the refusal to bury warriors who were excommunicates or peace-breakers, see Bachrach, *Religion and the Conduct of War*, 73.

[80] Cited by McLaughlin, *Consorting with Saints*, 87. The language of the charter recording this incident suggests Hugh believed the monks were under obligation to ransom him because of the bonds between them (cemented by Hugh's donation of land to the abbey): 'per fraternitatem que inter nos et eum erat, nobis mandavit ut eum redimeremus et in monachum orinaremus.' We can only speculate about Hugh's reasons for becoming a monk from the bare-bones narrative supplied in the document. For the charter, see *Collection des principaux cartulaires du diocèse de Troyes*, t. IV, ed. Charles Lalore (Paris, 1878), 187–8.

[81] Bouchard, *Sword, Miter, and Cloister*, 50.

[82] Such strategies did not preclude a sincere spiritual investment in the success of such foundations; many noble founders and patrons of monastic houses were concerned not merely to monopolize abbacies or priorates but to promote reform, and often greatly diminished their patrimonies to do so. See Joachim Wollasch, 'Parenté noble et monachisme réformateur: Observations sur les 'conversions' à la vie monastique aux XIe et XIIe siècles,' *Revue historique* 264 (1980), 3–24 (esp. 18f.); and Constance Brittain Bouchard, 'Noble Piety and Reformed Monasticism: The Dukes of Burgundy in the Twelfth Century,' in *Noble Piety and Reformed Monasticism: Sudies in Medieval Cistercian History VII*, ed. E. Rozanne Elder (Kalamazoo, MI: Cistercian Publications, 1981), 1–9.

in residence, and the same was true of women who entered the religious life.[83] Much has also been made over instances of what Constance Brittain Bouchard has termed 'dynastic suicide,' in which whole clans renounced the world for lives of prayer, or sent all surviving sons into the monastery, leaving their house without direct heirs.[84] Fiona Griffiths has found many examples of family groups who remained close after entering monastic life, often living together under a single roof or in neighboring communities, as well as instances of clerical men who provided female relatives living in the cloister with pastoral care.[85]

Although the taking of monastic vows theoretically mandated the abandonment of all worldly ties, including kinship bonds, studies of particular religious houses have brought to light many examples of individuals who continued to be actively involved in family affairs long after assuming the habit. In her work on the Chartrain, Amy Livingstone found that noblemen who became monks often continued to identify themselves by their old cognomens when they witnessed charters, sometimes even referring to family property as if it still belonged to them. She speculates that cutting themselves off from family concerns may have proven particularly difficult for monks who had spent decades as husbands, fathers, and household heads.[86] The transition may have been easier for an unmarried *miles* like Richard of Heudicourt, who became a monk at Saint-Évroul on the advice of his lord's lord. Carried into the monastery and given up for dead after being wounded by a lance, Richard survived to become a model monk. Though his wound never fully healed (earning him the grisly nickname *Vulneratus*), his zeal and generosity in endowing his new community made him a great favorite with the abbot, who even entrusted Richard with overseeing the construction of the new abbatial church.[87] As Penelope Johnson has suggested, commenting on the case of another eleventh-century *miles*, Robert of Moncontour, who as a monk of La Trinité, Vendôme, was appointed to oversee the very properties he had donated to the abbey, 'It was, indeed, eminently practical to appoint men like these to positions of authority and responsibility, since their secular lives had given them invaluable administrative experience.'[88] As we

---

[83] For male relatives professing in the same communities, see Bull, *Knightly Piety*, 141; and Livingstone, 'Brother Monk,' 95; for religious women, see Penelope D. Johnson, *Equal in Monastic Profession: Religious Women in Medieval France* (Chicago, 1991), 19–21.

[84] For examples and references, see Bouchard's *Strong of Body*, 150; and Wollasch, 'Parenté noble,' 10–11.

[85] Fiona J. Griffiths, 'Siblings and the Sexes within the Medieval Religious Life,' *Church History* 77 (2008), 26–53 (esp. 45–8).

[86] Livingstone ('Brother Monk,' 99–102) tells the wonderful story of Robert *Aculeus* ('the Sting'), a warrior who, after entering Saint-Père-de-Chartres, not only kept his nickname but 'continued to act as the head of his family,' even summoning his two sons to his new home and persuading them to renounce their rights to disputed family lands claimed by the monks.

[87] Orderic Vitalis, *Ecclesiastical History*, ed. Chibnall, 2: 132–3.

[88] Penelope D. Johnson, *Prayer, Patronage, and Power: The Abbey of la Trinité, Vendôme* (New York, 1981), 40. For similar conclusions, see Giles Constable, *Reformation of the Twelfth Century* (Cambridge, 1996), 77; and Livingston, 'Brother Monk,' 101–2. Many more references to knights entering the monastic life and, in some cases, continuing to

will see in Chapter 5, monastic hagiographers often claimed that many of the qualities that made arms-bearers successful in the world – such as loyalty and fortitude, even physical strength and bravery – made them exemplary monks following their conversions. Such hagiographical claims seem to be borne out by case-studies of these successful knightly converts.

As *oratores*, nobles who had entered the monastic life became intercessors for patrons and kin who continued to live in the world, as well as those who had died, and many monks would have recognized the names of blood relatives on the rosters of donors for whom they prayed.[89] Oblates and adult converts alike were expected to concern themselves with the spiritual wellbeing of family members and cultivate their continued patronage. Many monks exhibited concern for kinsmen who persisted in the worldly profession of arms, and entreated them by word and example to follow their lead in abandoning the world. Bernard of Clairvaux, who entered Cîteaux as a young man along with several of his brothers and his uncle, is undoubtedly the best-known example.[90] The nobleman and monastic reformer William of Volpiano, who had himself been given as an oblate by his father Robert, wrote urging his parent to give up martial pursuits and join him in the cloister. William also convinced two of his three brothers to collaborate in his foundation of a new abbey at Fruttuaria in 1003, which was built on family land and included both men in its original group of monks.[91]

In their new lives as *oratores*, these men did not simply renounce their familial obligations, although the nature of these obligations undoubtedly changed upon their entrance into monastic life; no longer permitted to defend their patrimony with arms, elite converts could, as monks, fight for the souls of their kin with the spiritual weapon of prayer. As we will see in the next chapter, this is just how new monks would have been taught (perhaps even by kinsmen) to view their calling, suggesting that the monastic identification with the soldiery of Christ may have helped smooth converted arms-bearers' transition to the religious life. The constant stream of elite oblates and knightly converts into monasteries also helped ensure that, even as church reformers defined monks and lay arms-bearers as opposites, members of both groups would likely have had difficulty accepting this view of society. After all, most of those whom reformers designated as 'men of peace' were the brothers, by blood, of worldly 'men of war' who might someday renounce bloodshed for the spiritual combat of the cloister.

---

manage lands and serve in a diplomatic capacity are provided by Christopher Harper-Bill, 'The Piety of the Anglo-Norman Knightly Class,' in *Proceedings of the Battle Conference on Anglo-Norman Studies* 2, ed. R. Allen Brown (Woodbridge, 1979), 63–77 (esp. 71–7).

[89] On the role of monastic communities as intercessors, see McLaughlin, *Consorting with Saints*.

[90] Specifics on the conversions and later careers of Bernard's kinsmen are provided by Anselm Dimier, 'Saint Bernard et le recrutement de Clairvaux,' *Revue Mabillon* 42 (1952), 17–30, 56–68, and 69–78 (esp. 19f.).

[91] For William's relationship with his father, see Erdmann, *Idea of Crusade*, 13. On the foundation of Fruttuaria, see Ralph Glaber, *Vita domni Willelmi abbatis*, c.9, in *Opera*, ed. Bulst, 278–9.

Becoming a monk

While stories abound of noble converts who became valued members of monastic communities, taking on leadership roles and eventually dying in the odor of sanctity, doubts about whether warriors could make good monks persisted in the minds of many contemporaries. As early as the sixth century, Gregory the Great had recommended no warrior be allowed to take monastic vows before his resolve had been tested for three years, and (though this was a lengthy novitiate by medieval standards) his eleventh-century successor and namesake Gregory VII invoked this piece of wisdom in a letter to Abbot Hugh of Cluny.[92] The canonist Ivo of Chartres (d.1116) echoed these sentiments, cautioning that warriors often adopted the habit rashly and without a sincere commitment to renounce their worldly obligations.[93] Fears that adult converts might change their minds and return to the world led many new orders to reject the traditional Benedictine practice of accepting aged or dying patrons *ad succurrendum* in the eleventh and twelfth centuries. And in fact noblemen did sometimes leave the cloister after taking their final vows, upon finding that they were not as near death as they had imagined![94] Some monastic writers complained of converted warriors that they brought with them into the cloister their worldly aggression and competitiveness, qualities which made them prone to excessive and ostentatious displays of asceticism. Giles Constable has posited that such men may have 'continued to wage against their own bodies the physical battle they had previously waged against their enemies in the world.'[95]

Writing in the eleventh century, Anselm of Canterbury likened monks raised in the cloister from childhood to the angels, and men who took vows in adulthood to the saints. 'But,' he cautioned, 'let not angels (i.e., *nutriti*) despise saints (i.e., *conversi*) because they have been overcome by temptation now and then, nor saints despise angels because they have never suffered from tempta-

---

[92] The background here was Duke Hugh I of Burgundy's sudden entrance into Cluny in 1079, a conversion which Gregory blamed Abbot Hugh for encouraging because he felt the duke could have better served the Church and its people as a pious warrior. For the text, see Gregory VII, *Registrum*, 6.17, in *Das Register Gregors VII*, ed. Erich Caspar, MGH Epist. selectae 2 (Berlin, 1920–3), 423–4.

[93] Ivo of Chartres, *Decretum*, c.124, PL 161: 728.

[94] Constable, *Reformation of the Twelfth Century*, 82–3. A remarkable example is the case of William Malevicino, who became a monk at Notre Dame, Coulombs in the 1130s after being seriously wounded in battle. Once he began to recover, however, William prepared to return to the world. But on the very day he put aside his habit and dressed again as a layman, his wound reopened, prompting him to seek admittance to yet another monastery! William's story is told in a charter of Coulombs; see the edition in *Cartulaire de l'abbaye de Saint-Martin de Pontoise*, ed. J. Depoin, 5 vols (Pontoise, 1895–1909), 3: 254; and for commentary, Richard Kaeuper, *Holy Warriors: The Religious Ideology of Chivalry* (Philadelphia, PA, 2009), 131–3.

[95] Giles Constable, 'Moderation and Restraint in Ascetic Practices in the Middle Ages,' in *From Athens to Chartres: Neoplatonism and Medieval Thought*, ed. Haijo Jan Westra (Leiden, 1992), 315–27 (here 322).

tion at all.'⁹⁶ Adult converts might possess greater maturity and resolve, but they brought the taint of the world into the cloister and threatened to pollute those who had been carefully preserved from sin since childhood. The earliest western monastic rules had made provision for oblates, and many, if not most, of the inhabitants of early medieval monasteries entered the religious life as children, who from their formative years received instruction in the texts, skills, and virtues that would enable them to function as adult monks.⁹⁷ In houses like Cluny, where the liturgy consumed a far greater proportion of the monastic day and required considerably more training than it had in Saint Benedict's day, adult converts might never acquire sufficient expertise to take their place in the monks' choir.⁹⁸ By the twelfth century, however, the proportion of oblates had declined substantially, with many orders rejecting the practice as tending to produce adult monks lacking in vocation.⁹⁹

Even for those who joined orders that did not accept oblates, the transition from the world to the cloister was rarely as rapid or as smooth as medieval hagiographers would have us believe. In her study of early Cistercian communities, Martha Newman identified two major challenges that faced men entering these houses: mastering the liturgical prayers and rituals that lent structure to the monastic life, and learning how to think like monks.¹⁰⁰ Many who joined reformed orders were priests or canons who, though they may have originally come from families of warriors, already possessed the skills needed to participate in the liturgy, but for arms-bearers who entered the monastery with no liturgical training and perhaps little Latin this part of the transition was far more difficult.¹⁰¹ Though *laicus* and *illitteratus* were synonymous in clerical parlance, scholars no longer accept that the majority of lay elites were ignorant of Latin. In the eleventh and twelfth centuries many young noblemen not destined for careers in the Church nonetheless studied grammar and acquired some knowledge of Latin either from clerical tutors or at cathedral schools. Still many, if

---

96 Anselm, *De humanis moribus*, ed. R.W. Southern and F.S. Schmitt in *Memorials of St. Anselm* (London, 1969), 68–9: 'Angeli enim sunt quasi nutriti, sancti vero quasi conversi. Sed nec angeli sanctos despiciunt, quia tentationibus aliquando victi sunt, nec sancti angelos, quia nullam quam vincerent tentationem passi sunt.' For commentary, see Grundmann, 'Adelsbekehrungen,' 325–6.
97 de Jong, *In Samuel's Image*; John Boswell, *The Kindness of Strangers: The Abandonment of Children in Western Europe from Late Antiquity to the Renaissance* (Chicago, 1988), 228–55, 296–321.
98 But see Giles Constable, '"*Famuli*" and "*Conversi*" at Cluny: A Note on Statute 24 of Peter the Venerable,' *Revue Bénédictine* 83 (1973), 326–350 (esp. 336–9), for Cluniac efforts to integrate adult converts into the liturgical life of the community, and for examples of *conversi* (not to be confused here with lay-brothers) who graduated to the status of full-fledged choir monks and rose to high positions in the order.
99 For this change, see Lynch, *Simoniacal Entry*, 37f.
100 Martha G. Newman, *The Boundaries of Charity: Cistercian Culture and Ecclesiastical Reform, 1098–1180* (Stanford, CA, 1996), 27–8.
101 Newman (*Boundaries of Charity*, 27) notes, however, that even clerics needed, as monks, to 'quell their ecclesiastical ambitions, redirect their intellectual interests, and attempt to extinguish the aggression and competitiveness that their background had encouraged.'

not the majority, of adult warriors who entered the monastic life would have required additional training before they could have been considered *litterati* by monastic standards.[102] Stories of holy men who struggled as adults to memorize the Psalms or even to learn their ABCs were told by hagiographers to demonstrate their subjects' discipline and humility, but also reflect the very real difficulties some adult converts faced.[103] Warriors may even have been drawn to the new orders of the eleventh and twelfth centuries in part because they placed less stress on elaborate liturgical performance and provided former arms-bearers with a wider range of outlets for their physical energy through their emphasis on manual labor.[104]

Adjusting to the monastic mindset and embracing humility, obedience, and stability could pose an even greater challenge for men raised to be aggressive and proud, especially if they had occupied positions of importance in the world. Orderic Vitalis described one such convert, Robert of Grandmesnil, a nobleman who joined Orderic's house of St-Évroul as a young man and rose to become prior and then abbot. Robert had left the world in the aftermath of a bloody feud that left his father dead and filled the young man with distaste for 'the perils of earthly warfare.' While he initially made himself popular, not least because he loaded his new home with lands and costly books and ornaments, as prior Robert behaved in a manner that showed he had not fully embraced monastic values:

> For this Robert, as I have explained [Orderic writes], was very highly born, being a brother of Hugh of Grandmesnil; he had still the shallowness of youth together with tremendous energy and worldly ambition. ... For if he thought anything, whether good or bad, desirable, he was after it at once; and if he saw or heard anything which displeased him he flew into a rage; he preferred to lead rather than to follow, and to command rather than to obey. Open-handed in both giving and receiving, he was quick to express his anger in violent utterance.[105]

---

[102] For medieval definitions of *litteratus* and *illitteratus* and the relationship of these to *laicus* and *clericus*, see Michael T. Clanchy, *From Memory to Written Record: England 1066–1307*, 2nd edn (London, 1993), 224f.

[103] For the memorization of the liturgy, see Clanchy, *Memory to Written Record*, 238–40. One nobleman who embarked on the monastic life with absolutely no degree of literacy (if his biographer Gilbert Crispin is to be believed) was Herluin of Bec; see the *Vita domni Herluini abbatis Beccensis*, ed. J. Armitage Robinson in *Gilbert Crispin, Abbot of Westminster* (Cambridge, 1911), 87–110 (at 91).

[104] This may explain why many knightly converts to the Cistercians preferred to remain lay brothers rather than monks until the General Chapter legislated against this practice in 1188; see Constance H. Berman, *The Cistercian Evolution: The Invention of a Religious Order in Twelfth-Century Europe* (Philadelphia, PA, 2000), 167, 184, 241. Marcus Bull (*Knightly Piety*, 130–3) describes how *milites* flocked to join Gerald of Corbie's foundation of La Sauve Majeure, where they particularly relished the back-breaking work of land-clearing and building.

[105] Compare Orderic's favorable view of Robert's conversion with these complaints about Robert's behavior during his priorate; see *Ecclesiastical History*, ed. Chibnall, 2: 40–3, 64–7.

Orderic's description of Robert as ambitious, proud, commanding, and irascible almost makes of him a noble stereotype, as all of these qualities are found in contemporary clerical critiques of powerful laymen. Ironically, what we know of noble culture in this period suggests that by acting in this manner Robert was only doing what he and his peers would have approved of – namely, demanding the treatment lay elites claimed as their birthright.[106]

Other monastic writers expressed doubts about the sincerity and constancy of highborn converts. Caesarius of Heisterbach told of a young noble who joined the Cistercians 'thoughtlessly and in distress and confusion of mind' as a way of escaping from gambling debts, and was soon persuaded by friends to return to the world.[107] Many held that warriors who entered the monastic life *ad succurrendum* on the assumption that their salvation was assured if they died as monks were just as bad.[108] In the *Vision of Gunthelm* discussed above, the Cistercian novice saw, among the legions of sufferers in Hell, a hypocritical knight-turned-monk who had thought to erase the sins of robbery and rape through a deathbed conversion. Since, however, the convert had 'not indeed been moved by the grace of penance' and had secretly planned to abandon his vows if he recovered, it had availed him nothing to die in a monk's habit. Instead he was condemned to resume his knightly garb as a form of torture: 'seated upon a flaming horse, and bearing a fiery shield upon his neck, he carried a goat upon his horse's neck, and dragged the habit of a monk after him bound to the horse's tail,' as a sign of how he had abused his vows.[109] As the monastic author of the *Visio* made clear, a warrior could not truly become a monk through a simple change of clothing.[110]

The rituals which marked an adult convert's entrance into the monastic life emphasized this very point.[111] But while these rites stressed the new monk's inner transformation, this transformation was symbolized and aided by visible changes to his physical appearance and renunciations of status and worldly ties represented by symbolically charged gestures. The shaving of the beard and

---

106 On the association of particular vices with nobles, see Lester K. Little, 'Pride Goes before Avarice: Social Change and the Vices in Latin Christendom,' *American Historical Review* 76 (1971), 16–49. For noble displays of anger, see Stephen D. White, 'The Politics of Anger in Medieval France,' in *Anger's Past: The Social Uses of an Emotion in the Middle Ages*, ed. Barbara H. Rosenwein (Ithaca, 1998), 127–52.
107 *Dialogus miraculorum*, 1.13, trans. Scott and Bland, 1: 19–20.
108 For examples, see Constable, *Reformation of the Twelfth Century*, 82.
109 The goat is a symbol of lust, perhaps a reference to the fact that the knight 'violently carried off a poor woman.' *Visio Gunthelmi*, ed. Constable, 110.
110 *Visio Gunthelmi*, ed. Constable, 110. The importance of clothing to social identity should not be underestimated, however; Jean Dunbabin has shown how noble clerks often dressed and wore their hair untonsured in order to 'pass' as knights; see 'From Clerk to Knight: Changing Orders,' in *The Ideals and Practice of Medieval Knighthood II: Papers from the Third Strawberry Hill Conference*, ed. Christopher Harper-Bill and Ruth Harvey (Woodbridge, 1987), 26–39 (at 31).
111 The definitive treatment of these rites is Giles Constable, 'The Ceremonies and Symbolism of Entering the Religious Life and Taking the Monastic Habit from the Fourth to the Twelfth Century,' in *Segni e riti nella chiesa altomedievale occidentale*, 2 vols (Spoleto, 1987), 2: 771–834.

tonsuring of the hair made one look like a monk, to be sure, but they also helped one to *become* a monk. As Odo of Cluny wrote of a *miles* named Adhegrin who joined the Cluniacs, 'after he laid aside the hair of his head and the practice of worldly warfare, he became forthwith a soldier of Christ (*Christi ... agonista*).'[112] In an equally powerful act of renunciation, some men who took their vows as adults ceremonially laid down their sword-belt (*miliciae cingulum*) in chapter or upon the high altar in their monastery's church to signify that they would never take up arms again, at least not in the service of any earthly lord.[113] As early as the ninth century, Hildemar of Corbie's commentary on the *Rule of Benedict* had specified that postulants must surrender their arms after a probationary period of two months, at which time they would be tonsured and assume the habit as a novice.[114] An eleventh-century charter from the Breton abbey of Redon suggests how this transition might actually have taken place. According to the text, Morvan, a '*quidam miles*' of noble birth, petitioned to enter the community and was duly accepted by the brothers. Entering the church armed (and presumably dressed in secular clothing), Morvan 'approached the holy altar and there left his knightly arms (*arma milicie*), laying aside the old man and putting on the new' (cf. Eph. 4:22–4).[115] The exact moment of Morvan's rebirth as a monk coincided not with his assumption of the monastic habit (although the verb *induere*, borrowed from Ephesians, evokes the act of dressing), or even with his taking of vows, but with his renunciation of arms.[116]

The disarming of new monks also emphasized that the transition to monastic life entailed the convert's rebirth as a man of peace, in the image of Christ.[117] As Mayke de Jong has observed, the deposition of arms was also a common element in the performance of public penance; along with the renunciation of

---

[112] Cited by Rosenwein, 'St. Odo's St Martin,' 321 and n.18: 'Deposita itaque capitis coma et saeculari militia, ex tunc Christi factus est agonista.' For the original text, see PL 133: 53. Odo's explicit comparison of the worldly and spiritual *militiae* is typical of monastic descriptions of warriors' conversions in the Central Middle Ages, as discussed in Chapter 5.

[113] Miramon, 'Embracer l'état monastique,' 841–3. See Chapter 5 for a discussion of the significance of the sword-belt (and its spiritual counterpart, the *cingulum duplex* of the monk) in monastic rules and hagiography.

[114] Hildemar of Corbie, *Commentarium in regulam S. Benedicti*, ed. Rupert Mittermüller (Regensburg, 1880), 535–6. The ritual, for which Hildemarus provides a lengthy script with questions and responses to be spoken by the abbot and postulant, is to take place in chapter 'in the presence of all the brothers.'

[115] *Cartulaire de l'abbaye de Redon en Bretagne*, ed. Aurélien de Courson (Paris, 1863), 312 (no. 361).

[116] Dominique Barthélemy sees this ceremony as a kind of 'un-dubbing'; see 'Qu'est-ce que la chevalerie en France aux Xe et XIe siècles?' *Revue Historique* 290 (1993), 15–74 (at 54). For more on the religious symbolism of these ceremonies, see Maurice Keen, *Chivalry* (New Haven, CT, 1984), 64–82, who argues (at p. 82) that 'knighting' rituals 'did not subordinate martial energy to ecclesiastical rule, and dubbing never became an eighth sacrament.'

[117] In many cases this would have been further underscored by the giving of the kiss of peace in the course of the ceremony, on which see Constable, 'Ceremonies and Symbolism,' 795–6, n.73.

sexual activity and office-holding, the putting aside of his weapons signaled a free man's voluntary entrance into a semi-monastic state for the duration of his penitential sentence.[118] Ritual disarmament thus underscored the penitential nature of the monk's life. Charles de Miramon sees in the martial symbolism of monastic profession rites evidence of 'the intrusion of the *milites*' values into the cloister,' and notes parallels between monastic rituals and ceremonies of arming and homage that served to cement bonds of loyalty between lay warriors.[119] There are hints in hagiography that the valuable military equipment converts laid aside at their professions might be preserved in their monasteries,[120] as in the *vita* of John of Montmirail (d.1217), a French nobleman and crusader who was a favorite of King Philip Augustus. His monastic biographer described how years after John joined the Cistercians of Longpont, when he had been elected abbot, he was struck by an impulse to see his old arms and armor, which had evidently been kept by the monks.[121] Upon being shown these instruments of war (*arma bellica*) however, all nostalgia for his past life disappeared in a flash as the memories of all the sins he had committed with them rushed into his mind.[122] This account is suggestive of how, following their entrance into the religious life, warrior-converts might have been encouraged to distance themselves from their previous martial exploits so that they could be reborn as monks.

Monastic colonization of sites of war

The transformation from man of war to man of peace represented by the gift of the self to a monastery was mirrored in the conversion of sites of violence and bloodshed into sanctuaries of prayer and repentance. As we saw in the preceding chapter, nobles viewed the endowment of a new monastic foundation as a remedy for sins committed in wartime, as the logic of patronage held that a spiritual

---

[118] Mayke de Jong, 'Power and Humility in Carolingian Society: The Public Penance of Louis the Pious,' *Early Medieval Europe* 1 (1992), 29–52 (esp. 43–4). For the laying down of arms as a form of penance, see Leyser, 'Beginnings of Knighthood,' 57–64.

[119] Miramon, 'Embracer l'état monastique,' 844. Constable ('Ceremonies and Symbolism,' 788–9) also compares the bond of *fidelitas* between the monk and abbot to that of the lay lord and his vassal.

[120] The secular clothing of converts was preserved in some houses so that it could be returned if they later decided to leave; see Giles Constable, 'Entrance into Cluny in the Eleventh and Twelfth Centuries According to the Cluniac Customaries and Statutes,' repr. in *Cluny from the Tenth to the Twelfth Centuries: Further Studies* (Aldershot, 2000), 335–54 (at 350n.).

[121] The fact of the weapons' preservation might be explained by their material value, their association with a famous convert, or both. For more examples of the preservation of converts' arms and armor in monastic communities, including instances where these attained the status of relics, see Chapter 5.

[122] John de Montmirail famously saved Philip II's life at Gisors in 1198, and went on the Fourth Crusade before withdrawing to the Cistercian abbey of Longpont in c.1209. See Murray, *Reason and Society*, 377–8; and for this episode, *Vita B. Johannis de Monte-Mirabili* [BHL 4415], c.29, AASS Sept 8: 218–35 (here col. 224).

army could more effectively fight for their patron's soul than he could himself. Some monasteries were even forged in battle, insofar as they owed their origins to a patron's battlefield vow or a desire to do penance for sins committed on campaign. Medieval Christians viewed pitched battles as mass trials by ordeal, and held that no victory could be won without God's aid; thus the foundation of a religious community in commemoration of a military triumph was one way of offering thanks for divine assistance in battle.[123] The most famous such foundation was, of course, Battle Abbey, founded by William I of England in c.1070 near the site of his victory at Hastings. The new king's endowment of Battle not only expressed his gratitude to God, but memorialized a decisive victory and served as a tangible monument to William's penance for the bloodshed that had accompanied the Conquest.[124] A twelfth-century chronicle composed by an anonymous monk of Battle held that William had in fact vowed to found the abbey *before* the battle, and described him announcing his intention in a pious battlefield speech to his men:

> And to strengthen the hands and hearts of you who are about to fight for me, I make a vow that on this very battlefield I shall found a monastery for the salvation of all, and especially for those who fall here, to the honor of God and of his saints, where servants of God may be supported: a fitting monastery, with a worthy liberty. Let it be an atonement: a haven for all, as free as the one I conquer for myself.[125]

William's speech, with its proclamation of the warrior's need for the monk, and open acknowledgment of the sinfulness of war, no doubt expresses the sentiments of the Battle chronicler better than it does those of the eleventh-century monarch. What is more interesting is that, far from being ashamed of the bloody origins of their community, the twelfth-century monks of Battle proudly proclaimed them to visitors, pointing out the high altar that was (they claimed) built upon the exact spot where Harold had fallen, and even undertaking an unsuccessful campaign to transform the battlefield itself into a pilgrimage destination.[126]

Whatever his true motives, William I was hardly the first or the only warrior to found a monastery as what Elizabeth Hallam has termed a 'war memorial.'

---

[123] On battle as 'a collective ordeal,' see Leyser, 'Warfare in the Western European Middle Ages,' 192; and Strickland, *War and Chivalry*, 58–68. Such an endowment could be simultaneously an historical commemoration of the victory and an expression of the temporal power of the victor, according to Elizabeth M. Hallam, 'Monasteries as "War Memorials": Battle Abbey and La Victoire,' in *The Church and War*, 47–57. Bernard S. Bachrach ('Combat Sculptures,' 67n.) has traced the practice back to Lombard Italy, where King Cunincpert built a monastery dedicated to Saint George following his victory at the Battle of Coronate (as related by Paul the Deacon in his *Historia Langobardum*, 6.17, MGH SS Rerum Langobardicarum, ed. L. Bethmann and G. Waitz [Hanover, 1878], 178).

[124] Hallam, 'War Memorials,' 50–3.

[125] *The Chronicle of Battle Abbey*, ed. and trans. Eleanor Searle (Oxford, 1980), 37. For critiques of this tale's historicity, see Searle's introductory comments (esp. 18–19); and Hallam, 'War Memorials,' 50–1.

[126] *Chronicle of Battle Abbey*, 18–19.

We know of numerous other examples that followed a similar pattern, and indeed the martial origins of many more monastic foundations have likely been obscured over time.[127] Those origin stories which have survived follow a common narrative: a great battle was won, and the victory commemorated by the construction of a generously endowed monastery on or near the site of the engagement. While such foundations were undoubtedly symbols of power as much as expressions of piety or repentance, it is this latter function that clerical writers naturally chose to emphasize. When Count Robert I of Flanders founded a community of canons dedicated to Saint Peter at Watten in c.1072, the cleric Lambert of Ardres explained that Robert had done so because 'he had enjoyed victory over Richilde [the former countess of Flanders who was Robert's main rival] on the day of the solemnity of the throne of Saint Peter, the prince of the apostles, through the intercession and merits of this same prince of apostles, to whom he and his men had commended themselves on the day of strife and battle, divine grace leading the way.'[128]

Ralph Glaber related the foundation of the monastery of Beaulieu-lès-Loches by Fulk Nerra, Count of Anjou, to the count's desire to do penance for sins of a martial nature:

> When he had shed much blood in many battles in many places, he was driven by fear of hell to go to our Savior's sepulcher at Jerusalem. Because he was an intrepid man he returned from there exultant, and for a time moderated his customary ferocity. It was now that he conceived the idea of building a church in the finest place on his domains and gathering there a community of monks who should intercede day and night for the redemption of his soul. Because he always made decisions carefully he consulted all religious persons on which saints he should honor when he dedicated his church, that they might pray to the Lord for the salvation of his soul.[129]

The site chosen by Fulk for his monastery, known in his day by the toponym *Belli Locus*, was a customary place for the staging of judicial duels as well as the execution of criminals. Bernard Bachrach has argued that Fulk intended the foundation to serve as a memorial to his 992 victory over the Breton count Conan I at Conquereuil, and that he deliberately chose a site which had, like the battlefield (located in enemy-held Brittany, and thus inaccessible as a building site), been soaked with the blood of Christians who had undergone divine judgment for their sins.[130] Constructed between c.1005 and 1012, the abbey church was adorned with friezes showing scenes from the Battle of Conquereuil as well as lions and carrion birds, symbols of courage and victory.[131]

---

[127] Bachrach, 'Combat Sculptures,' 74.
[128] Lambert of Ardres, *The History of the Counts of Guines and Lords of Ardres*, ed. and trans. Leah Shopkow (Philadelphia, PA, 2001), 75.
[129] Ralph Glaber, *Historiarum*, 2.4.5, in *Opera*, ed. Bulst, 61.
[130] Bachrach ('Combat Sculptures,' 66–8) argues that both Fulk Nerra and his opponent, Count Conan of Brittany, viewed Conquereuil as a mass ordeal in which God rendered his judgment on both parties and their supporters.
[131] Bachrach, 'Combat Sculptures,' 71.

In the following century the Flemish warrior-turned-hermit Oilard of Wimille affected a similar, though more modest, transformation of a site known as the 'Sinners' Field,' formerly a haven for a local gang of murderous robbers. Purchasing the place with alms collected from local people, Oilard built a hostelry and a church there, prompting local people to rechristen the spot the 'Field of Saints':

> Thus, in this way, the discernment of divine dispensation ordained that where the blood of the innocent had been frequently shed by malefactors, a daily sacrifice of the body and blood of Christ should be offered in perpetuity by Christian priests for the mystery of our salvation; that where there had been criminal conspiracies, the vigils of God's servants should be celebrated; that where death's destruction had daily threatened those passing by, an unlocked shelter should welcome the poor to a safe asylum and a comfortable place to recuperate....[132]

The chronicler believed that the power of peace, charity, and above all clerical prayer had the power to purify this place long polluted by the deeds of violent men. Tellingly, the site's new function as a sanctuary was presented not merely as a new stage in its history but as a neat inversion of its bloody past,[133] fittingly affected by a holy man who had himself begun life as a professional shedder of Christian blood.

Such purposeful transformations had a venerable history in the monastic tradition. The great Benedict himself had built Montecassino upon the site of an earlier fortress (*castrum*), and the abbey was accordingly referred to in the early Middle Ages as 'the citadel of Campania.'[134] But as castles attained ever-greater military and political importance in the West during the eleventh and twelfth centuries, these fortified places came to figure prominently among the practical and spiritual concerns of monks. Religious communities often viewed the citadels of neighboring lords as symbols of the lay oppression of the Church, and fought tooth and nail to prevent the construction (or bring about the demolition) of castles on or near their lands.[135] Some monastic superiors even took defensive matters into their own hands by building castles for themselves. As Markwald, a twelfth-century abbot of Fulda, explained, it is '[n]ot that it is proper that monks should inhabit anything but monasteries or fight battles other than spiritual ones, but the evil in the world cannot be defeated except

---

[132] Lambert of Ardres, *History of the Counts of Guines*, 86. Compare the similar narrative of the foundation of the Cistercian abbey of Clairvaux on a site formerly used as a lair by a gang of violent robbers, as told in William of Saint-Thierry et al., *Vita prima S. Bernardi*, 1.5, PL 185: 241–2.

[133] This is similar to Philippe Buc's concept of an 'oppositional conversion'; see 'Conversion of Objects,' *Viator* 28 (1997), 99–143 (here 104–7).

[134] Gregory I, *Dialogues*, ed. Vogüé and Antin, 2: 166. See also the comments in *The Life and Miracles of St. Benedict: Book Two of the Dialogues*, trans. Odo J. Zimmerman and Benedict R. Avery (Westport, CT, 1949), 74n.

[135] For examples, see Amy G. Remensnyder, *Remembering Kings Past: Monastic Foundation Legends in Medieval Southern France* (Ithaca, NY, 1995), 233–44.

by resistance.'[136] Such was evidently the philosophy of another abbot, Robert of Saint-Pierre-sur-Dives in Normandy, who during Henry I's 1106 invasion of the duchy found it necessary to fortify his monastery and hire a company of soldiers, paid with the house's jewels and plate, to defend it.[137] For a monastery or church to be captured by a layman and forcibly transformed into a citadel was viewed as the worst kind of sacrilege,[138] but the possession of castles by monastic lords was ingeniously defended by no less an authority than Peter the Venerable, on the grounds that 'if any castle is given to monks, from then on it ceases to be a castle and begins to be an oratory.'[139] Not content with such a conceptual transformation, the twelfth-century monks of Saint-Yvione (dép. Puy-de-Dôme) actually dismantled a stone *castrum* to obtain building materials for their new monastery.[140]

The transformation of places of war and bloodshed into refuges of peace and prayer was a hagiographical trope reflective of actual eleventh- and twelfth-century practice. In the decades following the Conquest some Norman lords wishing to import Continental monks to their new lands in England offered them churches adjoining or actually located within castles (*in castellaria*). Although an anonymous chronicler of the Angevin abbey of Saint-Florent, from which monks were sent to inhabit two new English castle-priories in the 1070s and 1080s, lamented that 'inhabiting a castle was burdensome, and extremely dangerous and damnable for the brothers' souls,' nevertheless the abbey accepted the bequests, as well as several similar ones closer to home.[141] A century later Aelred of Rievaulx recounted how Walter Espec, a nobleman and

---

[136] *Gesta Marcuardi abbatis Fuldensis*, ed. J.F. Böhmer (Stuttgart, 1853), 167; cited in Reuter, 'Prelates as Warriors,' 92–3 and n.63. For more examples of abbots and bishops as castle-builders, see Strickland, *War and Chivalry*, 73 and 82.

[137] As described by Orderic Vitalis, *Ecclesiastical History*, ed. Chibnall, 6: 74; cited in Strickland, *War and Chivalry*, 82.

[138] As happened in the twelfth century at Mozac (Remensnyder, *Kings Past*, 244) and at Gasny, a dependent house of Saint-Ouen (Orderic Vitalis, *History*, ed. Chibnall, 6: 184–6). For more examples, see Strickland, *War and Chivalry*, 76–7, 88.

[139] Cited in Remensnyder, *Kings Past*, 68n. Peter the Venerable, Letter 28, in *Letters*, ed. Constable, 1: 86: 'si castrum aliquod monachis detur, iam castrum esse desinit, et esse oratorium incipit.' If this seems somewhat disingenuous, it should be remembered that the castle was commonly employed as a metaphor for the cloister in this period, as described in Chapter 4.

[140] According to the twelfth-century foundation legend of the monastery, the *castrum* in question belonged to the priory's domineering mother-house, and so this was an act of destruction as well as a re-appropriation of the symbolic power of the castle. For this interpretation and discussion of the twelfth-century text (the *Additamentum de reliquiis S. Austremonii*, AASS Nov 1: 80–2), see Remensnyder, *Kings Past*, 68–9.

[141] Martindale, 'Monasteries and Castles,' 141–4, 152–4 (quoting 152). Martindale describes how Saint-Saumur accepted several more castle-donations in Northern France and Aquitaine in this period, but suggests the monks sought to transform or move these as soon as was feasible. For the Latin text of the anonymous chronicle, see *Historia Sancti Florentii Salmurensis*, in *Chroniques des églises d'Anjou*, ed. P. Marchegay and E. Mabille (Paris, 1869), 272: 'Habitatio castelli erat valde ei onerosa et animabus fratrum periculosa atque dampnosa....'

trusted *curialis* of Henry I, had decided to 'make Christ the heir of all his best possessions' by endowing a new community of Augustinian canons at Kirkham in Yorkshire. Not satisfied with merely granting the house some of his best lands, Aelred continued, Walter 'turned his castle, his rooms, and his storehouses into dwellings for the servants of Christ.'[142] In 1122, Count Geoffrey of Cappenburg defied his kinsmen by giving his castle, together with all the rest of his patrimony, to Norbert of Xanten to be transformed into a monastery of the fledgling Premonstratensians.[143] Along with his younger brother Otto, Geoffrey eventually joined the order as a monk, but only after spending two years quelling the uproar precipitated by his pious bequests. Twenty years following his death in 1129, Geoffrey's dying wish was belatedly fulfilled when his relics were translated to a new shrine in his former citadel at Cappenberg where, as his hagiographer wrote, the monks greeted Geoffrey as their protector and 'the captain of our army (*princeps exercitus*).'[144] In this case, the transformation of the donor's worldly fortress into a spiritual stronghold complemented his own enlistment in the *militia Christi*.

With few exceptions, the sources say little about the actual process by which a *castellum* could be remade as a religious house. The anonymous hagiographer of the hermit-turned-Cistercian abbot Stephen of Obazine (d.1159) offers us a rare glimpse of such a transformation in describing how Stephen, the lord of Monceaux, was so impressed by an encounter with the holy man, whom he received as a guest at his stronghold, that he joined the latter's fledgling community and made the monks a gift of the building where their leader had lodged.[145] On the day appointed for the transfer of property, Stephen and his family watched as monks from Obazine removed all of their household possessions, then gathered together all of the armaments which had been stored in the building to be smashed and burnt, and finally proceeded to tear down its fortifications in the castellan's presence. Only after the site had been purged of all martial associations, and thereby purified, could it be repurposed as a monastic

---

[142] *Relatio de Standardo*, c.2, in *Chronicles of the Reigns of Stephen, Henry II, and Richard I*, ed. R. Howlett, 4 vols (London, 1884–92), 2: 183; trans. Jane Patricia Freeland and ed. Marsha L. Dutton as *Battle of the Standard*, in *Aelred of Rievaulx: The Historical Works*, CF 56 (Kalamazoo, MI, 2005), 249–50.

[143] For the anonymous *Vita Godefridi comitis Cappenbergensis*, composed by a canon of Cappenberg in c.1150, see the edition by Philippe Jaffé in MGH SS 12: 513–30, and the translation by Theodore J. Antry and Carol Neel in *Norbert and Early Norbertine Spirituality* (New York, 2007), 92–117. The donation of Cappenberg is described in c.2 (MGH SS 12: 515–16; Antry and Neel, 94–5). For commentary on the text and the accuracy of Geoffrey's portrayal, see the comments by Antry and Neel, 85–91, and Gerlinde Niemeyer, 'Die Vita Godefridi Cappenbergensis,' *Deutsches Archiv für Erforschung des Mittelalters* 23 (1967), 405–67.

[144] *Vita Godefridi*, c.3–4 (MGH SS 12: 516–19; Antry and Neel, 96–101) and c.12 (MGH SS 12: 528; Antry and Neel, 116–17).

[145] This text and the identification of the donor (unnamed in the *vita*) are discussed by Miramon, 'Embracer l'état monastique,' 841–2.

grange, and only then, it seems, could its former master begin his new life as a monk.[146]

Reflecting on the ways in which castles figure in monastic foundation legends, Amy Remensnyder has suggested that such rites of destruction and reconstruction enabled religious communities to appropriate for themselves the authority these buildings represented, thus symbolically defeating would-be rivals who were as likely to be other monasteries as aggressive lay lords.[147] Accounts of castles transformed into monasteries might also be read as conversion narratives, which operate on the same set of assumptions as more conventional tales of this genre; any place, no matter how thoroughly soaked in blood, could – like a warrior stained by the sins of his *ordo* – be made anew in a guise infinitely more pleasing to God. But the remaking of a castle as a house of God was also, no doubt, conceptually facilitated by the longstanding association of monastic communities with spiritual warfare. As sites of constant liturgical combat, *all* monasteries were spiritual castles, whether or not they were founded on places where actual bloodshed had taken place.

Conclusion

Writing early in the thirteenth century, the French chronicler known as Guillaume le Clerc neatly summarized the respective functions of the two groups who have been the focus of this chapter:

> [W]hen the clergy have the task of leading knights, certainly that is contrary to the law. The clerk should recite aloud from his Scripture and his Psalms and let the knight go to his great battlefields. He [the clerk] should remain before his altars and pray for the warriors and absolve the sinners.[148]

These *ordines*, which were the conceptual bedrock of society for men like Guillaume, were construed at once in terms of mutual dependence and binary opposition. As Constance Brittain Bouchard has demonstrated, clerical theorists often represented the conversion of warriors to the monastic life 'as a radical and indeed abrupt change from one status to its diametric opposite.'[149] Dramatic acts of renunciation – setting aside secular clothing, laying down weapons, tearing down a castle – seem to be in keeping with this way of conceptualizing conversion. And, indeed, the rhetoric of church reformers starkly contrasted 'men of

---

146 *Vita S. Stephani Obazinensis*, c.29, ed. and trans. Michel Aubrun as *Vie de Saint Étienne d'Obazine* (Clermont-Ferrand, 1970), 88: 'Fratres vero qui convenerant, illo presente, munitiones et queque editoria deponentes, ex seculari habitatione religiosa et servis Dei opportuna habitacula construxerunt, que permanent usque in presentem diem. Quicquid telorum seu armorum fuit, quibus locus ipse instructissimus habebatur, aut minutatim concisum est, aut igne crematum, exceptis his que in meliores usus regidi potuerunt.'
147 See Remensnyder, *Kings Past*, 68–9.
148 Quoted by Siberry, *Criticism of Crusading*, 35; see *Le Besant de Dieu*, ed. P. Ruelle (Brussels, 1973), lines 2547–63.
149 Bouchard, *'Every Valley Shall Be Exalted'*, 76–7.

peace' with 'men of war,' even if these categories were not so clearly defined in reality. As we have seen, the actual process of conversion was complicated and often drawn out over years, as elite converts renegotiated relationships with family members who remained in the world, accustomed themselves to the rules and routines of their new lives, and learned to think like monks. In doing so, as their new companions in the cloister would have explained, former arms-bearers moved along a spiritual continuum, drawing steadily nearer to God and further from their former lives of comparative sinfulness.[150]

As we turn in the following chapters to an examination of how monastic authors used martial rhetoric to describe their calling, it will become apparent that the transition from battlefield or castle to monastery was not, ideologically speaking, a straightforward exchange of a violent life for a peaceful one. Men who gave up the battlefield to enter religious life did not so much give up being soldiers as channel their martial energies into another sort of warfare, learning to wield spiritual weapons against a new host of enemies. Learning to live as a monk entailed the acquisition of specialized skills and the cultivation of new virtues, but it also involved becoming a *tiro*, a soldier-in-training, all over again. For training in the combat of the spirit, converts looked to their new brethren, some of whom were themselves former arms-bearers, others lifelong monks with no personal experience of war. But, as we saw in the previous chapter, war entered the cloister not only in the memories of converts, but through the Scriptures, exegesis, and liturgies, all of which provided a rich store of military history and models of martial rhetoric. As a result, men who had lived in the cloister since childhood might be renowned *milites Christi*, who spoke the language of the battlefield with the facility of battle-hardened veterans. If many knightly converts learned to read, pray, and think like spiritual warriors from men who had never wielded secular weapons, however, men who had spent their entire lives in the monastery were, for their part, more interested in the technical and experiential aspects of worldly warfare than has generally been recognized. The story of how war shaped medieval monastic culture is, in a sense, the story of what these two groups – Anselm's saints and angels – were willing to learn from each other.

---

[150] Karl F. Morrison has emphasized that for monastic writers conversion was not an instantaneous transformation but a lifelong process, one in which *all* Christians participated as they sought to draw nearer to God; see *Understanding Conversion* (Charlottesville, VA, 1992). The topic of conversion is discussed in more detail in Chapter 5.

3

Spiritual Warfare: The History of an Idea to c.1200

Writers who wrestled with the moral dimensions of worldly military service recognized the inner warfare waged in the spirit as a fundamental part of the good Christian life. If engaging in spiritual combat kept one on the path to righteousness, winning a decisive victory in what Saint Augustine (d.430) called 'the narrow theater of the heart' marked one as a saint. Christ himself had taught men to do battle with the forces of evil, and those who wished to follow in his footsteps could find no better way than by devoting their lives to service in the *militia Christi*. But while the concept of spiritual warfare continued to fascinate Christian thinkers throughout the Middle Ages, its associations changed dramatically over time. This chapter delineates several key moments between the third and twelfth centuries when this idea was contested and reappropriated. For early Christian writers the soldier of Christ was the martyr, who fought beasts and gladiators in the arenas of the Roman Empire and won the prize of salvation through physical annihilation. In the fourth and fifth centuries the discourse of spiritual warfare was appropriated by promoters of the emerging monastic ideal, for whom the Christian soldier was the ascetic who warred against demons in the desert. Martial spirituality powerfully shaped the development of the coenobitic life, whose apologists were as confident as their predecessors in their identification of the real *milites Christi*: these were the members of the monastic militia, drawn up against vices and demonic forces in an unbreakable battle line. For the better part of a millennium, as the theory of spiritual warfare was elaborated by its self-proclaimed virtuoso practitioners, the *miles Christi* ideal remained inseparable from monastic models of spiritual progress and sanctity.

In the Central Middle Ages the concept of the *miles Christi* underwent its most radical change to date, as spiritual warfare became intertwined with papally sponsored holy wars and monks found themselves challenged by a series of newcomers to the spiritual battlefield: crusaders, members of the military orders, and pious arms-bearers more generally. Some aspects of this transformation have been exhaustively studied, so that we can now begin to trace a genealogy of holy war in the Latin West and to understand the emergence of Christian knighthood and crusading within this context.[1] Careful attention has

---

[1] On the genealogy of holy war and the First Crusade as a religious event, see the still-influential early study of Erdmann, *Idea of Crusade*, as well as H.E.J. Cowdrey, 'The Genesis of the Crusades: The Springs of Western Ideas of Holy War,' in *The Holy War*, ed. Patrick

been paid to the ecclesiastical rhetoric of crusading, as well as to the spiritual motivations of laymen who took the cross or joined the new military orders.[2] Monastic responses to the emergence of the new knighthood and the crusading movement have been, with a few notable exceptions, of much less interest to scholars.[3] These transformations have yet to be examined from the monastic perspective through the lens of spiritual warfare, or embedded in the longer history of the *miles Christi* ideal. This is what this chapter sets out to do, in the hope of offering a new way of looking at some themes and texts that have been among the most intensively studied by medievalists in recent decades.

The origins of the miles christi ideal

The earliest Christians living in the Roman Empire saw themselves as members of an elite corps of warriors, loyally awaiting the imminent return of their commander, Christ, and the onset of the war to end all wars. The earliest surviving Christian text outside of the New Testament, the *First Epistle of Clement* (c.96), exhorted believers at Corinth to 'do battle as soldiers,' serving in the spiritual army 'with order, habit, and submissiveness' to the orders of Christ and his earthly commanders.[4] The clear-cut hierarchy and strict discipline of the Roman military machine made it a particularly appealing institutional model for early church leaders, who sought to define a Christian chain of command in which all believers were soldiers subject to the leadership of 'generals': namely, bishops, deacons, and priests.[5] While the Epistles had identified the *miles Christi* with key virtues rather than with any particular group, a succession of groups

---

T. Murphy (Columbus, OH, 1976), 9–32; Bernard McGinn, 'Iter Sancti Sepulchri: The Piety of the First Crusaders,' in *Essays on Medieval Civilization: the Walter Prescott Webb Memorial Lectures*, ed. Bede Karl Lackner and Kenneth Roy Philip (Austin, 1978), 33–70; Riley-Smith, *Idea of Crusading*; Flori, *Guerre sainte*; and Horst Richter, '*Militia Dei.*'

[2] There has been an upsurge of interest in crusaders' spiritual motivations in the past two decades. See the provocative and influential essay by Jonathan Riley-Smith, 'Crusading as an Act of Love'; and idem, 'The State of Mind of Crusaders to the East, 1095–1300,' in *The Oxford History of the Crusades*, ed. Jonathan Riley-Smith (Oxford, 2002), 68–89. For a case-study that seems to affirm Riley-Smith's views, see William C. Jordan, 'The Representation of the Crusades in the Songs Attributed to Thibaud, Count Palatine of Champagne,' *The Journal of Medieval History* 25 (1999), 27–34. The work of Marcus Bull is also foundational here; see his *Knightly Piety*; and idem, 'The Roots of Lay Enthusiasm for the First Crusade,' *History* 78 (1992), 353–72.

[3] Most of this literature centers on the involvement of the Cistercians in the promotion of the crusading movement and military orders, and especially on Bernard of Clairvaux's *De laudae novae militiae*. See Penny J. Cole, *The Preaching of Crusades to the Holy Land, 1095–1270* (Cambridge, MA, 1991); *The Second Crusade and the Cistercians*, ed. Michael Gervers (New York, 1992); Newman, *Boundaries of Charity*; and Purkis, *Crusading Spirituality*.

[4] *First Epistle of Clement to the Corinthians*, c.37, ed. and trans. Bart D. Ehrman in *The Apostolic Fathers*, 2 vols, Loeb Classical Library 24–5 (Cambridge, MA, 2003), 1: 100–1.

[5] For analysis of this text, see Harnack, *Militia Christi*, trans. Grace, 40–1; Jean-Michel Hornus, *It is not lawful for me to fight: Early Christian Attitudes toward War, Violence, and the State*, trans. Alan Kreider (Scottdale, PA, 1980), 70.

within the early Church proclaimed themselves the true soldiers of Christ. The ideal of the *miles Christi* thus shaped the spiritual hierarchy of the Church in Late Antiquity by helping to define various spiritual elites – clerical leaders, martyrs, ascetics, and monks – even as the discourse of spiritual warfare became a way for Christians to demonize their enemies, be they pagan persecutors, heretics, desert-dwelling spirits, or vices.

By the third century the term *miles Christi* had become a veritable synonym for 'Christian,' and the phrase *militare deo* simply denoted that a person was living a pious life.[6] Indeed, early Christian writers developed an entire vocabulary of spiritual conflict by adding new shades of meaning to words originally devoid of martial overtones, and adapting specialized military terminology to discussions of spiritual progress.[7] In the ways in which early Christians spoke about themselves, especially in relation to non-Christians, we can discern a reliance on martial metaphors to describe what were for them the fundamental realities of life: the cohesion of the community of believers, expressed through rituals and prayer meetings; the individual's daily effort to overcome temptation; the struggle for orthodoxy against a bewildering profusion of heresies; and resistance to pagan authorities. To speak of spiritual warfare as merely a collection of metaphors, then, is to ignore the reality of membership in the *militia Christi* for early Christians, for whom identification with the *miles Christi* ideal was an important way of negotiating personal and collective identity.[8]

Spiritual warfare was often linked to the struggle to live a righteous life in the face of constant temptations and tribulations. For the third-century bishop Cyprian of Carthage, the world was a battlefield on which Christians were assailed by an army of enemies, including illness, ruin, and death. The mind was likewise 'besieged and surrounded on all sides by the assaults of the devil,' who continually sent reinforcements to carry on the attack, so that every time one vice was defeated another rose up in its place. Christians tested in this perpetual warfare were advised that only those who stood fast in the battle line would gain the crown of victory and the peace of heaven.[9] God and the angels rejoiced, Cyprian wrote, to behold such 'a sublime and a great and a glorious contest for the reward of the heavenly crown.'[10] The *Instructiones* of the poet Commo-

---

[6] Paolo Tomea, 'Il "*proelium*" cristiano: scene dai testi agiografici occidentali,' in *Militia Christi et crociata*, 573–623 (at 584).

[7] For two examples of adding military connotations to words, see the articles of Christine Mohrmann, 'Statio,' *Vigiliae Christianae* 7 (1953), 221–45; and eadem, 'Encore une fois "paganus",' *Vigiliae Christianae* 6 (1952), 109–21; and for an example of the adaptation of a primarily military concept (the *sacramentum*, or soldier's oath of loyalty), see eadem, '*Sacramentum* dans les plus anciens textes chrétiens,' *Harvard Theological Review* 47 (1954), 141–52.

[8] As discussed by Harnack, *Militia Christi*, trans. Grace, 35, and Hornus, *Early Christian Attitudes*, 69–70.

[9] Cyprian, *De mortalitate*, c.2, 4–5, 12, in PL 4: 584–6, 590–1; trans. Roy J. Deferrari in *Saint Cyprian: Treatises*, FC 36 (Washington D.C., 1958), 202, 208 (quoting 202).

[10] Cyprian, Letter 58.8, trans. Rose Bernard Donna, *Saint Cyprian: Letters 1–81*, FC 52 (Washington D.C., 1965), 169.

dian (fl.250) presented a similar vision of life in the world as a 'daily battle (*bellum cottidianum*)' against temptation, overseen by Christ in his capacity as commander of the heavenly militia:

> When you see the war raging, take up the nearest contest (*agon*). This is the king's glory, to see the soldier ready for battle. The king approaches – you should desire to conquer to fulfill his hopes. He prepares gifts, joyfully contemplates victory, and consecrates you as his own companion.[11]

The notion that the battle against sin constituted a performance of spiritual prowess was further developed by Augustine and others. In a sermon on the proto-martyr Stephen, for example, Augustine addressed the members of his audience as fellow soldiers: 'Know your enemy; know the one with whom you fight in the theater of your heart (*theatro pectoris*). It is a narrow theater, but God watches there, and it is there that you must conquer your foe.'[12]

Augustine's mentor Ambrose (d.397) recommended that believers train regularly, like professional soldiers, for spiritual battle.[13] In his *De officiis*, a handbook of Christian ethics, Ambrose combined Pauline spiritual warfare with a Stoic emphasis on self-control, creating a martially inflected program of meditation designed to appeal to the educated leadership of the Roman Church:[14]

> The man who wishes to acquire expertise in warfare (*disciplinam bellicam*) spends time every day in practice with his weapons (*cotidie exercetur armis*): he rehearses the whole scenario of a battle, imagining that he is there in the line of conflict, and he takes up his stance as though an enemy really were in position in front of him (*velut coram posito praetendit hoste*). To develop skill and strength at throwing the javelin, say, he will put his muscles to the test; or perhaps he will learn to dodge blows from opponents and to escape by keeping a sharp eye out.[15]

Through the cultivation of self-control, Ambrose wrote, Christians would become inured to the attacks of the enemy, and transform themselves into 'weapons of righteousness (*arma iustitiae*)' – not carnal weapons in which sin

---

[11] Commodian, *Instructiones adversus gentium deos pro christiana disciplina*, c.53, PL 5: 242: 'Cum videris bellum, agonia sume propinqua. / Haec gloria regis, militem videre paratum; / Rex adest, optato propter spem dominicaturum. / Ille parat dona, ille pro victoria laetus / Suscipit, et proprium satellum dedicat esse.' Cf. *Instructiones*, c.61 and 63, PL 5: 247–8 and 249–50.

[12] Augustine of Hippo, Sermo 315.7, PL 38: 1431: 'Agnosce inimicam tuam: agnosce cum qua pugnans in theatro pectoris tui. Angustum theatrum; sed Deus spectat: ibi doma inimicam tuam.' In this instance the Christian's enemy is the sin of anger, as Augustine is glossing Prov. 16:32 ('Melior est qui vincit iram, quam qui capit civitatem.')

[13] M.P. McHugh, 'Satan and St. Ambrose,' *Classical Folia* 26 (1972), 94–106 (esp. 96–8). See McHugh's notes for many more instances of Ambrose's use of martial imagery.

[14] For Ambrose's use of Stoic writers, particularly Cicero, see Marcia L. Colish, 'Cicero, Ambrose, and Stoic Ethics: Transmission or Transformation?' in *The Classics in the Middle Ages, Papers of the 20th Annual Conference of the Center for Medieval and Early Renaissance Studies*, ed. Aldo S. Bernardo and Saul Levin (Binghamton, NY, 1990), 95–112.

[15] Ambrose, *De officiis*, 1.32, ed. and trans. Davidson, 2: 134–5.

reigned, but 'weapons strong for God (*arma fortia Deo*),' able to destroy sin.[16] If Ambrose helped make spiritual warfare comprehensible to educated Romans by relating it to Classical philosophy, his younger contemporary Prudentius (d.413) adapted salvific history to the genre of epic poetry, transforming the Gospel into the 'glorious deeds of Christ (*gesta Christi insignia*)' and casting the Christian's struggle against sin as a heroic saga.[17] In his most original and influential work, the allegorical verse *Psychomachia* ('Soul-Battle' or 'Spiritual Warfare'), Prudentius transferred the inner contest between good and evil from the intimate setting of the soul to a sprawling battlefield where armies of virtues and vices clashed in a series of graphically violent single combats.[18]

As persecution spawned the martyr movement, the idea that the Christian life was a form of combat became a literal reality. The letters of Ignatius of Antioch (d.c.110) are our earliest evidence that the Epistles' call to spiritual arms supplied early Christians with a powerful vocabulary of resistance in the face of terrifying ordeals. En route to his martyrdom at Rome, Ignatius sent words of encouragement to his fellow bishop Polycarp of Smyrna, reminding him that 'it is the mark of a great athlete to bear up under blows, and still claim the victory.' Only by living in perfect singleness of heart with one another and in absolute obedience to Christ, Ignatius went on, would Christians find the strength to confront the trials awaiting them:

> Be pleasing to the one in whose army you serve, from whom also you receive your wages. Let none of you be found a deserter. Let your baptism remain as your weaponry, your faith as a helmet; your love as a spear; your endurance as a full set of armor.[19]

Though Ignatius' imagery is indebted to the Epistles (especially Eph. 6), he has adapted Paul's message to the specific circumstances of the embattled Christian community: baptism permanently enrolls believers in Christ's army, and apostates are rendered as deserters, a reference to the many Christians who renounced their faith when threatened with loss of property, torture, and death.

---

[16] Ambrose, *De officiis*, 1.186, ed. and trans. Davidson, 1: 226–7; cf. 1.16 and 1.20, 1: 126–9.

[17] A good introduction to Prudentius and the place of spiritual warfare in his works is Robert Louis Wilken, *The Spirit of Early Christian Thought* (New Haven, CT, 2003), 212–36.

[18] *Psychomachia*, in Prudentius, *Works*, 2 vols, ed. and trans. H.J. Thomson, Loeb Classical Library 398 (Cambridge, MA, 1949–53), 2: 274–343. This work was greatly admired by medieval Christians for its style and vivid imagery (though it has fared less well among moderns). In the ninth through eleventh centuries it was widely copied, glossed, and excerpted in the *florilegia* used to teach Latin grammar in monastic schools. On the *Psychomachia*'s reception, see Sinéad O'Sullivan, *Early Medieval Glosses on Prudentius' Psychomachia: The Weitz Tradition* (Leiden, 2004), chapter 1.

[19] Ignatius, Letter 6, c.3 and 6, in *Apostolic Fathers*, ed. and trans. Ehrman, 1: 312–13, 316–17. There are clear references here to Eph. 6:13–17, as well as hints of the athletic language of 1 Cor. 9:24–6 and 2 Tim. 4:7.

Spiritual warfare is a pervasive theme in the earliest works of Christian hagiography, the *passiones* of the martyrs.[20] Even as church leaders questioned whether Christians ought to serve in the Roman army, they exalted those willing to die rather than renounce their membership in the *militia Christi*. In his *Ad martyras* of c.203, Tertullian urged those awaiting execution to see their prison as a training ground, and reminded them that they 'have now been called to service in the army of the living God (*militiam Dei uiui*),' and must be prepared to exchange warmth for cold, soft clothes for armor, and quiet for tumult as long as Christ chose for their battle to last. On the day of the 'noble contest (1 Tim. 6:12),' their training complete, the Christians would enter the arena not as victims but as athletes 'built up by austerity' and prepared by virtue of their sufferings to win the crown of heaven.[21] Writing less than a decade before his own martyrdom at Carthage in 258, Cyprian envisioned the martyrs as a 'bright army of the soldiers of Christ (*militum Christi cohors candida*)' of both sexes and all ages, entering the gates of heaven in triumphal procession, loaded down with 'trophies of the vanquished foe.'[22] As Cyprian's description suggests, the experience of martyrdom transformed women as well as men into spiritual warriors. Even if, as Mathew Kuefler has shown, early Christians were reluctant to accord even the holiest of women the title of *miles Christi*,[23] later commentators sometimes recast the heroics of women martyrs in martial terms.[24]

The *passiones*' characterization of imprisonment and execution as glorious and of the martyrs not as passive victims but as agents of their own spiritual destinies relied on the judicious deployment of martial metaphors, many of which had their origins in the Epistles.[25] For instance, Bishop Fructuosus and his deacons, Augurius and Eulogius, martyred at Tarragona in 259, were described in their *passio* as archetypal Pauline spiritual warriors, 'clad in the breastplate of faith and the helmet of salvation (cf. Isa. 59:17, Eph. 6:14,17), crowned with a diadem and a crown that does not fade because they trod underfoot the Devil's

---

[20] See Peter Brennan, 'Military Images in Hagiography,' in *Reading the Past in Late Antiquity*, ed. Graeme Clark et al. (Rushcutters Bay, 1990), 323–45.

[21] Tertullian, *Ad martyras*, 3.1–3, *Quinti Septimi Florentis Tertulliani Opera*, 2 vols, ed. E. Dekkers, CCSL 1–2 (Turnhout, 1954), 1: 5; trans. Rudolph Arbesmann, Emily Joseph Daly, and Edwin A. Quain as *To the Martyrs*, in *Tertullian: Disciplinary, Moral, and Ascetical Works*, FC 40 (Washington D.C., 1959), 22–3. For commentary on this passage, see Eric Osborn, *Tertullian: First Theologian of the West* (Cambridge, 1997), 233.

[22] Cyprian, *De lapsis*, c.2, ed. and trans. M. Bévenot (Oxford, 1971), 2–5.

[23] Mathew Kuefler, *The Manly Eunuch: Masculinity, Gender Ambiguity, and Christian Ideology in Late Antiquity* (Chicago, MI, 2001), 114–15.

[24] For instance, in a sermon composed for the feast of the early-third-century martyrs Perpetua and Felicity, Augustine praised the two women for 'bearing in the battle (*in praelio*) the name of Christ, and in the prize of battle finding their own.' Augustine, 'In natali martyrum Perpetuae et Felicitatis (1),' 1.1, PL 38: 1281; trans. in *Medieval Saints: A Reader*, ed. Mary-Ann Stouck (Peterborough, Ont., 1999), 39.

[25] Much recent work has emphasized how the early Christian community drew power from martyrdom as an idea and spectacle; see Joyce E. Salisbury, *The Blood of the Martyrs: Unintended Consequences of Ancient Violence* (New York, 2004), 9–30.

head!'²⁶ Other *passiones* attest that in the struggle against the temptation to save oneself by apostasy, spiritual warriors felt themselves aided by Christ, under whose aegis all such combats were won.²⁷ This view was embraced by the most influential early historian of the church, Eusebius of Caesarea (d.c.339), whose *History* lauded the martyrs as 'noble combatants' who went to their deaths like eager warriors rushing into the fray.²⁸

Some of the most fully developed martial allegories in early hagiography appear in the passions of the so-called 'military martyrs,' Roman soldiers executed for putting their loyalty to the Christian God above their allegiance to the emperor.²⁹ Christian hagiographers inherited two conflicting literary images of the soldier: one represented him as brutal and immoral, a member of a social group tolerated only out of necessity; the other saw the soldier as an exemplar of the cherished Roman virtues of loyalty, bravery, and civic-mindedness. Both strands of thought informed the evolving relationship between the *militia Christi* and the *militia Caesaris* as well as the creation of competing models of Late Antique soldier-saints.³⁰

Some hagiographers took pains to show that worldly military service was not intrinsically evil, emphasizing that their heroes were put to death not for refusing to fight or kill on moral grounds but for declining to take part in pagan rites. Legends like that of the 'Thundering Legion,' Christian soldiers said to have won a great victory over Germanic tribes with the aid of a divinely sent storm, were also circulated as proof that God might work great miracles for pious warriors.³¹ Other *passiones*, however, describe soldiers rejecting their former calling on the grounds of its fundamental incompatibility with Christian morality, and often include commentaries on the evils of earthly military service.³² In the *Acts* of the third-century martyr Maximilian, when the hero is conscripted he proclaims simply, 'I cannot serve (*militare*) because I am a Christian.'³³ Sulpicius

---

26 'The Martyrdom of Bishop Fructuosus and his Deacons, Augurius and Eulogius,' in *The Acts of the Christian Martyrs*, ed. and trans. Herbert Musurillo, 184.
27 'The Martyrdom of Saints Marian and James' and 'The Martyrdom of Saints Montanus and Lucius,' both in *Acts of the Martyrs*, ed. and trans. Musurillo, 204 and 216.
28 See, for example, Eusebius of Caesarea, *The History of the Church*, 5.1 (describing the martyrs of Lyons and Vienne), 2nd ed., ed. and trans. G.A. Williamson and Andrew Louth (London, 1989), 139.
29 On the military martyrs, see Brennan, 'Military Images'; Hornus, 'Christian Soldiers and Soldier Saints,' in his *Early Christian Attitudes*, 118–57; and Jacques Fontaine, 'Le culte des martyrs militaires et son expression poétique au IVᵉ siècle: l'idéal évangélique de la non-violence dans le christianisme théodosien,' *Augustinianum* 20 (1980), 141–171.
30 Brennan, 'Military Images,' 325–7. The historical existence of many of these martyrs is highly doubtful; it seems to have been commonplace for hagiographers to invent soldier-saints out of whole cloth, or impose military pasts on martyred civilians, so that they might use the theme of conflicting loyalties as a narrative device. See Hippolyte Delahaye, *Les Légendes grecques des saints militaires* (Paris, 1909).
31 Brennan, 'Military Images,' 330–2. See, for example, the *passio* of Marinus in Eusebius' *History of the Church*, 7.15, ed. Williamson and Louth, 232–3.
32 Brennan, 'Military Images,' 330–2; Fontaine, 'Culte des martyrs militaries,' 156–65; Kuefler, *Manly Eunuch*, 107.
33 *Acta Maximiliani*, 1.2, ed. and trans. Musurillo, *Acts of the Martyrs*, 244.

Severus later put a nearly identical declaration into the mouth of his Saint Martin.³⁴ Another soldier-martyr, the centurion Marcellus, was said to have protested at his trial, 'it is not fitting that a Christian, who fights (*militare*) for Christ his Lord, should fight for the armies of this world (*militias saecularibus militare*),' and to have thrown down his soldier's belt in token of his renunciation.³⁵ The ambivalence suggested by these two models of the soldier-saint may reflect the diversity of Christian attitudes towards military service between the third and fifth centuries, during which time the faith rose to dominance in the Empire and the majority of believers came to accept military service as morally permissible, if irreconcilable with emerging ideals of sanctity.³⁶ In the long term, those *passiones* that espoused a view of earthly warfare as totally incompatible with service in the *militia Christi* were to exercise the greatest influence on the Christian hagiographical imagination.

Despite the vexed relationship between the two forms of warfare, the earthly and the spiritual, early hagiographers acknowledged that soldier-saints brought to the *militia Christi* the very qualities that had made them equally valuable members of the *militia Caesaris*. In one of many such accounts, the *passio* of Julius the Veteran, the eponymous character cites his military record to explain his unshakeable loyalty to the spiritual army of Christ:

> I cannot despise the divine commandments or appear unfaithful to my God. In all the twenty-seven years in which I made the mistake, so it appears, to serve foolishly in the army, I was never brought before a magistrate either as a criminal or a troublemaker. I went on seven military campaigns, and never hid behind anyone, nor was I the inferior of any man in battle (*nec alicuius inferior pugnaui*). My chief never found me at fault. And now do you suppose that I, who was always found to be faithful in the past, should be unfaithful to higher orders?³⁷

Even after the age of persecution had passed, hagiographers continued to find inspiration in the motif of the pious soldier torn between his spiritual and temporal lords. In the *Passio Acaunensium martyrum*, Eucherius of Lyons' fifth-century reworking of the legend of Saint Maurice and the Theban Legion, the unshakeable loyalty, bravery, and fellowship displayed by the martyred Christian soldiers formed a marked contrast to the cruelty and caprice of the pagan emperor Maximianus.³⁸ The founders of the monastic tradition also emphasized

---

34 Sulpicius Severus, *Vita S. Martini*, 4.3, in *Vie de Saint Martin*, ed. J. Fontaine, 1: 260: 'Christi ego miles sum; pugnare mihi non licet.'
35 *Acta Marcelli* (recension M), 1.1, 4.3, ed. and trans. Musurillo, *Acts of the Martyrs*, 250, 252.
36 A process described in Harnack, *Militia Christi*; Hornus, *Early Christian Attitudes*, chapter 5; L.J. Swift, *The Early Fathers on War and Military Service* (Wilmington, DE, 1983); and Kuefler, *Manly Eunuch*, 107–9.
37 'The Martyrdom of Julius the Veteran,' 2.1–2, ed. and trans. Musurillo, *Acts of the Martyrs*, 260–1.
38 Eucherius of Lyons, *Passio Acaunensium martyrum*, c.2–3, ed. C.B. Krusch, MGH SS RerMerov 3: 20–41 (at 33–4). The legionaries are 'viri in rebus bellicis strenui et virtute nobiles, sed nobiliores fide; erga imperatorem fortitudine, erga Christum devotione

these very virtues in their celebration of a new type of spiritual warrior, the holy ascetic, who achieved figurative martyrdom through daily combat with demons.

Hagiography and the making of the monastic warrior

Professing themselves the direct heirs of the martyrs, early Christian monks adopted the language of spiritual combat to describe their travails in the desert.[39] Glossing Paul (2 Tim. 2:3), the third-century theologian Origen had advanced the idea that a select few Christians might fight on behalf of the whole body of the faithful, wielding the weapons of prayer, fasting, and chastity, and later monastic writers identified themselves as this elite corps.[40] As opportunities to 'fight' for one's faith against pagan persecutors dwindled in the fourth century, Christian men and women sought new arenas of combat, first in the deserts ringing the eastern Mediterranean and later in the monastic communities which sprang up throughout what was by then ceasing to be the Western Empire. In the hermitage or monastery opportunities for spiritual combat abounded: in the ascetic war against the body, in violent confrontations with demons (often imagined as fully embodied opponents), and in the constant, grinding struggle against the vices of anger, pride, and acedia.

The monastic takeover of the *miles Christi* ideal was facilitated by the circulation of works of hagiography – *vitae* now rather than *passiones* – which presented the monastic life as a form of martyrdom and its practitioners as the new commanders of the *militia Christi*. A handful of *vitae* composed in Late Antiquity were instrumental in affecting this ideological shift by developing a cohort of heroic holy men – Athanasius' Antony, Jerome's Paul, Sulpicius Severus' Martin, and Gregory the Great's Benedict – whose example later monastic readers and hagiographers sought to follow (and indeed could hardly escape). These *vitae* remained living texts in the eleventh- and twelfth-century religious communities of the Latin West, where they formed the basis for private meditation, mealtime reading, and chapter-house preaching. Indeed, as the next two chapters will make clear, these early narratives' influence on later monastic sermons, liturgical texts, and especially hagiography was such that monks in the Central Middle Ages would have known Antony, Paul, Martin, and Benedict almost as well as they knew their living brethren.

---

certabant.' As David Woods points out ('The Origin of the Legend of Maurice and the Theban Legion,' *Journal of Ecclesiastical History* 45 [1994], 385–95), the drama revolves around the legionaries' conflicting loyalties to the emperor and Christ, rather than any perceived conflict between military service and the Christian life; indeed, after their martyrdom Maurice and his men do not abandon their calling but join the ranks of the 'angelic legions' in heaven.

[39] On this relationship, see Malone, *Monk and the Martyr*; and Brakke, *Demons and the Making of the Monk*, chapter 2.

[40] Origen, *Homélies sur les Nombres*, 25.4.1, ed. and trans. W.A. Baehrens et al., 3 vols, SC 415, 442, 461 (Paris, 1996–2001), 3: 204. This work, originally composed in Greek, was well known in the later medieval West in the Latin translation of Rufinus.

The martial symbolism of Athanasius' *Life of Antony*, the first work of Christian hagiography and 'the master text of Western asceticism,' hearkened back to the rhetoric of the *passiones* and thereby reinforced the monk-ascetic's status as heir to the martyr.[41] Both the original Greek text composed by Athanasius shortly after his hero's death in 356 and the free Latin translation of Evagrius of Antioch (made in c.374) promoted veneration and emulation of Antony as monk, ascetic, miracle-worker, and spiritual warrior *par excellence*.[42] Antony's figurative martyrdom, enacted through a rejection of the world and its comforts rather than torture and execution, is set against the background of the Great Persecution.[43] David Brakke has emphasized how, 'in Athanasius' presentation, the monk succeeds the martyr as the person on the front line in the conflict between Christ and Satan, between Christians and the demons.'[44] Almost from the moment the young Antony enters the desert he is assailed by the Devil, and in the violent encounters that follow readers familiar with later medieval *vitae* will recognize precedents for many familiar tropes. Since all Latin-speaking hagiographers had to come to terms with this first-ever saint's Life, the images of spiritual battle that fill Athanasius' narrative shaped the earliest paradigms of sanctity in the Western monastic tradition.

Given the frequency with which images of combat crop up in the text, Athanasius' narrative reads almost as military history, spanning as it does Antony's progression from untried recruit to hardened veteran, and narrating his countless engagements with evil spirits. Antony's encounters with demons are set against a backdrop of martial elements: the holy man becomes the sole defender of an abandoned Roman fort (*castrum*) in the desert; his subsequent moves deeper into the arid wastes are described as conquests of pagan–demonic territory; and demons appear to him in the guise of armed soldiers (*milites armati*).[45] Athanasius offered several lessons on spiritual warfare, none of which were lost on later authors. First, the holy man or woman could not hope to defeat the forces of evil single-handedly; Antony's first victory over demons was attributed to the power of Christ, and he received the Lord's assurance that he would

---

[41] Quoting Geoffrey Galt Harpham, *The Ascetic Imperative in Culture and Criticism* (Chicago, MI, 1987), 3.

[42] In the West Antony became the 'father of monks,' his example cited by monastic authors as indisputable proof of the orthodoxy of particular viewpoints or practices. See Jean Leclercq, 'S. Antoine dans la tradition monastique médiévale,' in *Antonius Magnus Eremita, 356–1956*, ed. Basilius Steidle, Studia Anselmiana 38 (Rome, 1956), 229–47; and Constable, *Reformation of the Twelfth Century*, 160f. The Latin text of Evagrius' translation of the *Vita Antonii* [BHL 609] is found in PL 73: 125–170; I have used the English translation of Evagrius by Carolinne White in *Early Christian Lives* (London, 1998), 7–70.

[43] Athanasius underscores how Antony actively seeks martyrdom and is inspired to greater heights of ascetic suffering by the martyrs' example; see E. Malone, 'The Monk and the Martyr,' in *Antonius Magnus Eremita*, ed. Steidle, 201–28 (at 213–15).

[44] Brakke, *Demons and the Making of the Monk*, chapter 2 (quoting 24); see also A.E.D. Van Loveren, 'Once Again: "The Monk and the Martyr" – Saint Anthony and Saint Macrina,' *Studia Patristica* 17 (1982), 528–38.

[45] *Vita Antonii*, c.11, 16, 20, 51, PL 73: 133, 138, 144, 162–3.

never fight alone.⁴⁶ But while the monk was assured of divine support in battle, his spiritual warfare was both a form of *imitatio Christi* and a continuation of Christ's fight against the devil and his followers, a campaign which fortunately weakened the latter to such a degree that mortals (at least, the holiest ones) could hope to defeat them.⁴⁷ Finally, ascetics are identified as the leaders of the *militia Christi*. In Antony's words, 'The demons are hostile to all Christians, but they especially hate those who are monks and virgins of Christ,' because their triumphs undermine the demons' influence in the world.⁴⁸ The more stringent the ascetic's discipline, as manifested in poverty, chastity, fasting, long vigils, and constant prayer, the greater his prowess in the daily contest against evil. An ascetic virtuoso, Antony 'destroyed the whole army of Satan on bended knee, using prayers as his weapons,' in an epic battle that set the desert echoing with war-cries and clashing arms.⁴⁹

Eager to portray his hero's ascetic achievement as a spiritual martyrdom, Athanasius co-opted the Pauline symbolism of struggle that had become synonymous with the martyrs. Antony himself was made to describe the monk's never-ending war against demons using language borrowed from Ephesians 6:12,⁵⁰ and, under demonic attack, was said to have meditated on the exhortations of this same passage.⁵¹ Athanasius presented Antony as the perfect embodiment of the Pauline *miles Christi*, showing his knowledge of how Christian writers had developed this archetype in the centuries after Paul. But the hagiographer went further, depicting Antony as a second Paul, even while making Paul, whose victory against 'the powers of the air' foreshadowed Antony's own, into an honorary monk.⁵² In the *Vita Antonii* martial rhetoric serves to draw together several strands of Late Antique thought: the association of spiritual combat with martyrdom and the fight against heresy; the belief that demons engaged Christians in a battle against temptation fought in the presence of, and with the aid of Christ; and finally, the growing conviction that chastity was a precondition of sanctity, to be defended at all costs.

The hagiography of Jerome, one of the earliest Latin writers to introduce firsthand knowledge of desert monasticism to a wider Roman audience, also

---

46 *Vita Antonii*, c.5, 9, and cf. 34, 52, PL 73: 130, 132–3, 154, 163–4.
47 *Vita Antonii*, c.28, 18, 40, PL 73: 151–2, 142–3, 156.
48 *Vita Antonii*, c.15, PL 73: 138: 'Hostile illis contra omnes Christianos, maxime vero contra monachos et virgines Christi, odium est. Eorum semitis laqueos praetendunt, eorum mentes impiis atque obscoenis cogitationibus nituntur evertere; sed nihil vobis in hoc terroris incutiant. Fidelium enim orationibus atque jejuniis ad Dominum statim corruunt; nec tamen si paululum cessaverint, prorsus plenam putetis esse victoriam.' Trans. White, *Christian Lives*, 23–4.
49 *Vita Antonii*, c.25, PL 73: 149–50: 'Illi enim tumultus et voces populi, armorumque sonitus, prorsus plenum montem daemonum multitudine sevidisse referebant: ipsum etiam quasi contra inimicos palam resistentem et fortiter colluctantem. Qui tamen et advenientes suo refovebat hortatu, et flexis genibus, armis quoque orationum omnem Satanae prosternebat exercitum.' Trans. White, *Christian Lives*, 40–1.
50 *Vita Antonii*, c.21, PL 73: 146.
51 *Vita Antonii*, c.37, and cf. c.25, PL 73: 155, 149–50.
52 This is especially clear in the *Vita Antonii*, c.37, PL 73: 155.

reflects an ascetic sensibility rooted in the understanding of the holy man or woman as spiritual soldier.⁵³ Jerome's enormously influential *vitae*, especially his *Life of Paul the First Hermit* (c.375), the first biography of a desert ascetic written for a Latin-speaking audience, ensured a place for the monk-as-warrior in the later hagiographical traditions of the West.⁵⁴ The survival of well over one hundred medieval copies of the *Vita Pauli* attests to the work's enduring popularity among later monastic readers.⁵⁵ Like the *Vita Antonii*, Jerome's narrative weaves martyrdom into the background, and uses the language of spiritual combat to link the monk to the martyr.⁵⁶

The *Vita Pauli* recounts Paul's visit to the dying Antony, who welcomes him into his desert retreat as a fellow soldier of Christ.⁵⁷ Despite his demotion in the *Vita Pauli* from founder of monasticism to Paul's protégé, it is Antony who exemplifies for Jerome the qualities of bravery, endurance, and self-control that by the fourth century had become the hallmarks of the *miles Christi*; he is a 'good soldier (*bonus praeliator*),' unshakeable in confrontations with desert-dwelling monsters, because he 'arms himself with the sign of salvation,' and is protected by the 'shield of faith and helmet of hope (cf. Eph. 6).'⁵⁸ Jerome revisited the theme of martial asceticism in his *Life of Hilarion* (c.390), in which a young monk, inspired by Antony's example, strikes out on his own into the Egyptian desert. Reflecting that the brave Antony had already won the victor's prize, while he himself 'had not yet begun to fight,' Hilarion sold his possessions and, 'armed with [the weapons of] Christ, entered upon a life of solitude.'⁵⁹ The *Life of Antony* was clearly a hagiographical touchstone for Jerome; even as he sought

---

⁵³ On Jerome's writings as a conduit for the transmission of eastern ascetic monasticism to the west, see Stefan Rebenich, *Jerome* (New York, 2002), chapter 2.

⁵⁴ For the *Vita Pauli* in the context of Late Antique hagiography, including its relationship to the *Life of Antony*, see Michael Stuart Williams, *Authorised Lives in Early Christian Biography: Between Eusebius and Augustine* (Cambridge, 2008), 119–28; and Stefan Rebenich, 'Der Kirchenvater Hieronymus als Hagiograph: Die *Vita S. Pauli primae eremitae*,' in *Beiträge zur Geschichte des Paulinerordens*, ed. Kaspar Elm (Berlin, 2000), 23–40.

⁵⁵ The majority of these date to the ninth through twelfth centuries. See John Frank Cherf, 'The Latin Manuscript Tradition of the *Vita Sancti Pauli*,' in *Studies in the Text Tradition of St. Jerome's Vitae Patrum*, ed. William Abbott Oldfather (Urbana, IL, 1943), 65–142. The *Vita Pauli* was often copied together with one or more of Jerome's other works of hagiography, as well as with Evagrius' Latin translation of the *Life of Antony*.

⁵⁶ Tellingly, the first *miles Christi* introduced in the *Vita Pauli* is not the monk Paul, but an unnamed martyr who bites off the end of his tongue in order to repulse the advances of a pagan prostitute, thus saving his soul by making war on his own body. Jerome, *Vita Sancti Pauli eremitae*, c.3, in PL 23: 17–28 (at col. 20).

⁵⁷ *Vita S. Pauli*, c.10, in PL 23: 25. Paul announces to Antony that Christ has miraculously supplied him with sufficient food to feed his unexpected guest: 'verum ad adventum tuum, militibus suis Christus duplicavit annonam.'

⁵⁸ *Vita S. Pauli*, c.7, 8, in PL 23: 22–3.

⁵⁹ Jerome, *Vita S. Hilarionis*, c.3, PL 23: 29–54 (at col. 30): 'Illum quasi virem fortem victoriae praemia accipere; se necdum militare coepisse.... Sic nudus, et armatus in Christo, solitudinem ... ingressus est.'

to revise and supercede Athanasius' model of the holy man, he himself preached a form of *imitatio Antonii*.⁶⁰

Jerome's correspondence, which is filled with meditations on his own (apparently considerably embellished) experiences in the desert, offers additional insight into his views on spiritual warfare.⁶¹ In a letter from which Bernard of Clairvaux and others would later borrow imagery,⁶² Jerome reproved Heliodorus, a former soldier who had come to regret his conversion to monastic life, as a deserter from Christ's army. Jerome warned Heliodorus that as a monk he had no business living as a 'pampered soldier (*delicate miles*)' in his father's house, where worldly comforts would inevitably destroy his martial spirit and render him unfit for service in the *militia Christi*:

> A body that is used to a tunic cannot support a breastplate (*lorica*), a head that has worn a linen hood shrinks from a helmet, a hand idleness has softened is galled by a hard sword-hilt. Hear your king's proclamation: 'He that is not with me is against me, and he that gathers not with me, scatters (Matt. 12:30).'⁶³

Given his addressee's former calling, there is a certain irony in Jerome's accusations of disloyalty and cowardice, and his reminders that Heliodorus has sworn an unbreakable oath to Christ (through baptism) and even accepted an enrollment bonus (*donativum*).⁶⁴ Underlying Jerome's rebukes is a comparison between the life of the worldly soldier, in which battles were interspersed with periods of rest and immoral indulgence, and the constant onslaughts, indeed the lifelong martyrdom, of those serving in the monastic *militia Christi*.⁶⁵

In Jerome's most famous letter, a treatise on virginity written in the form of an epistle to the thirteen-year-old girl Eustochium (c.384), he presented spiritual

---

60 As Michael Stuart Williams (*Authorised Lives*, 120–1) observes, 'despite Jerome's assertions of his importance ... Paul remains a secondary figure even in his own biography.' On Jerome's complex relationship to the *Vita Antonii*, see Virginia Burrus, 'Queer Lives of Saints: Jerome's Hagiography,' *Journal of the History of Sexuality* 10 (2001), 442–79 (esp. 447–8, 466–70).
61 For a recent reconsideration of Jerome's motivations in disseminating his letters, see Andrew Cain, 'Vox *clamantis in deserto*: Rhetoric, Reproach, and the Forging of Ascetic Authority in Jerome's Letters from the Syrian Desert,' *Journal of Theological Studies* 57 (2006), 500–25.
62 As a letter written by a mature man to a young protégé who had abandoned the monastic life, Jerome's piece offered a natural model for Bernard's Letters 1 and 2 (SBO 7: 1–22). Gerald of Wales also quotes this passage (in the context of his discussion of clerical celibacy) in his *Gemma ecclesiae*, 2.20, ed. and trans. John J. Hagen (Leiden, 1979), 203.
63 Jerome, Letter 14.2, in *Select Letters of St. Jerome*, ed. and trans. F.A. Wright (London, 1933), 28–53 (at 30): 'Corpus adsuetum tunica loricae non suffert, caput opertum linteo galeam recusat, mollem otio manum durus exasperat capulus. Audi edictum Regis tui: "Qui mecum non est, contra me est; et qui mecum non colligit, sparsit."' On Jerome's use of military imagery in this letter, see J.H.D. Scourfield, *Consoling Heliodorus: A Commentary on Jerome, Letter 60* (Oxford, 1993), 142–5; and Kuefler, *Manly Eunuch*, 275–6.
64 Letter 14.2, in *Select Letters*, ed. and trans. Wright, 30.
65 Letter 14.4, in *Select Letters*, ed. and trans. Wright, 34: 'Erras, frater, erras, si putas umquam Christianum persecutionem non pati; et nunc cum maxime oppugnaris, sit te oppugnari nescis.'

warfare as an integral part of the celibate life, a life which demands of women as well as men that they must comport themselves as though under perpetual attack.⁶⁶ Implicitly likening the dedicated virgin to the martyr, he demanded, 'Which of the saints was crowned without a battle (*certamine*)?' The celibate holy woman is a soldier fighting a battle against temptation, the stakes of which are unimaginably high:

> Is it not better to fight (*dimicare*) for a short space, to carry a camp stake (*vallum*), bear arms, live on rations, faint under the weight of a breastplate (*lorica*), and afterwards rejoice in victory, than to live in perpetual slavery as the result of a single hour's lapse?⁶⁷

Writing to a female subject, Jerome employed language similar to that he had used to exhort the apostate monk Heliodorus; whether the *miles Christi* was an enclosed virgin or a desert monk, he suggested, the ascetic contest against the flesh drew upon the same disciplinary reserves. It was also a lonely one, as Jerome implied he knew only too well: 'We are surrounded by the thronging hosts of our foes,' he wrote to Eustochium, 'our enemies are on every side,' and the weak flesh (*caro fragilis*), soon to be reduced to ashes, 'fights alone against a multitude.'⁶⁸ Jerome's definition of spiritual combat in terms of the taming of bodily desires – a prominent theme not only in his letters but throughout his hagiography – directly shaped later monastic understandings of what modern scholars have termed the 'battle for chastity.'⁶⁹ His acceptance that women, or rather virgins, possessed of a manly degree of *virtus*, could be worthy opponents for the devil, also reflected the consensus of his day.⁷⁰ Early hagiographers generally conceded that holy women could participate in the battle for salvation – in fact, the status of spiritual warfare as *imitatio Christi* meant that no woman (or man) could be considered a true follower of Christ if she did not 'fight' in this way.⁷¹

---

66 Letter 22, in *Select Letters*, ed and trans. Wright, 52–159.
67 Letter 22.39, in *Select Letters*, ed. and trans. Wright (slightly revised), 150–3: 'Quis sanctorum sine certamine coronatus est? ... Nonne melius est brevi tempore dimicare, ferre vallum, arma, cibaria, lassescere sub lorica et postea gaudere victorem, quam inpatientia unius horae servire perpetuo?'
68 Letter 22.3, in *Select Letters*, ed. and trans. Wright, 58–9: 'Magnis inimicorum circumdamur agminibus, hostium plena sunt omnia. Caro fragilis et cinis futura post modicum pugnat sola cum pluribus.'
69 Jacqueline Murray, 'Masculinizing Religious Life: Sexual Prowess, the Battle for Chastity and Monastic Identity,' in *Holiness and Masculinity in the Middle Ages*, ed. P.H. Cullum and Katherine J. Lewis (Toronto, 2004), 24–42. The origin of the phrase is Michel Foucault's essay on Cassian, 'Le combat de la chasteté,' *Communications* 35 (1982), 15–25.
70 David Brakke (*Making of the Monk*, chapter 8) has shown how hagiography of the fourth and fifth centuries portrayed monastics of both sexes as relatively masculine or feminine depending on their prowess in single combat against demonic adversaries. Just as a holy woman might display a spiritual manliness through displays of ascetic fortitude, it was imperative that monks avoid being effeminized by succumbing to temptation.
71 As argued by John Kitchen, *Saints' Lives and the Rhetoric of Gender: Male and Female in Merovingian Hagiography* (New York, 1998), 104–5.

In the introduction to his *Life of Martin* (begun c.396),[72] Sulpicius Severus expressed his hope that his work would 'rouse in the reader a desire for true wisdom, for heavenly warfare (*caelestem militiam divinam*) and for a valor (*virtus*) inspired by God.'[73] Sulpicius was more successful than he could possibly have hoped; in the following centuries his Martin came to fill a unique dual role as a model for pious laymen as well as monastic ascetics. As a soldier who 'abstained from those vices in which men of that class are prone to indulge,' Martin became a patron of the Frankish army and a natural reference point for later promoters of a model of knighthood that stressed restraint and service to the Church.[74] But Martin, who had continued to live as a monk even after his elevation to the episcopate, appealed just as strongly to monastic readers. Inscriptions at Martin's foundation of Marmoutier attest to his veneration as a spiritual warrior from an early period, and hagiographers of the Central Middle Ages praised their subjects as imitators of Martin.[75]

Sulpicius Severus was well acquainted with the *vitae* of Antony and Paul, and one of his central claims in Martin's Life was that his hero equaled these eastern predecessors in the perfection of his asceticism, even as he surpassed them in his ability to work miracles.[76] The son of a veteran, Sulpicius' Martin was conscripted into the Roman army at age fifteen and continued to serve even after his baptism, though his reputation for patience, humility, and self-denial was such that 'he was regarded as a monk, rather than a soldier (*non miles, sed monachus putaretur*).'[77] Even Martin's standard-issue sword was transformed into an instrument of Christian love, as he used it soley to cut his cloak in two so

---

[72] For the Latin text and extensive commentary, see Fontaine, *Vie de saint Martin*, 1: 248–317. I have used (with some modifications) the English translation by F.R. Hoare, 'The Life of Saint Martin of Tours,' in *Soldiers of Christ: Saints and Saints' Lives from Late Antiquity and the Early Middle Ages*, ed. Thomas F.X. Noble and Thomas Head (University Park, PA, 1995), 1–29. A comprehensive introduction to the text, its author, and his subject is Clare Stancliffe, *St. Martin and his Hagiographer: History and Miracle in Sulpicius Severus* (Oxford, 1983).

[73] *Vita S. Martini* 1.6, ed. Fontaine, 1: 252; trans. Hoare, *Soldiers of Christ*, 5.

[74] *Vita S. Martini* 2.6, ed. Fontaine, 1: 256; Ian S. Robinson, 'Gregory VII and the Soldiers of Christ,' *History* 58 (1973), 169–92 (at 178); and Rosenwein, 'St. Odo's St Martin,' 317–31 and figs 1, 3. In the Central Middle Ages, Martin was most often represented in art as a mounted warrior rather than a cleric. However, his flexibility as an exemplar is demonstrated by the fact that clerical critics of the crusading movement also cited Martin's *vita* in support of their position; see, for example, the anonymous twelfth-century Benedictine *Liber de poenitentia et tentationibus religiosorum*, PL 213: 863–904 (at col. 893).

[75] For Marmoutier, see Raymond Van Dam, 'Images of Saint Martin in Late Roman and Early Merovingian Gaul,' *Viator* 19 (1988), 1–27 (here 4 and n.18). For an example of *imitatio Martini*, see Adam of Eynsham's twelfth-century *vita* of the ascetic monk-bishop Hugh of Lincoln, *Magna Vita S. Hugonis*, 1.7, ed. and trans. Decima Douie and Hugh Farmer as *The Life of St. Hugh of Lincoln*, 2 vols (London, 1961–2), 1: 24.

[76] Stancliffe, *Martin and his Hagiographer*, 68–9, 96.

[77] *Vita S. Martini* 2.7, ed. Fontaine, 1: 256; trans. Hoare, *Soldiers of Christ*, 6. As Virginia Burrus observes (*The Sex Lives of Saints: An Erotics of Ancient Hagiography* [Philadelphia, PA, 2004], 95), 'Martin's baptism ... thus did not mark a break with soldiering, any more than soldiering compromised his monastic identity.'

that he might give half to a shivering beggar (who was, of course, Christ in disguise).⁷⁸ In his final renunciation of worldly soldiering before the emperor Julian, a scene that owes much to the passions of the military martyrs,⁷⁹ Martin was given the opportunity to prove that though he might be monkish, he was nonetheless a courageous warrior:

> 'I am Christ's soldier,' said Martin; 'I am not allowed to fight.' These words put the tyrant in a rage and he said that it was from fear of the battle that was to be fought the next day that he wanted to quit the service, not from religious motives. But Martin was undaunted; in fact he stood all the firmer when they tried to frighten him. 'If it is put down to cowardice,' he said, 'and not to faith, I will stand unarmed in front of the battle line tomorrow and I will go unscathed through the enemy's columns in the name of the Lord Jesus, protected by the sign of the cross instead of by shield and helmet.'⁸⁰

As it happened, Martin was not obliged to make good on his boast, since battle was miraculously averted by the enemy's surrender (though Sulpicius assured his readers that 'the good Lord could have kept his soldier safe even amid the swords and darts of the enemy.') The bloodless resolution of the conflict, however, was in itself a great victory won by God on Martin's behalf.⁸¹ His martyrdom was averted not because of his own weakness, but because, as becomes clear in the remainder of the *vita*, Martin was sorely needed in the ranks of the earthly *militia Christi*.

Martin is transformed in the course of the *vita* from a monkish soldier into a militant monk, and finally, the bishop of Tours.⁸² Many of the miracles reported by Sulpicius also have martial overtones; the fearless Martin wielded prayer and the sign of the cross as spiritual weapons, and even enlisted the help of angelic warriors in his campaign against one unfortunate group of pagans.⁸³ Up to the very moment of his death Martin remained a faithful soldier, whose dying words

---

78 *Vita S. Martini* 3, ed. Fontaine, 1: 256–8; trans. Hoare, *Soldiers of Christ*, 7.
79 Indeed, this scene constitutes a mini-passion within the *vita*; see Jacques Fontaine, 'Sulpice Sévère a-t-il travesti Saint Martin de Tours en martyr militaire?' *Analecta Bollandiana* 81 (1963), 31–58 (esp. 34–6); and Stancliffe, *Martin and His Hagiographer*, 141–7.
80 *Vita S. Martini* 4.3–5, ed. Fontaine, 1: 260: 'Christi ego miles sum: pugnare mihi non licet. Tum uero adversus hanc uocem tyrannus infremuit dicens eum metu pugnae, quae postero die erat futura, non religionis gratia detractare militiam. At Martinus intrepidus, immo inlato sibi terrore constantior: si hoc, inquit, ignauiae adscribitur, non fidei, crastina die ante aciem inermis adstabo et in nomine Domini Iesu, signo crucis, non clipeo protectus aut galea, hostium cuneos penetrabo securus.' Trans. Hoare, *Soldiers of Christ*, 8.
81 *Vita S. Martini* 4.7–9, ed. Fontaine, 1: 260–2; trans. Hoare in *Soldiers of Christ*, 8. Note that even in this description of worldly battle there is an echo of the spiritual warfare of Eph. 6:16 in the 'enemy's darts (*tela hostium*).'
82 See Fontaine, *Vie de saint Martin*, 1: 143–8; Raymond Van Dam, *Leadership and Community in Late Antique Gaul* (Berkeley, CA, 1992), 124–7, 136, 139; Burrus, *Sex Lives of Saints*, 91–103.
83 *Vita S. Martini* 12.3, 13.8, 22.1 (prayer/cross as weapons); 14.5 (angelic warriors), ed. Fontaine, 1: 278, 282, 300, 284.

affirmed his commitment to the *militia Christi* and his conviction that his whole life had been spent in combat:

> The battle of the bodily service (*corporeae pugna militiae*) is a weighty one, Lord, and I have already fought in it enough, but if you still require me to stand fast before your camps (*castris tuis*) in that effort, I do not refuse nor plead my weakened condition as an excuse. I will fulfill the duties you assign, I will serve beneath your standards as long as you will command (*sub signis tuis, quoadusque ipse tu iuserris, militabo*), and however much an old man wishes for a rest after his labors, the soul will still be the conqueror of years, unable to surrender to old age.[84]

Sulpicius' double-presentation of Martin as *miles* illuminates tensions and contradictions that would continue to preoccupy monastic writers in coming centuries. The first of these is the uneasy relationship between the worldly soldier and the spiritual warrior, whose callings seem at once to overlap and diverge; though Martin was said to have avoided the vices common among military men, the courage, steadfastness, and obedience that made him a valuable member of his cohort were the very qualities that rendered him a model monk. The hagiographer's concern with proving Martin's bravery, his *virtus*, points to another issue that many later monastic thinkers wrestled with: the reconciliation of Christian pacifism with martially inflected models of heroism rooted in the Classical tradition and the Hebrew Bible. Sulpicius' solution – to make Martin into a *heroic* pacifist, a man who refused to fight even as he showed no fear in the face of death – combined ingredients from the archetypes of the military martyr and desert ascetic with a new emphasis on miracles as proof of saintliness. The result was a new kind of Christian hero, whose militant sanctity was imbued with a decidedly monastic ethos.

In the *Dialogues* of Gregory the Great (d.604), a work composed two centuries after the *Life of Martin*, we find the identities of the martyr and the *miles Christi* have been thoroughly integrated into monastic ideals of sanctity.[85] Like Sulpicius before him, Gregory self-consciously defined his hero Benedict in relation to the great 'fathers of the monks': Benedict was Elisha to Antony's Elijah, an ascetic conqueror of lust on a par with Jerome's holy men, and, like Martin, a great miracle-worker.[86] As Athanasius had done in the *Vita Antonii*, Gregory presented his subject's spiritual victories as fulfillments of the precepts of the

---

[84] Sulpicius Severus, Lettter 3.13, ed. Fontaine, *Vie de Saint Martin*, 1: 340: 'Gravis quidem est, Domine, corporeae pugna militiae et iam satis est quod hucusque certaui; sed si adhuc in eodem labore pro castris tuis stare me praecipis, non recuso nec fatiscentem causabor aetatem. Munia tua deuotus inplebo, sub signis tuis, quoadusque ipse tu iuserris, militabo, et, quamuis optata sit seni remissio post laborem, est tamen animus uictor annorum et cedere nescius senectuti.'

[85] For the Latin text, see Gregory the Great, *Dialogues*, 3 vols, ed. Adalbert de Vogüé and trans. Paul Antin, SC 251, 260, 265 (Paris, 1978–80).

[86] Joan M. Petersen, *The Dialogues of Gregory the Great in their Late Antique Cultural Context* (Toronto, 1984), 27–8, 38 (and chapter 1 more generally); and the introduction to the *Dialogues* by de Vogüé, 1: 117–19, 120–4.

martyred apostle Paul.[87] Like his predecessors, Benedict's ascetic perfection marked him as a spiritual warrior and a conduit for heavenly *virtus*. In a scene destined to become a hagiographical commonplace, Gregory described how the holy abbot rolled naked in a patch of nettles as a means of quelling his lust, and thereby 'conquered sin (*vicit peccatum*).'[88] Benedict shook off the attacks of murderous monks and run-of-the-mill demons, and his prowess was such that the 'master of evil' himself eagerly engaged him in battle.[89] As in earlier holy men's Lives, Benedict's conquests served to expand Christian territory; but whereas Antony and Paul had driven demons out of the desert wastes, paving the way for monastic settlement, Benedict, like Martin, destroyed ancient groves and temples, and erected a Christian *castrum*, the abbey of Montecassino, on the site of a former stronghold of the pagan gods.[90] Benedict may be the mightiest spiritual warrior of the *Dialogues*, but he is by no means the only one: like the desert fathers of old, many of Gregory's holy men clash with demons and defend the 'citadel of chastity (*arx continentiae*)' against lust, armed only with the weapons of prayer.[91]

Like Antony, Paul, and Martin, Benedict and the other *milites Christi* of the *Dialogues* provided later monks with templates against which they could measure their own spiritual progress. From the Carolingian period onwards, monastic hagiographers often borrowed stories and lessons from Gregory's *vita* of Benedict.[92] Given the status of the *Dialogues* as an authoritative narrative of the origins of Benedictine monasticism, a text nearly on a par with the *Rule* itself, it is not surprising that many monks were so familiar with Gregory's words and images that they made them their own. A miracle recorded by Aimo, a tenth-century Benedictine monk of Fleury, illustrates how Gregory's stories became part of the mental wallpaper of later writers. Aimo described how Drogo, a monk of the abbey who had taken up the eremitic life, enlisted Benedict's aid to help him fight off demonic assaults, including an illusory fire that drove him from his hermitage. Remembering that the *Dialogues* contained a story of how demons had terrified Benedict's monks with just such a vision,

---

[87] *Dialogues* 2.3.11, ed. de Vogüé, 2: 148: 'Fortis etenim praeliator Dei teneri intra claustra noluit, certaminis campum quaesiuit.'

[88] *Dialogues* 2.2.2, ed. de Vogüé, 1: 138. This episode is re-enacted in countless later medieval Lives of holy men.

[89] *Dialogues* 2.8.10, ed. de Vogüé, 2: 166: 'Nam tanto post grauiora praelia pertulit, quanto contra se aperte pugnantem ipsum magistrum malitiae inuenit.'

[90] *Dialogues* 2.8.10–11, ed. de Vogüé, 2: 166–8. Fittingly, Benedict built an oratory dedicated to Martin on the site.

[91] *Dialogues* 1.10.1 (Fortunatus of Todi) and 3.7 (Andrew of Fondi), ed. de Vogüé, 2: 92–4, 278–80.

[92] On the text's reception and influence, see de Vogüé's Introduction to the *Dialogues*, 1: 141–3; and Jean Longère's study of the presentation of Benedict in sermons and liturgical texts; 'La prédication sur Saint Benoît du Xe au XIIIe siècle,' in *Sous la Règle de Saint Benoît: Structures monastiques et sociétés en France du moyen âge à l'époque moderne* (Geneva, 1982), 33–60.

the soldier of Christ (*miles Christi*), having recourse to a well-known protection, armed himself on the forehead with the sign of the cross and threw himself completely against the phantom fire, clearly mindful, we may conjecture, of the works of his lord and master Benedict, who, helped by the gift of divine grace, called his disciples into his presence and declared that the burning flames had been imaginary.[93]

For monks in the Central Middle Ages none of these saints was a long-dead figure from the distant past; each was a mentor and patron in the here-and-now, whose carved or painted visage they had seen innumerable times and who might at any moment make his wishes known by working a miracle or putting in a visionary appearance.[94] The *vitae* of these saints mediated their legacy in later centuries, ensuring that monks related their own experiences to incidents from these venerable texts, and spoke of the heroes of their own day in the words of Jerome, Sulpicius, and Gregory. Like the ancient Israelites, whose progress from historical warriors to soldiers of Christ was traced in Chapter 1, these 'fathers of monks' served as role models for later generations of monastic *milites Christi*. The concept of the ascetic life as a form of military service formed an especially sturdy bridge between past and present within the monastic tradition, as later hagiographers used martial rhetoric to situate their subjects within a long genealogy of spiritual combatants stretching back to the desert ascetics and beyond.

Monastic life as military service

The understanding of the monastic ideal as a spiritual military service was transmitted and elaborated in the various rules composed in the Latin West in the early Middle Ages. At the turn of the fifth century, when monasticism was as yet in its infancy in the West, Augustine warned of the sacrifices demanded of those who embarked on the 'holy warfare (*sancta militia*)' of monastic life, and urged the monks of his day to strive to fulfill Paul's command (2 Tim. 2:3–4) that the true soldier of Christ renounce all worldly concerns.[95] Early rules imported from the East, such as the fifth-century *Rule of Macarius*, echoed these sentiments.[96]

---

[93] *Miracula S. Benedicti*, 2.4, ed. de Certain, 102–3; trans. Head, *Hagiography and the Cult of Saints*, 119. The story alluded to is *Dialogues* 2.10.11, ed. de Vogüé, 2: 173. Aimo's text reads: 'Tunc miles Christi ad nota recurrens praesidia, signo crucis armat frontem, totemque se adversus phantasticum objicit incendium, memor utique, ut conjici datur, operum domini ac magistri sui Benedicti, qui, divinae gratiae praeventus munere, adurentes flammas, vocatis ad suos oculos discipulis, imaginarias fuisse declaravit.'

[94] For a discussion of the interplay of iconography and textual traditions, and how these in turn shaped one community's relationship to its saints, see Kirk Ambrose, *The Nave Sculpture of Vézelay: The Art of Monastic Viewing* (Toronto, 2006), chapter 3 (esp. 48–56 for the importance of Martin, Benedict, Antony and Paul as exemplars).

[95] Augustine, *De opere monachorum*, c.22.26, 25.32, 26.35, ed. in PL 40: 57–82 (at cols. 569, 571–2, 574).

[96] For the description of monks as *milites Christi* in the *Rule of Macarius*, see the excerpt in Benedict of Aniane's *Concordia regularum* 7.2, PL 103: 805.

In the *Admonitio ad filium spiritualium*, a text medieval readers attributed to Basil of Caesarea, the monastic author explained the nature of the wisdom he wished to impart to his spiritual son: 'I wish to instruct you about spiritual warfare (*spiritualis militia*), and teach you the way you should fight for the king.'[97] The *Rule of the Master*, composed in sixth-century Italy, employed military topoi familiar from earlier hagiography in its portrayal of monks as an 'order of holy warriors (*sanctae militiae ordo*).'[98] All of these texts circulated in the early medieval West, and, thanks to their inclusion in the massive *Codex regularum* compiled by the Carolingian reformer Benedict of Aniane, continued to be available to later monastic readers.[99]

Above all, it was the writings of Cassian (d.c.435) that introduced the militant asceticism of the eastern deserts into the monasteries of the early medieval West. His *Institutes* and *Conferences* exercised an enormous influence on the development of monastic spirituality, both directly, as these texts were widely read throughout the Middle Ages, and indirectly, as Cassian's ideas and language left their imprint on early Latin rules such as the *Rule of the Master* and the *Rule of Benedict*, as well as on the writings of Gregory the Great.[100] For Cassian, the successive stages of monastic development could be understood as battles, and the goals of each stage as victories to be won – against the flesh, the eight deadly vices, and the demons who harassed the monk at every turn.[101] Cassian

---

[97] *Admonitio ad filium spiritualium*, PL 103: 685–6 (quoting col. 685). The work is now thought to have been composed in c.500 by Abbot Porcarius of Lérins. For commentary, see James F. LePree, 'Two Recently-Discovered Passages of the Pseudo-Basil's *Admonition to a Spiritual Son* in Smaragdus' *Commentary on the Rule of St. Benedict* and the *Letters* of Alcuin,' *Heroic Age* 11 (2008), online at http://www.heroicage.org/issues/11/lepree.php (accessed 5 October 2010).

[98] *Regula Magistri*, ed. and trans. Adalbert de Vogüé as *La Règle du maître*, 3 vols, SC 105–7 (Paris, 1964–5). Depending on the dating of this text, which remains in question, the *Master's* references to spiritual combat may be read either as the inspiration for the martial language in the *Rule of Benedict* or as derivations from the latter work. Compare *Regula Magistri*, 1.1–5 (ed. de Vogüé, 1: 328–30), with RB 1.4–5, p.168. For the position that Benedict's *Rule* derives from that of the *Master*, see Marilyn Dunn, 'Mastering Benedict: Monastic Rules and their Authors in the Early Medieval West,' *English Historical Review* 105 (1990), 567–94; and for the counter-argument, Adalbert de Vogüé, 'The Master and St Benedict: A Reply,' *English Historical Review* 107 (1992), 95–103.

[99] The *Codex regularum monasticarum et canonicarum* is found in PL 103: 423–700. With the exception of the Pseudo-Basilian *Admonitio*, all of these texts were included in the *Codex* as well as in Benedict's *Concordia regularum*, a concordance of passages from various rules compiled with the intention of showing the universality of the *Rule of Benedict's* precepts. For the later circulation of Benedict of Aniane's works, see Pierre Bonnerue's Introduction to his edition of this work, *Benedicti Anianensis Concordia regularum*, CCCM 168 (Turnhout, 1999), 147–53.

[100] Though Cassian left no monastic rule *per se*, his advice was so highly regarded that Benedict of Aniane sought to create a rule out of excerpts from his writings. On Cassian's sources and the later influence of his works, see Columba Stewart, *Cassian the Monk* (Oxford, 1999), 24–7.

[101] See, for example, *Collationes* 4.11, 5.27, ed. and trans. Pichery, 1: 175–6, 216–17. Carol Straw emphasizes Cassian's tendency to externalize sin and its agents; see 'Gregory,

advised monks to model themselves on the faithful centurion of the Gospel (Matt. 8:5–13):

> If, therefore, we fight manfully (*viriliter dimicare*) against disturbances and vices and can bring them under our control, and if we fight and destroy the passions in our flesh, and subject the unruly cohort (*instabilis cohors*) of our thoughts to the rule of reason, and use the preserving standard (*vexillum*) of the Lord's cross to repulse the terrible host of opposing powers from the boundaries of our breast, as a reward for such triumphs we will be raised to the spiritual rank of that centurion....[102]

In other words, systematic progress in spiritual warfare would be rewarded with promotion through the ranks of the monastic militia. Significantly, Cassian also insisted that 'we can gain instruction about the spiritual contest by comparing it with the fleshly one,'[103] anticipating later monastic writers' engagement with the values and practical aspects of knightly combat.

For Cassian, as for his readers in later centuries, the monk's warrior status was symbolized by his clothing, understood as a suit of spiritual armor capable of deflecting sin, the most important component of which was the 'double belt (*cingulum duplicis*)' with which he girded his loins for battle. This belt represented, above all, the wearer's determination to extinguish the burning darts of lust with 'the frost of abstinence.'[104] At least some monastic readers must have been reminded of the *cingulum militaris*, the sword-belt worn by contemporary soldiers (and later by knights) as a badge of status, and may have seen Cassian's *cingulum duplicis* as a replacement of a spiritual, though still martial, nature. Later hagiographers continued to play with this theme, as we shall see in Chapter 5. For instance, William of Tocco wrote in his *vita* of Thomas Aquinas that when the holy scholar begged God to allow him to retain his virginity, a pair of angels appeared to tell him that 'God had heard him, and that he would achieve victory in this very difficult battle (*pugna tam difficilis*), and bound tight his loins, saying, "Behold, on behalf of God we gird you with a belt of chastity (*cingulum castitatis*)...."'[105]

Cassian, and the Cardinal Vices,' in *In the Garden of Evil: The Vices and Culture in the Middle Ages*, ed. Richard Newhauser (Toronto, 2005), 35–58 (esp. 44–6).

[102] *Collationes*, 7.5., ed. Pichery, 1: 250: 'Si igitur nos quoque uiriliter perturbationes et uitia dimicantes potuerimus ea dicioni nostrae discretionique subicere ac militantes in carne nostra extinguere passiones uel instabilem cogitationum nostrarum cohortem rationis imperio subiugare ac dominicae crucis salutari uexillo dirissimas aduersariarum potestatum turmas a terminis nostri pectoris propulsare, pro tantorum meritis triumphorum ad spiritalis huius centurionis ordinem prouehemur....'

[103] *Institutiones*, 6.7.1, ed. and trans. Guy, 271: 'ut posit nobis spiritualis agonis instructio conparatione carnalis adquiri.'

[104] *Institutiones*, 1.1.1–5 and 1.11.1–3, ed. Guy, 36–8, 52–4.

[105] Cited and discussed by Ruth Mazo Karras, 'Thomas Aquinas's Chastity Belt: Clerical Masculinity in Medieval Europe,' in *Gender & Christianity in Medieval Europe: New Perspectives*, ed. Lisa M. Bitel and Felice Lifshitz (Philadelphia, PA, 2008), 52–67 (quoting 62). For the Latin text, see William of Tocco, *Ystoria sancti Tome de Aquino*, 11, ed. Claire Le Brun-Gouanvic (Toronto, 1996), 112–13.

In Cassian's demanding regime of spiritual training personal asceticism took center stage and, although he wrote expressly for those living in communities, the monk of the *Conferences* and *Institutes* is often presented to the reader as a solitary figure, not unlike Athanasius' Antony or Jerome's Paul.[106] Cassian's monk was never truly alone, however, as he insisted, following earlier writers, that no victory could be won without God's support.[107] Finding himself 'under attack by day and night, and acknowledging that he cannot escape unless his protector comes to his aid,' the monk who cried out to God's for help would instantly be surrounded by an 'impregnable wall,' and defended by 'an impenetrable breastplate and the strongest shield.'[108] For Cassian the monk-ascetic's spiritual development was measured by the ferocity of the battles he fought, and by his victories – over gluttony, sadness, pride, and anger – each of which served only to bring his prowess to the attention of ever stronger and cleverer opponents.[109] As he explained, 'none but the weaker demons are sent to do battle with beginners and the weak, and when these demons have been defeated, progressively stronger ones take their place in the battle against the athlete of Christ.'[110] Many of the themes commonly found in later monastic writing on spiritual warfare are traceable to Cassian: these include the reliance on divine support in battle; the progression from novice-recruit to veteran ascetic; and the application of metaphors drawn from worldly warfare to monastic spirituality.

Like many earlier rules, the sixth-century *Rule of Benedict* envisioned the monastic community as a militia and the brethren's main occupations as battles.[111] Since this text formed the basis for communal life in most monas-

---

[106] Cassian is clearly influenced by eastern models of asceticism and eremitism, embodied in works like the *Vita Antonii* and the writings of Evagrius Pontius (and through the latter, those of Origen); see Stewart, *Cassian the Monk*, chapter 1.
[107] *Institutiones*, 6.5.1, ed. Guy, 268.
[108] *Conferences*, 10.10, ed. Pichery, 2: 85: 'Hic versiculus (Ps. 69:2) omnibus infestatione daemonum laborantibus inexpugnabilis murus est, et impenetrabilis lorica, ac munitissimus clypeus.' (Ps. 69:2 reads, 'Come to my help, O God; Lord, hurry to my rescue.')
[109] *Institutiones*, 5.19–20, ed. Guy, 222–4; *Conferences*, 7.20–1, ed. Pichery, 1: 261–5.
[110] *Conferences*, 7.20, ed. Pichery, 1: 261–2.
[111] The meaning of the language under consideration here has been the subject of heated debate. Eugène Manning ('La signification de *militare-militia-miles* dans la Règle de S. Benoît,' *Revue Bénédictine* 72 (1962), 135–8) has argued that Benedict's concept of *militia* has the meaning of 'service' or 'obedience,' and downplays the militaristic connotations of these passages. His argument follows the general lines of an earlier philological study by Christine Mohrmann ('La langue de Saint Benoît,' in *Sancti Benedicti Regula Monachorum*, ed. Philibert Schmitz [Maredsous, 1955], 9–39) which emphasized the associations of *militia* and *militare* with civil service in Late Antiquity. Although these meanings are certainly present in the text, Benedict was also aware of the long genealogy of spiritual warfare described here. Gregorio Penco has suggested that the martial imagery of the *Rule* should be read in the context of the many other sixth-century texts that describe monks as spiritual soldiers. See 'Il concetto di monaco e di vita monastica in occidente nel secolo VI,' *Studia monastica* 1 (1959), 7–50 (esp. 22–3). More recently, Benedict Guevin has argued for an acceptance of the martial overtones of the *Rule*'s language; see 'Benedict's "Military" Vocabulary Reconsidered,' *American Benedictine Review* 49 (1998), 138–47.

teries during the Central Middle Ages, and as such was read aloud each day in chapter, Benedict's words would have been as familiar to monks as those of the Scriptures. As he declared in his Prologue, Benedict wrote with an audience of monastic soldiers in mind: 'This message of mine is for you, then, if you are ready to give up your own will, once and for all, and armed with the strong and noble weapons of obedience to fight (*militare*) for the true King, Christ the Lord.'[112] For Benedict, the struggle to overcome the will – the central struggle of monastic life – was a battle each monk must fight within himself. At the same time, he added, 'We must prepare our hearts and our bodies for the battle of holy obedience (*sanctae ... oboedientiae militanda*),' in which soldier-monks collectively served under the generalship of Christ, or Christ's earthly representative, their abbot.[113] The collective warfare Benedict spoke of was fundamentally different from that celebrated by the martyrs, early desert ascetics, or the hermits of his own day, men who – in the words of the *Rule* – had shown themselves ready to 'go from the battle line (*acies*) in the ranks of their brothers to the single combat of the desert.'[114] As spiritual beginners, Benedict's monks were presumed to be novices in the daily battle that would henceforth consume their lives, and would gain experience in war by fighting as part of a cohort of *milites Christi* and thereby acquiring the soldierly virtues of obedience to superiors and loyalty to brothers-in-arms.[115]

Later monks' understanding of the *Rule* coalesced through their reading of a constellation of other texts seen as having a special relationship to Benedict's message. These included Cassian's works (which the *Rule* particularly recommended), the writings of Benedict's hagiographer Gregory the Great, and commentaries on the *Rule*. Gregory's *Dialogues* were often copied into manuscripts as an accompaniment to the *Rule*, and so monastic readers of the *Rule* would have been familiar with this work's depiction of Benedict as a spiritual warrior.[116] And indeed it seems impossible to separate Gregory's presentation of his hero from his own interpretation of the *Rule*. We catch a glimpse of Gregory's understanding of the obligations of the monastic militia in the following conversation from the third book of the *Dialogues*:

---

[112] RB Prol. 3, p. 156: 'Ad te ergo nunc mihi sermo dirigitur, quisquis abrenuntians propriis voluntatibus, Domino Christo vero regi militaturus, oboedientiae fortissima atque praeclara arma sumis.'

[113] RB Prol. 40, p.164.

[114] RB 1.4–5, p. 168. Hermits have gained their strength from living in community: 'eremitarum ... qui didicerunt contra diabolum multorum solacio iam docti pugnare, et bene extructi fraternal ex acie ad singularem pugnam eremi, securi iam sine consolatione alterius, sola manu vel brachio contra vitia carnis vel cogitationum, Deo auxiliante, pugnare sufficiunt.' Réné Dolle has traced the origins of this phrasing to the sermons of the fifth-century pope Leo I; see '"*Fraterna ex acie*": À propos du chapitre 1 (5) de la Règle Bénédictine,' *Studia Anselmiana* fasc. 44 (1959), 126–8.

[115] RB 2.20, p. 174: 'sub uno aequalem servitutis militiam baiulamus, quia non est apud Deum personarum acceptio (Rom. 2:11).' This emphasis on collective struggle represents a departure from the work of Cassian, one of Benedict's major influences, whose *Institutes* and *Conferences* focus to a greater extent on the individual ascetic's battle against sin.

[116] de Vogüé, Introduction to the *Dialogues*, 1: 143.

> Gregory: Without battle there is no palm of victory. None who do not fight to the end against the hostilities of the ancient enemy can be victors. This wicked spirit is ever mindful of our thoughts, words, and deeds, always seeking evidence with which he might accuse us on the day of judgment. [...]
>
> Peter the Deacon: It must be extremely exhausting and frightening to stand fast in the front battle line (*acies*), continually meeting the enemy's attacks.[117]

Peter's reply echoes the description of the spiritual battle line from the first chapter of the *Rule*, and reflects Benedict's presentation of the monastic life as a perpetual war.[118] And of course Gregory had anticipated Peter's objection to the strenuous, terrifying nature of monastic warfare; 'none who do not fight to the end,' he concluded, could hope to win the only victory that had any real meaning in the Christian life.

Of the commentaries on Benedict's *Rule* that began to appear in the Carolingian era, the most influential was the line-by-line *Expositio in regulam Sancti Benedicti* composed by the abbot Smaragdus of Saint-Mihiel in the early ninth century.[119] Widely copied and studied as an adjunct to the *Rule*, the *Expositio* shaped how later monastic readers perceived Benedict's intentions in much the way exegetical works influenced their understanding of the Scriptures. During the eleventh and twelfth centuries Smaragdus was enthusiastically read by traditionalists and reformers alike, and his work has been identified as a driving force behind the Cistercian rethinking of the *Rule*.[120] While modern scholars have disagreed about how to interpret Benedict's use of the terms '*militia*' and '*militare*,' Smaragdus left his reader in no doubt that the *Rule* intended these to be read in a military sense:

> For the world has its soldiers and Christ has his soldiers (*milites Christi*). Now the world's soldiers take up weak and slippery weapons, whereas Christ's soldiers take up strong and bright ones. The former fight against their enemies, and the result is they bring themselves and those they kill to eternal punishment; the latter fight

---

[117] *Dialogues* 3.19.5 and 3.20.3, ed. de Vogüé, 2: 348–50: 'Sine labore certaminis non est palma uictoriae. Unde ergo uictores sunt, nisi contra antiqui hostis insidias decertauerunt? Malignus quippe spiritus cogitationi, locutioni atque operi nostro semper insistit, si fortasse quis inueniat, unde apud examen aeterni iudicis accusator existat.... Laboriosum ualde atque terribile est contra inimici insidias semper intendere et continue quasi in aciem stare.'

[118] RB 1.4, p. 168. Note that elsewhere in the *Dialogues*, Gregory described a miracle in which dying monks were visited by angelic messengers on orders to 'enroll them in the heavenly militia,' as a reward for their faithful service in the *militia Christi*; see *Dialogues* 4.27.4, ed. de Vogüé, 3: 88–90.

[119] On Smaragdus, see Leclercq, *Love of Learning*, 44–6. The *Expositio* is ed. by A. Spannagel and P. Engelbert, Corpus consuetudinem monasticarum 8 (Siegburg, 1974); and trans. by David Barry as *Smaragdus of Saint-Mihiel: Commentary on the Rule of Saint Benedict*, CS 212 (Kalamazoo, MI, 2007).

[120] Daniel Marcel La Corte, 'Smaragdus of Saint-Mihiel: Ninth-Century Sources for Twelfth-Century Reformers,' *Cistercian Studies Quarterly* 41 (2006), 273–90; and Willibrord Witters, 'Smaragde au Moyen Âge: la diffusion de ses écrits d'après la tradition manuscrite,' *Études ligériennes d'histoire et d'archéologie médiévales* (Auxerre, 1975), 361–76.

against the vices, so that after death they may be able to gain eternal life and its rewards; the former fight, and the result is they go down into hell, the latter fight that they may ascend to glory; the former fight and so after death are enslaved with the demons in hell, ... the latter fight so that they may always rejoice with the angels; the former fight and so will always mourn with the devil, the latter fight so that they may always exult with Christ....[121]

Far from shying away from militaristic readings of the *Rule*, Smaragdus seems to have gone out of his way to make explicit what Benedict had left implicit. Where Benedict had urged monks to 'gird their loins with faith,' Smaragdus – drawing out the allusion to Ephesians 6, and likely thinking of Cassian's *Institutes* – explained that the master was referring to the 'double belt (*cingulum duplicis*) proper to monks' which enabled them to be 'manfully prepared for battle (*praelio viriliter praeparati*).'[122] The *Rule*'s reference to hermits who leave the security of the monastic 'battle line,' was likewise glossed in the *Expositio* in a way suggestive of the author's approval of this sort of martial imagery:

> The battle line is the line of soldiers (*ordo militum*) drawn up to wage war against the devil, and only this kind of monk leaves the battle line to fight. It is called fighting (*pugna*) because originally in a war people began to battle with their fists (*pugni*). For no one will be crowned without a contest (2 Tim. 2:5); nor does God's grace desert any if they fight against the vices of the flesh with alacrity and good will.[123]

Here, as elsewhere in the *Expositio*, Smaragdus linked Benedict's presentation of the monastic *miles Christi* to biblical passages which, as we saw in Chapter 1, were commonly invoked in discussions of spiritual warfare, lifting imagery of competition and combat from Job and especially the Epistles.[124] The resulting

---

[121] *Expositio*, Prol. 3, ed. Spannagel and Engelbert, 13–14: 'Sunt enim milites saeculi, sunt et milites Christi. Sed milites saeculi infirma et lubrica arma, milites autem Christi fortissima sumunt atque praeclara. Pugnant illi contra hostes, ut se et interfectos aeternam perducant ad poenam; pugnant isti contra vitia, ut post mortem aeternam vitam consequi possint et praemia; illi ut descendant ad tartara, isti ut ascendant ad gloriam; illi ut post mortem cum daemonibus mancipentur in inferno, ... isti ut cum angelis semper laetentur; illi ut cum diabolo semper lugeant, isti cum Christo semper exultent.' Trans. Barry, *Commentary*, 58–9. Note that Smaragdus here expressed the view of most early medieval churchmen that all worldly warfare is evil and its practitioners damned.

[122] *Expositio*, Prol. 21, ed. Spannagel and Engelbert, 35; trans. Barry, *Commentary*, 88.

[123] *Expositio*, 1.5, ed. Spannagel and Engelbert, 57. 'Acies dicitur instructus ordo militum ad bellandum contra diabolum, ex qua iste solus monachorum ordo egreditur pugnaturus. Pugna vocata, eo quod primitus in bello pugnis praeliare incipiebant. Nullus enim absque certamine coronabitur; neque gratia dei deserit quemquam, si cum alacritate et bona voluntate pugnaverit contra vitia carnis.' Trans. Barry, *Commentary*, 118. This philological approach to the *Rule* is typical of Smaragdus. Cf. the similar imagery in Smaragdus' collection of meditations on the monastic life, the *Diadema monachorum*, c.76, PL 102: 671–2.

[124] *Expositio*, 1.2 (Job 7:1, Ps. 35:1–2), 1.4–5 (2 Tim. 2:5, Eph. 6:11–16), 2.20 (Job 7:1), ed. Spannagel and Engelbert, 56–8, 69; trans. Barry, *Commentary*, 117–18, 136.

exegetical argument – that the individual monk's prowess as a spiritual warrior was essential to the success of the communal life – was to become particularly meaningful after c.1000, as new monastic orders claimed authority by professing themselves the true spiritual warriors of the *Rule*, and groups from outside the monastic *ordo* laid claim to membership in the *militia spiritualis*.

Throughout the early medieval centuries, the monastic monopoly of the *miles Christi* ideal went largely unchallenged. The *vitae* of eremitical ascetics foregrounded their single combats with the devil,[125] and hagiographers of abbesses as well as abbots described their subjects as commanders of spiritual armies.[126] Reinforced through rules, commentaries, and works of hagiography written for consumption in the cloister, spiritual warfare became synonymous with a monastic ideal of sanctity based on ascetic self-denial, courageous defense of the Church's privileges, and willingness to sacrifice one's life (if only figuratively) for the faith. This model of monastic sainthood celebrated virtues that would not have been out of place in a secular military setting – loyalty, bravery, physical strength and endurance – even as it subverted them. For what could be stronger or braver, asked Smaragdus of Saint-Mihiel, than to meet violence with peace, freely subjecting oneself, body and soul, to another's rule, and rendering good for evil, all the while stoically enduring the poverty, hunger, and other hardships that were the monk's lot?[127]

New groups on the spiritual battlefield

While the *miles Christi* ideal had become inseparable from monastic identity in the early Middle Ages, by the ninth and tenth centuries there were intimations of how the rhetoric of spiritual warfare might be adapted to a Christian model of the secular warrior as defender of the Church. As we have seen, spiritual warfare did not originate as a monastic ideal, but was gradually assimilated to the monastic *ordo* by generations of hagiographers and exegetes. Moreover, the early Christian idea that *all* pious Christians, laypeople as well as clerics, could attain the status of spiritual warriors never completely fell out of favor. The cults of military martyrs like Maurice and the exegetical transformation of Old Testament warriors into spiritual soldiers may also have inspired Carolingian churchmen to describe warriors who resisted pagan invaders as *milites*

---

[125] In these Lives, the theme of spiritual battle is, unsurprisingly, often linked to the preservation of virginity, as observed by John Bugge, *Virginitas: An Essay in the History of a Medieval Ideal* (The Hague, 1975), 50–5; and Matthäus Bernards, *Speculum virginum: Geistigkeit und Seelenleben der Frau in Hochmittelalter* (Cologne and Vienna, 1982), 102–6.

[126] See these Carolingian examples: Anon., *Vita* of Ansegisus of Fontenelle, c.5, PL 105: 735–50 (at col. 737); Eigil of Fulda, *Vita Sturmi*, c.7, ed. Pius Engelbert in *Die Vita Sturmi des Eigil von Fulda* (Marburg, 1968), 139.

[127] Paraphrasing *Expositio*, Prol. 3, ed. Spannagel and Engelbert, 14–15; trans. Barry, *Commentary*, 60–1.

Christi.[128] The scholar-abbots Alcuin of York (d.804) and Hrabanus Maurus (d.856) theorized that pious noblemen and rulers could be considered spiritual warriors provided they renounced certain violent behaviors (upon which, alas, their power traditionally depended). Alcuin wrote that warriors who aspired to this ideal must abandon the bloodfeuds that were the prerogative of men of their class and devote themselves instead to serving legitimate authorities and following Christ's precepts.[129] Several decades later, when Hrabanus Maurus dedicated his collection of poems, *De laudibus sanctae crucis*, to Louis the Pious, he identified the emperor as a 'universal victor' endowed by Christ with spiritual weapons to be wielded against the enemies of the church.[130] While Hrabanus elsewhere associated the *miles Christi* with the monk, his definition of the term left room for its application to pious laymen: 'Those are rightfully called soldiers of Christ,' he wrote, 'who fight against the devil and struggle against the vices.'[131]

During the tenth and early eleventh centuries, as the Church sought to restrict and redirect the violence of warrior elites, monastic hagiographers began to offer up the most pious of these men as spiritual exemplars for their peers to emulate. Undoubtedly the best-known example is the Frankish count Gerald of Aurillac, who was the subject of two widely read *vitae*: a brief Life composed by Odo of Cluny soon after Gerald's death in the early tenth century, and a much longer *vita* which was probably the work of an early-eleventh-century monk with ties to Cluny.[132] Gerald was, as his biographers realized, an unusual candidate for sanctity: a nobleman who neither died fighting the heathen nor

---

[128] For Old Testament heroes as spiritual warriors, see Chapter 1. On the use of one particular group, the Maccabees, as models for rulers and aristocratic warriors, see Jean Dunbabin, 'The Maccabees as Exemplars in the Tenth and Eleventh Centuries,' in *The Bible in the Medieval World: Essays in Memory of Beryl Smalley*, ed. Katherine Walsh and Diana Wood (Oxford, 1985), 31–41.

[129] Mary Alberi ('"The Sword Which You Hold in Your Hand"') has posited 'a connection between [Alcuin's] exegesis and political ideals derived from the monastic tradition of *militia* as disciplined service to Christ.'

[130] Elizabeth Sears, 'Louis the Pious as *Miles Christi*: The Dedicatory Image in Hrabanus Maurus's *De laudibus sanctae Crucis*,' in *Charlemagne's Heir: New Perspectives on the Reign of Louis the Pious (814–840)*, ed. P. Godwin and Roger Collins (Oxford, 1990), 605–28.

[131] *De rerum naturis*, 16.3, PL 111: 451: 'Milites autem Christi illi esse dimicuntur, qui contra diabolum pugnant, et contra vitia dimicant.' Cited by Sears, 'Louis the Pious,' 623.

[132] Though Odo of Cluny has traditionally been credited with the composition of both Lives, and many scholars continue to treat both texts as Odo's work, other scholars have distinguished between an earlier *vita* by Odo (the *Vita brevior*) and a later one (the *Vita prolixior*) by another author. I am indebted to Mathew Kuefler, who is completing a study of Gerald's cult, for sharing his unpublished essay on the 'Dating and Authorship of the *Vitae* of Saint Gerald of Aurillac' with me and helping me see this material in a new light. The *Vita prolixior*, which (following most previous scholars) I have focused on here, has recently been re-edited by Anne-Marie Bultot-Verleysen (who attributes the work to Odo) as *Vita sancti Geraldi Auriliacensis*, Subsidia hagiographica 89 (Brussels, 2009). For an older translation of this second Life (again, attributed to Odo), see Sitwell, *St. Odo of Cluny*. My reading of the uses of war in the *Vita prolixior* is indebted to two articles in particular: Rosenwein, 'St. Odo's St Martin'; and Stuart Airlie, 'The Anxiety of Sanctity: St. Gerald of Aurillac and His Maker,' *Journal of Ecclesiastical History* 43 (1992), 372–95 (esp. 384–7).

entered a monastery, he was, in the words of his second *vita*, 'powerful and rich (*potens et dives*) and lived in luxury (*in divitiis*).'[133] True, Carolingian hagiographers had elevated other warriors to the status of saints, but these were men who, like William of Gellone, had ended their days in a monastery, or, like Gangulf of Varenne, could at least be portrayed as martyrs.[134] War is a recurring theme in the Lives (particularly the second Life) of Gerald: it causes Christians to shed one another's blood and oppress the poor, and promotes the sin of pride (whereas *patientia*, endurance, breeds humility); but war is also potentially an instrument for restoring order and protecting the innocent, provided warriors fight defensively rather than for vengeance or gain. To demonstrate this point, his eleventh-century biographer famously described how Gerald contrived to avoid the sinfulness of bloodshed while upholding his obligation to defend the poor against less conscientious *potentes*:

> Sometimes, when the unavoidable necessity of fighting lay on him, he commanded his men in imperious tones, to fight with the backs of their swords and with their spears reversed. This would have been ridiculous to the enemy if Gerald, strengthened by divine power, had not been invincible. And it would have seemed useless to his own men, if they had not learnt by experience that Gerald ... was always invincible. When, therefore, they saw that he triumphed by a new kind of fighting (*novus praeliandi genus*) mingled with piety, they changed their scorn to admiration, and sure of victory they readily fulfilled his commands.[135]

Georges Duby has seen Gerald's cult as part of a Cluniac campaign to 'monasticize' the laity,[136] and indeed his biographers praised Gerald for renouncing the very pollutants – sex, money, and armed violence – which were believed to compromise the purity of those living under monastic vows. While Gerald may have been an unusually monkish layman, however, his hagiographers' purpose

---

[133] *Vita sancti Geraldi Auriliacensis*, Preface to Book 1, ed. Bultot-Verleysen, 131. On widespread skepticism about Gerald's sanctity, see the preface to the *vita* more generally (*ibid.*, 130–6), and for commentary, Airlie, 'Anxiety of Sanctity.'

[134] On William, see Ardon Smaragdus, *Vita Benedicti Abbatis Anianensis et Indensis auctore Ardone*, c.30, ed. G. Waitz, MGH SS 15/1: 200–20 (at 211–13) (which, unlike the saint's later hagiographical dossier, casts William as a holy Benedictine on the model of Benedict of Aniane); for commentary, Victor Saxer, 'Le culte et la légende hagiographique de Saint Guillaume de Gellone,' in *La chanson de geste et le mythe carolingien: Mélanges Réné Louis*, 2 vols (Saint-Père-sous-Vézelay, 1982), 2: 565–89. On Gangulf (an eighth-century nobleman 'martyred' at the hands of his wife's lover), see *Vita Gangulfi martyris Varennensis*, ed. W. Levinson, MGH SS RerMerov 7: 142–74; for commentary, Airlie, 'Anxiety of Sanctity,' 385.

[135] *Vita sancti Geraldi*, 1.8, ed. Bultot-Verleysen, 144: 'Aliquoties autem cum inevitabilis ei praeliandi necessitas incumberet, suis imperiosa voce praecepit, mucronibus gladiorum retroactis, hastas inantea dirigentes pugnarent. Ridiculum hoc hostibus foret, nisi Geraldus vi divina roboratus, mox eisdem hostibus intolerabilis esset. Quod etiam suis valde videbatur ineptum ni experimento probassent, quod Geraldus ... vincebat invincibilis semper esset. Cum ergo viderent quod novo praeliandi genere mista pietate triumpharet, irrisionem vertebant in admirationem. Etiam victoriae securi, servabant alacres quod jubebat.' Trans. Sitwell, *Odo of Cluny*, 100.

[136] Duby, *Three Orders*, 97–8.

in writing was to encourage more warriors to lead a quasi-monastic life, rather than to inspire monks, for whom Gerald was felt to be an unsuitable model.[137] Was Gerald a *miles Christi*? Though his hagiographers never used this terminology, the longer *vita* does employ language that would have identified Gerald to monastic readers as a spiritual warrior: 'the athlete of the heavenly militia (*athleta coelestis militiae*), long struggling in the arena of this earthly life, fought manfully against the forces of evil.'[138] And the inspiration behind the 'bloodless battle' in Gerald's *vita* seems to have been Sulpicius Severus' *Life* of Martin, who, as suggested above, continued to be greatly admired as a spiritual warrior by later monks.[139] If Gerald was no ordinary nobleman, neither did he fit the mold of the early medieval *miles Christi*. He was, as many scholars have recognized, representative of a new Christian ideal – perhaps not a proto-crusader,[140] but certainly an ancestor of the hybrid spiritual-temporal warriors who emerged in the two centuries after Gerald's death.

It should be noted that, by the time Gerald was celebrated as a saint, the words *miles* and *militia* had acquired meanings they had not possessed in the age of Saint Martin. While we can trace the continuous usage of the phrases *miles Christi* and *militia Christi* in relation to (especially monastic) spiritual warfare from Late Antiquity through the Middle Ages, the use of the terms *miles* and *militia* as descriptors of secular warriors seems to have fallen into abeyance between the end of the Roman Empire and the tenth century, when they began to reappear with great frequency in charters and chronicles. By the turn of the eleventh century, the *miles* had come to refer to a mailed, mounted combatant who fought with sword and lance, usually on behalf of a more powerful warrior (and who was thus quite different from the *milites* of Roman Antiquity) – in other words, a knight.[141] Dominique Barthélemy has emphasized that from the Carolingian period onward the title *miles* (as in '*miles secularis*') was used by clerical and especially monastic writers as a way of articulating the hierarchical relationship between secular and spiritual warriors. In the view of the monastic authors of chronicles and charters, the *militia secularis* and the *militia spiritualis*

---

[137] *Vita sancti Geraldi*, Preface to Book 2, ed. Bultot-Verleysen, 196. The text makes it clear that laymen simply could not be held to the same standards as monks, and that Gerald was a saint *in spite of* being a nobleman: 'Nam laico homini multa licent quae monacho non licent.'

[138] *Vita sancti Geraldi*, 2.1, ed. Bultot-Verleysen, 198: 'Athleta coelestis militiae dudum in palestra mundanae conversationis agonizans, cuneos vitiorum viriliter debellavit.'

[139] Rosenwein, 'St. Odo's St Martin,' 324.

[140] Against reading Gerald as a proto-crusader, see H.E.J. Cowdrey, 'Cluny and the First Crusade,' *Revue Bénédictine* 83 (1975), 285–311 (at 288–9).

[141] For the evolving meaning of *miles* and related terminology, see (for France) Georges Duby, 'Origins of Knighthood,' in his *The Chivalrous Society*, trans. Cynthia Postan (Berkeley, CA, 1977); Jean Flori, *L'essor de la chevalerie: X^e et XIe siècles* (Geneva, 1986), chapter 2; and (for England) Richard Barber, 'When is a Knight Not a Knight?' in *The Ideals and Practice of Medieval Knighthood V: Papers from the Sixth Strawberry Hill Conference*, ed. Stephen Church and Ruth Harvey (Woodbridge, 1995), 1–17.

were indissolubly bound to one another, but there was no doubt that the latter was a higher calling, superior to worldly soldiery in both prestige and power.¹⁴²

We can identify two stages in the emergence of a new, non-clerical *miles Christi* between the late tenth and mid twelfth centuries.¹⁴³ The first of these, spanning c.970–1073, roughly coincides with the renewal of ecclesiastical authority that drew strength from a number of sources, including the convening of local peace councils and the promotion of an increasingly coherent reform agenda. The second, encompassing the period from the papacy of Gregory VII (r.1073–85) to the composition of Bernard of Clairvaux's *De laudae novae militiae* in c.1130, encompasses the investiture crisis, as well as the First Crusade and the foundation of the earliest military orders. The offspring of initiatives by the papacy and local collectives of bishops and abbots, this new model was articulated in chronicles, *vitae*, letters, and sermons composed by clerical writers fluent in the language of spiritual warfare. This was a process by which a new identity was projected onto members of one group (arms-bearers) by another (church leaders), and was thus quite different from the last major transformation of the *miles Christi* ideal, in which early monastic writers had self-consciously appropriated the martial rhetoric of martyrdom to define their calling.

As described in Chapter 2, local ecclesiastical authorities became increasingly concerned from the later tenth century with limiting the violence of lay *potentes* and enlisting the latter group's military might in defense of the Church. One early manifestation of these aims was the Peace movement, an ideological project which 'blurred the distinctions between secular and sacred power.'¹⁴⁴ While the peace councils of the tenth and eleventh centuries did not explicitly develop the idea that laymen could be simultaneously worldly arms-bearers and spiritual warriors, they helped lay the framework for a new model of Christian knighthood which would ultimately adopt this viewpoint. Just as importantly, the promotion of peace sometimes resulted in a blurring of the boundaries between spiritual and temporal warfare, as in the 'peace-war' led by Archbishop Aimon of Bourges against lay peace-breakers in the Berry in the late 1030s.¹⁴⁵

If the Peace movement blurred boundaries between ecclesiastical authority and secular power on the local level, papal reformers sought nothing less than the restructuring of Christian society. Whereas bishops had curbed the violence of *potentes* with peace oaths and threats of excommunication, and monasteries had used the power of saints to fend off predatory warriors, eleventh-century popes emphasized the rich spiritual rewards of warriors who served the Church's

---

¹⁴² Dominique Barthélemy, *The Serf, the Knight, and the Historian*, trans. Graham Robert Edwards (Ithaca, NY, 2009), 143–4, 151–2.
¹⁴³ This is the same period that scholars have traditionally associated with the development of Christian knighthood and chivalrous ideals; for example, see Keen, *Chivalry*, 44–5.
¹⁴⁴ Thomas Head, 'The Development of the Peace of God in Aquitaine (970–1005),' *Speculum* 74 (1999), 656–86 (quoting 686); and for the 970s as a turning point in the relationship between the Church and lay authorities in Aquitaine, *ibid.*, 659–61.
¹⁴⁵ The term 'peace-war' comes from Erdmann, *Origins*, 64. For monastic disapproval of Aimon, whose makeshift 'army' of peasants and clerics won several bloody victories before being defeated by Odo of Déols, see Head, 'Judgment of God.'

interests. The use of papal armies by Leo IX (r.1049–54) against the Normans of Apulia in 1053, and by the rival popes Alexander II and Honorius II during the Cadalan Schism of the early 1060s, raised thorny moral questions about church-sanctioned war, and prompted some churchmen to condemn lay participants as wicked mercenaries.[146] But others maintained that warriors who died while serving in the papal armies were assured a place in heaven. The earliest Life of Leo IX, written by an anonymous Lotharingian monk, reports that Leo's distress after his defeat at Civitate was eased by a vision of his fallen soldiers 'united in heavenly glory with the holy martyrs,' and by the proliferation of miracles at their burial site.[147] The claim that these warriors had achieved not only salvation but veritable sainthood through the bearing of arms would have seemed extraordinary a century earlier, but was soon to become a commonplace of crusading chronicles.[148]

By the accession of Gregory VII in 1073, the groundwork had been laid for a new definition of the *miles Christi* as a layman willing to die in defense of the Church, whose sacrifice made him the heir of the martyrs.[149] In Gregory VII's letters and polemical works by members of his circle the *miles Christi* continued to be identified with clerics, but also with the 'vassals of Saint Peter,' lay arms-bearers who supported the papacy against its enemies both within and outside Christendom.[150] Gregory recognized the existence of two sorts of warfare: the first (which was, regrettably, by far the most common) was fought for worldly advancement and was thus spiritually degrading to practitioners; the second, waged in defense of the church's interests, was a form of *imitatio Christi* that

---

[146] On Leo IX's wars, see Erdmann, *Idea of Crusade*, 123–4; on the Cadalan Schism, see H.E.J. Cowdrey, *Pope Gregory VII, 1073–1085* (Oxford, 1998), 49–54. For a contemporary view of these developments, see Peter Damian, Letters 87–9 and 100, ed. Reindel, *Briefe*, 2: 504–72 and 3: 101–15.

[147] Versions of this story were reported by all of Leo's hagiographers. For the text, begun during Leo's lifetime and completed in the 1060s, see *Vita Leonis Papae* (here attrib. to the archdeacon Wibert), 2.11, in *Pontificum Romanorum Vitae*, ed. J.M. Watterich (Leipzig, 1862), 166; and for translation and commentary, Ian S. Robinson, *The Papal Reform of the Eleventh Century: Lives of Pope Leo IX and Gregory VII* (Manchester, 2004), 17–29 and 181 (text).

[148] For the 'martyrs' of Civitate as precursors of martyred crusaders, see Robinson, *Papal Reform of the Eleventh Century*, 9; Colin Morris, 'Martyrs on the Field of Battle Before and During the First Crusade,' in *Martyrs and Martyrologies*, ed. Diana Wood, Studies in Church History 30 (London, 1993), 93–104.

[149] The emphasis on martyrdom which we find in the writings of eleventh-century reformers as well as chronicles of the First Crusade becomes especially significant when we remember that the martyrs were the original soldiers of Christ, and that the concept of spiritual warfare was introduced into monastic discourse by writers borrowing from the *passiones* of the martyrs.

[150] See Robinson, 'Soldiers of Christ.' It is hardly coincidental that several of the commanders of the First Crusade had fathers who had been, or had been themselves, '*milites Sancti Petri*,' as pointed out by Jonathan Riley-Smith, 'The First Crusade and St. Peter,' in *Outremer: Studies in the History of the Crusading Kingdom of Jerusalem*, ed. B.Z. Kedar, H.E. Mayer, and R.C. Smail (Jerusalem, 1982), 49.

elevated laymen to the status of soldiers of Christ.[151] Rather than supplanting clerical warriors, Gregory's lay *milites Christi* were to join them on the spiritual battlefield. Soon after his accession, Gregory encouraged Bishop William of Pavia and the knight Erlembald, leader of the Pataria of Milan, to 'join manfully in fighting God's warfare (*bellum Dei*)' against the opponents of papal reform.[152] Like Leo IX before him, Gregory also promoted the idea that papal allies killed fighting for the cause of reform were to be regarded as martyrs.[153]

Nor was Gregory's promotion of the 'warfare of Saint Peter' without its clerical detractors. Perhaps the most unsettling aspect of Gregory's new martial theory was its failure to distinguish clearly between spiritual and temporal warfare and their respective practitioners. The pope now wielded *both* the spiritual and the material sword, and threatened his enemies simultaneously with the familiar clerical weapon of anathema and with flesh-and-blood armies.[154] In a new twist, some noblemen who converted to the monastic life during Gregory's reign were not praised for exchanging the evils of the *militia temporalis* for the glorious *militia Christi*, but actually reproached for renouncing the worldly power they could have used in the Church's service.[155] Gregory himself was a former monk whom admirers compared to the humble biblical hero (and model spiritual warrior) David, and yet he saw no contradiction between his dual roles as leader of the *militia spiritualis* and organizer of worldly military expeditions.[156]

In the next century several new groups, including crusaders and members of the military orders, laid claim to the title of soldier of Christ. The undertaking historians have come to call the First Crusade (1096–99) marked a major turning point in the history of the *miles Christi* ideal. In promoting his armed pilgrimage to the East, Pope Urban II (r.1088–99) clearly distinguished between

---

[151] Cowdrey, 'Gregory VII and the Bearing of Arms,' in *Montjoie: Studies in Crusade History in Honor of Hans Eberhard Mayer*, ed. Benjamin Z. Kedar, Jonathan Riley-Smith and Rudolf Hiestand (Aldershot, 1997), 33; also see idem, *Gregory VII*, 650–8.

[152] Gregory VII, *Registrum*, 1.28, ed. Caspar, 1: 45–6. Cited by Cowdrey, 'Bearing of Arms,' 31.

[153] Robinson, *Papal Reform of the Eleventh Century*, 51; H.E.J. Cowdrey, 'Martyrdom and the First Crusade,' in *Crusade and Settlement*, ed. Peter Edbury (Cardiff, 1985), 46–56 (at 48).

[154] Robinson ('Soldiers of Christ,' 179) notes that Gregory's military terminology is extremely ambiguous, so much so that it is sometimes difficult to tell if he is referring to spiritual or temporal warfare (or both). But Cowdrey cautions (*Gregory VII*, 564) that this ambiguity may reflect that of the words *militia* and *militare*, and that 'Gregory's use of this group of words calls for care in not exaggerating the degree to which he used them of armed warfare in a temporal sense; other forms of service, both temporal and spiritual, might be intended.'

[155] See, for example, Gregory's 1078 letter to Hugh of Cluny in which he scolded the abbot for encouraging the conversion of Duke Hugh I of Burgundy, whom the pope felt was sorely needed in the world. For the text, see Gregory VII, *Registrum*, 6.17, ed. Caspar, 423–4; and for commentary, see Bouchard, 'Noble Piety and Reformed Monasticism.'

[156] On Gregory's monastic background, see Cowdrey, *Gregory VII*, 28–9. None of the campaigns he planned (and proposed to lead himself) – most notoriously a 'proto-crusade' to the East – came to fruition. On this last expedition, see H.E.J. Cowdrey, 'The Gregorian Papacy, Byzantium, and the First Crusade,' in *Byzantium and the West, c.850–1200*, ed. J. Howard-Johnston (Amsterdam, 1988), 145–69.

participation in this new military venture and spiritual warfare, and in so doing defined the two activities as the rightful prerogatives of different groups.[157] He wrote to the monks of Vallombrosa that the expedition to the Holy Land should be composed of knights, 'since they might be able to restrain the savagery of the Muslims by their arms and restore the Christians to their former freedom: we do not want those who have abandoned the world and who have vowed themselves to spiritual warfare either to bear arms or to go on this journey; we go so far as to forbid them to do so.'[158] Nevertheless, many who heard the pope's call did not accept the neat division he proposed: as shown in the previous chapter, significant numbers of monks joined the expedition to the Levant, and many would-be crusaders hesitated over the choice between joining the pope's army and entering a monastery. Most significantly, both crusaders and monastic chroniclers seem to have understood the undertaking to entail a combination of temporal *and* spiritual warfare.

If the surviving accounts of Urban's call to arms at the Council of Clermont have been studied from almost every imaginable angle,[159] they have yet to be situated in the history of spiritual warfare. In contextualizing Clermont in this way I am not so much trying to recover the pope's true motivations or his actual language – though as a former monk he would have been quite familiar with the monastic concept of the *militia Christi* and its literary pedigree – as to reconstruct the interpretive processes by which clerical observers tried to make sense of the armed pilgrimage Urban preached in 1095. While our five contemporary or near-contemporary sources for the pope's speech are marked by significant differences in emphasis, three of them affirm that Urban used the rhetoric of spiritual warfare to promote the expedition.[160] Each of these authors was either a monk, like the abbot Guibert of Nogent, or had been trained in a monastic milieu, as were the abbot-turned bishop Baldric of Dol and the chaplain Fulcher

---

[157] As a former Cluniac monk from a knightly family, Urban was well-equipped to assess the relationship between *milites saeculares* and *milites spirituales*.

[158] Quoted in Riley-Smith, *Idea of Crusading*, 26; and Purkis, *Crusading Spirituality*, 12. Urban even threatened disobedient monks with 'the sword of apostolic excommunication.' The Latin text is ed. by W. Wiederhold, 'Papsturkunden in Florenz,' *Nachrichten von der Gesellschaft der Wissenschaften zu Göttingen, Phil.-hist. Klasse* (1901), 313–14 (no. 6).

[159] These studies give some sense of the range of modern interpretations of Urban's motives and message: Augustus C. Krey, 'Urban's Crusade: Success or Failure?' *American Historical Review* 53 (1948), 235–50; H.E.J. Cowdrey, 'Pope Urban's Preaching of the First Crusade,' *History* 55 (1970), 177–88; and Marcus Bull, 'The Pilgrimage Origins of the First Crusade,' *History Today* 47 (1997), 10–15.

[160] The exceptions are the anonymous *Gesta Francorum*, the only near-contemporary source possibly composed by a layman, who would have presumably been less familiar with the concept of the *militia Christi*, and the *Historia Hierosolymitana* of Robert of Reims. For the authorship of the *Gesta*, see Kenneth Baxter Wolf, 'Crusade and Narrative: Bohemond and the *Gesta Francorum*,' *Journal of Medieval History* 17 (1991), 207–16; and for a recent reappraisal, Jay Rubenstein, 'What is the *Gesta Francorum*, and Who was Peter Tudebode?' *Revue Mabillon* 16 (2005), 179–204.

of Chartres.¹⁶¹ Further, Guibert and Baldric employed tropes from monastic exegesis and hagiography to reinforce the identification of the crusaders with *milites Christi*.

First, the chroniclers identified the crusaders with the Hebrew patriarchs, who were widely regarded as both pre-Christian spiritual warriors and monastic exemplars. According to Guibert, Urban II encouraged his audience to emulate the bravery and piety of the Maccabees, while in Baldric's version the pope likened the proposed expedition to the Israelites' campaign against the Jebusites.¹⁶² Baldric's depiction of crusaders 'struggling for Jerusalem in an invincible Christian battle line (*acies invictissima*),' under the generalship of Christ brings to mind imagery from the Benedictine *Rule* as well as martial rhetoric found in contemporary monastic letters and hagiography.¹⁶³ There is even an allusion in Baldric's *Historia* that indicates he may have understood the act of taking the cross as akin to monastic conversion. Baldric wrote that Urban offered the assembled warriors two options: they could 'either lay down the sword-belt of earthly knighthood (*cingulum militiae*), or boldly go forth as knights of Christ (*milites Christi*), and make haste to defend the eastern Church.'¹⁶⁴ One is reminded of monastic profession rites that featured the warrior's renunciation of the *cingulum militiae* and the symbolic assumption of the spiritual double-belt of the monk; and indeed, according to Baldric, the choice Urban offered his listeners was that between becoming a monk and joining the crusade.¹⁶⁵ In contrasting the wickedness (*malitia*) of warfare between Christians with the spiritual benefits to be gained by fighting infidels as a member of the holy army,¹⁶⁶ monastic accounts

---

[161] Guibert served as abbot of Nogent-sous-Coucy from 1104 until his death in 1125, and composed his *Gesta Dei per Francos* in c.1108 (though he continued to revise it over the next few years). Baldric of Dol was abbot of Bourgeuil from 1079 until his ascension to the see of Dol in 1107, and wrote his *Historia Hierosolimitana* in c.1108–10. Fulcher of Chartres was educated and likely trained as a priest in the cloister school at Chartres, and accompanied the First Crusade as chaplain to Baldwin of Boulogne. His *Historia Hierosolymitana* dates to c.1100–06.

[162] Guibert of Nogent, *Gesta Dei per Francos*, 2.4, ed. R.B.C. Huygens, CCCM 127A (Turnhout, 2002), 112–13; Baldric of Dol, *Historia Hierosolimitana*, 1.4, RHC Occ. 4: 15. And see Fulcher of Chartres' Prologue for another comparison of the crusaders to the Maccabees; *Historia Hierosolymitana*, Prol. 3, ed. H. Hagenmeyer (Heidelberg, 1913), 116–17. (Baldric's analogy may be suggested by the statement in Josh. 15:63 that the Jebusites could not be driven out of Jerusalem.)

[163] Baldric of Dol, *Historia Hierosolimitana*, 1.4, RHC Occ. 4: 15: 'et sub Jesu Christo, duce nostro, acies Christiana, acies invictissima, melius quam ipsi veteres Jacobitae, pro vestro Jerusalem decertetis ....'

[164] Baldric of Dol, *Historia Hierosolimitana*, 1.4, RHC Occ. 4: 14: 'aut istiusmodi militiae cingulum quantocius deponite, aut Christi milites audaciter procedite, et ad defendendam Orientalem Ecclesiam velocius concurrite.'

[165] For another explicit comparison of the spiritual benefits of crusading and monastic profession, see Guibert of Nogent, *Gesta Dei per Francos*, 1.1, ed. Huygens, 87.

[166] Baldric of Dol, *Historia Hierosolimitana*, 1.4, RHC Occ. 4: 14: 'Non est haec militia Christ, quae discerpit ovile Redemptoris. Sancta Ecclesia ad suorum opitulationem sibi reservavit militiam, sed vos eam male depravatis in malitiam.' Cf. Fulcher of Chartres, *Historia Hierosolimitana*, 1.3.7, ed. Hagenmeyer, 136.

of Clermont acknowledged the existence of a new form of spiritual combat, one carved out within the space that had traditionally separated the monastery from the world and monastic soldiers of Christ from lay warriors.

The equation of the *miles Christi* with the crusader persists in clerical narratives of the expedition to Jerusalem, which, unsurprisingly, often employed scriptural language or metaphors to describe the events of 1096–99. The Christian army's exploits were likened to those of the ancient Israelites, especially the Maccabees, though it was generally agreed that the crusaders far surpassed their predecessors in their courage and enjoyment of divine favor.[167] In characteristic exegetical fashion, monastic chroniclers pronounced the bloody conquest of Jerusalem in the summer of 1099 to be a fulfillment of biblical prophecies.[168] They also used the theme of martyrdom to link the crusaders to the martyrs of the early Church who were the first *milites Christi*.[169] Describing how a bold *miles* named Fulcher won glory on the walls of Antioch, the monk Robert of Reims employed Pauline athletic–military language of the sort common in the martyrs' *passiones* and monastic hagiography: 'I will go up the ladder first in the name of Jesus Christ,' Fulcher declared, 'ready to brave whatever God may please to send me, whether martyrdom or the prize of victory (*victoriae bravium*).'[170] Roman soldier-saints were claimed to have lent their patronage to the expedition, appearing in blinding celestial garb to help rout the Turks.[171] According to the cleric Raymond of Aguilers, Saint George appeared to a priest to identify

---

[167] Raymond of Aguilers, *Historia Francorum qui ceperunt Iherusalem*, c.6, RHC Occ. 3: 245; Fulcher of Chartres, *Historia*, 2.54.5, ed. Hagenmeyer, 589; Guibert of Nogent, *Gesta Dei per Francos*, 2.4, 6.8, ed. Huygens, 112–13, 240; Gilo of Paris, *Historia Vie Hierosolimitane*, ed. and trans. Grocock and Siberry, 160–1. The theme of the Maccabees in crusading chronicles and sermons is discussed in Jonathan Philips, *The Second Crusade: Extending the Frontiers of Christendom* (New Haven, CT, 2007), 56.

[168] Sylvia Schein, *Gateway to the Heavenly City: Crusader Jerusalem and the Catholic West (1099–1187)* (Burlington, VT, 2005), 24. For example, see the German Benedictine abbot Ekkehard of Aura's *Hierosolymita*, c.20, RHC Occ. 5: 11–40 (at 26). Guibert's *Gesta Dei* is particularly interesting in this regard; for example, in book 7.21 (ed. Huygens, 302) he describes the sack of the city as a fulfillment of Zech. 12:2–3 (which predicts that Jerusalem will be besieged, 'rent and torn,' and 'all the kingdoms of the earth gathered together against her.') Jay Rubenstein has shown that Guibert's *Gesta Dei* is fundamentally exegetical in its approach to the crusade; see *Guibert of Nogent: Portrait of a Medieval Mind* (London, 2003), 98–101.

[169] Morris, 'Martyrs on the Field of Battle'; Cowdrey, 'Martyrdom and the First Crusade'; Riley-Smith, *Idea of Crusading*, 114–19; and idem, 'Death on the First Crusade,' in *The End of Strife*, ed. D.M. Loades (Edinburgh, 1984), 14–31.

[170] Robert of Reims, *Historia Iherosolimitana*, 5.12, RHC Occ. 3: 799–800: 'Ego in nomine Jesu Christi primus ascendam ad quodcumque me Deus vocaverit suscipiendum, sive ad martyrium, seu ad obtinendum victoriae bravium.' Trans. Carol Sweetenham, *Robert the Monk's History of the First Crusade (Historia Iherosolimitana)*, Crusade Texts in Translation 11 (Aldershot, 2006), 145. Cf. Raymond of Aguilers, *Historia Francorum*, c.16, RHC Occ. 3: 276; Ekkehard of Aura, *Hierosolymita*, c.35, RHC Occ. 5: 39.

[171] Riley-Smith, *Idea of Crusading*, 105; Bachrach, *Religion and the Conduct of War*, 125–8; and James B. MacGregor, 'Negotiating Knightly Piety: The Cult of the Warrior-Saints in the West, ca.1070–ca.1200,' *Church History* 73 (2004), 317–45 (esp. 324–38).

himself as the expedition's 'standard-bearer (*vexillifer*).'[172] Theodore, Maurice, and Demetrius, all Late Antique military martyrs like George, were said to have been sent from heaven to aid the crusaders at Antioch, a feat Robert of Reims explained as a reprisal of their earthly 'fight' against unbelievers several centuries earlier.[173]

Throughout the chronicles, the crusaders are referred to as *milites Christi* and *athletae Christi*, terms traditionally used for monks, and are credited with possessing the very qualities – humility, righteousness, and even chastity – from which the latter drew their spiritual authority.[174] That such terminology is most often found in descriptions of the Christian army's battles with the Turks is not surprising; earlier instances in which arms-bearers were described as soldiers of Christ usually involved wars against non-Christian invaders. The Poitevin priest Peter Tudebode regularly portrayed the crusaders as soldiers of Christ in their confrontations with the Turkish enemy (and even with Byzantine troops under the walls of Constantinople).[175] For Raymond of Aguilers, the crusaders most truly embodied the ideals of the *militia Christi* when they remained focused on the goal of reaching Jerusalem in the midst of defeat, famine, and faltering leadership.[176] Clerical chroniclers also endowed their subjects with spiritual arms and armor. For Peter Tudebode, the crusaders were 'knights of the true God, protected on all sides by the sign of the cross.'[177] Gilo of Paris, a cleric who joined the Cluniacs in the early twelfth century, wrote that the crusaders had no fear of the Turks because they were 'protected by the arms of faith (*arma fidei*).'[178]

This new model of the arms-bearer as *miles Christi* seems at first glance to be a radical departure from the monastic tradition we have traced, insofar as the monk's warfare was internalized and invisible, while the crusader fought real, flesh-and-blood opponents. But I would argue that the relationship between the two models should not be construed in neatly oppositional terms. First, it is anachronistic to discount the monk's struggles as not 'real'; as we shall see in the next chapter, spiritual warfare informed nearly every aspect of monastic identity and helped constitute the reality of the monastic experience. Second, the crusader's battles were understood as outward manifestations of his own inner

---

[172] Raymond of Aguilers, *Historia Francorum*, c.18, RHC Occ. 3: 290.
[173] Robert of Reims, *Historia*, 5.8, RHC Occ. 3: 796–7; trans. Sweetenham, 141–2. Most of the chroniclers replace Maurice with Mercurius; for a summary of the various sources, see MacGregor, 'Negotiating Knightly Piety,' 324–31.
[174] On the use of *miles Christi* and related terminology in the chronicles, and for additional examples not considered here, see Riley-Smith, *Idea of Crusading*, 118–19; Richter, 'Militia Dei,' 117ff.; and D.H. Green, *Crusading Epic*, 318, 325, 387. For the crusaders' 'monastic' virtues, see Purkis, *Crusading Spirituality*, 20–2.
[175] Peter Tudebode, *Historia de Hierosolymitano itinere*, c.1.1.6, 2.2.3, 2.3.2, 2.5.4, 5.14.1, RHC Occ. 3: 15, 19, 25, 36, and 103.
[176] Raymond of Aguilers, *Historia Francorum*, c.15 and 20, RHC Occ. 3: 276, 295. These descriptions pertain to crusaders' actions at, respectively, the sieges of Arqah and Jerusalem.
[177] Peter Tudebode, *Historia de Hierosolymitano itinere*, c.5, PL 155: 763–821 (at col. 784): 'Milites igitur veri Dei undique signo crucis protecti....'
[178] Gilo of Paris, *Historia Vie Hierosolimitane*, ed. Grocock and Siberry, 82.

fight against evil, not unlike the 'conquests of the self' so frequently described in contemporary monastic hagiography. Further, like countless generations of ascetics, the crusaders were said to have fought side-by-side with Christ, trusting in divine aid rather than relying solely on their own strength. As the Norman commander Bohemond reminded his knights in Guibert of Nogent's *Gesta Dei per Francos*,

> Thus far you have fought for the faith against the infidel, and have emerged triumphant from every danger. Having already felt the abundant evidence of Christ's strength should give you pleasure, and should convince you beyond all doubt that in the most severe battles it is not you, but Christ, who has fought.[179]

Apart from its reference to the 'infidel,' this speech could have been lifted from a letter, sermon, commentary, or *vita* written by any number of Guibert's monastic contemporaries.

The foundation of the first military orders, especially the Order of the Temple in c.1120, reflected the willingness of some contemporaries to attempt a synthesis of temporal and spiritual warfare, knightly and monastic life, within a single ideal.[180] If the crusaders' warfare had been implicitly double, that of the Templars was explicitly so. Moreover, while the first crusaders had been linked to the *miles Christi* ideal primarily through their perceived imitation of the warriors of the Hebrew Bible and the martyrs, the Templar's identity as a soldier of Christ stemmed from what seemed to some contemporaries an unnatural dual status as monastic spiritual warrior and knightly vassal of the Church. It is undeniable that the Templars' foundation created anxiety among some contemporary monastic leaders,[181] and it was partly in an effort to assuage such misgivings that Bernard of Clairvaux composed his treatise *De laude novae militiae* in around 1130.[182]

---

[179] Guibert of Nogent, *Gesta Dei per Francos*, 4.13, ed. Huygens, 185–6: 'Fidei hactenus contra perfidiam bella gessistis et inter omnia discrimina felices exitus habuistis. Delectare vos profecto iam debuit Christi fortitudinis sepissime evidens experimentum, presertim cum certo certius noveritis, in illis quae potissimum urgebant preliis non vos pugnasse, sed Christi.' Trans. Levine, 82–3.

[180] While the Hospitallers pre-dated the Templars, unlike the latter group their charitable function was never overshadowed by their involvement in military matters. The foundation of the Templars is described in detail by Malcolm Barber, *The New Knighthood: A History of the Order of the Temple* (Cambridge, 1994), chapter 1.

[181] For ambivalence about the Templars, see Barber, *New Knighthood*, 41–4; Helen Nicholson, *Templars, Hospitallers and Teutonic Knights: Images of the Military Orders, 1128–1291* (Leicester, 1993), 35–41; and Giles Constable, *Crusaders and Crusading in the Twelfth Century* (Burlington, VT, 2008), 80.

[182] For the Latin text, see '*Liber ad Milites Templi: de laude novae militiae*,' in SBO 3: 212–39. All quotes are from the translation by M. Conrad Greenia (with minor modifications), *In Praise of the New Knighthood*, CF 19B (Kalamazoo, MI, 2000). There is a huge literature on the *De laude novae militiae*. See Barber, *New Knighthood*, chapter 2; Flori, *L'essor de la chevalerie*, 209–14; Newman, *Boundaries of Charity*, 184f.; M.L. Bulst-Thiele, 'The Influence of St. Bernard of Clairvaux on the Formation of the Knights Templar,' in *The Second Crusade and the Cistercians*, ed. Gervers, 57–65; P. Cousin, 'Les débuts de l'Ordre

Bernard began by insisting on the novelty of the Templars, calling them 'a new knighthood and one unknown in ages past,' and explaining that this novelty derived from the 'twofold combat' to which they devoted themselves.[183] He went on to employ what Constance Brittain Bouchard has characterized as a 'rhetoric of opposition' to situate the Knights of the Temple in relation to ordinary (i.e., evil) lay warriors and good Christians (i.e., monks), and explain how they could combine the normal functions of each group, fighting and praying.[184] The Templar fought the earthly enemies of the Church, but also contended 'against spiritual hosts of evil in the heavens'; he wore the two swords of the Gospel (Luke 22:38); and was protected by two hauberks (*loricae*), one forged of faith and the other of steel.[185] Like earlier crusaders, Bernard's 'new knight' was a *miles Christi*, an *athleta* in the tradition of the martyrs, and the heir to the 'true Israelites,' particularly the Maccabees.[186] But in the end Bernard intended the Templar 'as an exemplar, or at least an embarrassment, for those of our knights who are apparently fighting not for God, but for the devil,' and certainly not as a model for monks.[187] And if the Templar combined in a single individual the best attributes of the monk and the knight, there is little doubt as to which Bernard would have considered the better part of his *novus miles*. Bernard never wavered in his conviction that the monastic life was the surest path to salvation, and even in the *De laude* he reaffirmed the monastic prerogative to 'wage war (*bellum indicere*) with spiritual strength against vices and demons.'[188]

Bernard's monastic contemporaries shared his fascination with the double nature of the Templars' warfare, as well as his uncertainty as to whether they were to be considered monks, knights, or both.[189] Writing to Everard of Barres,

---

des Templiers et saint Bernard,' in *Mélanges Saint Bernard* (Dijon, 1953), 41–52; and E. Delaruelle, 'L'Idée de croisade chez saint Bernard,' *ibid.*, 53–67.

[183] *De laude novae militiae*, c.1, SBO 3: 214: 'Novum, inquam, militiae genus, et saeculis inexpertum, qua gemino pariter conflictu atque infatigabiliter decertatur, tum adversus carnem et sanguinem, tum contra spiritualia nequitiae in caelestibus.' Trans. Greenia, *New Knighthood*, 33.

[184] Bouchard, *'Every Valley Shall Be Exalted'*, 83–7.

[185] *De laude*, c.1, SBO 3: 214: 'Ceterum cum uterque homo suo quisque gladio potenter accingitur ... quis hoc non aestimet omni admiratione dignissimum, quod adeo liquet esse insolitum? Impavidus profecto miles, et omni ex parte securus, qui ut corpus ferri, sic animum fidei lorica induitur. Utrisque nimirum munitus armis, nec daemonem timet, nec hominem.' Trans. Greenia, *New Knighthood*, 33–4.

[186] *De laude*, c.1, 7, 8, SBO 3: 214–215, 219, 221; trans. Greenia, *New Knighthood*, 34, 45, 47.

[187] *De laude*, c.7, SBO 3: 219: 'Sed iam imitationem seu confusionem nostrorum militum, non plane Deo, sed diabolo militantium ....' Trans. Greenia, *New Knighthood*, 45.

[188] *De laude*, c.1, SBO 3: 214: 'Sed et quando animi virtute vitiis sive daemoniis bellum indicitur, ne hoc quidem mirabile, etsi laudabile dixerim, cum plenus monachis cernatur mundus.' Trans. Greenia, *New Knighthood*, 33. Particularly useful here are the comments by Flori (*L'essor de la chevalerie*, 209–10) and Newman (*Boundaries of Charity*, 86). It is also worth noting that Bernard insisted that the Cistercians refuse admittance to former Templars, although other religious orders apparently accepted them.

[189] See *De laude*, 4.8, SBO 3: 221; trans. Greenia, *New Knighthood*, 48. For this debate in medieval texts and modern scholarship, see Constable, 'Place of the Crusader.' For a spirited defense of the Templars status as dual spiritual–temporal warriors by one Hugh

then Master of the Temple, the abbot of Cluny Peter the Venerable stressed that it was their 'double conflict (*duplex conflictus*)' which made Everard and his fellows 'monks in virtues and knights in deeds.'[190] In a letter he intended as a sermon to the Templars, Guigo, prior of La Grande Chartreuse (d.1137), exhorted their co-founder Hugh de Payns that spiritual combat was the best possible form of training for physical battle against the infidels. While Guigo acknowledged that 'We have no idea how to encourage you, dear friend, in physical battles and combats,' he informed Hugh that 'we desire at least to advise you on spiritual battles, in which we engage on a daily basis.'[191] Refusing to cede a jot of spiritual authority to these new *milites Christi*, Guigo went on to offer Hugh and his comrades a sort of beginner's manual, in which he outlined the basics of how to fight against the vices and overcome the flesh, and provided relevant Scriptural passages, complete with very straightforward glosses.[192] The lessons and tone are reminiscent of contemporary letters written by older, experienced monks to novices or new converts, which is what Hugh and his fellows – their prowess in worldly battle notwithstanding – must have seemed like to a renowned ascetic like Guigo.

Looked at within the long history of monastic writing on spiritual warfare, the ideological underpinnings of the crusade and the military orders seem startlingly familiar; from this perspective, the most radical aspect of the new holy war was its displacement of the traditional heroes of the spiritual battlefield in favor of those who had formerly stood on the sidelines. Jonathan Riley-Smith has hypothesized that the First Crusade would have seemed to contemporaries like 'a military monastery on the move,' and that crusading rhetoric served to 'monasticize' arms-bearers.[193] The extent to which the crusading movement and the foundation of the military orders blurred the boundaries between the secular and the monastic becomes apparent when we focus our attention on the role of the *miles Christi* ideal in crusading chronicles and related writings by monastic authors. These works helped ensure that in the twelfth century the definition of the *miles Christi* became inextricably bound up with the ideology of crusading in the minds of both clerics and arms-bearers.

Peccator (possibly an early member of the Order), see 'Un document sur les débuts des Templiers,' ed. Jean Leclerq, in *Revue de l'histoire ecclésiastique* 52 (1957), 81–91 (text at 86–9).

[190] Peter the Venerable, Letter 172, in *Letters*, ed. Constable, 1: 407–9 (quoting 408): 'Estis monachi virtutibus, milites actibus, illud spiritualiter implendo, istud corporaliter exercendo.' On this text, written c.1150, see Constable, 'Place of the Crusader,' 397; Purkis, *Crusading Spirituality*, 102.

[191] Guigo of La Grande Chartreuse, Letter 2.2, in *Lettres des premiers Chartreux*, ed. and trans. by 'a Carthusian,' 2 vols, SC 88, 274 (Paris, 1962–80), 1: 154–61 (at 154): 'Ad corporea quidem bella pugnasque visibiles dilectionem vestram exhortari nequaquam novimus: ad spiritualia vero in quibus et quotidie versamur, etsi excitare idonei non sumus, admonere saltem desideramus.' For commentary, see Barber, *New Knighthood*, 149–50.

[192] Guigo of La Grande Chartreuse, Letter 2.3–6, in *Lettres des premiers chartreux*, 1: 154–60.

[193] Riley-Smith, *Idea of Crusading*, 2; also see Constable, 'Place of the Crusader,' 380–4; and Brundage, 'Crusades, Clerics, and Violence.'

In the process of defining a divinely sanctioned role for Christian *bellatores* as protectors of the weak and defenders of Christendom's boundaries, churchmen had seriously undermined their own longstanding monopoly on spiritual warfare. But not all monks were willing to concede the spiritual battlefield without a fight. As noted in the previous chapter, many contemporary monastic writers emphasized the superiority of life in the monastery to participation in the crusade, and others openly doubted whether taking the cross had any spiritual value at all. The lack of crusading fervor shown by Anselm of Canterbury (d.1109), for instance, has often been noted.[194] Would-be crusaders who applied to Anselm for advice were told to shelve their plans and instead convert to the monastic life so that they could attain the true heavenly Jerusalem, rather than bloody their hands and imperil their souls by attempting to conquer the earthly one.[195] An anonymous twelfth-century Benedictine echoed these sentiments, using Scriptural examples as well as the *vita* of Saint Martin to argue that the true *miles Christi* fought exclusively in the spiritual sense: 'it is not by fighting for Jerusalem with a sword that one is granted salvation.'[196]

Conclusion

In the early Church the title of *miles Christi* became shorthand for all those qualities most admired in a Christian, as well as a designation for the spiritual elites who 'fought' the devil and his worldly representatives, the pagan authorities, on behalf of the entire community of believers. Through spiritual combats Christians self-consciously lived out the words of Paul and demonstrated their loyalty to the commandments of their faith above worldly obligations. As members of the *militia Christi*, believers were not merely soldiers of Christ but soldiers *like* Christ, who had, in the words of Cyprian, 'walked first in that very warfare, so that what He taught was to be done, He did first,' by triumphing over death and the devil.[197] The first warrior elites to emerge from the ranks of the faithful were the martyrs, whose *passiones* are filled with tales of spiritual struggle. With the triumph of Christianity in the Roman world, the ascetic's body became the new arena for spiritual combat, now fought against temptation rather than gladiators and wild beasts. The mantle of the *miles Christi* was taken up by the early desert ascetics, and passed from them into the monastic traditions of the early medieval West.

The clergy, and especially monastic orders, maintained a near-monopoly on the role of *miles Christi* throughout the early Middle Ages. Spiritual warfare helped shape monastic identity, defining the monk in relation to other members

---

194 James Brundage, 'St. Anselm, Ivo of Chartres, and the Ideology of the First Crusade,' repr. in *The Crusades, Holy War, and Canon Law* (Aldershot, 1991), 175–87.
195 Anselm, Letters 2.19, 2.25, in PL 158: 1167–70, 1175–6.
196 *Liber de poenitentia et tentationibus religiosorum*, c.27–28, PL 213: 894. Cited by Schein, *Gateway to the Heavenly Jerusalem*, 135.
197 Cyprian, Letter 58.2, in *Letters 1–81*, trans. Donna, 165.

of Christian society (who were, spiritually speaking, non-combatants) and delineating the boundaries between the monastery and the world. But in the eleventh century the traditional model of the *miles Christi* as a monastic warrior of the spirit gave way to a new ideal of the pious layman who fought physically against the Church's enemies, and spiritually against the forces of unbelief. At once temporal and spiritual warriors, crusaders and members of the military orders colonized the middle ground between the *bellatores* and the *oratores*, an intermediate space that was no longer supposed to exist in the neatly ordered society envisioned by ecclesiastical reformers. But while reformers had succeeded in closing some gaps between the orders, new hybrid groups soon sprang up in the grey areas which reform inadvertently created. Casting lay crusaders and Templars as *milites Christi* enabled clerical apologists to identify these new defenders of the Church with what was to them a hallowed form of *imitatio Christi* and simultaneously distance them from the *malitia* of ordinary worldly warfare. If one result of the new knighthood and the crusading movement was a 'monasticization' of lay warriors, another was an unprecedented irruption of non-monastic competitors onto the spiritual battlefield.

In the midst of these shifts, however, monastic writers did not relinquish their claim to be the true *milites Christi*; as we shall see in the next chapter, they clung more tenaciously than ever to this martial rhetoric, developing increasingly elaborate military metaphors to describe their vocation and function within Christendom. Designated as men of peace, monks evinced a strong interest in evolving conceptions of holy war. In the wake of the First Crusade monastic chroniclers theorized new forms of double warfare and debated larger questions the successful expedition to Jerusalem had raised about the relationship between physical and spiritual combat. But monastic engagement with contemporary warfare was not merely theoretical. In their conviction that studying secular warfare and its living practitioners could lead to a better understanding of the *militia Christi*'s obligations, these chroniclers of the crusade (all of whom wrote in Latin for clerical audiences) were following a centuries-old precept articulated by Cassian and other patristic authors. And, as shown in Chapter 2, opportunities for first-hand observation of warriors, including former crusaders, abounded in monasteries during this period, when adult conversion to the religious life was becoming the norm. But the conclusion monastic writers arrived at (and expressed in their letters to crusaders and members of the military orders) reaffirmed their privileged position at the head of the army of Christ. However meritorious the double warfare of crusaders and members of the military orders – as compared with the traditional wicked warfare of knights – it was nonetheless inferior to the bloodless, purely spiritual combat which could be fought only in the hermitage or cloister.

4

Martial Imagery in Monastic Texts

Even as the clerical creation of a new model of Christian knighthood threatened the long-held monastic monopoly on spiritual warfare, monks clung tenaciously to their identification with the true *milites Christi* and continued to present their calling as a form of military service superior to any other. 'Do not yearn to be sent forth to the place of battle,' the Cistercian abbot Aelred of Rievaulx (d.1166) told his monks, 'for *this* is the place of battle.'[1] A survey of sermons, letters, and works of hagiography by monastic authors of the eleventh and twelfth centuries turns up this sort of martial rhetoric at seemingly every turn; indeed, one can hardly find an author who never used military language in reference to the religious life, and it is not unusual to encounter allegories involving monk-soldiers, demonic armies, and monastery-citadels under siege which are far more elaborate (and bloody) than anything to be found in patristic or Carolingian texts. Modern scholars have often noted the presence of this material, and a handful of studies have examined the use of military imagery by individual authors or members of particular orders.[2] With the goal of gaining a better understanding of how martial rhetoric both reflected and shaped monastic identities in the Central Middle Ages, this chapter casts a wider net across orders and genres, seeking to identify rhetorical patterns and to connect these, in turn, to specific contemporary practices and concerns. What might at first glance seem to be nothing more than a collection of tropes reveals itself, upon closer examination, as a distinctly monastic language of warfare with its own conventions and specialized vocabulary. While this language drew upon earlier traditions of martial rhetoric traced in the previous chapter – reflecting the continued popularity of patristic commentaries and hagiography – it also engaged with present-day realities, those of the cloister as well as the outside world. Monastic

---

[1] Aelred of Rievaulx, Sermon 15, *Sermones*, PL 195: 294: 'Nolite dimittere ad locum pugnae. Hic est locum pugnae.' (Emphasis mine).

[2] Nearly all of these have concerned works produced by twelfth-century Cistercians, especially Bernard of Clairvaux. While the Cistercians were by no means the only group to use elaborate martial analogies, they were prolific, and their works accessible. These factors, along with their close involvement with the knightly class and the crusading movement, have combined to create interest in Cistercian writings on warfare (spiritual and otherwise). See Jean Leclercq, *Monks and Love in Twelfth-Century France* (Oxford, 1979), chapter 5; Martha G. Newman, *Boundaries of Charity*, chapter 1; and Rudolph, *Violence and Daily Life*, 42–56.

writers of the Central Middle Ages applied the language of spiritual warfare to contemporary debates concerning, among other issues, the value of communal life, the training of novices, and the role of the abbot. They also spiced their allegories with military details drawn from the violent world beyond the monastery: vats of boiling oil, feigned retreats by mounted knights, and dank dungeons all feature in sermons monks delivered to their brethren, suggesting that the spiritual warriors of monastic imagination looked and acted a good deal like contemporary lay arms-bearers.

Previous scholarship has viewed the martial imagery in monastic texts through two lenses: psychology and the history of rhetoric. According to the psychological interpretation, the military imagery in sermons, letters, and hagiography provided men who were banned from actual fighting with a much-needed outlet for their aggression.[3] Scholars sensitive to questions of historical gender identity have built on this view, contending that whereas medieval lay elites demonstrated their manliness by (among other things) doing battle with peers, clerical men 'fought' with words to prove their masculine status.[4] While concurring with these historians' insistence that readings of martial rhetoric should take into account changing patterns of monastic recruitment in the eleventh and twelfth centuries, in particular the influx into many houses of adult converts from families of arms-bearers, my reading has also been influenced by a second group of scholars who have privileged the rhetorical functions of symbolic language. This approach seeks to understand how the historical uses of particular metaphors (be they military, domestic, environmental, etc.) might reflect authorial self-perceptions or bolster larger ideological claims.[5] Applied to the material at hand, such an interpretive strategy seeks to discover what martial rhetoric reveals about medieval writers' understanding of how individuals progressed toward the divine, and how various settings (the coenobium or hermitage) and practices (such as prayer, study, ascetic self-denial) aided this progress. Sensitivity to the rhetorical nature of much monastic writing also enables us to appreciate how the *miles Christi* ideal and related allegories served not merely to describe the religious life but to construct particular arguments about the superiority of certain orders, practices, and models of sanctity.

Because an undertaking of this sort is in some sense a history of the monastic imagination, it has the potential to shed light on tensions, anxieties, and desires that are often elusive; for the same reason, it has the potential to meander off

---

[3] Leclercq, *Monks and Love*, chapter 5.
[4] For examples, see Murray, 'Masculinizing Religious Life'; Andrew Taylor, 'A Second Ajax: Peter Abelard and the Violence of Dialectic,' in *The Tongue of the Fathers: Gender and Ideology in Medieval Latin*, ed. David Townsend and Andrew Taylor (Philadelphia, PA, 1998), 14–34.
[5] For examples of this approach, see Newman, *Boundaries of Charity*, 29–37; Caroline Walker Bynum, 'Jesus as Mother and Abbot as Mother,' ch. 4 in her *Jesus as Mother: Studies in the Spirituality of the High Middle Ages* (Berkeley, CA, 1982); eadem, Review of Jean Leclercq, *Monks and Love in Twelfth-Century France*, *Speculum* 55 (1980), 595–7; Mary Carruthers, *The Craft of Thought: Meditation, Rhetoric, and the Making of Images, 400–1200* (New York, 1998).

into the realm of speculation. Aiming to avoid the latter outcome, the following discussions anchor particular rhetorical patterns to specific historical concerns that shaped the monastic experience in the Central Middle Ages: the novitiate, which received unprecedented attention as a distinct stage in this period; the debates over various models of community life that attended the eremitic revival and explosion of new orders; the roles of monastic superiors; and the definition of boundaries between the monastery and the world, and between their respective value systems. Monastic writers addressed each of these subjects using distinct *picturae*, detailed descriptions meant to evoke vivid, memorable images in the mind's eye of readers or listeners. Violent images of duels, battles, and sieges made for particularly effective *picturae* which held the attention and could be stowed away in the memory for future contemplation.[6] Sermons and letters of instruction encouraged monks to imagine themselves fighting in full armor, or even to recreate in their minds scriptural or historical scenes of combat, in effect mapping out a distinctly monastic meditative practice based on the conception of the monk as a spiritual warrior.

Learning to fight

From the moment novices passed through the gates of the monastery, whether they arrived as young children or worldly wise adults, they were exposed to the martial imagery that, their seniors believed, would help them learn to talk, act, and think like monks. The terms commonly used to describe a novice or newly professed monk (*tiro*) and his term of probation and early spiritual development (*tirocinium*) were the same as those used by non-monastic authors for young knights and their activities; the *tiro* was an untested warrior, a young *miles* whose military training was not yet complete, while the term *tirocinium* could refer to knight's service, or even, by the end of our period, a tournament.[7] As *tiro*, the new monk was a raw recruit to the *militia Christi* who, whatever his previous experiences in the world, had to learn the rudiments of spiritual warfare if he hoped to succeed in monastic life. While the conception of the novitiate

---

[6] On monks' use of *picturae* as mnemonic and meditative tools, and the utility of violent imagery, see Carruthers, *Craft of Thought*, Introduction, 101f., 203–5.

[7] Charles Du Cange et al., *Glossarium mediae et infimae Latinitatis*, 2nd ed., 10 vols (Niort, 1883–7; repr. Graz, 1954), 8: 221. Du Cange quotes the eleventh-century grammarian Papias' definition of *tiro*: 'Strong boys are called *tirones* who are destined for military service, and who are considered suitable for it (*Tirones dicuntur fortes pueri, qui ad militiam deliguntur, atque habiles existunt*).' These terms do not appear in the Vulgate, but Cassian spoke in his *Collationes* (1.1, ed. Pichery, 1: 78) of his affection for a certain Germanus, who, he said, 'had been with me from the time when we were recruits (*ab ipso tirocinio*) acquiring the skills needed for spiritual warfare (*rudimentis militiae spiritalis*).' Sometimes *tiro* was contrasted with *miles Christi*, the latter title indicating a status the new recruit had not yet earned, as in the anonymous twelfth-century *vita* of Gaucher, founder of the canons of Aureil; *Vita beati Gaucherii primi pastoris Aurelii*, c.8, ed. Jean Becquet as 'La vie de S. Gaucher, fondateur des chanoines réguliers d'Aureil en Limousin,' *Revue Mabillon* 54 (1964), 25–55 (at 49).

differed from order to order in terms of its length and the emphasis placed on it as a distinct stage,[8] authors from all of the major old and new orders – Benedictines and Cluniacs, regular canons, Cistercians, Carthusians, and others – used martial analogies to describe initial spiritual progression within the monastic life. To some extent, this reflects the common sources of such rhetoric explored in the previous three chapters, namely the Scriptures and liturgy, patristic exegesis and hagiography, but it also points to shared concerns about how the transition from the world to the cloister was to be made. These concerns, especially as reflected in sermons, *vitae*, handbooks for novices, and personal letters of direction, centered on the need to acclimate oneself to chastity, fasting, solitude (especially in semi-eremitic orders), and to learn how to repel the attacks of invisible enemies. While these challenges would have been instantly recognizable to Jerome, Cassian, or Benedict, later medieval authors did not simply echo the good counsel of earlier authorities but offered advice grounded in the specific concerns of their own day.

One learned to fight through study, especially through holy reading and meditation on the foundational texts that presented the religious life as a *militia spiritualis*. In the words of the twelfth-century canon Geoffrey of Breteuil, 'A cloister without a library is like a castle without an arsenal.'[9] The Cluniac abbot Peter of Celle (d.1183) explained that every book the monk read became a shield to fortify his cell and a projectile to hurl at demonic attackers. Most importantly, he wrote, reading 'tells of the clash of virtues and vices,' offering edifying examples of how the saints conquered temptation, which in turn help prepare the monk for his own battles.[10] The study of Scripture introduced novices to a legion of spiritual exemplars, many of whom their teachers identified as *milites Christi* and encouraged them to imitate. Predictably, Paul was often presented as the archetypal *miles Christi* and the ideal instructor, via the Epistles, for warriors-in-training. Writing to his nephew, the young monk Marinus, Peter Damian admonished him to master Paul's precepts thoroughly, because 'the raw recruit (*rudis tiro*) is easily defeated in his first taste of combat in battle, unless he uses

---

[8] Although the *Rule of Benedict* prescribed a year-long novitiate, broken into three stages (RB 58, pp. 266–70), later Benedictines often imposed much shorter probationary periods. This was the case at Cluny through the early eleventh century, though under Saint Hugh greater attention began to be paid to the novitiate; see Isabelle Cochelin, 'Peut-on parler de noviciat à Cluny pour les Xe–XIe siècles?' *Revue Mabillon* n.s. 9 (1998), 17–52. In accordance with their strict interpretation of the Benedictine Rule, the Cistercians reinstated the one-year novitiate; see Joseph L. Lynch, 'The Cistercians and Underage Novices,' *Cîteaux* 24 (1973), 283–97.
[9] Geoffrey of Breteuil, Letter 18, *Epistolae*, PL 205: 845: 'Claustrum sine armario, quasi castrum sine armamentario.'
[10] Peter of Celle, *De afflictione et lectione*, ed. J. Leclercq in *La spiritualité de Pierre de Celle* (Paris, 1946), 231–9 (at 233–4): 'Exarmat enim propugnacula sua mille clypeis pendentibus ex eis (Song of Sol. 4:4) qui non uacat lectionibus diuinis. O quam cito et sine labore capietur ciuitatuta cellae, nisi se defenderit auxilio Dei et scuto diuinae paginae! ... Lectio ista docet quia uirtutum et uitiorum congressum tam continue narrat, ut paene nusquam hic sileat.' Trans. Hugh Feiss as 'On Affliction and Reading,' in *Peter of Celle: Selected Works*, CS 100 (Kalamazoo, MI, 1987), 131–41 (at 134–5).

beforehand the good offices of the drillmaster (*campidoctor*).'[11] The twelfth-century Cistercian abbot Guerric of Igny reminded his monks that they should remember Paul's defeats as well as his victories, lest they forget that no mortal warrior was invincible.[12] Sermons preached on the feast of Saints Peter and Paul might also be occasions for discussions of the theme of spiritual warfare in the Epistles.[13] Next to Scripture, the *Rule of Benedict* was perhaps the most valuable source of instruction on the obligations of the *militia Christi*. If the significance of the martial imagery in the *Rule* was lost on new monks, it would have been made clear to them through conferences with *seniores*, the reading of commentaries on the *Rule* during chapter, and sermons honoring Benedict, which often featured exegesis of his *Rule*.[14] For instance, in a sermon composed for the saint's feast, Odo of Cluny told his monks that it was through Benedict's guidance that they 'were enrolled in the ranks of recruits (*tirocinium*) of the heavenly army,' and that they would gain admittance to the heavenly kingdom only by 'fighting under his leadership': that is, by cultivating obedience to his *Rule*.[15]

Tirones were especially vulnerable to attack, writers of all orders agreed, because they entered the monastery with little or no knowledge of spiritual warfare, and thus could not guard against the various enemies of the cloistered.[16] As suggested by the military imagery that pervades the letters of encouragement written by mature men to their spiritual protégés, teaching them to defend themselves was synonymous with teaching them how to be monks.[17] So consistent is the rhetoric of these letters that they may be considered as a distinct epistolary genre,[18] one reflecting a widespread perception of the monastic life as the

---

[11] Peter Damian, Letter 132, ed. Reindel, *Briefe*, 3: 438–52 (at 439).

[12] Guerric of Igny, Sermon 24.2, in *Sermones*, 2 vols, ed. John Morson and Hilary Costello, SC 166, 202 (Paris, 1970–3), 2: 78; trans. Monks of Mount Saint Bernard Abbey as *Guerric of Igny: Liturgical Sermons* (Spencer, MA, 1970–2), 2: 19.

[13] For example, see Aelred of Rievaulx's Sermon 15, *Sermones*, PL 195: 294–8.

[14] On the reading of commentaries and sermons on the *Rule* in chapter, see Beverly Mayne Kienzle, 'The Twelfth-Century Monastic Sermon,' in *The Sermon*, ed. Kienzle, Typologie des sources du Moyen Âge occidental 81–3 (Turnhout, 2000), 271–323 (at 271 and 278). For monastic preaching on Benedict, see Longère, 'La prédication sur saint Benoît.'

[15] Odo of Cluny, Sermo 3, in *Sermones quinque*, PL 133: 724–5: 'Gaudent, quia per ejus magisterium, ad coelestis militiae tirocinium sunt asciti. Sperant sub ejus ducatu militantes, ad superni regis palatium intromitti.'

[16] One of the few handbooks for novices written before 1200, the Benedictine *De novitiis instruendis*, explicitly warned that the devil loved to assail the novice with the sin of pride, and offered suggestions for safeguarding one's humility against these *bella inimici*; see *De novitiis instruendis: Text und Kontext eines anonymen Traktates vom Ende des 12. Jahrhunderts*, ed. Mirko Breitenstein (Münster, 2004), 113.

[17] While most of these letters contain stylized literary phrasing and could not be considered 'personal' in the modern sense of the word, they undoubtedly shed light on contemporary views of spiritual formation, if not on relationships between individual writers and their addressees. On the differences between medieval and modern approaches to letter-writing, see Giles Constable, *Letters and Letter Collections*, Typologie des sources du Moyen Âge occidental 17 (Turnhout, 1976), 11–16.

[18] These letters are comparable in some ways with letters of vocation written by professed religious to encourage friends or relatives to enter the monastery; see Jean Leclercq,

worthiest kind of military service. Writers often began by hailing the recipient as a fellow soldier, welcoming him into the *militia Christi*. In a typical opening, Anselm of Canterbury addressed a newly arrived monk at Bec as 'his once most longed-for friend, now his dearest fellow-monk and brother and son, Ralph, the new soldier of Christ (*novus miles Christi*).'[19] An explanation of the military nature of the monastic life generally came next. As the bishop Herbert of Losinga (d.1116) wrote to his 'dearest son,' the monk Odo, 'our religious life is a warfare (cf. Job 7:1), and under the gaze of God, with the angels as spectators, we contend in the arena of this world with beasts, who are all the more dangerous because they are invisible.'[20]

Many novices would have entered the monastery as *adolescentes* (in medieval terms, between the mid teens and mid twenties), and older letter-writers recognized that such youths were particularly prone to what John of Fruttuaria's eleventh-century manual for novices called 'the many and harsh wars of the body (*corporis bella*).'[21] Writing to a fellow superior, Peter Damian evoked the trials of young manhood with an immediacy one suspects may have come from personal experience:

> To be sure, every hostile impulse attacks you in a direct assault; upon you all the power of war presses. Hailstorms thick with every kind of dart assail you and, once the iniquitous spirits have been gathered against you, then the most violent storms assail you with the vices of the flesh. Wars rage (*fervent ... bella*), they rage in your bones, and the furnace of your body spews out balls of fire just like restless Vesuvius or smoking Aetna.[22]

Knowing the weakness of their flesh, the devil sought to destroy the resolve of young monks by making them hate their vows of chastity and the harshness of monastic life. 'Often,' Anselm wrote to the Cluniac novice Lanzo, 'when the malicious one cannot openly annihilate Christ's new recruit (*tiro*) by inflicting a wound of ill will, the sly devil tries to destroy him by maliciously offering him a cup of toxic reason to slake his thirst,' thus inspiring him with disgust for the

---

'Lettres de vocation à la vie monastique,' in *Studia Anselmiana* 37, Analecta monastica, 3rd ser., fasc. 27 (1955), 169–97 (and 175 and 180 for examples of martial rhetoric).

[19] Anselm, Letter 10, in *Epistolae*, PL 158: 1159; trans. Walter Fröhlich as Letter 99 in *The Letters of St. Anselm*, 3 vols, CS 96–7, 142 (Kalamazoo, MI, 1990–4), 1: 248–9.

[20] Herbert of Losinga, Letter 13, in *Epistolae Herberti de Losinga, primi episcopi norwicensis*, ed. Robert Anstruther (London, 1846), 23: 'militi est vestrae religionis vita, et praesente Deo, prospectantibus angelis, in circo hujus mundi invisibilibus et ideo crudelioribus bestiis exponimur.' Here the monastic warrior is explicitly presented as the heir of the martyr.

[21] On adolescence as a stage of life in medieval thought, see J.A. Burrow, *The Ages of Man: A Study in Medieval Writing and Thought* (Princeton, 1986). John of Fruttuaria (d.c.1050), *Liber de ordine vitae et morum institutione*, c.4, PL 184: 563; and for commentary, see Caroline Walker Bynum, *Docere verbo et exemplo* (Missoula, MT, 1979), 119.

[22] Peter Damian, Letter 153, ed. Reindel, *Briefe*, 4: 54: 'In vos siquidem recto cursu omnis belli robur incumbit. In vos omnigenum telorum densissimae grandines et constipatis adversum vos iniquis spiritibus cum viciis carnis turbulentissimae vobis ingruunt tempestates. Fervent, fervent in ossibus bella, et tamquam vagus Vesevus vel Ethna vaporati corporis vestri caminus flammarum globos eructat.' Trans. Blum and Resnick, *Letters*, 5: 57–8.

religious life.²³ What the older men wished to convey was that the renunciation of the world, difficult as it may have been for these youths, was not the culmination, but only the beginning, of their spiritual journeys.

God supplied, in Guerric of Igny's words, 'an abundant grant of arms for those who are to fight,'²⁴ and it was urgent that vulnerable recruits master this spiritual arsenal as quickly as possible. There were no better teachers than fellow monks and superiors who had attained the status of battle-hardened veterans. So often did Romuald of Ravenna's disciples entreat him for guidance on spiritual combat that the holy man finally composed a treatise (*libellus*) entitled '*De pugna daemonum*' that they might study in his absence.²⁵ In a letter urging 'a certain Peter' to abandon the schools for the monastic life, Peter the Venerable eloquently expressed the obligation of *seniores* to tutor new monks in the art of war:

> I will arm you with heavenly arms (*armes caelestes*) among the multitude of recruits (*tirones*), and urge you to spiritual warfare (*spiritualis militia*) as much as is permitted, and I will fight (*pugnare*) alongside you against the enemy. With heavenly aid, fighting the enemy together in the heavenly camps (*castra caelestes*), we will triumph and be crowned victors ....²⁶

Peter Damian echoed this sentiment in his letter of advice to his nephew Marinus, who had recently 'enrolled in the junior squadrons (*pueriles alae*),' urging him to seek out as mentors older monks who would make 'worthy instructors' for one newly arrived in the 'spiritual encampments.'²⁷ 'My soul will have no peace within me,' Anselm wrote to Ralph at Bec, 'until my eyes have seen him whom I long for, and my mouth has spoken to my dearest son, and my heart has armed my new fellow-soldier (*commilito*) against the devil's arrows.'²⁸ While emphasizing the obligation of *tirones* to learn, and the reciprocal duty of *seniores* to instruct newcomers, letter-writers also sought to impress upon their young charges a sense of the camaraderie of the spiritual army. Since all monks were soldiers for life, not even the holiest of them could lay aside his weapons until death. As the Carthusian monk Stephen of Chalmet (d.1177) wrote to

---

²³ Anselm, Letter 29, PL 158: 1095: 'Saepe namquam dum tironem Christi vulnere malae voluntatis aperte malevolus non valet perimere, sitentem eum poculo venenosae rationis malevole callidus tentat exstinguere. Nam, cum monachum nequit obruere vitae quam professus est odio, nititur eum conversationis, in qua est, subruere fastidio.' Trans. Fröhlich as Letter 37 in *Letters*, 1: 134.

²⁴ Guerric of Igny, Sermon 7.3, in *Sermones*, ed. Morson and Costello, 1: 182; trans. Monks of Mount Saint Bernard, *Sermons*, 1: 45.

²⁵ Unfortunately this work has not survived; its existence is known only through Peter Damian's *Vita S. Romualdis abbatis*, c.33, PL 144: 953–1008 (at col. 984).

²⁶ Peter the Venerable, Letter 9, ed. Constable in *Letters*, 1: 16; for a discussion of the identity of the recipient, whom some scholars have identified as Peter Abelard, see *ibid*., 2: 101–2.

²⁷ Peter Damian, Letter 132, ed. Reindel, *Briefe*, 3: 439.

²⁸ Anselm, Letter 10, PL 158: 1159: 'non habebit anima mea requiem in me, donec videatur oculi mei desideratum meum, et alloquator os meum dilectissimum filium meum, et instruat cor meum contra diaboli jacula noum commilitonem meum.' Trans. Fröhlich, *Letters*, 1: 248.

the novices of the nearby Cistercian priory of Saint-Sulpice, 'I do not offer advice to recruits (*tirones*) as a veteran (*veteranus*) whose own military service is finished, but rather as a soldier even now struggling in new wars, and merely offer some words that might serve for my own as well as your exhortation and encouragement.'[29]

Enumerating and glossing the *miles Christi*'s spiritual weapons was an excellent way for superiors to impress on new recruits the fundamental values of the cloister. Such descriptions had the added virtue of being memorable, and, because they made use of objects that were familiar (especially to those raised in aristocratic households), easy to hold as *picturae* in the mind's eye. 'Arms must be prepared for your early training in warfare (*rudimentum militiae*),' wrote Herbert of Losinga to the young Odo, 'and equipped with these you may go on your way and succeed in avoiding the hidden snares of your enemies.'[30] Like many other authors, Herbert carefully labeled each component of the spiritual soldier's kit with a corresponding monastic virtue; sometimes writers paraphrased Paul (Eph. 6:14–17), but more often they customized the Epistles' *armatura Dei* to suit their own needs and better reflect the realities of their day.[31] For instance, in his letter to Odo, Herbert replaced the scriptural meaning of each weapon with a characteristically monastic one; the shield of faith became the shield of obedience, and the sword of the spirit the sword of patience.[32] Bernard of Clairvaux's *Sentences*, thought to approximate how the great abbot preached to his monks in chapter, similarly tailored the meaning of spiritual arms to the values of the coenobium, identifying the virtues of patience, humility, and charity as the *miles Christi*'s most potent weapons.[33]

The basic Pauline formulation of spiritual armor had consisted of the Roman soldier's cuirass (*lorica*), shield (*scutum*), helmet (*galea*), and sword (*gladius*), but later monastic writers embellished and updated this very basic outfit to bring it in line with the equipment of contemporary warriors, and thereby ensure that their allegorical discussions would easily translate into mental *picturae*. As the Benedictine preacher Julian of Vézelay (d.c.1160) told his fellow monks, 'you should know what the arms of God are so that you can go out to meet the enemy. Observe the arms of the secular knight (*eques saecularis*) and arm yourself

---

[29] Stephen of Chalmet, Letter to Monks of Saint-Sulpice, in *Lettres des premiers chartreux*, 2: 212: 'Igitur non ego tanquam emeritae militiae veteranus, tirones instruo, sed quasi miles adhuc ad nova bella rudis, quae ad meam aeque sicut ad vestram vel confirmationem vel exhortationem valeant, profero.'

[30] Herbert of Losinga, Letter 13, ed. Anstruther, *Epistolae*, 22–3: 'Tuae rudimentis militiae praeparanda sunt arma, quibus et munitus incedas et tuorum hostium latentes insidias evitare pervaleas ....'

[31] For the changing symbolism of spiritual weaponry in medieval thought, see Evans, 'An Illustrated Fragment,' 17–20; and Katherine Allen Smith, 'Saints in Shining Armor: Martial Asceticism and Masculine Models of Sanctity, ca. 1050–1250,' *Speculum* 83 (2008), 572–602 (esp. 576–81).

[32] Herbert of Losinga, Letter 13, ed. Anstruther, *Epistolae*, 23.

[33] *Sententiae* 1.32, SBO 6/2: 18; trans. Francis R. Swietek in *The Parables & Sentences*, CF 55 (Kalamazoo, MI, 2000), 131. See also the comments on the original context of the *Sentences* by John R. Sommerfelt, *ibid.*, 111–14.

according to his example.'³⁴ By the twelfth century, through the sort of careful observation Julian recommended, the *miles Christi* had acquired a warhorse, spurs, lance, and banner, and exchanged his cuirass for a hauberk of mail, all of which were markers of knightly status whose use was forbidden to clerics.³⁵ We can see how monastic writers embellished and glossed the spiritual warrior's equipage in an early-twelfth-century treatise entitled *Similitudo militis*, produced in the circle of Anselm of Canterbury.³⁶ This short piece contains an extended comparison between the *miles temporalis* and his counterpart, the *miles spiritualis*, whose battlefield was his own soul. The author opened with the following proposition:

> Just as the worldly knight is fortified with worldly arms, so the spiritual knight should be fortified with spiritual arms. For whatever is necessary for a worldly knight [to fight] against a visible enemy, those intellectual [arms] are very necessary for the spiritual knight who [fights] in the spirit against an invisible enemy.³⁷

There followed a catalogue of the equipment required by a contemporary warrior – a horse, bridle, saddle, spurs, hauberk, helmet, shield, lance, and sword – and analogues for each were given in the form of a list of the arms required by *milites spirituales*. The knight's horse was equivalent to the body of the spiritual warrior, who went into battle on foot, holding in one hand the bridle of chastity and wielding the sword of patience with the other. His hauberk was justice, 'for the works of justice are like the rings of the hauberk (*annuli loricae*).³⁸ Just as worldly knights armed themselves before battle, new monks learned to practice a medita-

---

34 Julian of Vézelay, Sermon 26, in *Sermones*, ed. and trans. Damian Vorreux, 2 vols, CS 192–3 (Paris, 1972), 2: 600: 'Sed nosse debes quae sit armatura Dei (Eph. 6:11) ut congrediaris hosti. Et attende armaturam equitis saecularis ut simili tu quoque armeris exemplo.'
35 For examples of these additions, see Bernard of Clairvaux, *Sententiae* 1.32, and *Parabola* 2, SBO 6/2: 18 and 267f.; Herbert of Losinga, Letter 13, ed. Anstruther, *Epistolae*, 23; Julian of Vézelay, Sermon 26, ed. Vorreux, *Sermones*, 2: 598; Galand of Regny, Parable 10, in *Parabolaire*, ed. and trans. Colette Friedlander, Jean Leclercq and Gaetano Raciti, SC 378 (Paris, 1992), 176; and the Pseudo-Anselmian *Similitudo militis* (n.36 below).
36 Evans ('An Illustrated Fragment,' 20) calls this piece 'the first systematic comparison between the arms of a knight and the spiritual weapons of a Christian.' The text is edited by R.W. Southern and F.S. Schmitt as an appendix to *De humanis moribus*, in *Memorials of Saint Anselm*, Auctores Britannici Medii Aevi 1 (London, 1969), 97–102 (commentary at 12–17). The editors conclude that the work in its current form was completed by c.1130 by monastic disciples of Anselm. While the author was clearly inspired by contemporary knights in developing his catalogue of arms, he also shows an awareness of exegetical traditions related to Ephesians 6 that stretched back through the Carolingian age to patristic writers (on which, see Chapter 1).
37 *Memorials of St Anselm*, 97: 'Sicut miles temporalis armis munitus est temporalibus, sic miles spiritualis debet armis munitus esse spiritualibus. Quaecumque enim temporali militi contra hostem visibilem sunt necessaria, ipsa eadem spiritualiter intellecta et spirituali militi contra hostem invisibilem sunt pernecessaria.'
38 *Memorials of St Anselm*, 101. One wonders if the image of the *miles Christi* walking into battle reflects contemporary criticism of monks riding horses.

tive arming in preparation for private prayer, participation in the Divine Office, and confession and punishment of faults during chapter meetings.[39]

Almost immediately upon their entrance into monastic life, new monks were taught to see themselves as warriors and to view their transition to the cloister as a period of training for a new kind of warfare. They would, no doubt, have been introduced to a number of allegorical interpretations of the religious life – monasteries were often depicted as tombs, prisons, storm-tossed ships, and bridal chambers in this period – but the martial allegory possessed a certain degree of utility that these others lacked. As the letters of encouragement and related texts show, the concept of the *tirocinio* allowed new monks and their mentors to acknowledge the difficulties of adjustment to monastic life and to depict this time of transition as a distinct stage in the individual's spiritual growth. The eleventh and twelfth centuries, when all of these authors wrote, saw a heightened conceptual interest in the novitiate, as well as in the practical difficulties attendant on adult conversion to monastic life. But, just as importantly, martial rhetoric wreathed the monastic life in glory, presenting it as a worthy, indeed superior, alternative to any life that could be lived in the world; it gave meaning to the new monk's sacrifices and struggles, and allowed him to conceive of the stages of his training in heroic terms.

Brothers-in-arms

The training new recruits received during their first months and years in the monastery enabled them to take their place in what Benedict's *Rule* termed the fraternal battle line (*acies*). While for a few the coenobium was merely a training ground where they would hone their skills before going on to the single combat of the hermitage or recluse's cell, most would never leave the security of the *militia Christi*. Monastic theorists built upon Benedict's analogy, as well as a handful of Scriptural passages (especially Gen. 32:2 and Song of Sol. 3:7–8, 6:3), to create martial allegories and related *picturae* which emphasized the unity, discipline, and mutual support that should bind together those living in community. The eleventh-century customary of Fleury, for instance, opened with a description of the duties of membership in the abbey's monastic army, where communal life was synonymous with unceasing war against demonic legions, and the atmosphere of heroism inspired each individual to 'strive to acquit himself more perfectly.'[40] Peter of Celle's *Adhortatio ad claustrales* (written c.1179) also utilized

---

[39] On the wielding of spiritual arms in prayer, see Chapter 1. The Cistercian Stephen of Sawley's *Speculum novitii*, c.10, gave this advice to novices: 'In the Chapter Room, put on the armor of God with diligence: the helmet of providence, the breast-plate of patience, and the shield of mercy. Use them to dispose of both just and undeserved accusations.' Trans. as 'A Mirror for Novices,' in *Stephen of Sawley: Treatises*, ed. Bede K. Lackner and trans. Jeremiah F. O'Sullivan, CF 36 (Kalamazoo, MI, 1984), 101–2.

[40] *Consuetudines Floriacenses antiquiores*, Prologue, ed. Anselmus Davril and Linus Donnat, in *Consuetudinum saeculi X/XI/XII monumenta non-Cluniacensa*, Corpus Consuetudinem Monasticarum 7/3 (Siegburg, 1984), 8: 'Quis enim illic non studeat perfectius inveniri,

the concept of the battle line to describe the perfect order that should prevail in a house of monks or regular canons:

> Be a battle line (*acies*), be terrible (cf. Song of Sol. 6:3). No battle line that is not well ordered can be terrible, and if it is not terrible, then it cannot be the Lord's battle line.... You know how those concerned with worldly military operations arrange the slingers and archers in their proper positions, and place the standard-bearers in suitable spots; the strongest troops in support and the weaker ones, who cannot bear the onslaught of the enemy, in protected places. And so the well ordered battle line is terrible to enemies, because it offers no weak point at which it may be breached. Thus the battle line of God's encampments (Gen. 32:2) must make an orderly advance through the level and rough places of the world, so it will present no weakness to the enemy who wishes to make an assault.[41]

The monastic battle line could thus accommodate soldiers of varying strengths without losing cohesion; indeed, its strength derived from the brothers' willingness to support and protect one another. 'For the devil greatly detests those whom he sees joined and united in love (*caritas*),' Peter explained, 'but he confidently attacks those lacking in this love.'[42]

As with the identification of new monks as *tirones*, descriptions of professed religious as brothers-in-arms (*commilitones*) are not simply instances of tacking on military metaphors to the monastic life, but reflect careful thinking about the virtues undergirding the coenobitic ideal. Such imagery often appears in conjunction with discussions of *caritas*, the selfless love for God and neighbor that mirrored God's love for humanity.[43] The Benedictine *Rule* insisted that the personal bonds upon which communal harmony depended must be built on a firm foundation of *caritas*, and spoke of the monk's 'pure love' for his brothers, his 'humble love' for the abbot, and the abbot's 'equal love' for all his spiritual

---

ubi in tanti patris presentia trecentorum et eo amplius monachorum diatim cuneata visitur frequentia? Qui omnes in commune degentes dyabolicas acies fide armati, spe loricati, verbo veritatis galeati (cf. Eph. 6:12–17) indefatigato certamine infringere solent totumque....'

[41] Peter of Celle, *Adhortatio ad claustrales*, PL 202: 1145: 'Estote acies, estote terribiles. Omnis acies quae ordinata non est, terribilis non est; et si terribilis non fuerit, acies Domini esse non poterit. ... Scitis qui de rebus militaribus agunt, funditores, sagittarios in suis locis disponunt, signiferos in sibi competentibus, robur belli in subsidiis, debiliores in locis tutioribus, quia impetum adversantium ferre non valent; et propter hoc ipsa acies ita ordinata, terribilis est hostibus, quia ingrediendi ei aditum in se non relinquit. Sic acies castrorum Dei per plana et aspera hujus mundi ordinata incedere debet, ne aditum hosti incursare cupienti ullatenus relinquat ....' Trans. based on Feiss, *Peter of Celle: Selected Works*, 129–30.

[42] Peter of Celle, *Adhortatio ad claustrales*, PL 202: 1146: 'quos enim diabolus charitate compactos et unitos videt, vehementer abhorret, quaque carentes secure invadet.' Trans. Feiss, *Selected Works*, 130.

[43] The term appears with great frequency in the Epistles, where it is used especially to signify the believer's love for God (e.g., Rom. 5:5, 2 Cor. 5:14), and described as the greatest of virtues, akin to patience, kindness, and selflessness (e.g., 1 Cor. 13:4, 13:13; Gal. 5:22; Phil. 1:9).

sons.⁴⁴ While the *Rule* did not explicitly link *caritas* to the image of the monastic battle line, this connection may be found in patristic works that continued to influence later monastic writers. In his *Homilies on Ezekiel*, for example, Gregory the Great had written that 'when we position ourselves in battle formation to wage spiritual war against evil spirits, it is necessary above all that we be always united and governed by love (*caritas*), and resolve never to be broken apart by discord.' Without this unifying love, Gregory continued, no matter how well individual spiritual warriors had mastered the virtues of chastity, abstinence, and poverty, their battle line could not possibly withstand demonic attacks.⁴⁵

Not surprisingly, we find most explanations of communal spiritual warfare in the writings of members of coenobitic orders, including Cluniacs, Cistercians, traditional Benedictines, and regular canons. Odo of Cluny counted all those living under the *Rule* in every land as sworn members of a single *militia*, marching forward in unison under their founder's banner.⁴⁶ And the satirical description of the Cluniacs as knights by the eleventh-century bishop Adalbert of Laon may reference martial rhetoric in the Cluniacs' own writings. While the bloodthirsty Cluniac monk of Adalbert's *Carmen ad Rotbertum*, who rides a spirited horse and proudly sports the sword-belt of a lay warrior, certainly embodies concerns about the enormous power and wealth of the Cluniac 'kingdom,' the poet's symbolic vocabulary is not so very different from that found in contemporary monastic celebrations of spiritual warfare, and the drama in both cases revolves around monks who are simultaneously warriors.⁴⁷

Writers of the eleventh and twelfth centuries likened the religious communities of their own day to the 'armies' of apostles and martyrs who had spiritually conquered pagan adversaries, the church fathers aligned in battle formation against heretics, and armies of virtues waging war on the vices.⁴⁸ For the last of these analogies, monastic authors drew directly or indirectly upon the bloody

---

44 RB 72.8, 72.10, 68.5, 2.22, pp. 294 (bis), 290, 174.
45 Gregory the Great, *Homiliarum in Ezechielem prophetam libri duo*, 8.5, PL 76: 857: 'Et nos ergo cum contra malignos spiritus spiritalis certaminis aciem ponimus, summopere necesse est ut per charitatem semper uniti atqe constricti, et nunquam irrupti per discordiam inveniamur quia quaelibet bona in nobis opera fuerint, si charitas desit, per malum discordiae locus aperitur in acie, unde ad feriendos nos valeat hostis intrare.' Peter of Celle references this commentary in his *Adhortatio ad claustrales*, showing it still resonated with later monastic ideals of community.
46 Odo of Cluny, Sermon 3, in *Sermones quinque*, PL 133: 729: 'Quis unquam rex aut imperator in tantis mundi partibus imperavit, aut ex tam diversis nationibus sibi tantas legiones conduxit, quantas videlicet iste, cujuslibet sexus et aetatis in Christi militia, voluntarie juratas disponit? Quem quasi praesentem intuentes, et vexillum institutionis sequentes, diabolicas acies viriliter infringunt.'
47 Adalbéron of Laon, *Carmen ad Rotbertum francorum regem*, ed. and trans. Claude Carozzi as *Poème au roi Robert* (Paris, 1979), 8 (lines 93–114).
48 These analogies effectively historicized coenobitic 'warfare' by creating for it a long pre-Benedictine history. For the battle against vices as a model for monastic combat, see Peter of Celle, Sermon 39.16, PL 202: 766; for the apostles, martyrs, and fathers as proto-monastic armies, see Bernard of Clairvaux, *Sententiae* 3.122, SBO 6/2: 232; and Aelred of Rievaulx, Sermon 23, *Sermones*, PL 195: 340–1.

struggle described in the early-fifth-century *Psychomachia* of Prudentius.[49] Perhaps because the *Psychomachia* depicted the virtues fighting duels against individual opponents, yet simultaneously emphasized their unity as a cohort, Prudentius appealed to monks who conceived of themselves as spiritual warriors in similar terms. The career of the Benedictine Ademar of Chabannes (d.1034) demonstrates the power of the *Psychomachia* to capture the monastic imagination. While studying as a young monk in the scriptorium at Saint-Martial, Limoges, Ademar was assigned the task of producing a copy of the poem complete with glosses and accompanying drawings, and, throughout the rest of his prolific career, Prudentius' work remained a touchstone to which he returned for inspiration and imagery.[50] The *Psychomachia*'s instructional value was likewise recognized by Herrad, the Augustinian abbess of Hohenbourg (d.1195), who had it included in her *Hortus Deliciarum*, a wide-ranging theological compendium designed for educational use in the cloister.[51] As Fiona Griffiths has shown, the glosses and illustrations accompanying the psychomachia cycle in the *Hortus* were carefully planned to work together with Prudentius' text to encourage Herrad's canonesses to contemplate spiritual warfare.[52]

Like Prudentius, later monks wove together violent images to create *picturae* of group combat that were simultaneously edifying and memorable. Monastic writers tailored patristic descriptions of spiritual battle to contemporary ideals of community and military practices, just as they had updated the Pauline spiritual arms and armor to suit the expectations of a medieval audience. For instance, preachers like Bernard of Clairvaux used the concept of the feigned retreat, a military tactic responsible for turning the tide of many battles, as a technique for encouraging listeners to imagine themselves in the thick of spiritual combat.[53] So taken was Julian of Vézelay with accounts of the crusader king Baldwin II's victory at Ascalon in 1125, an engagement in which Baldwin's knights feigned

---

[49] For the popularity of Prudentius in the Central Middle Ages, see Carruthers, *Craft of Thought*, 143f.; and Catherine E. Karkov, 'Gender and Voice in the Cambridge, Corpus Christi College 23 *Psychomachia*,' *Anglo-Saxon England* 30 (2001), 115–36 (esp. 115–18).

[50] Remarkably, Ademar's copy of the *Psychomachia* is extant; see the images and commentary in Danielle Gaborit-Chopin, 'Les dessins d'Adémar de Chabannes,' *Bulletin du Comité des Travaux Historiques et Scientifiques* n.s. 3 (1967), 163–225 (esp. 168–78). For the influence of Prudentius on Ademar, see Richard A. Landes, *Relics, Apocalypse, and the Deceits of History: Ademar of Chabannes, 989–1034* (Cambridge, MA, 1995), 97–9.

[51] For the illustrated *Psychomachia* cycle in the *Hortus Deliciarum* (which exists in the form of copies made prior to the destruction of the original ms. in the Franco-Prussian War), see *The Hortus deliciarum of Herrad of Hohenbourg*, ed. Rosalie Green et al., 2 vols (London, 1979), 1: 190–6, 2: figs 258–85 (fols 199v-204).

[52] Fiona J. Griffiths, *The Garden of Delights: Reform and Renaissance for Women in the Twelfth Century* (Philadelphia, PA, 2007), 121 and 185.

[53] The feigned retreat was a favorite tactic used by mounted knights to make the enemy break ranks or lead opponents into an ambush; see Helen Nicholson, *Medieval Warfare* (Houndsmills, 2004), 141–2. Probably the best-known instance was the Normans' feigned retreat at Hastings, on which see Bernard S. Bachrach, 'The Feigned Retreat at Hastings,' *Mediaeval Studies* 33 (1971), 264–7. Bernard mentioned the feigned retreat in *Parabola* 3.2, SBO 6/2: 268–9.

retreat in order to draw the Turkish garrison out of the city into an ambush, that he used it as the basis for a chapterhouse sermon on spiritual combat.[54] Another common cognitive image used by monastic preachers was the pitched battle, a scenario that continued to stir the monastic imagination even as actual pitched battles remained fairly rare in the world beyond the cloister.[55] The following extract from another sermon by Julian of Vézelay conveys a sense of how monastic preachers sought to imbue their battle scenes with a sense of immediate danger:

> A terrible war assails us. Knights of Christ (*milites Christi*), seize your arms! ... The enemy is approaching, and at any moment we must be ready to fight with self-control and eager hands. Our enemies are numerous, and they shoot flaming arrows (*ignita specula*) at us from all directions. If they discover us unprepared and unarmed, they will only brandish their lances and unsheathe their swords all the more boldly, and launch their assault against us more rapidly. With such enemies as these we cannot enter upon even the shortest truce.[56]

It is noteworthy that, while many monastic sermons were delivered in the second-person plural, here Julian consistently used the first-person plural, a rhetorical device that allowed him to address his listeners directly while also reminding them that they were brothers-in-arms fighting in a common cause. To appreciate the effect the sermon was intended to have, we must remember that Julian would have preached in chapter, with all of his brothers seated in a circle around him, the intimacy of the setting reinforcing the sermon's message about the communal nature of spiritual combat.[57]

---

[54] Julian of Vézelay, Sermon 9, ed. Vorreux, *Sermons*, 1: 208–25, and for the identification of this battle as Julian's source, 208n. The parallels suggested by Julian's sermon are particularly interesting: his monks imaginatively become crusaders, and the crusaders' victory is both a contemporary re-enactment of Joshua's victory over the people of Hai (Josh. 8) and of Christ's victory over the devil. Comparison with the description of the battle by William of Tyre suggests Julian did some embellishing to make the Christian victory seem even more glorious (e.g., crediting Baldwin's army with the capture and sack of Ascalon, which eluded them in reality); see *Historia rerum in partibus transmarinis gestarum* 13.7, ed. R.B.C. Huygens, 2 vols, CCCM 63–63A (Turnhout, 1986), 1: 606–8.

[55] In this period protracted sieges (which, as we shall see, were also of great allegorical interest to monks) were more common than pitched battles, which commanders generally sought to avoid if possible; see Nicholson, *Medieval Warfare*, chapter 5.

[56] Julian of Vézelay, Sermon 26, ed. Vorreux, *Sermons*, 2: 594: 'Magnum contra nos bellum ingruit. Corripite arma, milites Christi! ... Assunt hostes, et sine mora continenter et consertis minibus est pugnandum. Multi hostes nostri sunt, in nos undique ignita specula iaculantur. Qui si nos imparatos uiderint et inermes, audentius tela corripient et exsertis in nos gladiis, impetum facient citiorem. Hostes autem isti tales sunt cum quibus nec indutias quantulascumque aut foedus aliquod ualemus inire.'

[57] Kienzle ('Twelfth-Century Monastic Sermon,' 278, 297–8) discusses the use of the second-person plural, as well as the delivery of sermons in chapter. On the 'intimacy' of chapter sermons, see Chrysogonus Waddell, 'The Liturgical Dimension of Twelfth-Century Cistercian Preaching,' in *Medieval Monastic Preaching*, ed. Carolyn Muessig (Leiden, 1998), 335–49 (at 339).

Some of the most vivid descriptions of the coenobitic militia appear in defenses of communal life against promoters of the contemporary eremitic revival. In his letter to Gilbert of Senlis, a Cluniac monk who had become a recluse, Peter the Venerable inserted, amidst his warnings about the perils of single combat, a celebration of the fraternal battle line his correspondent had abandoned:

> The common life of the cloistered might be compared to a multitude of camps ordered for battle, in which each contends against the adversary the more securely, since he trusts in the aid of his fellow-fighters (*commilitones*) close at his right hand. In that [community] no one presumes to go forth to battle alone, relying on his own strength, but places his trust in the right hands of his fellow-fighters (*compugnantes*) more than in his own. There individual [monks] labor, and their helpers (*coadjutores*) defend them in every way against the [enemies] lying in wait to destroy their salvation.[58]

Peter's assurances that Cluny's monks fought not only for themselves but in support of one another, and his use of the rhetoric of military brotherhood (*commilitones, compugnantes, coadjutores*) pointed back to the virtue of *caritas* which was the foundation for spiritual well-being within the coenobium.[59]

The term *commilito*, frequently used in monastic writing on spiritual combat, was, like *tiro*, a term with distinctly worldly connotations. Though it appears twice in the Epistles, and was occasionally used in the early Church to describe martyrs,[60] by the Central Middle Ages its primary meaning was secular. *Milites* who served a single lord and lived together in his household were *commilitones*, as were members of the military orders who lived and fought together.[61] The appeal of this terminology to monastic writers may reflect their awareness that the knights of a *mesnie*, like individuals in a religious community, were bound by oaths of loyalty to one another and their lord, and were supposed to treat one another in a manner befitting their quasi-familial relationship.[62] In its weaving together of Scriptural and contemporary military imagery, the following description of Cistercian monks from a letter of Nicholas of Clairvaux (d.1178) evokes

---

[58] Peter the Venerable, Letter 20, ed. Constable, *Letters*, 1: 31: 'Nam claustralium communiter uiuentium cohabitatio castrorum ad pugnam ordinatorum multitudini uidetur comparari, ubi quisque tanto securius aduersarium dimicat, quanto sibi uicinius adiutorium de commilitonis dextera sperat. In illo enim praelio non solum de sua quilibet praeliator uirtute praesumit, sed etiam de aliorum dextera leuaque compugnantium uiribus quandoque magis quam de suis confidit. Laborant ibi singuli, et saluti suae insidiantes perimere, et coadiutores modis omnibus defensare.' For background on this letter, *ibid.*, 2: 107–8.

[59] See also Ivo of Chartres' letter to the then-hermit Robert of Arbrissel (below, n.78).

[60] Fellow Christians are termed *commilitones* in Phil. 2:25 and Philem. 2. For examples of patristic usage, see Tertullian, *De corona*, c.1, in PL 2: 77; and Eucherius of Lyon, *Passio Agausensium martyrum* (the Theban Legion as *commilitiones*), PL 50: 829–30.

[61] For the definition of *commilito*, see Jan Frederik Niermeyer, *Mediae Latinitatis lexicon minus* (Leiden, 1976), 217; and Barthélemy, *Serf, the Knight, and Historian*, 233; for the Templars as *commilitones*, see Bernard of Clairvaux, *De laude novae militiae*, Prologue, SBO 3: 213.

[62] On the bonds of the *mesnie*, see David Crouch, *William Marshal: Knighthood, War, and Chivalry, 1147–1219*, 2nd edn (London, 2002), 29–31.

this understanding of the monastery as a brotherhood of warriors, unwavering in their unity and wholly dedicated to their lord's service:

> I saw the armed soldiers of Christ standing around the little bed of Solomon, every man with his sword on his thigh, on account of the fears of the night (Song of Sol. 3:7–8); I saw them standing on guard for the Lord for entire days and nights, each wearing the hauberk of justice and the helmet of salvation, holding the shield of faith and the sword of the spirit, which is the word of God (cf. Eph. 6:14–17).[63]

For the author and his medieval readers, these words would have summoned up exegetical and iconographical memories of the Song of Songs which deepened their understanding of the passage; for instance, they might have remembered that Solomon's 'little bed' traditionally represented the Church, which all *milites spirituales* were bound to defend, and perhaps envisioned the verses as medieval artists depicted them, as a chamber within a turreted castle, in which a company of mailed knights stood guard around their sleeping lord.[64]

If descriptions of spiritual warriors fighting as a cohort promoted the virtue of *caritas*, those who abandoned the monastic militia were denounced as cowardly deserters who had betrayed their brothers-in-arms and lord. When Robert of Châtillon fled the rigors of the Cistercian order for the comparative comforts of Cluny, his kinsman and former abbot Bernard of Clairvaux composed an open letter of reproach intended to demonstrate the superiority of the Cistercian way of life to the errant monk as well as the leaders of his new order.[65] Writing to Robert at his new home, Bernard spoke not merely as a monastic superior to an apostate but as a military commander to a soldier, insisting that in leaving Clairvaux for Cluny, Robert had deserted his army of fellow monks in the midst of a great battle, exchanging 'the arms of fighting men (*arma pugnantium*)' for 'comforts for the weak,' namely soft clothing and abundant food, and leaving himself open to accusations of cowardice and weakness. It was Robert's sworn duty, Bernard reminded him, to return and fight beside his brothers-in-arms, the monks of Clairvaux:

---

[63] Nicholas of Clairvaux, Letter 45, in *Epistolae*, PL 196: 1645: 'Vidi milites Christi armatos stare, et ambire lectulum Salomonis, uniuscujusque ensis super femur suum propter timores nocturnes; vidi stare super custodias Domini totis diebus et totis noctibus, indutos lorica justitiae et galea salutis, habentes scutum fidei et gladium spiritus, quod est verbum Dei....' This verse was often used by Cistercian writers as a way of speaking about the warfare of monastic life; see, for instance, Gilbert of Hoyland, Sermon 16.4–6, *Sermones in Cantica Canticorum*, PL 184: 83–5.

[64] See, for example, the depiction of the verses in the *Hortus deliciarum*, ed. Green et al., 1: 197 and fig. 279.

[65] Bernard of Clairvaux, Letter 1, SBO 7: 1–11. While this letter has traditionally been dated to c.1119, soon after Robert's flight, Adriaan Bredero has forcefully argued for a later dating of 1124/5, and characterizes the piece not as a private communication but as an 'open letter' intended to stimulate discussion of the monastic ideal. See Bredero, *Bernard of Clairvaux: Between Cult and History* (Grand Rapids, MI, 1996), 218–21. Compare the similar rhetoric of desertion in Bernard's Letter 2, also written to a young man who had abandoned his vows; SBO 7: 12–22 (esp. 22).

> Arise, soldier of Christ (*miles Christi*), arise! Shake off the dust and return to the battle from which you fled.... Do you think that because you fled the battle line (*acies*) you will escape the enemies' clutches? The enemy pursues you more eagerly when you flee than he would one who fought back, and more daringly ambushes you from behind than he would oppose you to your face. Are you safe, now you have thrown down your arms, and are sleeping away the morning, even at that hour when Christ rose again? Do you not know that unarmed you are more timid and less intimidating to your enemies? A host of soldiers is besieging the house, and you are sleeping? They are already climbing the walls, destroying the barriers, charging through the rear gates. Would you not be safer with others than alone? Would you not be safer armed in camp than lying naked in bed? Go, take up arms, and flee to your fellow soldiers (*commilitones*) whom you deserted by running away.[66]

By deserting his brother-soldiers, Robert had forfeited the spiritual benefits of their companionship, but, just as importantly, had failed in his duty to support them in their own spiritual struggles. But Bernard also used military imagery to assert the superiority of the Cistercian ideal of community, with its greater austerity, over the Cluniac model, which subordinated asceticism to the demands of the liturgy and thereby produced weaker spiritual soldiers. When Robert rejected the hardships of poverty, manual labor, meager food and rough clothing that set the Cistercians apart, he cast aside the best weapons at the monk's disposal for fighting the devil.[67] This view was echoed by the Cistercian author of the *vita* of Amedeus of Hauterive (written c.1160), a nobleman who entered the house of Bonnevaux with a number of his knights, only to decamp after a short while to Cluny, and finally return to Bonnevaux after suffering an acute crisis of conscience. According to the *vita*, Amedeus was tormented with guilt because of his cowardly desertion of his fellow soldiers:

> Alas! What have I done?' [he lamented]. 'I have deserted my brothers in arms (*commilitones*). They are girded for battle, while I have disgracefully fled my post.

---

[66] Bernard of Clairvaux, Letter 1.13, SBO 7: 10–11: 'Surge, miles Christi, surge, excutere de pulvere, revertere ad proelium unde fugisti.... An quia fugisti ex acie, putas te manus hostium evasisse? Libentius te insequitur adversarius fugientem quam sustineat repugnantem, et audacius insistit a tergo quam resistat in faciem. Securus nunc, proiectis armis, capis matutinos somnos, cum illa hora Christus resurrexit, et ignoras quod exarmatus, et tu timidior, et hostibus minus timendus sit? Armatorum multitudo circumvallaverunt domum, et tu dormis? Iam ascendunt aggerem, iam dissipant saepem, iam irrunt per postitium. Tutiusne est ergo tibi ut te inveniant solum quam cum aliis, nudum in lectulo quam armatum in campo? Expergiscere, sume arma et fuge ad commilitones tuos, quos fugiens deseruas ....' Trans. based on James, *Letters*, 8–9.

[67] Bernard of Clairvaux, Letter 1.13, SBO 7: 11: 'Quid armorum refugis pondus et asperitatem, delicate miles? Adversarius instans et circumvolantia specula facient clipeum non esse oneri, loricam non sentiri vel galeam. Et quidem subito procedenti de umbra ad solem, de otio ad laborem, grave cernitur omne quod incipit....' See also *ibid.* (7: 10) for Bernard's juxtaposition of hardship and luxury within the monastery. In this portion of the letter Bernard drew heavily upon Jerome's Letter to Heliodorus, another missive sent to a 'deserter' from the monastic camp (on which see Chapter 3, n.63) which he would undoubtedly have known.

They are struggling vigorously, so that after the victory is won they will receive the eternal prize (cf. 1 Cor. 9:24). Wishing to evade the spears of my adversaries, deceived by the clever enemy's wiles, I have run straight into the demons' many traps.'[68]

To grasp the ideological significance of these descriptions of monks as *commilitones* we must read them in the context of evolving conceptions of *caritas*, which encouraged individual spiritual progress toward the divine even while stressing each monk's duty to minister to his spiritual brothers. This model was particularly emphasized by the Cistercians, whose hagiography and sermons identified such selfless love as a key trait, and even a potential weapon, of the *miles Christi*.[69] But such imagery also reflects larger changes taking place in the religious landscape as these authors wrote. In an age when new orders were being founded at a dizzying rate and competing interpreters of the monastic ideal vied for patronage and recruits, it is no wonder that eleventh- and twelfth-century writers were preoccupied with defining – and debating – the truest and best forms of community.[70] Even if most churchmen were accepting of the increasing diversity of religious ideals and institutions they nonetheless viewed these in hierarchical terms, typically placing their own order or way of life at the conceptual pinnacle.[71] The centuries-old image of the fraternal battle line may have possessed a special immediacy for Benedictines, Cluniacs, and Cistercians living in an age when many of the best and brightest young recruits were being drawn to new semi-eremitic orders and informal settlements of hermits. Such imagery affirmed the fundamental values of the coenobium, and the spiritual rewards of community, all the while surrounding them with an appealing aura of valor. The martial allegory was a particularly effective way of reinforcing the *Rule*'s emphasis on obedience and mutual support and driving home the lesson that while the communal life was designed with the goal of helping each monk

---

[68] *Vita venerabilis Amedaei Altae Ripae († c.1150)*, c.5, ed. Anselme Dimier, *Studia monastica* 5 (1963), 265–304 (at 287): 'Heu! Heu quid feci? Prodidi, inquam, prodidi commilitones meos. Illos in procinctu constitui, ego autem turpiter victus aufugi. Illi nunc strenue dimicant, ut post victoriam, bravium perenne recipiant (cf. 1 Cor. 9:24); ego vero cum adversantium tela evadere volui, hostis callidi arte deceptus, multiplices daemonum laqueos incurri.'

[69] For the Cistercian understanding of *caritas*, see Newman, *Boundaries of Charity*, chapter 2, and for examples of how Cistercian writers linked *caritas* to the practice of spiritual warfare, ibid., 29–37. In addition to the texts cited by Newman, see Walter Daniel's *vita* of Aelred of Rievaulx, in which the hagiographer describes how, 'during the time of his training (*tirocinio*) in Christ,' the future abbot 'excelled all his comrades and fellow-soldiers (*commilitones*) in humility,' triumphing over himself by *caritas* even as he submitted himself to his fellows and encouraged them. See Walter Daniel, *Vita Ailredi abbatis Rievall'*, c.8, ed. and trans. F.M. Powicke (Oxford, 1950), 17.

[70] For the range of options represented by new orders and independent reformers, as well as contemporary responses to these, see Constable, *Reformation of the Twelfth Century*, chapter 2; Caroline Walker Bynum, 'The Cistercian Conception of Community,' in *Jesus as Mother*; and John Van Engen, 'The Crisis of Cenobitism Reconsidered,' *Speculum* 61 (1986), 68–89.

[71] Constable, *Reformation of the Twelfth Century*, 47–50.

achieve salvation, this goal could only be reached if he was willing to support, and in turn be supported by, his brethren.

Single combat

All members of the monastic *militia Christi* fought their own battles against worldliness, demonic temptations, and the body, but only a select few ventured to leave the safety of the battle line for a life of single combat (*certamen singulare*) in the 'desert.' Those who took this radical step may have been inspired by the example of the earliest desert monks, who were claimed as progenitors not only by hermits and the new semi-eremitic orders like the Carthusians and Vallombrosans, but also by coenobitic monks, especially Cistercians, who conceived of the individual monk as a single combatant drawing strength from his community.[72] The great resurgence of eremitism which began in the tenth century meant that those seeking to follow in the footsteps of Athanasius' Antony or Jerome's Paul hardly lacked for contemporary models. Like their Late Antique prototypes, the *vitae* of solitaries composed in the eleventh and twelfth centuries presented their subjects as great champions, single-handedly triumphing over the devil and his minions.[73] The monastic hagiographers who composed most of these *Lives* viewed heroic hermits as worthy spiritual exemplars for those living in community; after all, even those who enjoyed the support of *commilitones* earned their salvation by fighting as individuals within the monastic army. Allegories of single combat can thus shed light on monks' perceptions of the solitary life as well as their understanding of individual spiritual development within the community of the cloister.

In the Central Middle Ages the line between monks and hermits seems to have been thin, and the movement of individuals between the two identities fluid. New orders like the Carthusians and Grandmontines combined Benedictine communal elements with eremitic ideals, many hermits and especially recluses were bound to monasteries by ties of friendship and support, and coenobites often undertook temporary solitary retreats. Generally speaking, a heightened value was placed on solitude in this period by the 'new monks.'[74] While Benedict's *Rule* had described a progression from coenobitic battle line to eremitic single

---

[72] For the Desert Fathers as models for later monks, see Leclercq, 'S. Antoine dans la tradition monastique médiévale'; Peter Jackson, 'The *Vitas Patrum* in Eleventh-Century Winchester,' in *England in the Eleventh Century: Proceedings of the 1990 Harlaxton Symposium*, ed. Carola Hicks (Stamford, 1992), 119–34; and for the Cistercians, Benedicta Ward, 'The Desert Myth: Reflections on the Desert Ideal in Early Cistercian Monasticism,' in *One Yet Two: Monastic Tradition East and West*, ed. M.B. Pennington (Kalamazoo, MI, 1976), 183–9; and Bede K. Lackner, *Eleventh-Century Background of Cîteaux*, CS 8 (Washington D.C., 1972), 146–7, 204.

[73] For example, see Peter Damian, *Vita Sancti Romualdi*, c.7 and 17, PL 144: 962, 970; and Stephen of Lissac, *Vita Sancti Stephani dicta et facta* (Life of Stephen of Muret, founder of Grandmont), c.2, PL 204: 1071–86 (at col. 1074).

[74] Lackner, *Background of Cîteaux*, 215.

combat, many later hermits reversed this order, founding monastic communities or even new orders and becoming monks after a period of living alone or with a few companions in the wilderness.[75] The spiritual trajectory of Gregory the Great's *vita* of Benedict, in which the holy man begins, rather than ends, his saintly career as a hermit, also appears to have been a source of inspiration for later hermits and their biographers.[76] But the course prescribed by the *Rule* continued to influence monastic views of eremitism,[77] so that individuals who bypassed the recommended period of training in the monastery might encounter stern disapproval. Soon after the itinerant preacher Robert of Arbrissel took up the life of a hermit in the forest of Craon during the 1090s, Ivo of Chartres wrote to warn him that he lacked adequate spiritual preparation for this sort of life:

> For you are to fight against evil spirits, and if you wish to fight in safety (cf. Eph. 6:12), introduce yourself into Christ's encampments among the ranks of soldiers arranged in battle-formation, lest if you contend in single combat (*certamen singulare*) as an untrained soldier against experienced opponents, you may be overwhelmed by a countless number of your adversaries. Afterwards, armed with the spirit of counsel and fortitude (cf. Isa. 11:2), accustomed to avoiding the ancient enemy's traps, and now more experienced in spiritual battle, you will be able to take on any enemies at all, since you will have learned to counter their attacks in the battle line (cf. RB 1.5).[78]

Ivo's concern, which many of his contemporaries shared, was not with the legitimacy of the eremitic ideal *per se*, but rather with the dangers such a life held for

---

[75] Those familiar with Benedict's *Life* by Gregory the Great (i.e., nearly all monks) would have known that Benedict himself had been a cave-dwelling hermit at Subiaco before embarking on a career as a founder and abbot. For many examples of the movement from hermit to monk in the eleventh and twelfth centuries, see Henrietta Leyser, *Hermits and the New Monasticism: A Study of Religious Community in Western Europe, 1000–1150* (New York, 1984).

[76] John Howe, 'St Benedict the Hermit as a Model for Italian Sanctity: Some Hagiographical Examples,' *American Benedictine Review* 55 (2004), 42–54.

[77] The Benedictine Rule's distinction between eremitic single combat and the fraternal battle line was often used by later writers to summarize the difference between hermits and monks; for example, Otto of Freising, *Chronica sive historia de duobus civitatibus*, 7.35, ed. Adolf Hofmeister, MGH SS 40 (Hanover, 1912), 373; John of Fécamp, Letter 6, in *Epistolae*, PL 147: 473; and the *Lives* of the Italian hermit Dominic of Sora (d.1032) (on which see John Howe, *Church Reform and Social Change in Eleventh-Century Italy* (Philadelphia, PA, 1997), 36 and n.47).

[78] Ivo of Chartres, Letter 34, in *Yves de Chartres: Corréspondance*, ed. J. Leclercq (Paris, 1949), 140. Although Leclercq identifies the recipient as a canon of Saint-Quentin, the letter is commonly believed to have been written to Robert of Arbrissel; see Berenice M. Kerr, *Religious Life for Women, c.1100–c.1350* (Oxford, 1999), 6. The text reads: 'Contra spirituales itaque nequitias pugnaturus, si securus vis pugnare, castris Christi militum ordinate pugnantium te insere, ne si certamine singulari contra exercitatos inexercitatus pugnare contenderis, innumera adversariorum tuorum multitudine comprimaris. Postquam vero, spiritu consilii et fortitudinis armatus, callidates antiqui hostis evitare consueveris, jam exercitatior in spirituali certamine poteris solus, si ita contingat, contra quoslibet hostes certamen inire, quorum impetus didiceris sustinere in acie.'

those who lacked sufficient strength and experience.[79] Those who went to live as hermits because, 'after mastering the skills of the claustral army (*claustralis exercitus*), they yearned for the single combat of the desert,' were almost universally admired.[80]

Hermits and recluses, many of whom followed modified versions of his *Rule*, also represented themselves in Benedict's terms, as veterans who surpassed their coenobitic counterparts in martial prowess. The tenth-century *Regula solitariorum*, composed by a certain Grimlaicus (who was probably, like many of his intended readers, a recluse and former monk),[81] cited Benedict nearly word for word in its description of how recluses often began their careers as monks, and 'learned through long experience how to fight the devil' in the communal battle line before leaving for the single combat of the desert.[82] In a letter to an unnamed Benedictine abbot (possibly John of Fécamp), Peter Damian developed an exegetical reading of the *Rule* that ranked coenobitic monks as inferior fighters:

> Therefore, the brothers who practice stability by living in the monastery are to be tolerated, but those who with a spirit of fervor transfer to the hermitage deserve the highest praise. The former seek shelter behind the shield of God's protecting hand, while the latter go forth into the field of battle (*campus certaminis*) and are awarded the badge of victory. The former defend what is theirs, but the latter bring back the spoils. With God as their defender, the former are invincible (*insuperabiles*), but the latter are content each day merely to tread on the necks of their enemies. Ensconced within their walls, monks battle to keep their attackers from entering, but hermits drive the threatening ranks of the enemy far from their lines and force them to flee.[83]

---

[79] Constable, *Reformation of the Twelfth Century*, 63. It is noteworthy that, only a few years after receiving Ivo's letter, Robert founded the double-monastery of Fontevrauld, a community in which, in the words of his hagiographer, both women and men came together to became 'Christ's recruits (*tirunculi*)' and serve in the 'great armies of Christians (*agmina Christianorum*)' the former hermit placed under the rule of an abbess. See Baldric of Dol, *Vita B. Roberti de Abrissello*, c.19 and 24: PL 162: 1053 and 1056.

[80] The quote, from a twelfth-century *vita* of Robert of Molesme, describes how four men of unusual spiritual strength, Stephen Harding, Alberic of Cîteaux, and two unnamed companions, left Molesme to become hermits at a place called Vivicus: 'Erant autem inter illos quatuor viri spiritu fortiores, scilicet Albericus et Stephanus et alii duo, qui post claustralis exercitii rudimenta ad singulare certamen eremi suspirabant.' *Vita S. Roberti, abbatis Molesmensis*, PL 157: 1277. Regardless of the veracity of this account (on which see Lackner, *Eleventh-Century Background of Cîteaux*, 235 and n.), it attests to the influence of Benedict's model of spiritual progression.

[81] For the text of the *Regula solitariorum*, see PL 103: 573–664; on authorship and dating, see Phyllis G. Jestice, *Wayward Monks and the Religious Revolution of the Eleventh Century* (Leiden, 1997), chapter 3.

[82] Grimlaicus, *Regula*, c.1, PL 103: 579: 'qui jam didicerant per multa experimenta contra diabolum pugnare, ipsi quoque bene instructi, atque sicut aurum in fornace probati, fraterna ex acie ad singularem pugnam eremi, securi jam sine consolatione alterius, sola manu vel brachio contra vitia carnis vel cogitationum, Deo auxiliante, dimicaturi pergebant.' Cf. RB 1.4–5, p. 168, which the author has paraphrased here.

[83] Peter Damian, Letter 152, ed. Reindel, *Briefe*, 4: 12 (and for the possible identity of

While enclosed monks were able merely to defend themselves as though besieged, those unhindered by the demands of community could take the offensive against demonic adversaries. As this letter shows, the martial allegory could be used to make a powerful argument for the superiority of hermits to traditional monks.

Solitaries were often renowned ascetics, their self-imposed sufferings regarded by contemporaries as a figurative martyrdom that made them into living saints.[84] Monastic writers used the language of martial struggle to link this eremitic model of sanctity to the tradition of the earliest martyrs, and urged the solitaries of their own day to emulate the martyrs' example in single combat. The *Liber Confortatorius*, an eleventh-century spiritual guidebook written by the monk Goscelin of Saint-Bertin for Eva, a young English nun of Wilton who had become a recluse, presented the martyrdom of the third-century Roman matron Perpetua as a worthy subject for contemplation for a recluse training for spiritual battle.[85] After detailing first the famous vision in which Perpetua fought as a gladiator in the arena, and then her actual martyrdom, Goscelin explained how such an example might prove useful to Eva. While the recluse might not have to face public execution, he wrote, she was no less threatened by enemies than the martyr, and indeed her entire life was a spiritual re-enactment of the scene she had just been 'shown.' If she hoped to avoid defeat she 'must keep watch in the armor of prayer on the ramparts of [her] confinement,' and be ready to 'open a path with the sword (*ferrum*) through the densely clustered ranks of the enemy.'[86]

---

the addressee, 4, 6n.): 'Fratres itaque in monasterio immobiliter permanentes tolerandi sunt, ad heremum vero fervido spiritu transmigrantes, plausibus ac praeconiis efferendi. Illi siquidem sub divinae protectionis clipeo delitescunt, isti vero in campum certaminis prodeuntes victoriae titulis decorantur. Illi defendunt sua, isti referunt spolia. Illi Deo se protegente sunt insuperabiles, isti cottidie satagunt hostium suorum calcare cervices. Illi intra moenia constituti obsidentes ne ingrediantur obsistunt, isti minaces hostium cuneos procul de suis finibus terga cedentes expellunt.' Note how in the last sentence Damian's use of the passive in reference to monks and the active in reference to hermits drives home his overall message. Trans. Blum and Resnick, *Letters*, 5: 12–13.

[84] Jestice, *Wayward Monks*, 104–5; Heinrich Fichtenau, *Living in the Tenth Century: Mentalities and Social Orders*, trans. Patrick Geary (Chicago, MI, 1991), 250–1.

[85] The Latin text has been edited by C.H. Talbot as 'The *Liber Confortatorius* of Goscelin of Saint Bertin, *Studia Anselmiana* 37, Analecta Monastica, 3rd ser. (1955), 2–117 (for Perpetua, see 50–1); and trans. Monika Otter, *Goscelin of St Bertin, The Book of Encouragement and Consolation* (Cambridge, 2004). While the *Liber* has received attention for its confessional style and erotically charged language, the elaborate discourse on spiritual warfare in its second book has drawn few comments from modern readers. The most extensive study of the work to date, *Writing the Wilton Women: Goscelin's Legend of Edith and Liber Confortatorius*, ed. Stephanie Hollis et al. (Turnhout, 2004), comments only briefly on the theme of spiritual warfare at 372–4 and 393–4.

[86] *Liber Confortatorius*, ed. Talbot, 51: 'Quanquam non sit gladiator, non deerit materies uictorie persecutor, et omnes qui pie uolunt uiuere in Christo persecutionem patientur (2 Tim. 3:12).... Aerie potestates et principes tenebrarum omnem celi regionem densis agminibus occluserunt, nulli aditum nisi expugnati concedunt. Quocunque ire uolueris, ferro iter aperiendum est, per glomerosos hostium cuneos erumpendum est.' Trans. Otter, *Book of Encouragement*, 55–6.

Similarly, in the sermons he wrote for his hermit-monks, Peter Damian identified the martyrs as archetypal *milites Christi* and urged his listeners to imitate their fortitude.[87] Peter recounted the martyrdom of Saint Christopher, as he told his audience, 'so that through the mystery of sacred history I might teach you the spiritual combat in which the blessed Christopher distinguished himself as a celebrated victor.'[88] He described how

> the new soldier snatched up the sword of the spirit, which is the word of God (Eph. 6:17), and went forth into battle; and so he contended in implacable battle against the enemy of humankind.... The fierce warrior joined hand-to-hand combat (*comminus dimicat*), and mowing down whatever was in his way cut down the proud necks of the enemy. Armed with the hauberk of faith and relying on a citadel (*arx*) raised up not from a mountain but from the mind, although the battle line of the foe raged and gnashed its teeth on every side, the strongest athlete knew not how to fear the assault of his opponents.[89]

Here, as elsewhere in his letters and sermons, Peter offered his audience a battle scenario (what he called a *spectaculum*) for them to 'contemplate with the eyes of faith,' and encouraged them to insert themselves into the scene imaginatively.[90] It was not enough for his brethren to celebrate or passively contemplate these martyred warriors; each of them must re-enact their predecessors' struggles, 'bravely resolving to imitate the martyrs of Christ by taking up arms among the soldiers of Christ.' Further, as Peter explained, the recluse had to be simultaneously martyr and executioner: 'Are external enemies lacking? Turn your hand against yourself, and you will discover many seditious citizens. Conquer pride, cut the throat of wrath, restrain avarice, slay envy.'[91]

But if the eremitic life offered opportunities for greater glory, solitaries were also at greater risk of attack; after all, they lived outside the safety of the battle

---

[87] Peter Damian, Sermon 3, 17/1, 17/2, 30, ed. Giovanni Lucchesi in *Petri Damiani sermones*, CCCM 57 (Turnhout, 1983), 11–12, 85–6, 97, 105–6, 172, 177.

[88] Peter Damian, Sermon 33.10, ed. Lucchesi, *Sermones*, 201: 'Haec vobis, fratres carissimi, quasi per excessum diximus, ut spiritale certamen in quo beatus Christophorus insignis triumphator enituit, etiam per sacrae historiae mysterium doceremus.'

[89] Peter Damian, Sermon 33.2, ed. Lucchesi, *Sermones*, 196: 'Nouus adhuc miles corripit gladium spiritus, quod est uerbum Dei (Eph. 6:17), et protinus in bella congreditur; et sic aduersus humani generis inimicum infoederabili certamine colluctatur ... feruidus bellator cum hoste committit. Consertis armis comminus dimicat, et obuia quaeque metens, superbas aduersantium hostium ceruices optruncat. Fidei quippe lorica munitus et excelsa non montis sed mentis arce subnixus, licet undique fremat ac frendeat acies hostium, nescit athleta fortissimus impetum formidare bellorum.'

[90] Peter Damian, Sermon 30.1, ed. Lucchesi, *Sermones*, 172. Here Peter's repetition of 'uidimus' shows how he sought to make his audience visualize the scene he was describing in detail.

[91] Peter Damian, Sermon 30.6, ed. Lucchesi, *Sermones*, 177: 'Quisquis ergo gaudes fortiter egisse martyres Christi, corripe et ipse arma inter milites Christi. Desunt exterius hostes? Verte manus in te, et multos seditiosos inuenies ciues. Doma superbiam, iugula iracundiam, extingue libidinem, reprime auaritiam, occide inuidiam.'

line, and their way of life made them prone to indulge in excessive asceticism or become puffed up with pride. Self-denial, when accompanied by humility, was the recluse's best defense against such assaults. Aelred of Rievaulx wrote to his sister, an anchoress, advising her 'to engage in battle with the wily foe' by fasting, but simultaneously warned her from personal experience against waging unrelenting war against the flesh.[92] The Carthusian monk Bernard of Portes (d.1158) cautioned the recluse Reynald that the devil never ceased to test and torment solitaries, forever implanting impure thoughts in their minds, causing them to become melancholy or bored, and, worst of all, inciting them to pride. The recluse must accordingly arm himself with the weapons of tears and prayer for his battles (*certamina*) against the invisible enemies (*invisibiles inimici*) who prowled his cell while he recited the Psalms, hoping to distract him with thoughts of his own holiness.[93] The Benedictine Adam of Eynsham's *vita* of Hugh of Lincoln, who lived for years as a Carthusian before becoming bishop of Lincoln in 1186, detailed his hero's protracted war with the devil, an epic struggle fought entirely within the confines of Hugh's cell at La Grande Chartreuse. From the moment Hugh crossed the threshold of the cell, where, according to the order's custom, he was to spend the majority of his time in solitary prayer, 'the tempter directed all his ancient wicked weapons (*malitie instrumenta*)' against him, even shooting him with bolts 'as if from a mighty crossbow (*balista robustissima*)' to incite his flesh to rebellion against his spirit.[94] Only after years of campaigning did Hugh finally defeat his enemy, and he accomplished this feat only with the spiritual

---

[92] Aelred of Rievaulx, *De institutione inclusarum*, c.18, 31, ed. C.H. Talbot in *Aelredi Rievallensis Opera omnia*, Vol. 1: *Opera ascetica*, ed. Anselm Hoste et al., CCCM 1 (Turnhout, 1971), 653–4, 665. Alexandra Barratt has shown the indebtedness of Aelred's *De Institutione* to the Carthusian *Constitutions*, pointing to a wider interest among twelfth-century Cistercians in the semi-eremitic orders; see 'The "De Institutione Inclusarum" of Aelred of Rievaulx and the Carthusian Order,' *Journal of Theological Studies* 28 (1977), 528–36.

[93] Bernard of Portes, Letter to Reynald, c.13–14, in *Lettres des premiers chartreux*, 2: 71: 'Tu vero adversus haec et omnia omnino tentationum genera, adversus quoque nocturnas illusiones, virtute orationis armare, et clypeum illum arripe, de quo Apostolus ait (cf. 2 Eph. 6:16).... Sincerus enim amor et fervens fides crucis Christi universa machinamenta inimici irrita facit; et effusa cum lacrymis oratio omne genus tentationis superat et repellit. Haec sunt spiritualia instrumenta atque certamina militiae tuae coram Rege, cui militare coepisti ... Ieiunanti tibi, oranti, psallenti, non deerunt invisibiles inimici, applaudentes tibi et dicentes: "Euge, euge, quis similes tibi? Quis ita placet Deo? O se scirent hominess sanctitatem tuam!"'

[94] Adam of Eynsham, *Life of St Hugh*, 1.9, 2 vols, ed. and trans. Douie and Farmer, 1: 28: 'immo nouam ingresso militiam omnia temptator innouauit antique sue malitie instrumenta; precipue, quasi balistam robustissimam et eo, ut sperabat, insuperabilem, quo michi inseparabilem tetendit, immo accendit contra me stimulum carnis mee.' Here the hagiographer (or possibly Hugh, whose words Adam purports to record here) seems to have updated the devil's traditional 'fiery darts' (Eph. 6:16) for his medieval audience. Note too the respective associations of the devil with *malitia* and Hugh with *militia*, which may be an allusion to the *malitia/militia* pun so popular among monastic writers.

support of Christ and his prior.⁹⁵ As Hugh's *vita* emphasized, even those who lived in solitude did not – and could not – fight completely alone.⁹⁶

Hugh's conclusive victory over his flesh and the devil was, as his hagiographer made clear, proof of his sanctity; for the majority of solitaries and monks alike, peace came only with death. Like the hermit, the individual monk also engaged in a sort of single combat; as Guerric of Igny told his brethren, the flesh and spirit were like two men standing on opposite sides of a road, perpetually fighting with one another and blocking one's path.⁹⁷ 'Let us not grieve for that soldier who is now safe,' the Cistercian abbot Stephen Harding reminded the brothers of Cîteaux after the death of his predecessor Robert of Molesme, 'but for ourselves, who are still in the midst of the battle (*in praelio*).'⁹⁸ Sermons and works of instruction encouraged monks to be mindful of this ongoing struggle, indeed, to meditate on it regularly, and supplied *picturae* designed to facilitate their contemplation. John of Fruttuaria suggested monks cultivate humility by envisioning themselves battling a fearsome three-headed dragon (*draco*) representing the related vices of pride, vainglory, and envy. Since this monster had 'killed and cast down and trampled underfoot many men,' John advised monks to arm themselves with all the spiritual armor and weapons prescribed in Ephesians and told them how to recognize each of the beast's terrible heads.⁹⁹ Each head is described in gruesome detail: Pride has a three-pronged tongue and 'breath as deadly as that of the deadliest serpent'; Vainglory 'emits fearful voices and terrible roars from a swollen throat'; and Envy 'belches forth flames' to scorch the careless soldier.¹⁰⁰ Through such 'signs (*indicia*)' John painted a gruesome

---

95 *Life of St Hugh*, 2.2, ed. and trans. Douie and Farmer, 1: 50–2. Hugh's prior and mentor, Basil, continued to aid him in his struggles even after death, even appearing in a vision, knife in hand, to spiritually castrate Hugh and thereby cure his temptations!

96 As Adam of Eynsham wrote of Hugh in his *Life* (1.10, ed. and trans. Douie and Farmer, 1: 30–2), 'Sedebat uero solitarius, qui tamen non erat solus; set erat cum eo Dominus, per quem erat in cunctis prospere agens.'

97 Guerric of Igny, Fifth Sermon for Advent, c.3, ed. and trans. Morson and Costello, *Sermones*, I: 158. Compare the contemporary parable by another Cistercian, Galand of Reigny, in which the flesh and spirit are two fighters (*pugili*) engaged in a duel (*duellum*); Parable 10, ed. Friedlander et al., *Parabolaire*, 176–83.

98 Stephen Harding, *Sermo in obitu praedecessoris sui*, PL 166: 1376: 'Non doleamus super militem securum, doleamus super nos constitutos in praelio, et tristes moestasque voces in orationes vertamus, deprecantes triumphatorem Patrem, ne rugientem leonem, et saevum adversarium de nobis triumphare patiatur.'

99 John of Fruttuaria, *Liber de ordine vitae*, c.31, PL 184: 579: 'Arripiendum namque tibi est totis viribus juge certamen contra crudelissimam et triformem bestiam, id est superbiam, inanem gloriam, et invidiam, cujus in corpore tria capita, et in ipsis capitibus dentes ferrei comminuentes omnia. O quam multos viros haec immanissima bestia momordit et dejecit, atque sub pedibus suis conculcavit! Circumda itaque tibi fortem armaturam, ut possis stare contra tantam nequitiam (cf. Eph. 6:13).'

100 John of Fruttuaria, *Liber de ordine vitae*, c.31–2, PL 184: 579–80: 'Caput superbiae sicut caput viperae, furor ejus ut furor draconis, et flatus ejus lethifer, ut insanabilis flatus reguli. ... Cenodoxiae alterum caput, multiforme prodigium, et multiplex malum, diras voces et rugitus terribiles ex turgidis faucibus quadripartitito modo altius afflat. ... Ipsa quoque invidia duplices evomit flammas. Hoc namque caput tertium ....'

picture in the mind's eye of his reader, while through his consistent use of the second-person singular, he emphasized that the soldier battling the beast was none other than the reader himself.

John was hardly alone in his insistence on the value of such meditative training. Many contemporaries would have agreed with Peter Damian's sentiment, expressed in a sermon, that only if 'the mind is constantly trained in spiritual combat ... would it be inflamed with a love of battle (*amor certaminis*)' and eagerly seek out the enemies that lurked in the dark regions of the soul.[101] Bernard of Clairvaux encouraged each of his monks to train by imagining himself as the protagonist of a famous combat often glossed as a spiritual battle, David's confrontation with Goliath. In monastic thought, David was traditionally associated with the virtue of humility, and his contest with Goliath read as an allegory of the soul's single combat with pride, the root of all vices and the deadliest enemy of monks. Bernard asked each monk to imagine himself as David facing Goliath, felling the giant with stones hurled from the sling of 'long suffering,' and finishing him off in a bloody fashion just as the young hero had done:

> Now come up closer, lest perhaps he rise again; and, standing over him, cut off his head with his own sword's point, destroying vainglory with the very vainglory that assails you. You have slain (*peremisti*) Goliath with his own sword if, struck by that haughty thought, from it you take the material and occasion for humility....[102]

Here again we see the use of direct address, which was intended to make each monk feel the preacher was speaking to him alone, and to ease the transition from listening to Bernard's words to 'seeing' oneself engaged in the violent confrontation being described.[103]

Such martial meditation would have drawn upon, and been facilitated by, familiar images of battle that were to be found in the monastery, perhaps carved into the capitals of the cloister or church or painted upon the pages of manuscripts in the scriptorium. Bernard of Clairvaux's monks, for example, would have likely 'seen' David and Goliath's confrontation as it was depicted in contemporary Cistercian manuscripts, with Goliath as a huge mailed knight.[104]

---

101 Peter Damian, Sermon 74, c.3, 7, ed. Lucchesi, *Sermones*, 444, 447.
102 Bernard of Clairvaux, Sermo in dominica IV post Pentecosten, SBO 5: 205; trans. Beverly Mayne Kienzle in *Sermons for the Summer Season* (Kalamazoo, MI, 1991), 118. For commentary on this passage, see Jean Leclercq, 'Le thème de la jonglerie chez S. Bernard et ses contemporains,' *Revue d'histoire de la spiritualité* 48 (1972), 385-99 (esp. 387 and 396). Bernard's interest in the David and Goliath story as an allegory of spiritual warfare is attested by his use of it to describe his own confrontation with Abelard (Letter 239.3-4, SBO 8: 14) and in his Sentences (2.68, 3.42, SBO 6/2: 39, 89).
103 In my reading of the sermons of Bernard and his contemporaries, I am inclined to follow Christopher Holdsworth's argument that the written texts do reflect, albeit imperfectly, the actual words the authors would have spoken to their monks; see 'Were the Sermons of St Bernard on the Song of Songs Ever Preached?' in *Medieval Monastic Preaching*, ed. Muessig, 295-318.
104 A famous example, which Bernard would certainly have seen as a young monk, is in the Bible of Stephen Harding (Dijon, Bibliothèque municipale, MS 14, fol. 13r); fig. 6 in Newman, *Boundaries of Charity*; and fig. 43 in Yolanta Zaluska, *L'enluminure et le*

Verbal *picturae* were sometimes accompanied by complementary images of spiritual combat, as in the *Moralia in Job* produced in the scriptorium at Cîteaux in 1111.[105] To accompany Gregory the Great's text, which we have seen was a landmark work in the history of spiritual warfare,[106] the monastic illuminator created a visual program full of scenes of violent spiritual struggle. A medieval reader would have found much here upon which to meditate, in the form of men grappling with fantastic beasts, a mounted knight battling a dragon, and mailed warriors defending a tower, interspersed with images of Cistercian monks – in short, a rich array of *picturae* that invited contemplation on the monk's daily warfare against earthly temptation and vice.[107] Another example of how the effect of word-pictures could be heightened by accompanying images may found in the St Albans Psalter, a richly illuminated manuscript produced by the Benedictines of that abbey, probably for the recluse Christina of Markyate in the 1140s.[108] The beginning of the biblical text is heralded in the manuscript by a large historiated capital showing David in his role as composer of the Psalms, enthroned beneath two mounted warriors who ride at one another full-tilt with unsheathed swords.[109] An inscription identifies these men, who could otherwise be taken for contemporary knights, as 'heavenly athletes (*celestes athletae*)' engaged in a duel (*duellum*), and instructs the reader to use them as the starting point for a meditation on the spiritual combat of the religious life:

> Whoever wishes to be a son of God and a worthy heir of heaven, and whoever wishes to gain the glory and inheritance which the demons lost in their fall from the kingdom of God, let her watch carefully by night and day, with eye and mind, that war and mounted combat (*equitatio*) which she sees depicted here. Just as

---

    scriptorium de Cîteaux au XIIᵉ siècle (Cîteaux, 1989). The young David is shown here doing exactly what Bernard urged his monks to do: felling Goliath with a stone from his sling and, in the next frame, sawing energetically away at the giant's neck with his huge sword.

[105] For the date and circumstances of the manuscript's production, see Zaluska, *L'enluminure de Cîteaux*, 64–73; Conrad Rudolph, *Violence and Daily Life*, Introduction and 97n.

[106] For Job as a spiritual warrior and a model for monks, and for the enduring popularity of the *Moralia in Job*, see Chapter 1.

[107] On the ways in which monastic readers might have used the manuscript, see Rudolph, *Violence and Daily Life*, chapters 4–5, and for representative images of struggle, *ibid.*, figs 2, 4, 12, 21–2, 25, 30–2.

[108] For commentary on this imagery, see Openshaw, 'Weapons in the Daily Battle,' 34–7. For an image of this leaf of the manuscript (fol 36v) and transcription of the Latin text, see Otto Pächt, C.R. Dodwell and Francis Wormald, *The St. Albans Psalter* (London, 1960), 163–4 and plate 41. Though most recent scholarship has suggested that the Psalter was created for Christina, Donald Matthew has recently argued that it may have originally belonged to her spiritual mentor, the monk-turned-hermit Roger ('The Incongruities in the St Albans Psalter,' *Journal of Medieval History* 34 (2008), 396–416), for whom this imagery of spiritual battle would have been equally well-suited.

[109] Illuminated Psalters of the period often contain illustrations of the enemies of the righteous who are described in many of the prayers, and depict David not only as a king but battling Goliath; see Alexander, 'Ideological Representation of Military Combat,' 15; Howard Helsinger, 'Images on the *Beatus* Page of Some Medieval Psalters,' *Art Bulletin* 53 (1971), 161–76 (esp. 165–8).

these visible arms have been made from iron and wood ... it is necessary for each of us settled in [a life of] warfare and penance (*in bello et penitentia*), to be armed with faith and love (*caritas*), so that we may approach the heavenly blessings and gain the angelic crown of life. ... Let the cloistered, and those with hearts that are manly, temperate, and chaste, and every faithful disciple, meditate by day and night upon that war and divine inheritance.[110]

After studying the text and accompanying images over a period of years, would the image of Christina as a spiritual warrior, tilting against the devil in spiritual armor, have arisen unbidden in her mind's eye? This certainly seems to be what the manuscript's creator intended.

Allegories of single combat shed light on a lively dialogue about different forms of religious life in which coenobitic monks, members of the new semi-eremitic orders, and hermits all took part. This imagery reveals that the ambivalence some living in community felt about the solitary life was balanced by the great admiration other monks felt for hermits as elite fighters within the spiritual army. These allegories also help us understand how monks and hermits defined themselves in relation to one other, with members of both groups accepting and defending Benedict's assessment that solitaries were possessed of greater fortitude than their coenobitic counterparts. The ideal of the *miles Christi* as single combatant underscored the necessity for individuals to develop defenses against the devil, even within the security of the claustral battle line, and reminded those who lived alone that even in the seclusion of the cell they had only to call upon divine aid for it to be present. Finally, the prominence of martial rhetoric in instructional works composed by monks for female solitaries, who figured prominently in the eremitic revival of this period, indicates that churchmen did not seek to bar women from spiritual combat, though they exhorted female protegées to cultivate 'masculine' qualities in order to compete with male *milites Christi*.[111]

---

[110] Pächt et al., *St. Albans Psalter*, 163–4: 'Quicumque vult esse filius dei et dignus heres celorum et quicumque vult adimere gloriam et hereditatem, quas diaboli a regno dei elapsi amiserunt, nocte ac die occulo et corde speculetur illud bellum et equitationem quae hic viderit protracta. Sicut hec visibilia arma ferro et ligno sunt parata ... similiter autem quemque nostrum in bello et penitentia constitutum, fide et caritate oportet armari, ut celestibus bonis appropinquemus et coronam vitae angelicam percipiamus. ... de illo bello et divina hereditate meditantur die ac nocte boni claustrales et virilia corda sobria et casta et quisque fidelis discipulus.'

[111] Exhortations to 'act manfully (*viriliter agite*)' are common in these works. See, for example, Goscelin of Saint-Bertin's *Liber Confortatorius*, book 2, ed. Talbot, 47; and, if we accept that the *Saint Albans Psalter* was intended for the use of Christina of Markyate, the treatise on spiritual combat in that work (see above, n.108–10). For a fuller discussion of the gendering of spiritual combat, see Katherine Allen Smith, 'Spiritual Warriors in Citadels of Faith: Martial Rhetoric and Monastic Masculinity in the Long Twelfth Century,' in *Negotiating Clerical Identities: Priests, Monks, and Masculinity in the Middle Ages*, ed. Jennifer D. Thibodeaux (London, 2010), 86–110.

Jesus as warrior, abbot as warrior

If each monk was an armored spiritual warrior, his monastic superior was a courageous general, standing in the place of Christ, the supreme commander of the heavenly armies. Like the other clusters of imagery considered above, depictions of abbots and Christ as warriors or war leaders drew upon scriptural themes and exegetical and hagiographical conventions even while they reflected contemporary concerns. As we saw in Chapter 1, the portrayal of Christ as a warrior triumphing over death became common in Late Antiquity and persisted throughout the early Middle Ages. Patristic and Carolingian exegesis, particularly commentaries on the Psalms and Revelation, also encouraged the interpretation of Christ as a triumphant war leader.[112] The latter book's description of the 'faithful and true' rider upon a white horse, leading the heavenly armies to victory over the armies of the Beast (Rev. 19:11–21), was originally read as an allegory of the resurrected Christ or of the Church triumphant. But from the Carolingian period monastic exegetes like Haimo of Auxerre had associated these verses with spiritual warfare and encouraged the reader to imitate the Christ-warrior's combat with the devil by 'first conquering the devil in himself, so that he may conquer him afterwards in others.'[113] Later exegetes followed early medieval precedent in their Christological readings of the apocalyptic horseman.[114] The Psalms' many references to God as an armed warrior, leading his people into battle and visiting destruction upon their enemies, were also natural points of departure for monastic meditations on Christ as war leader.

Sources for the figure of the abbot as warrior are more elusive, although the topos is found in hagiography by the Carolingian period, and may well have earlier roots.[115] Unlike the conception of the abbot as mother, depictions of the abbacy in military terms pre-date the monastic reform movements of the Central Middle Ages, although they may reflect the new emphasis placed on the abbot as *magister* and spiritual trainer by members of many new religious orders.[116] Neither Cassian nor Benedict presented the abbot in this way, though Benedict emphasized that Christ was made present in the monastery through

---

[112] For medieval exegesis of the Psalms' martial imagery, see Chapter 1.

[113] For this citation and commentary, see Douglas W. Lumsden, *And Then the End Will Come: Early Latin Christian Interpretations of the Opening of the Seven Seals* (London, 2001), 88–9. The quote is from Haimo of Auxerre, *Expositio in Apocalypsin B. Joannis*, 2.6, PL 117: 1025: 'Vincens primo diabolum in seipso, ut vinceret illum postea in aliis ....'

[114] The broad continuity of this interpretation is suggested by a comparison of the works of two Benedictines separated by several centuries: Ambrose Autpert (d.778/9), *Expositio in Apocalypsin*, in *Ambrosii Autperti Opera*, ed. Robert Weber, 3 vols, CCCM 27, 27A-B (Turnhout, 1975–9), 2: 719f.; and Rupert of Deutz (d.1129), *Commentaria in Apocalypsim*, 11.1, PL 169: 1162–3.

[115] For pre-1000 examples, see Chapter 3, n.128.

[116] For the rise of this imagery, see Daniel Marcel La Corte, 'Abbot as *Magister* and *Pater* in the Thought of Bernard of Clairvaux and Aelred of Rievaulx,' in *Truth as Gift: Studies in Cistercian History in Honor of John R. Sommerfeldt*, ed. Marsha Dutton, CS 204 (Kalamazoo, MI, 2004), 389–406.

the person of the abbot, who 'holds the place of Christ' for his monks and was, in recognition of this relationship, to be addressed as 'father (*abbas*)' or 'lord (*dominus*).'[117] This aspect of the superior's identity was the very bedrock of the coenobitic ideal,[118] and likely encouraged the application of metaphors initially associated with Christ to the figure of the abbot. At the same time, it seems probable that the association of the abbacy with military leadership was influenced by the venerable traditions of reading the monk as *miles Christi* and the monastic community as a cohort of *commilitones*.

The abbot-as-war-leader idea reflected a belief that superiors should serve as spiritual exemplars for their monks, modeling the virtues of the *militia Christi* in word and deed. Commemorative poems and sermons composed to mark the passing of holy abbots memorialized them in martial rhetoric, recounting how abbots had led their troops in battle as long as they lived and joined the saints in prayer for their soldiers' victories after their deaths. Odilo of Cluny (d.1048) was remembered to have been like 'a strong tower, fortified above with a shield and ringed around with seven battlements, from which hung the strong arms of men (cf. Song of Sol. 4:4),' making him impregnable to the assaults of the devil.[119] The epitaph Peter the Venerable wrote to honor his late prior, Bernard of Morlaix, reminded all who read it that Bernard's steadfastness in the struggle (*agon*) of religious life had earned him a place alongside the angels in the 'fortresses of heaven (*coelestia castra*).'[120] In a eulogy for Robert of Molesme, the second abbot of Cîteaux, Stephen Harding (d.1134) remembered his predecessor as a paternal figure with whom he had shared a close martial camaraderie, and lamented that he had lost 'not only a father and ruler, but a companion and fellow-soldier (*commilito*), and a remarkable athlete in God's war.'[121] Similar descriptions of abbesses, including the renowned mystic Hildegard of Bingen and Matilda, first abbess of La Trinité, Caen, suggest that female superiors, like their male counterparts, were expected to embody what we might call martial virtues if they were to command the perfect obedience of their charges.[122]

---

[117] For this idea, see RB 2.2, p. 172: 'Abbas autem, quia vices Christi creditur agere, dominus et abbas vocetur, non sua assumptione sed honore et amore Christi; ipse autem cogitet et sic se exhibeat ut dignus sit tali honore.' Cf. RB 63.13–14, p. 278.

[118] Adalbert de Vogüé, *Community and Abbot in the Rule of St Benedict*, trans. Charles Philippi, CS 5/1 (Kalamazoo, MI, 1979), 110–13.

[119] *Planctus de transitu Odilonis abbatis*, PL 142: 1045: 'Dilectus turri comparatur, et mysticis armis munitur. Odilo, dum vixit, virtutum sparsit odores, / Turris erat fortis, clypeus munita supernis, / Quam circumcingebant propugnacula septem, / Fortia pendebant ex illis arma virorum, / Nullus et hanc hostis potuit superare malignus.' For another, slightly earlier Cluniac example of this sort of rhetoric applied to an abbot, see the *Sermo de beato Maiolo*, ed. Dominique Iogna-Prat in *Agni immaculati: Recherches sur les sources hagiographiques relatives à saint Maieul de Cluny (954–99)* (Paris, 1988), 288–9.

[120] *Vita altera (Petri venerabilis abbatis)*, PL 189: 40: 'Hic post militiam coelestia castra subintrans, / Consenuit, certans hoc in agone diu.'

[121] Stephen Harding, *Sermo in obitu praedecessoris sui*, PL 166: 1375.

[122] For Hildegard, see Guibert of Gembloux, Letter 38, in *Guiberti Gemblacensis epistolae*, ed. Albert Derolez, CCCM 66A (Turnhout, 1989), 368–9; for Matilda, see her epitaph in *Rouleaux des morts du IXe au XVe siècle*, ed. Léopold Delisle (Paris, 1866), 181. Abelard

Besides serving as spiritual exemplars, abbots were tasked with training and protecting the monks in their care. While these functions were often articulated through metaphors of shepherding or fathering (both of which occur in the *Rule*), or mothering, medieval authors employed the image of the abbot as militant defender of the community for the same purpose. The twelfth-century Benedictine Peter of Dives praised Boso, fourth abbot of Bec, because during the twelve years he held office he had tirelessly stood guard (*invigilare*) over the monastic encampment, warding off the devil's attacks with spiritual arms.[123] Geoffrey of Auxerre, a secretary of Bernard of Clairvaux who later succeeded his mentor as abbot, preached a sermon to his monks on the anniversary of Bernard's death in which he reminded them how, whenever the great man had returned to the abbey after a trip abroad, he rushed to visit his new recruits (*tirones*), and, despite his frequent absences, had 'trained some eighty men in spiritual arms to serve in his Lord's army.'[124] The failings of unworthy superiors were also interpreted in military terms. Venting his scorn for abbots who shirked their duties, Peter Damian wrote that every superior should not only *appear* to be, but be in truth a 'war leader (*dux belli*),' who bore Christ's battle standard in his lord's absence and refused to be routed. Abbots who fled the spiritual battlefield, showing themselves unworthy even to bring up the rear of their cohort, were reminded of Benedict's warning that they would someday be called to account for all their actions before God.[125] But abbots who lovingly trained new recruits and bravely led them into battle truly stood in the place of Christ to their monks.

As the many images of Christ as a warrior in hagiography and sermons from this period attest, abbots led the monastic army only in Christ's stead, and were themselves soldiers in the *militia Christi*. Monastic authors retold Christ's victory over death and the devil in martial allegories in which he became a conquering king, a brave general, and a stern but generous leader of his troops. As the Cistercian abbot John of Ford (d.1244) preached to his monks, 'Christ's cross and death were formerly his weapons of war, and now they are his victory-

---

also likened the abbess to an *imperator* leading her army of nuns; see Letter 7 to Heloise, PL 178: 266.

[123] Peter of Dives, *Gesta septem abbatum Beccensium*, PL 181: 1717: 'Taliter egregius Boso pastorque peritus, / Invigilans castris Domini ter quattuor annis, / Justitiae tectus lorica vir bene doctus, / Neumatis at gladio sancti praecinctus actuo, / Tum clypeo fidei tutus galeaque salutis, / Fortis ut athleta non segniter intus agebat, / Hostis ab incursu servando suos satagebat.'

[124] Geoffrey of Auxerre, *Sermo in anniversario obitus S. Bernardi*, c.3, PL 185: 575: 'Regressus denique de via, tirones Domini sui confestim visitat, quos ad militiam ejus (si bene memini) circiter octoginta armis spiritualibus instruebat.'

[125] See RB 2.37, p. 178. Peter Damian, Letter 105, ed. Reindel, *Briefe*, 3: 161: 'Illi praecipue qui, ut laborem militiae fugiat, ad eiusdem militiae ducatum inhianter anhelat. Dumque dux belli esse humanis oculis cernitur, in conspectu occulti arbitris malefidus transfuga iudicatur. Fugit enim, qui ut revera pugnandi valeat vitare periculum, simulat se antesignani vice specietenus portare vexillum.'

banner.'¹²⁶ Herbert of Losinga described the Incarnation in terms of the arrival of badly needed reinforcements in the midst of a battle:

> Thus the long-awaited captain (*imperator*) came to the aid of his weary troops, charged the enemy forces, cut them down, captured them, punished them, destroyed them, and consigned that first parricide and father of sin to a shameful punishment in eternal fires.'¹²⁷

The image of the devil as a defeated, disgraced tyrant (likely inspired by Rev. 20: 2–3) was a common one; Goscelin of Saint-Bertin, for instance, envisioned him as bound in chains and imprisoned for eternity, while his demonic troops, deprived of their leader, tried in vain to regroup.¹²⁸

In spite of the victory of the resurrection, Christ's spiritual battle with evil was an ongoing one in which no quarter could be given. To use a common medieval analogy, there could be no peace between the rulers of Jerusalem and Babylon.¹²⁹ This was the struggle of the monk writ on a cosmic scale, and individual *milites Christi* could ask for no better model of soldierly perfection. A parable by the twelfth-century Cistercian Galand of Reigny suggests how the image of Christ's combat with the devil might lend itself to the creation of gruesomely memorable *picturae*. Galand presented his reader with a scene of single combat (*singulare bellum*) between two giant knights (*milites gigantes*) whose sword-blows made the very ground shake.¹³⁰ The wicked knight (i.e., the devil) is of a type often found in monastic chronicles of the period – a cruel villain who delights in indiscriminate slaughter of innocents – while his virtuous opponent (i.e., Christ) seems to reference the emerging model of Christian knighthood with its obligations to protect the defenseless.¹³¹ After providing a blow-by-blow narration of this epic contest, Galand ended with a flourish worthy of the goriest contemporary *chanson de geste*: the good giant, with a single mighty stroke of his

---

126 John of Ford, Sermon 23.3, in *Super extremam partem Cantici Canticorum sermones CXX*, 2 vols, ed. Edmund Mikkers and Hilary Costello, CCCM 17–18 (Turnhout, 1970), 1: 195: 'crux Christi et mors olim quidem arma ei fuerint potentiae, nunc autem uexilla uictoriae.'
127 Herbert of Losinga, Letter 13, ed. Anstruther, *Epistolae*, 24: 'Suis laborantibus copiis expectatus superuenit imperator, hostilibus irruit manibus, cedit, expugnavit, afflixit, extinxit, ipsumque primum paricidam et peccati patrem igniominiosa condemnatione perpetuis in incendiis colligavit.'
128 Goscelin of Saint-Bertin, *Liber Confortatorius*, ed. Talbot, 50–1. Cf. this description of Christ as a warrior in the *Liber* with that in another of Goscelin's works, his *Historia translationis Sancti Augustini* [BHL 777], c.1, PL 80: 50.
129 Bernard of Clairvaux, Parable 2.1, SBO 6/2: 267–8; Honorius Augustodunensis, *Speculum ecclesiae*, PL 172: 1093.
130 Galand of Reigny, Parable 12, ed. Freidlander et al., *Parabolaire*, 208–21. Like all of Galand's parables, this one is provided with a detailed authorial gloss designed to guide the reader's interpretation.
131 The villain's black deeds are described in detail: 'innumeras cotidie populorum cateruas prosternebat. Pueros aeque iuuenes, iuuenes ut senes caedebat, excepto quod aliis hos, aliis illos confodiebat missilibus.' Galand de Reigny, Parable 12.1–2, ed. Friedlander et al., *Parabolaire*, 208–10.

sword, neatly cut the evil knight in two from his head downwards, so that the corpse's two halves fell separately to the ground!¹³²

Christ was also characterized as a warrior in his role as intercessor, fighting on behalf of mankind, winning a great victory, and drawing strength from the faithful, past and present, even as he lost his mortal life. Monastic writers supplied this Christ-knight with a full set of spiritual arms and armor; Peter Damian described how Christ 'constructed a hauberk (*lorica*) for himself out of our frailty, in which, exulting in battle like a strong and powerful giant, he waged war against the powers of the air.'¹³³ Bernard of Clairvaux asked his monks to imagine Christ as a brave warrior who, 'striding, as it were, onto the plain of the world to be anointed for combat with the oil of the Holy Spirit, exulting like a hero to *run the race* (1 Cor. 9:26) for the ransom of humanity,' nonetheless allowed himself to be 'taken captive and bound by the devil.'¹³⁴ John of Ford also glossed Christ's submission as a powerful act of heroism. 'What could display his might more resplendently,' he asked his monks, 'than to have the power to lay down his life as and when he chose, and to take it up again at the time and in the manner of his choosing (John 10:18)?'¹³⁵ Christ not only campaigned against the devil, but lovingly made war on the souls of the faithful. In Bernard of Clairvaux's *Sentences*, Christ was said to be armed with three arrows – chaste fear, devout love, and virtuous desire – with which 'he wounds those whom he invites to taste the sweetness of his love.'¹³⁶ John of Ford called upon the God of the Psalms, with his sword girded on his thigh (cf. Ps. 43:4), to stab his soul and fill it with divine beauty and love, and rejoiced at the thought of being taken captive by Christ.¹³⁷

Monks were no passive observers of Christ's war; on the contrary, they fought under his command, shoulder to shoulder with hermits, martyrs, and angels – all the members of the spiritual armies past and present. Like knights, Julian

---

¹³² Galand of Reigny, Parable 12.3, ed. Friedlander et al., *Parabolaire*, 210–12: 'Nam melioris illius bellatoris framea per medium huius caput librata ita eum usque ad terram fidit medium, ut corporis pars altera ad dexteram, alia rueret ad laevam.' This sort of improbable but highly memorable image frequently appears in contemporary vernacular epics; for examples, see Kaeuper, *Chivalry and Violence*, chapter 7.

¹³³ Peter Damian, Sermon 35, ed. Lucchesi, *Sermones*, 211: 'Loricam quippe sibi de nostra fragilitate composuit, in qua exultans ut gigas et potens ac fortis in praelio (cf. Ps. 18:6, 23:8) potestates aerias debellauit.'

¹³⁴ Bernard of Clairvaux, *Sententia* 3.70, SBO 6/2: 103: 'Itaque inter Deum et hominem medium se faciens, qui recedens a Deo, captus et ligatus est.' Trans. Swietek, *Parables and Sentences*, 242.

¹³⁵ John of Ford, Sermon 23.3, ed. Mikkers and Costello, *Sermons*, 1: 195: 'Quid enim hac uirtute praeclarius qua potestatem habuit ponendi cum uoluit et prout uoluit animam suam, et quando uoluit et quomodo uoluit iterum sumendi eam?' Trans. Wendy Beckett, in *John of Ford: Sermons on the Final Verses of the Song of Songs*, 7 vols, CS 29, 39, 43–7 (Kalamazoo, MI, 1977–84), 1: 190–1.

¹³⁶ Bernard of Clairvaux, *Sententia* 2.13, SBO 6/2: 27: 'Sunt et aliae tres sagittae, quibus Dominus etiam eos sauciat, quos ad degustandum dulcedinem suae dilectionis invitat.' Trans. Swietek, *Parables and Sentences*, 142.

¹³⁷ John of Ford, Sermon 4.1, ed. Mikkers and Costello, *Sermons*, 1: 55–6; cf. Sermon 33.5–6, *ibid.*, 1:258–59. For the theme of captivity: Sermon 63.7–8, *ibid.*, 1: 445–6.

of Vézelay preached, monks went forth under Christ's command against their mortal foes ('evil spirits and bad men'), inflicting upon the latter a terrible defeat, burning the enemy city (the 'city of chaos and confusion') to the ground and putting to the sword all who refused to surrender.[138] In a letter to the prior of Clairvaux, Peter of Celle borrowed from Revelation in his depiction of the Cistercians as a company of knights mounted upon white horses, their white robes stained red because they 'have made their robes white in the blood of the Lamb by resisting vices even unto blood and by attaining even to the suffering of the immaculate Lamb.'[139] Aelred of Rievaulx encouraged his monks to envision themselves marching in battle formation under Christ's command as part of the great army of the saints:

> Behold, today our king, that captain of ours, is coming to see us with his entire army. Let us contemplate, to the best of our ability, all those in his battle line, how beautiful they are, and how well-ordered; let us long for their fellowship, but first let us not flee from the toil that was theirs. The fight is indeed a desperate one, but the thought of eternal reward should make us rejoice. We do not lack support in this battle. All around us are the angels and archangels. Let us look at that captain of ours, standing in the vanguard of his troops, and hear how he exhorts his knights. 'In this world,' he says, 'you shall face persecution (John 16:33).'[140]

Though Aelred broke off without completing the scriptural quotation, his listeners could have supplied the next verse for themselves: 'Take courage, for I have conquered the world.'

The ultimate goal of this great spiritual army was nothing less than the siege and conquest of the kingdom of heaven, an undertaking suggested by Christ's words in Matthew 11:12: 'From the days of John the Baptist until now the kingdom of heaven has suffered violence, and the violent take it by force.' Since mankind's fall, the way to heaven had been blockaded by armies of demons, Goscelin of Saint-Bertin wrote to the anchoress Eva, and only by the 'violence

---

[138] Julian of Vézelay, Sermon 9, ed. Vorreux, *Sermones*, 1: 214–25.
[139] Peter of Celle, Letter 46, ed. and trans. Haseldine, *Letters*, 190–1: 'considero alium in equis albis (Rev. 19:14) chorum certantem non iam pro uictoria sed ad coaceruanda pretiosiora spolia…. Isti sunt qui stolas suas dealbauerunt in sanguine agni (Rev. 7:14) resistendo usque ad sanguinem uitiis et pertingendo usque ad patientam agni immaculati.' Note the play on the word '*chorus*,' which can mean a monastic choir or a troop of soldiers (and here has both meanings).
[140] Aelred of Rievaulx, Sermon 23, PL 195: 340–1: 'Ecce hodie rex, ipse imperator noster, cum omni suo nos visitat exercitu. Consideremus, quantum possumus, omnes acies ejus, quam sunt pulchrae, quam sunt ordinatae; desideremus eorum societatem, sed primo non refugiamus eorum laborem. Gravis quidem est pugna, sed debet nos delectare corona. Non deest nobis auxilium in hac pugna. Sunt circa nos angeli, archangeli …. Videamus ergo in prima fronte ipsum imperatorem nostrum; audiamus quodmodo hortatur milites suos. In hoc, inquit, mundo pressuram habebitis (John 16:33).' Trans. based on Theodore Berkeley and M. Basil Pennington, *Aelred of Rievaulx: The Liturgical Sermons: The First Clairvaux Collection*, CF 58 (Kalamazoo, MI, 2001), 356.

of virtues (*violentia virtutum*)' could spiritual soldiers hope to break through and carry off the rich spoils of salvation.[141] 'Be armed,' Guerric of Igny commanded his monks, 'with the power of love, if you would force your way into the kingdom of heaven as a pious invader (*pius invasor*).' He instructed them to imagine themselves as a cohort following John the Baptist into heavenly battle:

> Gird yourselves, I say, men of courage; and follow the leader and master of this happy militia – I speak of John the Baptist – from whose days heaven begins to be open to assault (*expugnabile*).... Follow, I say, this leader, whose banners are red with his own blood, whose deeds and triumphs you have chanted today with proper veneration.[142]

In a letter to Fulk, an apostate canon, Bernard of Clairvaux warned that Fulk's *commilitones* would conquer the kingdom of heaven without him unless he speedily returned to his community. 'The Lord himself is present as our supporter and guardian (*adiutor et susceptor*),' Bernard assured him, 'who teaches our hands to fight and our fingers to make war (Ps. 143:1).' If Christ, the commander leading the siege of his own citadel, did not recognize Fulk in the heat of the battle, he would certainly not remember him on the Last Day.[143]

For monastic writers, depicting Christ as a warrior was a way of articulating particular truths about salvation and intercession, and insisting on the limited power of evil. Just as Christ might be invoked in a maternal guise by writers wishing to emphasize his 'feminine' capacity for nurturing and unconditional love, and to promote these virtues within the monastery,[144] casting Christ as a powerful war leader enabled these same writers to promote 'masculine' qualities, such as fortitude and bravery, which were no less essential to the monk. As the commander of the monastic militia Christ modeled martial *virtus* for his soldiers, and contemplating Christ's triumphs – or even meditatively partici-

---

[141] Goscelin of Saint-Bertin, *Liber Confortatorius*, ed. Talbot, 51: 'Quia ex quo homo peccando illud perdidit, iam indebitum longe aufertur, nisi per violentam virtutum rapiatur. Aerie potestates et principes tenebrarum omnem celi regionem densis agminibus occluserunt, nulli aditum nis expugnati concedunt.'

[142] Guerric of Igny, Second Sermon for John the Baptist, c.3–4, ed. Morson and Costello, *Sermones*, 2: 332–4: ' Virtute igitur dilectionis armatus sis, quicumque es ille pius invasor qui rapere contendis regnum coelorum .... Accingimini, inquam, viri virtutis; et sequimini ducem ac magistrum felicis huius militiae, Ioannem Baptistam loquor, a diebus cuius coelem esse coepit expugnabile.... Sequimini, inquam, ducem istum, cuius vexilla proprio rutilant sanguine, cuius hodie virtutes ac triumphos debita decantastis veneratione.' Trans. based on Monks of Mount Saint Bernard, *Sermons*, 2: 334. Note Guerric's use of the second-person plural as a hortatory device.

[143] Bernard of Clairvaux, Letter 2.12, SBO 7: 22: 'adest ipse Dominus adiutor et susceptor, qui doceat manus tuas ad proelium et digitos tuos ad bellum (Ps. 143:1). Procedamus in adiutorium fratrum, ne si forte sine nobis pugnent, sine nobis vincant, sine nobis ingrediantur, novissime, cum clausa fuerit ianua, sero pulsantibus de intus nobis repondeatur: Amen dico vobis, nescio vos (Matt. 25:12). ... Sic te Christi agnoscit in bello, recognoscet in caelo ....'

[144] Bynum, 'Jesus as Mother, Abbot as Mother: Some Themes in Twelfth-Century Cistercian Writing,' in *Jesus as Mother*, 110–69.

pating in them – was in itself a form of *imitatio Christi*. If Christ was the ultimate spiritual warrior, a more accessible martial role-model was the abbot who led the *militia Christi* in Christ's stead. Images of superiors as military commanders, like comparisons of them to parents or shepherds, had a special meaning within monastic culture. As a spiritual war leader the abbot commanded unquestioningly obedience, but was in turn bound to train and protect his faithful soldiers and prove himself worthy of their loyalty.

Citadels of faith besieged

The imaginations of their inhabitants transformed monasteries, and even monks themselves, into fortresses, modeled on the Scriptural *castra Dei* defended by angelic warriors (Gen. 32:2) and the tower of David hung all over with the shields of heroes (Song of Sol. 4:4).[145] But monastic writers who outfitted their model spiritual warriors with the latest arms and armor and found homiletic inspiration in contemporary battles were hardly unaware that they were living in a great age of castle-building and innovations in military architecture and siege warfare.[146] As we saw in Chapter 1, the relationship between castle and monastery was too complicated to be described in terms of simple opposition; religious communities were founded within fortresses or upon sites where these had once stood (and sometimes built with the very same stones), abbots controlled and built castles to protect the interests of their communities, and even fortified claustral buildings in dangerous times. Various castle allegories developed by monastic writers combined exegetical sophistication with vivid *picturae* as a means of addressing the spiritual concerns particular to monks. In the first place, the monastery or hermitage was likened to a fortress surrounded by demonic hordes and defended by spiritual knights armed with prayer and virtue.[147] Monastic sermons also encouraged monks to meditatively fortify their souls, making them stronger than any castle constructed of wood or stone, as indeed they needed to be; unlike its worldly counterparts, the fortress of the soul was perpetually under siege. Once built, such strongholds could be used indefi-

---

[145] For a handlist of castle imagery in medieval ecclesiastical writing, see Roberta D. Cornelius, 'The Figurative Castle: A Study in the Mediaeval Allegory of the Edifice with Especial Reference to Religious Writings' (Unpub. PhD thesis, Bryn Mawr, 1930), 82–3.

[146] Malcolm Hebron has shown that the proliferation of castles and increase in siege warfare in the Central Middle Ages was accompanied by a heightened interest in allegorical sieges on the part of ecclesiastical writers, who filled their descriptions with very contemporary details; see *The Medieval Siege: Theme and Image in Middle English Romance* (Oxford, 1997), 142–3.

[147] Such descriptions seem to evoke the function of religious communities as strongholds of peace in times of civil strife; for example, William of Newburgh wrote that an unusually large number of monasteries were founded as '*castra Dei*' in England during the civil-war-torn reign of Stephen (*Historia rerum anglicarum*, 1.15, in *Chronicles of the Reigns of Stephen*, ed. Howlett, 1: 53).

nitely as settings for the drama of spiritual warfare,[148] where monastic warriors could test the martial skills they had developed as new recruits and honed as members of the *militia Christi*.

Allegorical castles descended in an exegetical genealogy from the detailed descriptions of the temple of Solomon in Ezekiel 40–44 and the heavenly Jerusalem in Revelation 21:12–27.[149] Although these passages do not feature siege imagery – and, in fact, the latter text expressly described a future in which the end of wars would render all fortifications unnecessary – later writers who knew their audiences would be familiar with these settings often borrowed their features for use in *picturae* of spiritual sieges. The theme of the soul-siege appeared in patristic treatises as early as the third century, when Cyprian spoke of the devil prowling around the ramparts of the soul, testing the strength of its gates and seeking a weak point by which he might force an entrance.[150] Cassian, in his *Institutes*, warned that vices harbored in one's mind would attack the 'citadel of virtues (*arx virtutum*)' therein, sack the city of the soul, and enslave its inhabitants.[151] The exegetical works of Gregory the Great, which, as we have seen, profoundly shaped the monastic *miles Christi* ideal, repeatedly returned to the theme of the besieged soul. Gregory also laid the groundwork for what would become a popular contemplative exercise in later monastic culture: the meditative siege of the heavenly Jerusalem, which pitted attacking vices and temptations against defending virtues.[152] Looking forward to the eleventh and twelfth centuries, we see an unprecedented explosion of architectural allegory, including castle allegories, in monastic texts, many of which moved beyond Scriptural models to incorporate familiar features from contemporary buildings.[153]

Comparisons of the monastery, or the Church more generally, to a castle reflected the belief that the cloister was both a refuge from worldly wickedness – the 'strong tower' of the Psalms[154] – and a tempting target for demonic armies.

---

[148] For the more general use of architectural forms in monastic meditation, see Carruthers, *Craft of Thought*, 237–40, 257–69, who emphasizes how buildings once created in the mind were often 'revisited' and even 'remodeled,' so to speak, in meditation.

[149] For overviews of allegorical buildings in Christian tradition from the Scriptures to the later medieval period, including some of the references discussed here, see Hebron, *Medieval Siege*, 136–42; Jill Mann, 'Allegorical Buildings in Medieval Literature,' *Medium Ævum* 63 (1994), 191–210 (esp. 191–7); and Christiania Whitehead, *Castles of the Mind: A Study of Medieval Architectural Allegory* (Cardiff, 2003), 87–116.

[150] Cyprian, *Liber de zelo et livore*, c.2, PL 4: 639: 'Circuit ille nos singulos, et tamquam hostis clausos obsidens, muros explorat, et tentat an sit pars aliqua murorum minus stabilis et minus fida, cujus aditu ad interiora penetretrur.'

[151] Cassian, *Institutiones*, 12.3.2, ed. Guy, 452–4.

[152] Gregory the Great, *Moralia in Job*, Preface 4, ed. Adriaen, 1: 14; cf. idem, *Homiliarum in Evangelia libri duo*, 7.1, PL 76: 1100. For the meditative building and besieging of the heavenly city, see the *Regula pastoralis*, 2.10, ed. Floribert Rommel and trans. Charles Morel as *Règle pastorale*, CS 381–2 (Paris, 1992), 1: 244–8.

[153] Christiania Whitehead, 'Making a Cloister of the Soul in Medieval Religious Treatises,' *Medium Ævum* 67 (1998), 1–29 (at 2).

[154] For this comparison, see Odo of Cluny, Sermon 2, in *Sermones quinque*, PL 133: 716. The reference is to Ps. 60:4 ('Esto mihi turris fortitudinis, a facie inimici.') Cf. the Benedictine

Evil spirits were thought to desire the conquest of this holy fortress as ardently as spiritual warriors themselves wished to capture the heavenly city. Having fled the world for the *castra Dei*, monks were henceforth obliged to defend these spiritual strongholds.[155] In one of his most influential works, the *Liber qui dicitur 'Dominus vobiscum*,*'* Peter Damian offered a breathtakingly vivid description of the monastic cell as a fortress:

> O cell, you are the tent of the holy army, the battle line of the victorious array, the camp of God (cf. Gen. 32:2), the tower of David, built as a fortress, hung round with a thousand bucklers, and each the shield of a hero (Song of Sol. 4:4)! ... You are a rampart (*vallum*) for those rushing to battle, a bulwark (*munitio*) for the brave, a defense for fighters who know not the word 'surrender.' Let the barbarous fury of the surrounding enemy rage, let them advance under cover and hurl their missiles, and let the brandishing swords press all around you like a forest. Those who stand within you, armed with the breastplate of faith (cf. Eph. 6:14), dance for joy under the unconquerable protection of Christ their commander and celebrate their victory over an enemy who has already gone down to certain defeat.[156]

Bernard of Clairvaux encouraged his monks to think of their church as a recognizably twelfth-century fortress, the various elements of which he described with great precision: at the center was a castle (*castrum*), well-stocked with arms and supplies, and surrounded by an inner wall (*murus*) of chastity and an outer wall (*antemurale*) of patience, which served to hold back the enemies swarming on all sides.[157] Another Cistercian, Galand of Reigny, likened the monastery to a 'fortified city (Ps. 30:22)' in which the abbot and his officers were the towers and the thick walls, 'bound together by the cement of love,' the monks.[158] *Picturae* like these were meant to convey the need for vigilant self-control within the cloister,

---

abbot-bishop Bruno of Asti's depiction of the Church as a fortress defended by armies of angels and virtues; *Commentarium in Lucam, Pars 1*, 10.22, PL 165: 390–1.

[155] For this sentiment, see Hildebert of Lavardin, Sermon 29, *Sermones*, PL 171: 876; Abelard, Letter 7 (*Regula monialum*), PL 178: 266.

[156] Peter Damian, Letter 28, ed. Reindel, *Briefe*, 1: 273–4: 'O cella sacrae miliciae tabernaculum, procinctus triumphatoris exercitus, castra Dei, turris David, quae aedificata es cum propugnaculis: mille clipei pendent ex te, omnis armatura fortium (Song of Sol. 4:4)! ... Tu vallum in expeditione currentium, tu munitio fortium, tu praesidium cedere nescentium bellatorum. Fremat hostium circumfusa barbaries, accedant vinea falaricis, millilia iaculentur, vibrantium gladiorum silva densescat. Qui in te sunt, lorica fidei praemuniti sub imperatoris sui invicta protectione tripudiant, et de hostium suorum certa iam deiectione triumphant ....' Trans. Blum, *Letters*, 1: 282–3. Cf. Peter the Venerable's similar, though much briefer, description of Cluny (above, n.58).

[157] Bernard of Clairvaux, *In dedicatione ecclesiae, sermo 3*, c.1, SBO 5: 379–80; discussed in Leclercq, *Monks and Love*, 95. Cf. the imagery of the *castra* of Wisdom in *Parabola* 1.5, SBO 6/2: 264–5; and the soul-fortress in the Pseudo-Bernardine sermon *In Assumptione B. Mariae Virginis*, PL 184: 1001–10. Aelred of Rievaulx also described the monastery (or rather, monastic life) as a fortress in which each monk and superior was assigned a particular post to defend; see Sermon 15, PL 195: 294.

[158] Galand de Regny, *Petit livre de proverbes*, 37, ed. and trans. Jean Châtillon, Maurice Dumontier, and Alexis Grélois, SC 436 (Paris, 1998), 88: 'In cenobio monachorum, uelut in ciuitate munita (Ps. 30:22).... Porro huius urbis turres tam abbates quam ceteri

which, though it might be taken for a safe haven, was in fact as dangerous as any worldly battlefield.

The soul of the individual *miles Christi* was understood to be a fortress against which the devil brought to bear his vast collection of siege-machines.[159] Monastic meditations on this theme often built on exegesis of the story of Mary and Martha as told in Luke 10:38–42, which begins: 'Now it came to pass, as they went, that [Jesus] entered into a certain town (*castellum*).' Though the term *castellum* had referred to a walled town when Jerome made his translation, later readers saw in this verse a reference to the military strongholds (*castra* or *castelli*) of their own day.[160] In a sermon for the feast of the Assumption, Aelred of Rievaulx exhorted his monks to 'make ready a spiritual castle (*castellum*)' within themselves, complete with tower (*turris*), wall (*murus*), and moat (*fossatum*), in order that Christ might dwell there as he had within the *castellum* of the Virgin Mary.[161] The preacher led his listeners through each step of the construction process, labeling the *castellum*'s features with virtues indispensable to the monk: first, the moat was created by hollowing out the heart, removing the dirt of human frailty to lay bare the low ground of humility (*humilitas*); then a strong wall, symbolizing chastity (*castitas*), was erected around it; and finally, a tall tower of love or charity (*caritas*) was erected above the rest. Aelred used various military scenarios to explain how the three virtues supported one another. Without a wall to defend it enemies could fill in the moat with earth, but even if the enemy were to scale the wall those within the tower would remain secure.[162] Like the castle-body of the Virgin, the soul of the monk was thus fortified with humility and love, its gates permanently sealed by chastity so that none but Christ could enter.[163] With its connotations of unyielding strength and sealed-off invulnerability, the castle was a significant choice of metaphor for the monastic

---

priores uel prelati sunt.... Murus autem, ex ipsis fratribus ordinatim distributis, et amoris cemento ligatis fit.'

[159] For a brief genealogy of this motif, see J.F. Doubleday, 'The Allegory of the Soul as Fortress in Old English Poetry,' *Anglia* 88 (1970), 503–8.

[160] As pointed out by Wheatley, *Idea of the Castle*, 179.

[161] Aelred of Rievaulx, Sermon 17, *Sermones*, PL 195: 303–4; trans. Berkeley and Pennington, *Liturgical Sermons*, 264. Cf. Aelred's Sermon 14, PL 195: 290–1. On the symbolism of this sermon, see Wheatley, *Idea of the Castle*, pp. 78–89; and Cornelius, *Figurative Castle*, 49–50.

[162] Aelred of Rievaulx, Sermon 17, *Sermones*, PL 195: 304–5: 'Ille est murus, qui servat istud fossatum, de quo locuti sumus, ut non possit impleri ab hostibus. Nam, si quis perdit castitatem, statim cor totum impletur sordibus et immunditiis, ut humilitas, id est spirituale fossatum omnino pereat in corde. ... Sine ista turri infirmum est istud spirituale castellum, do quo loquimur.... quia non habet turrim, inimicus ejus transit murum, et occidit animam ejus.'

[163] Cistercian writers may have developed this idea from a Benedictine tradition exemplified by Ralph d'Escures (d.1122), who presents this interpretation as an exegetical reading of Luke 10:38 ('ipse intravit in quoddam castellum'); see his *Homilia de assumptione Mariae* (pub. as a work of Anselm: *Homiliae*, 9), PL 158: 644–9 (esp. 645). Cf. the similar reading of this verse by the Benedictine abbot Geoffrey of Admont (d.1165), Homily 65, *Homiliae Festivales*, PL 174: 959–71 (esp. 964). For more examples of the Virgin as *castellum*, see Fulton, *From Judgment to Passion*, 248–9 and 259–61.

community, and by extension, the monastic body; purged of internal enemies and tirelessly policed from within, the monk's body (or body of monks) was an impregnable citadel of virtue.

But the devil was always watching and waiting, as Bernard of Clairvaux warned, for his chance 'to assault the walls of virtue and cast down the citadel of reason.'[164] Moreover, the enemy army which had invested the walls of the soul-castle knew well how to turn its defenders into traitors. Honorius Augustodunensis described the passions and vices as factions of mutinous citizens who would, if given the chance, overwhelm the garrison of virtues and surrender the soul-castle to the enemy.[165] The monk must take care to fortify his citadel with the words of Scripture, the sacraments, and good works, wrote the Cistercian Thomas of Perseigne (d.1190), and, equipped with spiritual arms, prepare to do battle against the devil on its ramparts.[166] If the interior castle fell through the weakness of its defenders, the soul would be carried off into captivity, cast into a hellish dungeon and guarded by demons. John of Ford spun a cautionary tale for his monks about the dangers of letting down one's guard for even a moment:

> How often it happens, Lord Jesus, that I feel the castle of my soul is beset by an oppressive siege and hemmed in on all sides, on one hand the pains of death, on the other, the pains of hell (cf. Ps. 17:5–6)! Then there are the torrents of iniquity, more terrible than an army in battle array (cf. Song of Sol. 6:9), that ring me round and blockade me in and mount an attack. At the sight of so mighty a host, my soul is seized with trembling, I cannot withstand the length of the siege, and all of a sudden I hand myself over as a prisoner, afflicted by immeasurable pain. I am swept off, loaded with chains, and hurled into a narrow dungeon, into the thick darkness of passionate grief.[167]

---

[164] On the interior castle taken over by sin, and retaken by virtue with Christ's aid, see Bernard of Clairvaux, *Sententiae* 3.12, 3.24, 3.98, SBO 6/2: 27, 82–3, 163 (here 163): 'Virtutum muros arietes huiusmodi concutiunt, arcem deiciunt rationis.' Trans. Swietek, *Parables & Sentences*, 323. Cf. the account of the siege of the city of Wisdom in Parable 1.6, SBO 6/2: 265.

[165] Honorius Augustodunensis, *Speculum ecclesiae*, PL 172: 1097: 'Hoc castellum a turba hostium exterius obsidetur, a factione civium interius commovetur dum proximi exteriora damna ei inferunt, vicia autem et carnis desideria interiora bona obruunt.'

[166] Thomas of Perseigne, *Cantica Canticorum* (commenting on Song of Sol. 4.4), PL 206: 410–12, 415.

[167] John of Ford, Sermon 22.10, ed. Mikkers and Costello, *Sermons*, 1: 191–2: 'Quotiens mihi, Domine Iesu, cum castrum mentis meae graui quadam obsidione uallari sentirem et circumdarent illud undique hinc dolores mortis (cf. Ps. 17:5–6), inde dolores inferi, sed et torrentes iniquitatis, quae est terribilior acies hostium (cf. Song of Sol. 6:9), in giro obsiderent et expugnarent illud, mens mea ante faciem tanti exercitus tremefacta et longam obsidionem non sustinens, subito in captiuitatem immensi doloris manus dedit. Raptusque et catenatus in carcerantes angustias ac densissimas tenebras tristitiae uehementis proiectus sum....' Trans. Beckett, *Sermons on the Final Verses*, 2: 112–13.

While conversion to the monastic life was itself a form of liberation from the 'prison of captives' that was the world, those living in the cloister needed to be as vigilant as any worldly castellan.[168]

If the soul-fortress was to be defended unto death, monastic warriors were, as we have seen, equally strongly encouraged to attack the heavenly city of Jerusalem, batter down the heavenly gates and take their salvation by force. The meditative besieging of paradise, which had long been represented as a citadel in Christian texts,[169] was suggested by the command of Ezekiel 4:1–2: 'Take a tile, and lay it before you, and draw upon it the plan of the city of Jerusalem. And lay siege to it, and build fortifications, and cast up a mount, and set up a camp against it, and place battering rams around it.' Early medieval writers had associated this passage with struggle against vices and demons,[170] and later monks used it as the basis for meditations on spiritual sieges of the heavenly city, in which they were as likely to be defenders as assailants. Julian of Vézelay recommended that monks contemplatively construct the heavenly Jerusalem within their hearts, beginning, as Aelred of Rievaulx's spiritual castle-builder had, by digging up earth to make a ditch with a tall rampart (*agger*) all around, even knowing that as soon as the castle's defences began to be erected an enemy army would arrive and invest it. But though the enemy placed their battering rams all around the perimeter and shook the walls with great blows of temptation (*tentationum crebres ictus*), Julian assured his listeners that the ramparts could not be breached, because both the inner and outer walls were built out of Christ himself.[171]

The construction and defense of mental fortresses was an integral part of contemplative practice within the monastery, and, by extension, of monastic spirituality. Castles were by no means the only allegorical buildings used for such exercises – churches and cloisters were also employed in meditations on monastic life and virtues in this period[172] – but the castle, like other types of martial *picturae*, served a didactic function these other edifices did not. A castle allegory was a uniquely effective means of conveying to monks a sense of the fragile, precious nature of their souls and reminding them how dangerous it was to lower their defences against evil. Comparisons of the monastery or soul to a

---

[168] For the world as a 'prison of captives (*carcer captivorum*),' and hell as a perpetual imprisonment, see Bernard of Clairvaux, *Sententiae* 3.91, SBO 6/2: 142.

[169] Pierre Riché, 'Les représentations du palais dans les textes littéraires du Haut Moyen Âge,' *Francia* 4 (1976), 161–71 (esp. 168–9).

[170] See the highly influential reading by Gregory the Great in his *Homiliarum in Ezechielem*, 1.12.23, PL 76: 929–32.

[171] Julian of Vézelay, Sermon 5, ed. Vorreux, *Sermones*, 1: 146: 'aggerat aggerem et cordis intima replet terra ut nil caeleste cogitare possit homo interior, circa terrena curis multiplicibus occupatus. Dehinc ad murum urbis intimae conquassandum arietes ponuntur in giro (cf. Ezek. 4:1–2) et tentationum crebris ictibus propulsatur. Sed si Saluator in urbe murus est et antemurale (Isa. 26:1), pulsari murus potest, subrui non potest.'

[172] The most widely read of these was probably the mid-twelfth-century *De claustro animae* by Augustinian Hugh of Fouilloy (d.c.1172), PL 176: 1017–82; on which see Christiania Whitehead, 'Making a Cloister of the Soul,' 3–9.

fortress ultimately stemmed from Scripture and exegetical traditions, but new developments in the world beyond the monastery lent these a new immediacy after c.1000. When professed religious encountered allegorical fortresses in the Bible, liturgy, or sermons preached in chapter, they quite naturally 'saw' these in their mind's eye in familiar, contemporary guises, as moated wooden towers or stone keeps surrounded by curtain walls. Once constructed in the mind, such edifices, likely modeled on castles which the visionaries had seen or even lived in, could be endlessly visited, added to, and defended. Like the monastery itself, the soul-castle served a two-fold function: it was both a place of refuge for the inner self and a stage for the enactment of epic spiritual battles. This latter function allowed the monk's spiritual self to don spiritual armor and confront enemies even while his physical self remained peacefully at prayer in the cloister.

Conclusion

Medieval writers employed martial metaphors to describe every imaginable aspect of the monastic experience. But this language is more significant than the term 'metaphor' implies; monks were *like* warriors, but they also *were* warriors, insofar as constant use of elaborate martial imagery helped shape monastic self-perception.[173] Spiritual progress within the religious community was understood in military terms, daily activities and obligations such as private prayer, communal liturgical performances, and ascetic practices cast as battles, and martial analogies used to define hierarchies and explore relationships within the monastery. Martial rhetoric was applied to Christ and abbots as a way of emphasizing particular qualities – strength, fortitude, courage – that monks should cultivate as part of their *imitatio Christi*. The language of spiritual warfare, which veteran monks spoke fluently, possessed its own specialized vocabulary and particular turns of phrase which would have set off long chains of association in the minds of initiates accustomed to thinking exegetically. We can also speak of a distinctly monastic practice of martial meditation which encouraged professed religious to imagine the experience of battle, and even build castles in their minds, in so doing learning to fight off temptation and cultivate virtue. As a concept and a practice, spiritual warfare was an integral part of monastic culture in the Central Middle Ages.

As we saw in the previous chapter, the concept of spiritual combat informed Christian life from the Church's earliest beginnings, but in the eleventh and twelfth centuries it gained a level of prominence, especially in monastic circles, it had previously held only in the age of the martyrs. During this period monks filled their letters, sermons, and *vitae* with military allegories that were more

---

[173] On metaphors as more than mere words, but mediators between the ideal and the real, and in this sense constitutive of reality, see Constable, 'Medieval Latin Metaphors,' 19; and for a more theoretical discussion on which Constable builds, George Lakoff, 'The Contemporary Theory of Metaphor,' in *Metaphor and Thought*, 2nd edn, ed. Andrew Ortony (Cambridge, 1993), 202–52 (esp. 245–50).

elaborate, and more graphic in their depiction of violence, than anything their patristic or Carolingian predecessors had imagined.[174] While the conceptual framework and exegetical tools for understanding the monastic life as a war of the spirit had been put in place by patristic writers, these earlier thinkers seem to have written about spiritual warfare less, and certainly less vividly, than their later medieval successors. How, then, can we explain the veritable explosion of military metaphors and related meditative practices after c.1000? It seems to have been the result of a confluence of factors, reflecting changes within monastic life as well as developments in the world outside the monastery. One of the most significant internal shifts involved recruitment to the religious life, as most new orders rejected child oblates in favor of older adolescents and adult converts. As we saw in Chapter 2, most of these converts came from families of arms-bearers, and many would have entered the religious life with personal experience of military training and combat.[175] Several scholars have hypothesized that martial rhetoric was specifically directed at such men, and that it helped to ease their transition from a life dedicated to war to one centered on prayer and the cultivation of humility. According to this argument, military imagery demonstrated the value of certain 'knightly' virtues within the monastic life, such as loyalty, camaraderie, and fortitude, and helped to explain new theological ideas to converts in familiar, readily understandable terms.[176]

While such an explanation is quite convincing with regard to writings by members of the Cistercians and other new orders, it cannot explain the significance of similar rhetoric in the writings of Cluniacs and traditional Benedictines (who were likely to be surrounded by, and to be themselves, monks who were former oblates), or authors with neither familial connections to nor firsthand experience of the world of arms-bearers. Considering martial rhetoric thematically, as this chapter has done, shows that particular themes cut across orders, and were linked to particular challenges, values, and stages of development within the monastic experience. That similar images appear in the writings of monks and hermits of varying personal backgrounds and affiliations reflects, to be sure, the shared heritage of Scripture, patristic exegesis and hagiography, and Benedict's *Rule*, as well as the fact that no order constituted a hermetically sealed thought-world. But the martial rhetoric used by monastic authors of all orders also reflects their engagement with the world outside the cloister. Consider that Julian of Vézelay opened a sermon by reminding his fellow monks of the *Rule*'s warning that 'one does not repeat within the monastery what one has seen or heard in the outside world,' but then proceeded to share the news of a military

---

[174] I am grateful to Matt Kuefler, whose expertise in the earlier material far exceeds my own, for this observation.
[175] On this shift, see Chapter 2.
[176] For this position, see Newman, *Boundaries of Charity*, 33 and 268–9, n.47; and Hugh M. Thomas, *Vassals, Heiresses, Crusaders, and Thugs: The Gentry of Angevin Yorkshire* (Philadelphia, PA, 1993), 142.

victory recently won by Christians in the crusader states, because he felt his brother-monks could learn a great deal from this event.[177]

Such an attitude is hardly surprising when we remember that by Julian's day church leaders had been holding up pious arms-bearers as models of Christian virtue and behavior for a century and more. The expansion of the concept of the *miles Christi* in the early crusading era theoretically allowed lay and monastic combatants to meet on the spiritual battlefield, even as most worldly warfare continued to be condemned as *malitia* and the ritual purity of all clerics ensured by their distancing from actual bloodshed. By creating and meditating on military allegories monks imaginatively indulged in activities forbidden to them in practice, but, more importantly, they asserted their status as the true *milites Christi* and claimed their traditional place at the front line of the spiritual army. What is more, these monastic soldiers of Christ appeared at the front lines bearing arms and armor borrowed, metaphorically speaking, from contemporary knights, ready with battlefield orations that mingled biblical exegesis with tales of recent martial heroics. In an age when lay arms-bearers were exposed to the influence of monastic spirituality through various avenues, the martial rhetoric considered above offers evidence that monks were equally willing to appropriate symbols and scenarios from the world of arms-bearers. As the next chapter will demonstrate, warriors could even be worthy spiritual exemplars for monks.

---

[177] Julian of Vézelay, Sermon 9, ed. Vorreux, *Sermones*, 1: 208: 'Licet beatus Benedictus interdicat et vetet ne quis quae foris uiderit uel auderit in monasterio referat (cf. RB 67.5, p. 288), nos tamen quae audiuimus, uobis, fratres, referimus, ad aedificationem uestram plurimum ualitura.'

5

Warriors as Spiritual Exemplars

As members of an elite corps of spiritual warriors, medieval monks modeled the virtues of the true soldiery of Christ for other members of Christian society, and held themselves to be superior to all lay arms-bearers, even the most pious crusaders and members of the military orders, whose spiritual warfare was tainted by physical violence and bloodshed. Historians have long recognized the role of clerics in the promotion of saintly warriors as exemplars for pious arms-bearers and have linked the cults of various warrior-saints to the development of Christian knighthood and crusading ideology. What has been less appreciated is the extent to which monastic writers also found in holy warriors spiritual role models worthy of celebration and emulation by fellow religious. We have already seen that the warriors of the Hebrew Bible, their military campaigns spiritualized by medieval exegetes, were embraced as models for monks. This chapter will survey other groups of warriors who attracted the admiration of monastic writers in the Central Middle Ages: the legendary warrior-saints of Late Antiquity; lay arms-bearers of the distant and not-so-distant past who had renounced the world to enter the cloister; and the *loricati* ('mailed ones'), ascetics who donned actual armor to engage in spiritual combat with the forces of evil.

The following discussions are based largely on the evidence of hagiography, and specifically consider how saints' Lives articulated new models of spiritual development. Though concerned primarily with the miraculous, monastic *vitae* evince an active engagement with lived experience. Many Lives of holy warriors demonstrate knowledge of (even, on occasion, a relish for) medieval combat, the obligations of arms-bearers to wives, lords, and brothers-in-arms, and the various circumstances under which men of war entered the cloister. But the focus of this chapter is not on what hagiography can reveal about the lives of warrior elites, but how monastic writers remembered and manipulated the memory of saintly warriors for their own purposes. Paramount among these was the desire to show that the life of the monk or hermit was the highest mode of Christian existence, a goal hagiographers accomplished by equating warriors' journeys from the world to the monastery or hermitage with their souls' progress toward God. By hagiographic convention, such a conversion was defined as a transition from a life dedicated to an inferior form of warfare to one devoted to a superior type of battle in Christ's service, an interpretation which reflects the longstanding monastic self-identification with the *miles Christi* ideal and the practice of spiritual combat explored in previous chapters. While professed religious may have written these *vitae* partly in the hope that such stories might inspire other would-be converts among the *bellatores*, these works also show that warriors could serve as spiritual exemplars for monks. Above all, hagiographical evidence underscores the extent to which warfare as a concept shaped the monastic experience, and reveals how easily the boundary between the identities of monk and warrior could be blurred, even dissolved, in the monastic imagination.

Warrior-saints and saintly warriors

In their identification with the *miles Christi* ideal, monks proclaimed themselves the heirs of countless spiritual warriors who had gone before them. The warriors of the Hebrew Bible, their earthly campaigns spiritualized by generations of exegetes, served as exemplars for clerics and lay arms-bearers alike. And if the combats of these ancient secular warriors could be reimagined in spiritual terms, long-dead spiritual warriors might also take part in worldly battles when their places of cult or their earthly guardians were threatened. The medieval reality was that *every* saintly patron was potentially a warrior. Modern scholars have traditionally used the term 'warrior-saints' to describe a handful of martyred Roman soldiers, including Maurice, George, and Sebastian, but medieval Christians would hardly have defined this category so narrowly; these ancient warrior-martyrs comprised but a small subsection of a much larger, more heterogeneous cohort which included knights who had renounced the world to become monks and even legendary epic heroes who embraced the spiritual warfare of religious life.

Most studies of soldier-saints have focused on clerical attempts to promote these figures as models of Christian conduct for lay arms-bearers, in conjunction with the articulation of a model of Christian knighthood from the eleventh century onwards.[1] But warrior-saints were also revered as embodiments of monastic virtues. In some cases, holy warriors were conversionary models, their rejections of worldly warfare testaments to the superiority of monastic life; others, who died as soldiers in the world, nevertheless displayed qualities such as humility and obedience which allowed them to be seen as both *milites Christi* and honorary monks. It is possible to distinguish three groups of non-biblical holy warriors upheld as spiritual exemplars by monastic hagiographers: long-venerated Roman military martyrs of the distant past like the members of the Theban Legion; semi-legendary heroic warriors like William of Gellone who moved freely between epic *chansons de geste* and the hagiographical imagination; and finally, knightly converts from the recent past who had abandoned worldly

---

[1] Erdmann, *Idea of Crusade*, is foundational and still influential; more recent examples include John Edward Damon, *Soldier Saints and Holy Warriors: Warfare and Sanctity in the Literature of Early England* (Aldershot, 2003); and MacGregor, 'Negotiating Knightly Piety.' It should be noted, however, that this interpretation assumes a level of passivity on the part of lay elites that has increasingly been called into question, most recently by Kaeuper, *Holy Warriors*.

military service for the spiritual soldiery of religious life. This section will focus on the first two of these groups, while the last group will be the subject of the chapter's remaining sections.

A well-known story from Orderic Vitalis' *History* recounts how the chaplain Gerald of Avranches used tales of the Roman military martyrs to bring about the conversion to religious life of several *milites* belonging to the household of his master, Hugh of Avranches.[2] Himself the son of a Norman lord, Gerald might well have grown up hearing these 'vivid stories of the conflicts of Demetrius and George, of Theodore and Sebastian, of the Theban Legion and Maurice its leader, and of Eustace, supreme commander of the army' in his father's household. But Gerald's purpose in retelling these martyrs' passions was not to exhort his knightly listeners to greater feats of strength or courage, but to encourage them to do something none of his legendary exemplars had done – namely, to take monastic vows and abandon the world.[3] As shown in Chapter 3, medieval monks' appropriation of the *miles Christi* ideal reflected their claim to be direct descendants of the martyrs, and this ancient association of monastic life with figurative martyrdom would hardly have been lost on Gerald (or, for that matter, on Orderic). Orderic's account of Gerald's ministry has often been cited as evidence of the military martyrs' appeal for medieval knights, but it also attests to the acknowledged status of these soldier-saints as spiritual warriors, admired not only for their military exploits but also for such decidedly unknightly virtues as humility and obedience, and thus equally worthy models for clerics.

In the Central Middle Ages, the cults of many military martyrs centered on monastic shrines where their relics were exhibited, their *vitae* written and rewritten, and liturgies composed in honor of their feasts. Maurice was a special patron of the monks of Agaune and Saint Gall, both of which communities possessed his relics; Sebastian's relics were venerated at the great Benedictine houses of Fleury and Saint-Médard, Soissons; and the cult of another Roman soldier-martyr, Julian, flourished at the abbey dedicated to him at Brioude in the Auvergne.[4] While these shrines attracted knightly pilgrims seeking the soldier-martyrs' favor, their monastic guardians also strongly identified with their patron saints as fellow *milites Christi*. Recounting the arrival of Sebastian's relics at Soissons a century earlier, for instance, a tenth-century hagiographer at Saint-Médard described how the local people had turned out 'to pay homage to the most glorious victory by which [the saint], protected by the armor of virtue, learned to do battle against that cruelest of enemies, and, enobled by his wounds, won the martyr's crown and everlasting triumph.' It was particularly

---

[2] Orderic Vitalis, *Ecclesiastical History*, ed. Chibnall, 3: 216.
[3] A point discussed in detail by James B. MacGregor, 'The Ministry of Gerold d'Avranches: Warrior-Saints and Knightly Piety on the Eve of the First Crusade,' *Journal of Medieval History* 29 (2003), 219–37.
[4] For the cults of these and other military martyrs, see Erdmann, *Idea of Crusade*, 273–81; and Flori, *Guerre sainte*, 127f. For the cult of Maurice at Agaune and Saint Gall, see AASS Sept. 6: 152–64; for Sebastian's cult at Saint-Médard, *Translatio S. Sebastiani martyris*, AASS Jan. 2: 278–93; for Fleury: *Miracles de saint Benoît*, 3.20, ed. Certain, 65; and Julian's cult at Brioude, *Passio S. Juliani martyris Brivatensis*, AASS, Aug. 6: 169–88.

fitting that Sebastian be delivered to the monastery by his new 'legion (*legio*),' the writer continued, which consisted of Abbot Hilduin and his delegation of relic-seeking monks.[5]

Although the Roman military martyrs were honored because they had gone to their deaths for refusing to fight, later hagiographers made no attempt to conceal their patrons' pre-conversion military careers. In fact, as the entrance of adult warriors into the religious life became increasingly common, monastic authors often invented military pasts, along with dramatic conversion scenarios, for obscure saints.[6] Later hagiographers also dusted off ancient warriors and outfitted them with new *vitae* that reflected the spiritual preoccupations of later centuries, such as penance and preaching. A case in point is the Life of Avitus of Sarlat, which makes of the saint – a Visigothic warrior said to have fought against Clovis at Vouillé – a figure more at home in the early twelfth century than his native sixth.[7] The hagiographer, who wrote around 1118, the year Avitus' relics were translated to the newly built church of the canons of Saint-Avit-Sénieur, described how the saint's conversion from warrior to wandering hermit-preacher was effected by a vision in which God ordered him henceforth to 'fight (*certare*)' as a spiritual warrior against paganism and never again bear arms against men.[8] His monastic hagiographer sought to fit Avitus into an emerging archetype: the warrior-saint as convert rather than martyr.

While the original model of the warrior-saint-as-martyr retained its appeal throughout the Central Middle Ages – as demonstrated by the ethos of martyrdom that permeated early crusading culture – a new kind of warrior-saint, the heroic *miles*-turned-monk, appeared around the turn of the first millennium. These new figures were regarded as the heirs of the Roman military martyrs, as illustrated by Orderic Vitalis' inclusion of one of the most famous, William of

---

[5] *Translatione S. Sebastiani martyris*, c.9, AASS Jan. 2: 285: 'Sic gratanter uiam legentes ad diu praeoptati ruris fines perueniunt, sexto ab urbe miliario stationem collocantes, donec in obuiam caelestis militis legio se praeparet omnis, gloriosissimo uictoria obsecutura, per quem et ipsa uirtutum loricis obtecta discerent contra hostem saeuissimum inexpugnabilia sumere certamina, et eius sancta digne excolendo uulnera, adquireret lauream et trophea perennia.' This view of churchmen as honorary legionaries is echoed by an anonymous clerical chronicler of the Fifth Crusade, whose *Historia de expeditione Friderici imperatoris* (MGH SRG n.s. 5: 85) characterized the priests and bishops accompanying the expedition as 'a holy legion of select soldiers, who are to be compared in every respect to the legion of Theban martyrs, each of them prepared and with free will, bravely standing firm and yearning to pour forth his blood for Christ.' Cited by Bachrach, *Religion and the Conduct of War*, 139.

[6] For numerous examples, see John Howe, 'Greek Influence on the Eleventh-Century Western Revival of Hermitism,' 2 vols (unpub. PhD thesis, UCLA, 1979), 1: 91–2.

[7] *Vita S. Avito eremita in Sarlatensi apud Petracoricos diocesi* [BHL 884], AASS Jun. 3: 360–5. Avitus' *vita* casts him in the mold of a Robert of Arbrissel or Bernard of Tiron. Other recognizably later elements include the saint's devotion to the Virgin Mary and his pre-conversion 'knighting' ceremony.

[8] For Avitus' conversion, see *De S. Avito eremita*, c.4–5, AASS Jun. 3: 361–2. These passages are shot through with the monastic rhetoric of spiritual warfare: Avitus, an *athleta Dei*, is to become a *tiro* in the heavenly militia; Christ will defend him against the 'spears of his enemies,' he will 'bear the banner of faith,' etc.

Gellone, in his list of the warrior-saints whose stories Gerald of Avranches told his knightly audience.⁹ But unlike the soldier-saints of Late Antiquity, these holy warriors conformed to contemporary models of spiritual development by seeking salvation through the figurative martyrdom of monastic profession. This new kind of warrior-saint was brought to life in the *moniage*, a genre that resists easy classification, hovering at the boundaries between hagiography and epic, Latin and vernacular literature, the cloister and the battlefield.¹⁰ Since, nearly a century ago, Joseph Bédier identified a number of such narratives, many extant in both 'clerical' versions (i.e., Latin hagiographical works) and 'lay' versions (i.e., vernacular *chansons*),¹¹ scholars have debated these conversionary tales' origins and meaning. While Bédier's contention that the *moniage* genre was monastic in origin has long been contested,¹² there can be no doubt that in the eleventh and twelfth centuries monasteries were overrun, figuratively speaking, by epic hero-converts. As the narratives of these heroes' conversions were being composed in the eleventh and twelfth centuries, hordes of epic warriors were being elevated to the status of saints; the tombs of the legendary martyrs of the *Chanson de Roland* attracted pilgrims to monastic shrines across southern France, while Charlemagne himself, reinvented as a crusader-king, was formally canonized in 1165.¹³

The Latin counterpart to the vernacular *moniage* was the *conversio*, an account of a hero's entrance into monastic life that melded epic themes with hagiographical tropes. The composition of such a text constituted a claim to the special patronage of its protagonist, who was typically said to have made his profession at the author's own monastery. The drama of these *conversiones*, which range from short narratives inserted into larger texts to lengthy freestanding *vitae*, unfolds according to standard hagiographical trajectories, with the heroes' sinful lives giving way to contrition, conversion, and finally salvation achieved through prayer and ascetic self-denial. But the Latin texts are also informed by the action-packed *chansons de geste* in their concern with warriors' loyalty to their overlords and companions-in-arms, the defense of personal honor, and, of course, the actual practice of war. A partial roll-call of the converts celebrated in vernacular *moniages* and Latin *conversiones* (and sometimes both) reads like

---

⁹ Orderic Vitalis, *Ecclesiastical History*, ed. Chibnall, 3: 218–26.

¹⁰ The term, which means 'monastic profession,' derives from the Old French *monie* (the equivalent of the modern *moine*). On this genre, see Charles de Miramon, 'La guerre des récits: autour des *moniages* du XIIᵉ siècle,' in *Guerriers et moines: Conversion et sainteté aristocratiques dans l'Occident médiéval*, ed. Michel Lauwers (Antibes, 2002), 589–636; and D.A. Trotter, *Medieval French Literature and the Crusades (1100–1300)* (Geneva, 1988), 86–9.

¹¹ Joseph Bédier, *Les légendes épiques: Recherches sur la formation des chansons de geste*, 4 vols (Paris, 1908–13), 4: 403–33.

¹² Ferdinand Lot, *Études sur les légendes épiques françaises* (Paris, 1958), 17–22.

¹³ On Charlemagne as a saint, see Remensnyder, *Kings Past*, 195–8; and Jace Stuckey, 'Charlemagne as Crusader? Memory, Propaganda, and the Many Uses of Charlemagne's Legendary Expedition to Spain,' in *The Legend of Charlemage in the Middle Ages: Power, Faith, Crusade*, ed. Matthew Gabriele and Jace Stuckey (New York, 2008), 137–52.

a list of the all-stars of medieval epic: Walter of Aquitaine, a legendary Visigothic warrior-king; Ogier the Dane, fearless companion of Charlemagne in the *Chanson de Roland*; William of Orange, loyal vassal of Charlemagne and hero of an entire epic cycle; and William's faithful companion, the Saracen-slaying giant Rainoart.[14]

The earliest tale of an epic hero's conversion is found in the *Chronicon Novaliciense*, composed at the Piedmontese abbey of Novalesa in the 1020s. It purports to describe the monastic conversion of a certain Walter, whom the chronicler conflates with Walter of Aquitaine, the protagonist of a Latin epic called the *Waltherius* composed a century earlier by the monk Ekkehard of Saint Gall (who in turn seems to have been inspired by earlier epic traditions).[15] The chronicler, who envisioned his work as a sequel to the *Waltherius*, continued the hero's story along quite plausible eleventh-century lines; an aging Walter, his mind turning more and more to spiritual matters, took the habit at Novalesa in hopes of atoning for his many sins.[16] While Walter approached his change of life with great seriousness, and even won praise for his careful tending of the monks' garden, when a band of robbers attacked the abbey's servants the former *miles* within him yearned to punish the offenders. He begged the abbot's leave to ride after them on his faithful warhorse (which had, like its master, humbled itself, and been hard at work in the monks' mill).[17] Walter rode forth with the blessing of his abbot, and soon tracked down the criminals. The chronicler, who was evidently a great connoisseur of epic, outdid himself in his description of how Walter, having dutifully allowed his opponents to attack him first rather than strike the first blow, punished the criminals:

> And when he began to attack them most violently, Walter stealthily drew forth a stirrup-rope from his saddle, and struck one of the men with it so hard that he fell to the ground as though already dead. Snatching up the fallen man's weapons, he rained down blows to the right and left. Then, catching sight of a calf grazing beside him, he seized it and tore off its [leg at the] shoulder and beat his enemies with it, pursuing them and scattering them across the field. Some of them fled, but there was one whom Walter pursued more ruthlessly than the rest, and when he

---

[14] For a full list, see Bédier, *Légendes épiques*, 4: 419–20. All of these characters feature in the various *chansons de geste* which focused on or incorporated Charlemagne's military exploits.

[15] The *conversio* of Walter is found in the *Chronicon Novaliciense*, 2.7–15 (of which 2.8–9 alternately summarize and directly quote from the *Waltherius*), ed. George Pertz (Hanover, 1846), 13–33. On the relationship between the *Waltherius* and the *Chronicon*, see John K. Bostock, Kenneth C. King and D.R. McLintock, *A Handbook on Old High German Literature* (Oxford, 1976), 265–7; for a compilation of all the texts related to Walter's epic career, see Marion Dexter Learned, 'The Saga of Walther of Aquitaine,' *Proceedings of the Modern Language Association* 7 (1892), 1–129 and 207–8; and for translations of many of these, *Walter of Aquitaine: Materials for the Study of His Legend*, ed. Francis Peabody Magoun and H.M. Smyser (New London, CT, 1950).

[16] *Chronicon Novaliciense*, 2.7, ed. Pertz, 13–14: 'Hic post multa prelia et bella, que viriliter in seculo gesserat, cum iam prope corpus eius senio conficeretur, recordans pondera suorum delictorum, qualiter ad rectam penitentiam pervenire mererentur.'

[17] *Chronicon Novaliciense*, 2.7, 2.10–11, ed. Pertz, 14, 27–9.

turned around, Walter dragged him back by his shoes and struck him a great blow on the neck so that he sank down with a crushed throat.[18]

Satisfied that he had brutally dispatched most of the malefactors, Walter returned home with the monastery's recovered property and again settled down to a life of prayer. In spite of this bloody episode, the chronicler concluded his narrative with a paean celebrating Walter as a model convert, who was remembered for his love of obedience and passionate devotion to the discipline of the *Rule*.[19]

The Novalesa narrative contains many elements commonly found in later examples of both the *moniage* and *conversio* genres: the author dwells at length on the hero's unmatched physical strength and martial prowess; the change of life from warrior to monk is termed a '*conversio militiae*,' a transfer from one kind of military service to another; and the new convert struggles, often in vain, to subdue his bellicose impulses in his new life. All of these features are present in two twelfth-century accounts of the most famous epic hero-convert of all, William of Gellone (aka Guillaume d'Orange), the *Vita Willelmi Gellonensis* and the Old French *Moniage Guillaume*.[20] The author of the *vita*, composed at the abbey of Gellone in the 1120s, wrote with the aim of identifying William, a Carolingian nobleman who had founded Gellone in the early ninth century, with Guillaume d'Orange, the epic hero credited with driving the Saracens out of Provence. While earlier traditions at Gellone had identified the house's founder merely as a pious patron and an exemplary convert, the twelfth-century Life makes of William a larger-than-life figure whose conversion is only the last and most glorious of his many campaigns.[21]

Like the monastic biographer of Walter of Aquitaine, the composer of the *Vita Willelmi* used extracts from epic material to establish William's heroic credentials before moving on to the 'spiritual exploits (*spiritualia gesta*)' of his later years. The rhetoric of spiritual warfare is applied to William even before

---

[18] *Chronicon Novaliciense*, 2.11, ed. Pertz, 30: 'Cumque coepissent illi vehementissime vim facere, Waltharius clam abstrahens a sella retinaculum, in quo pes eius antea herebat, percussit uni eorum in capite, qui cadens in terram, velut mortuus factus est: arreptaque ipsius arma, percutiebat ad dexteram sive ad sinistram. Deinde aspiciens iuxta se vidit vitulum pascentem; quem arripiens, abstraxit ab eo humerum, de quo percutiebat hostes, persequens ac dibachans eos per campum. Volunt autem nonnulli, quod uni eorum, qui Waltario plus ceteris inportunius insistebat, cum se inclinasset, ut calciamenta Waltharii ab pedibus eius extraeret, hisdem Waltharius ilico ex pugno in collum eius percutiens, ita ut os ipsius fractum in gulam eius caderet.'

[19] *Chronicon Novaliciense*, 2.12, ed. Pertz, 31. Walter is remembered as follows: 'in predicto monasterio post militie conversionem amoris obedientiae et regularis discipline oppido fervidissimus fuisse cognoscitur.'

[20] For these texts, *Les deux rédactions en vers du 'Moniage Guillaume,'* 2 vols, ed. Wilhelm Cloetta (Paris, 1906–11); and *Vita Willelmi Gellonensis* [BHL 8916], AASS May 6: 811–20; and for commentary, Bédier, *Légendes épiques*, vol. 1; Saxer, 'Guillaume de Gellone'; Kaeuper, *Holy Warriors*, 151–2; and Joan Ferrante, 'Introduction,' *Guillaume d'Orange: Four Twelfth-Century Epics* (New York, 1974), 8–12. The *Moniage Guillaume* exists in two twelfth-century versions: an older, longer version, and a later, shorter version, which is incomplete.

[21] Saxer, 'Saint Guillaume de Gellone,' 580–1; Remensnyder, *Kings Past*, 55–60, 189–91.

his entrance into the monastery, wreathing his worldly victories in an aura of divine approval; as a crusader, William is a *miles Christi* and the 'conqueror and standard-bearer of Christ (*triumphator et signifer Christi*),' whose divine hand guides his sword.[22] But the hagiographer makes clear that even the most glorious worldly victories over infidels could not assure William's place in heaven; only by becoming a monk – in the words of the *vita*, giving himself as 'an offering to God (*holocausta Deo*)' – could he be confident of winning salvation.

The *Vita Willelmi* characterizes William's transition from warrior to monk as a successful transfer from one form of military service to another. After countless years of campaigning, finding he has literally run out of worldly enemies to defeat and is surrounded (somewhat to his alarm) by peace and quiet, William embarks on a series of spiritual battles as a 'new knight (*novus miles*)' in the soldiery of Christ at his new foundation of Gellone.[23] When William makes his intention to become a monk known to his lord Charlemagne, the emperor receives William's petition with a piety and generosity characteristic of his appearances in the *chansons de geste*,[24] bestowing on his faithful friend a number of valuable relics which, he says, will henceforth serve as William's 'weapons':

> Now take these, dearest friend, as gifts for your new Lord; these will be very strong and powerful arms (*praeclara atque fortissima armae*) for you to bear against evil spirits and all other adversaries (cf. RB Prol. 3). Undertake to do your duty for your new king, with these newest rewards for your military service (*militia*).[25]

Armed with these spiritual weapons, William had no more need of his well-used knightly gear. In a subsequent scene that links William to the tradition of the Roman military martyrs surveyed in Chapter 3, the convert travels to the shrine of Julian at Brioude and offers up his arms on the warrior-saint's altar in token of his resolution to become a monk.[26] After taking monastic vows at Gellone,

---

[22] *Vita Willelmi*, 1.7, AASS May 6: 811–12.
[23] *Vita Willelmi*, 1.7, 2.24, AASS May 6: 812, 817. Compare this language to the descriptions of new monks as 'new recruits' and of the Templars as members of a 'new knighthood,' both discussed in Chapter 4.
[24] Pierre Chastang emphasizes the hagiographer's desire to demonstrate a strong connection between William (and hence his foundation at Gellone) and the Carolingian dynasty; see 'La fabrication d'un saint: La *Vita Guillelmi* dans la production textuelle de Gellone au début du XIIe siècle,' in *Guerriers et moines*, ed. Lauwers, 429–47. This scene, which provides provenances for a number of relics belonging to Gellone, seems to grow out of the cultic concerns of the abbey and is not included in either version of the *Moniage Guillaume*.
[25] *Vita Willelmi*, 2.17, AASS May 6: 815: 'Suscipe nunc, dilectissime, haec Domini tui dona; contra malignos spiritus et contra adversa omnia, praeclara atque fortissima armae; suscipe Regis tui munera, novissima militiae tuae praemia.' Here the epic king is made to speak the monastic language of spiritual warfare, and even to quote the Benedictine Rule! Cf. RB Prol. 3, p. 156: 'Ad te ergo nunc mihi sermo dirigitur, quisquis abrenuntians propriis voluntatibus, Domino Christo vero regi militaturus, oboedientiae fortissima atque praeclara arma sumis.'
[26] *Vita Willelmi*, 2.20, AASS May 6: 816: '[William says] Noi, sancte Juliane, novi et certum habeo, quam miles, quam armis strenuus fueris in seculo, numquam victus, numquam

William wages war on his own flesh as strenuously as he had previously fought mortal enemies, achieving a figurative martyrdom by means of the most stringent asceticism.[27] William's transformation from proud warrior to humble monk is all the more wondrous, the hagiographer comments, when one remembers the nature of the convert's previous life:

> How changed, how humbled [William] is! He who formerly rode the most wonderful horses, sought out and carefully selected from every corner of the world, whose many servants and even his servants' servants went about on fine horses and in costly carriages. Now this same man does not blush to ride about on a lowly ass carrying little barrels! Nor is he content to abase himself in this way; if any of the brothers is occupied in a lowly or distasteful task, or anything that might seem dangerous or demeaning, Brother William may be counted upon to offer to do the job himself, as a lightener of burdens, a humble laborer, who assists all without distinction.[28]

As this passage shows, the *Vita Willelmi* never loses sight of William's epic past; by emphasizing his former wealth and power the hagiographer underscored the miracle of his self-abasement, while the great victories he won in his former life as a crusading hero serve in the *vita* as preludes for his final war against himself.

As Amy Remensnyder has shown, the hagiographical remaking of William at Gellone in turn influenced the presentation of the epic hero's conversion in the Old French *Moniage Guillaume*, which existed in its present versions by about 1180.[29] Like the earlier *vita*, these narratives explain William's conversion in terms of his remorse for a life of violence; concerned that even his crusading exploits cannot guarantee his salvation, he resolves to become a monk as the best way to make amends to God for his sins.[30] In the *Moniage*, however, it quickly

---

derelictus a Deo: ideoque coram altari tuo arma haec derelinquo, quae Deo omnipotente dimitto, tibique ea committo: insuper vero animam meam tibi instanter commendo, et viam istam, qua nunc ad Deum vado, ut tu serves me a malo, custodias a delicto, salves ab hoste maligno.' Bédier (*Légendes épiques*, 4: 411) points out that Saint-Julien, Brioude, was identified in later *chansons* as the place where the hero Bertrand the Paladin deposited his arms, and where William's legendary companion, the giant Rainoart, offered his war-club and made his *moniage*. In the shorter version of the *Moniage Guillaume* (ed. Cloetta, 1: 54–5, lines 80–90), William offers Julian only his shield, with the provision that if he should ever be called upon to fight the Saracens again he will be able to reclaim it!

27 *Vita Willelmi*, 3.30–2, AASS May 6: 819.
28 *Vita Willelmi*, 3.26, AASS May 6: 818: 'Quantum mutatus, quantum humiliatus! Qui enim quondam decentissime utebatur equis mirabilibus, electis et exquisitis de multis mundi partibus; cujus etiam servi numerosi et servi servorum ejus equis ibant et curribus pretiosis et pluribus; hic modo non erubescebat vili asello gestari cum suis flasconibus! Necque vero his contentus, si quis fratrum in officio vili et quasi contemptibili detineretur, in quo etiam quasi locus injuriae vel contumeliae videretur; hujus nimirum Frater Willelmus mox aderat vicarius, sublevator oneris, humilis operarius, et omnibus indiscrete unus hebdomadarius.'
29 Remensnyder, *Remembering Kings Past*, 192.
30 *Moniage Guillaume II*, ed. Cloetta, 2: 43–4 (lines 45–8, 50–1): 'Dont s'apensa Guillaumes au cort nés / Que mout a mors Sarrasins et Esclers, / Maint gentil home a fait a fin aler; / Or se vaura envers Dieu amender. ... / Ne li plaist mais au siecle converser, / Ains sera moines, ce li vient en penser.'

becomes apparent that William is not cut out for the religious life. His initial encounter with the monks of Aniane is decidedly unpromising: seeing William ride up to the gates on his warhorse, fully accoutered as though for battle, the monks flee in panic, eliciting loud curses from their would-be brother.[31] Even after taking his vows William insists on wearing his own rich clothing rather than a habit, chafes at the *Rule's* restrictions on the consumption of food and wine, and uses his fists to intimidate any fellow monks who dare admonish him. His pronouncement, 'I *will* be a monk, whomever it annoys,' sums up William's approach to salvation as a prize to be won by force, rather than through obedience and humility.[32]

Desperate to be rid of him, the abbot and monks send William on what they hope will prove a deadly errand along a bandit-infested road, but, in a scene which echoes the *conversio* of Walter of Aquitaine, William makes short work of the robbers. He then returns to the abbey where, finding the gates barricaded against him, he breaks in and kills several of the monks in a rage! Luckily for all concerned, an angel presently appears to William and orders him to leave the house and become a hermit (on the future site of Gellone), a plan to which the abbot readily accedes, even offering William a pile of gold as a bribe never to return.[33] Unlike the *Vita Willelmi* or the *conversio* of Walter of Aquitaine, the *Moniage Guillaume* offers a satirical view of the coenobitic life more generally – the monks of Aniane are proud, greedy, and vengeful[34] – and depicts William's conversion as merely one of his many adventures. At the end of the narrative, when William abandons his vows and leaves his hermitage to resume the fighting life, he does so with the author's – and God's – blessing.

On one level, the *moniages* may be read as monastic comedies starring huge, brutish warriors who don't know their own strength, with supporting casts of unfortunate monks forced to put up with their bumbling attempts to become holy men.[35] But while there is no shortage of comic moments in the texts – Walter fighting off a gang of robbers in his underwear, William eating his fellow monks out of house and home – these cannot be classified as purely satirical works. The Latin and vernacular narratives alike bring to the fore the very serious matter of salvation, and their epic heroes (despite sometimes behaving

---

31 *Moniage Guillaume II*, ed. Cloetta, 2: 45–8 (lines 90–145).
32 (Emphasis mine). *Moniage Guillaume II*, ed. Cloetta, 2: 49 (line 166): 'Jou serai moines, qui qu'en doie anuier.'
33 *Moniage Guillaume*, ed. Cloetta, 2: 53–137 (lines 254–2034). An equally disastrous tale of conversion is found in the *Moniage Rainouart*, composed c.1190/1200, which describes the trials of William's companion, the giant Rainouart, in his efforts to adjust to the religious life. For the text, which forms part of the Guillaume d'Orange cycle, see *Le Moniage Rainouart I*, ed. Gérald A. Bertin (Paris, 1973).
34 As Wilhelm Cloetta points out (Introduction to *Moniage Guillaume*, 2: 28–58), the text's negative depiction of the monks of Aniane, the arch-rival of Gellone, reflects similar views in the historical writings of the latter house. The abbey is named as Aniane only in the longer version of the *moniage*.
35 Norman Daniel has argued that the *moniages* function on multiple levels: as comedies, serious commentaries on conversion, and folk-tales with fantastic elements. See his *Heroes and Saracens: An Interpretation of the Chansons de Geste* (Edinburgh, 1984), 227–36.

like, well, epic heroes) are unquestionably sincere in their contrition for past sins and their desire to do penance. Both genres also manifest a genuine understanding, even sympathy, for the challenges faced by men who sought late in life to transform themselves into *milites Christi*. The epic heroes are made to face many of the difficulties that confronted real knightly converts in this era; they must negotiate the terms of their conversion with their overlords, take leave of beloved kin and friends, and even struggle with the lack of learning which bars them from taking part in the all-important monastic liturgy.

The *conversiones* are, as one would expect, deeply rooted in hagiographical convention and monastic values, but the *moniages* likewise engage with the values of the cloister (e.g., the love of peace, obedience, and humility) even as they satirize them. Perhaps the most significant difference between the *moniages* and the Latin hagiographical texts is that the former present the characters and values of the lay warrior and the monk as irreconcilable, and discount the possibility of a successful transition from one identity to the other. The *conversiones*, by contrast, are steeped in the monastic ethos of spiritual warfare that viewed a knight's entrance into religious life with greater optimism, as a transfer from one military service to another that could be successfully accomplished, provided the convert's motives were sincere. According to the dominant monastic view of conversion even the most hardened lay warrior could be redeemed and, through self-abasement and ascetic suffering, become a spiritual exemplar for monks as well as laymen. In their tales of epic heroes' successful conversion to the religious life, as in the *vitae* of ordinary knights considered in the following section, monastic writers presented lay arms-bearers not as their evil opposites but as inferior soldiers, and as potential recruits to the *militia Christi*.

Warrior-converts to the monastic army

Knights are everywhere in the hagiography of the Central Middle Ages. They make predictable appearances as villains who treat one another cruelly, despoil the property of the poor and the Church, and scorn the power of saints. But lay warriors, as we have seen, were not always vilified by monastic hagiographers; *milites* crowd the periphery of *vitae* as patrons and deserving recipients of miracles, and often take center stage as converts to the religious life.[36] While noting the existence of multiple conversionary models in medieval Europe, Karl Morrison has seen in monastic texts of the eleventh and twelfth centuries a dominant view of conversion as a gradual, indeed lifelong process, in which individuals' hearts drew gradually nearer to God.[37] More than any other social

---

[36] For a survey of this subject, see Dominique Barthélemy, *Chevaliers et miracles: La violence et le sacré dans la société féodale* (Paris, 2004). Treatments of warriors' conversion to the religious life that address the evidence of hagiography include: Miramon, 'Embracer l'état monastique'; Wollasch, 'Parenté noble'; Murray, *Reason and Society*, chapter 13; and Grundmann, 'Adelsbekehrungen im Hochmittelalter.'

[37] Morrison, *Understanding Conversion*; see also the companion case-studies in his *Conversion and Text: The Cases of Augustine of Hippo, Herman-Judah, and Constantine Tsatsos*

group in medieval Christendom, Morrison writes, professed religious were 'specialists in the ideology and techniques of conversion,' an experience they understood to be fundamental to, even synonymous with, spiritual development within the monastic life.[38] According to the trajectory defined by monastic thinkers, converts progressed towards the divine through three main stages; initial contrition for past sins was followed by increasing devotion to God, and finally, sustained contemplation of heavenly things.[39] Though they called themselves Christians, many of those who lived their entire lives in the world never progressed beyond the first of these three stages, if indeed they reached it at all.

Saints' *vitae* testify to hagiographers' interest in exploring the conceptual boundary between the monk and lay warrior and meditating on the experiences of those who, by exchanging the military service of the world (the *militia saecularis*) for that of Christ (the *militia spiritualis*), irreversibly crossed this divide. For a penitent arms-bearer who abandoned the world for the cloister, the initial stage of conversion involved, in Constance Brittain Bouchard's words, 'not merely a transition from one status to a different one, but a radical and indeed abrupt change from one status to its diametric opposite.'[40] But was the transition from knight to monk really a movement between two neatly opposed poles of existence? Insofar as monastic conversion entailed warriors' radical rejection of their worldly standing, wealth, and relationships, it seems we should answer in the affirmative. But in the sense that conversion did not necessarily entail a wholesale rejection of the qualities that had ensured warriors' success in the world, the secular *miles* was not simply the monk's opposite. A close reading of the hagiographical evidence reveals an important continuity between the pre- and post-conversion identities of knights who became monks: the persistent desire for battle. In the eyes of hagiographers, warriors who became members of religious communities did not simply cease to be warriors, though they had to master a new kind of combat. Their new lives as monks, their biographers emphasized, required former knights to draw upon their martial prowess to fight spiritual battles against vices, demons, and the flesh, and to put to good use the strength and courage they had acquired in worldly battles.

The conversions of adult warriors entailed not only the transformation of converts themselves but, potentially, of the communities which received them, and in doing so opened themselves to the world and its dangers.[41] Although any

---

(Charlottesville, VA, 1992). In his work on Anglo-Norman monastic writers of the eleventh and twelfth centuries, Charles de Miramon ('Embracer l'état monastique') has found an emphasis on conversion as the culmination of a gradual journey towards God, marked along the way by offerings of ever-increasing value (i.e., alms, one's goods and properties, and ultimately oneself).

[38] Morrison, *Understanding Conversion*, xix.
[39] Morrison, *Understanding Conversion*, 79.
[40] Bouchard, *'Every Valley Shall Be Exalted'*, 76–7.
[41] As Charles de Miramon writes ('Embracer l'état monastique,' 826), 'La conversion est l'un des moments où le monastère s'ouvre sur la société extérieure. L'histoire de la conversion a donc un cadre plus large: celui de la société. Le discours monastique est peu loquace à ce sujet car la rupture avec le monde forme l'une des pierres angulaires du monachisme.'

attempt to reconstruct the personal experiences of knightly converts themselves is complicated by the fact that they rarely speak to us directly in the sources, it is possible to reconstruct monastic hagiographers' theoretical understanding of such conversions, as revealed in the *vitae* of saints who had begun their lives as arms-bearers. These texts, written during a period of dramatically changing ideas about war, exhibit a variety of attitudes towards war and the spiritual status of warriors, ranging from outright condemnation (the traditional clerical view of *militia* as *malitia*) to approval of the bearing of arms under certain circumstances. Surveying these Lives as a group, it becomes apparent that in hagiography, as in reality, a bloody past was not necessarily a bar to a successful career in the monastic army of Christ.

Predictably, some monastic writers sought to gloss over their subjects' martial training and participation in combat prior to their entrance into the cloister, insisting that the men in question had been repulsed by violence and bloodshed from an early age. Born into a family of warriors in Champagne, Thibaud of Provins (d.1066) rebelled against his boyhood training in arms and fled home just before he was to be knighted, initially going to live as a hermit and finally dying as a Benedictine monk in Polesina.[42] As a young *miles*, the future abbot Adelelme of La Chaise-Dieu (d.1097) reluctantly allowed himself to be knighted, but only in order that he might inherit his portion of his father's wealth, which he promptly gave away to the poor.[43] Though he was destined to lead the greatest spiritual army in Christendom, Hugh of Cluny (d.1109), the eldest son of a noble Burgundian clan, similarly resisted his father's efforts to train him to 'ride a horse, wield a spear, bear a shield, injure rather than be injured, and all the other nonsense pertaining to knighthood in which men of that sort foolishly exert themselves and unhappily die.' As his monastic biographer Gilo made clear, Hugh's distaste (and, the *vita* hints, lack of aptitude) for worldly warfare was as clear a proof of his sanctity as his disdain for fine clothes or his love of solitary prayer.[44]

Other future converts were acknowledged to have gone further along the path of wickedness, shedding the blood of fellow Christians until they experienced dramatic spiritual awakenings. Everard of Breteuil, viscount of Chartres (d.aft.1095), 'came to his senses' at the pinnacle of worldly power and, realizing 'that he was doing nothing else in the world but destroying (*dampnare*) and being destroyed, polluting (*foedare*) and being polluted,' abruptly left his castle to follow the same path his hero Thibaud of Provins had several decades earlier: after living for some time in the forest as a humble charcoal-burner, he took the habit at the ancient abbey of Marmoutier under the patronage of the greatest

---

[42] *Vita S. Teobaldi* [BHL 8032], 1.3, AASS June 5: 592–5 (at col. 593).
[43] Ralph of La Chaise-Dieu, *Vita Adelelmi Casae Dei* [BHL 71], c.1, in *La España Sagrada*, 51 vols, ed. H. Florez (Madrid, 1743–1886), 27: 425–34 (at 426).
[44] Gilo of Cluny, *Vita S. Hugonis abbatis* [BHL 4007], 1.2, ed. H.E.J. Cowdrey in *Two Studies in Cluniac History, 1049–1126*, Studi Gregoriani per la storia della 'Libertas Ecclesiae' 11 (Rome, 1978), 49–50 (quoting 49).

of soldier-saints, Martin.[45] We find an even more dramatic volte-face in the *vita* of Robert of Molesme, which tells of two knights, brothers-in-arms as well as by birth, who secretly plotted to kill one another, each wishing to seize the other's wealth for himself. But as they passed through the forest near the dwelling-place of a holy hermit both were suddenly seized by compunction and, cured of their greed, vanity, and pride (the latter sins manifested in their addiction to 'those accursed fairs called tournaments') by confession, they were able to prepare in their hearts 'an interior dwelling-place for God.' Thereafter, 'despising the pomp of the world, and treading underfoot all its display,' they begged leave to join the hermit, whose prayers had helped bring about their conversion, and 'began to live a spiritual life in company with him, humbly bending the necks of their hearts to carry the sweet yoke of Christ.'[46]

Some *milites* were said to have been diverted from the path of wickedness after participating in or witnessing particularly horrific acts of war. Reinfrid, a Norman *miles* who served in the army of William I in the years following the Norman Conquest, resolved to leave his calling after taking part in the ferocious 'Harrying of the North' in the winter of 1069–70. It was the sight of the lonely ruins of Whitby Abbey, abandoned two centuries earlier in the wake of Viking raids, that moved Reinfrid's heart to sorrow for the sins of his peers and made him vow to resettle the site as a man of God.[47]

Occasionally hagiographers even emphasized warriors' pre-conversion cruelty and brutality as a prelude to their miraculous transformation into loyal servants of God. Pons of Léras (d.c.1140) founded the abbey of Silvanès and there devoted himself to atoning for the sins of his early life, which his Cistercian biographer Hugh Francigena narrated in detail: for years, Pons had been driven by greed to attack and rob countless fellow Christians, neighbors as well as strangers, who passed by his mountain stronghold.[48] Equally shamefully, before joining the Cistercians and rising to the office of abbot, Henry of Waverley

---

[45] For Evrard's story, see Guibert of Nogent, *De vita sua*, 1.9, ed. E.R. Labande as *Autobiographie* (Paris, 1981), 52–8 (quoting 52); trans. John F. Benton as *Self and Society in Medieval France* (Toronto, 1984), 54–6. For the spread of Thibaud's cult, and reflections on Guibert's comparison of Thibaud and Evrard, see Dominique Iogna-Prat, 'Évérard de Breteuil et son double: morphologie de la conversion en milieu aristocratique (v.1070–v.1120),' in *Guerriers et moines*, ed. Lauwers, 537–55.

[46] *Vita S. Roberti abbatis Molesmensis* [BHL 7265], c.2, in PL 157: 1272–3.

[47] Reinfrid initially entered the abbey of Evesham (which had become a safe haven for refugees in the North) before embarking on a career as a hermit and monastic founder. His story is told in the cartulary of Whitby, *Cartularium abbathiae de Whiteby ordinis S. Benedicti*, c.1, ed. J.C. Atkinson, 2 vols, Surtees Society Publications 69, 72 (Durham, 1879–81), 1: 1–2. For commentary, see Janet Burton, *Monastic and Religious Orders in Britain 1000–1300* (Cambridge, 1994), 32–3.

[48] Hugh Francigena, *Tractatus de conversione Pontii de Laracio et exordii Salvaniensis monasterii vera narratio*, ed. Beverley Mayne Kienzle, *Sacris erudiri* 34 (1993), 273–311; trans. Kienzle as 'The Tract of the Conversion of Pons of Léras and the True Account of the Beginning of the Monastery at Silvanès, in *Medieval Hagiography: An Anthology*, ed. Thomas Head (London, 2001), 495–513. On the remaking of Pons as a Cistercian saint after Silvanès' incorporation into that order, see Berman, *Cistercian Evolution*, 110f.

(d.1182) had been a lawless English knight during the anarchy of Stephen I's reign, one of those enemies of peace (*pacis inimici*) 'who loved war and, like beasts of the forest creeping forth from their lairs by night, spread out across the whole land to commit brigandage.'[49]

Repentant warriors are given voices in these narratives the better to proclaim the superiority of the cloister to the castle. In the mid-twelfth-century *vita* of Amedeus of Hauterive, a work composed at the Cistercian abbey of Bonnevaux (where the castellan had taken the habit), the hero preaches an impromptu sermon to his comrades-in-arms, warning them of the fate awaiting unrepentant warriors:

> Now do you see those young knights (*tirones*), and those over there? How strong, how vigorous, how eager, how comely, how wise, how virtuous they are, and how they make merry! Yet not one of their number will escape the fatal trial of death. That one will hurry off in perfect health to a tournament where he will be run through with a lance and killed.... That one will die of an arrow wound; another, thrown headlong from his horse, will pass over into Hell.... That one will lack a proper tomb for his sins; another, stuffed into a wine-cask, will be cast into the waves of the Rhône by his own kinsmen. What good, I ask you, will their worldly distinction have done those men, if they are to be condemned to eternal captivity?[50]

The hagiographer went on to report that Amedeus' words had their intended effect, and no fewer than sixteen of his knights followed their lord into the monastery.[51] Herluin of Bec's biographer Gilbert Crispin, himself raised as an oblate at Bec during Herluin's abbacy, recounted the impassioned speech with which his hero had taken leave of his worldly lord to enter the Church. During his years of loyal service, as Herluin explained to Count Gilbert of Brionne, he had elevated his knightly obligations above his duties to God, and neglected his soul even as he cultivated great physical strength. 'Allow me to spend the rest of

---

[49] For what purports to be a first-person account of Henry's conversion, see John of Ford, *Vita beati Wulfrici Haselbergiae* [BHL 8743], c.50–1, ed. Maurice Bell, Somerset Record Society 47 (London, 1933), 68–73 (quoting 68), and xxxii–xxxvii (commentary).

[50] *Vita venerabilis Amedaei Altae Ripae*, c.2, ed. Dimier, 276: 'Num vidistis tirones illos et illos? Quam fortes, quam strenui, quam alacres, quam decori, quam sapientes, quam probi, quam largi fuerunt convivae? Horum tamen omnium fatales mortis periculum nullus evasit. Ille ludis circensibus incolumis properavit ubi lancea perforatus interiit.... Ille sagitta transfixis obiit; suus alterum equus ad Tartara praecipitando transmisit.... Ille sepultura caruit pro suis sceleribus; propinqui sui alterum vasculo vinario conditum exposuerunt Rhodani fluctibus. Quid, rogo, temporalis illis profuit probitas, si nunc eos retinet aeterna captivistas?'

It is also worth noting that the monastic hagiographer had his knightly subject uphold the superiority of traditional monastic life to that of the new military orders, specifically the Templars (*ibid.*, c.4, p. 282), telling his knights that the Cistercian life is far more demanding (and thus offers far greater spiritual rewards), and that 'To join the Order of the Temple is not to give up luxuries but merely to change the color of one's clothing.'

[51] For commentary, see Chrysogonus Waddell, 'Simplicity and Ordinariness: The Climate of Early Cistercian Hagiography,' in *Simplicity and Ordinariness*, Studies in Medieval Cistercian History 4, ed. John R. Sommerfeldt (Kalamazoo, MI, 1980), 14–25.

my life in a monastery,' he begged Gilbert, 'with your love for me intact. Give to God, with me, what I owned.'[52]

All of the narrative approaches considered thus far reflect a traditional early medieval view of warfare as synonymous with evildoing. According to this line of thought, knights might be good Christians only in spite of – never by means of – their bloody occupation.[53] But not all hagiographers were so strident in their condemnation of their subjects' violent pasts. The *vitae* of crusaders who had fought in the East before becoming monks do not portray these men's military service as evil, but rather as a form of spiritual preparation for the better warfare of monastic life. Hugh of Lacerta (fl.c.1150), an early disciple of Stephen of Muret, was praised for having left behind his possessions in his youth to become a *miles Dei* in the Holy Land in the wake of the First Crusade. Hugh's religious conversion was depicted as a natural next step after his participation in the holy war.[54] Another crusader-turned-monk, Adjutor of Tiron (d.1131), was said to have 'earned eternal triumph by means of his double warfare (*duplex militia*)' – that is, his military service in the East and his subsequent spiritual combats in the monastery.[55] Such converts – and their biographers – embraced the monastic life as the surest path to salvation, but in doing so they did not simply reject the fighting life as evil. This hagiographical trend, which becomes increasingly pronounced from the late eleventh century onwards, seems to reflect the emerging view that fighting men could do good through their calling by putting their strength at the service of the Church.[56]

Although, as we saw in Chapter 2, many warriors entered the religious life because illness, age, or injuries prevented them from fulfilling their worldly responsibilities, the knightly converts of monastic hagiography were vigorous men who entered the cloister in the prime of their lives. It was no great sacrifice, as Gilbert Crispin wrote, for a *miles* to lay down his arms and become a monk late in life, 'when he had grown weary of arms and was satiated with worldly

---

[52] Gilbert Crispin, *Vita Herluini*, ed. Robinson, 90; trans. Sally N. Vaughn in *The Abbey of Bec and the Anglo-Norman State, 1034–1136* (Woodbridge, 1981), 70–1. For commentary on the *vita*, see Christopher Harper-Bill, 'Herluin, Abbot of Bec, and His Biographer,' in *Religious Motivation*, Studies in Church History 15, ed. Derek Baker (Oxford, 1978), 15–25.

[53] The comments by the anonymous author of the *vita* of the nobleman Bobo of Provence (d.986) summarize this position: 'Puer autem bonae indolis crescendo, paternum morem quasi hereditario jure non morabatur amplecti, exercens se arcu et pharetra et equestri luctamine; ut si quando necessarium foret arcum cognosceret, et si equitandum equum non ignoraret; fide tamen Catholica eruditus, studebat ut Christianus in omnibus haberetur.' Vita S. Bobonis [BHL 1383], c.1, AASS May 5: 184–91 (at col. 185).

[54] William Dandina of Saint-Savin, *Vita Hugonis de Lacerta* [BHL 4017], c.9, in *Vetera scriptorum ... amplissima collectio*, ed. Edmond Martène and Ursin Durand (Paris, 1724–33), 6: 1143–86 (at 1146–7).

[55] Hugh of Amiens, *Vita S. Adjutoris* [BHL 81], PL 192: 1347.

[56] For discussion and additional examples, see Bernard Hamilton, 'Ideals of Holiness: Crusaders, Contemplatives, and Mendicants,' *International History Review* 17 (1995), 693–712; Constable, *Reformation of the Twelfth Century*, 75–6; and Erdmann, *Idea of Crusade*, chapters 2 and 9.

pleasure,' but a knight who offered himself to God at the peak of his prowess, as Gilbert's hero Herluin had done, proved himself truly worthy of salvation.[57] Such thinking may have led Odo of Saint-Maur, in his eleventh-century *vita* of Count Burchard of Vendôme, to rewrite the historical circumstances of Burchard's entrance into religious life, making the convert into a virile man in his prime rather than an elderly postulant seeking admittance to the community of Saint-Maur-des-Fossés *ad succurrendum*.[58]

Contemporary writers mocked knights who lacked martial skill, and laymen often derided clerics as weak, cowardly, and effeminate men who would never have made good warriors.[59] Needless to say, monastic authors did not share this view, and the hagiography of converted warriors anticipated and pre-emptively countered accusations of this sort. Almost without fail, the *vitae* insist that their subjects had been 'the most vigorous of knights (*milites strenuissimi*)' before taking monastic vows.[60] Many future monks were said to have been what one might call knights' knights: possessed of remarkable skill in riding and the use of arms, heroic on the battlefield, and courtly in their bearing. 'When he was only in the first flush of youth,' his hagiographer wrote of the converted nobleman Simon of Crépy (d.1081/2), 'he excelled many men in martial skill (*ars militaris*), and in all those things in which almost everyone in the world sets store.'[61] Count Geoffrey of Cappenberg (d.1129), who joined the Premonstratensians, was described in his *vita* as 'easy of speech, prudent of counsel,' and 'powerful in knightly skill,' though he yearned throughout his youth 'to fight for the highest King' rather than bear arms against fellow Christians.[62] Far from being cowards or weaklings, these men were the best and bravest of worldly soldiers before their conversions, and naturally ranked among the greatest of spiritual warriors afterwards.

Even as warriors living in the world, some knightly converts were said to have possessed humility, obedience, steadfastness, compassion – personal quali-

---

[57] Gilbert Crispin, *Vita Herluini*, ed. Robinson, 94–5; trans. Vaughn, *Abbey of Bec*, 74.

[58] On the historical Burchard, see Dominique Barthélemy, 'Sur les traces du comte Bouchard: Dominations châtelaines a Vendôme et en *Francia* ver l'an Mil,' in *Le roi de France et son royaume autour de l'an Mil*, ed. Michel Parisse and Xavier Barral i Altet (Paris, 1992), 99–109. In the *vita* (c.11, ed. de la Roncière, 26–7), the decision by Burchard to enter monastic life is met with 'luctus ingens ab omnibus Francorum,' including 'cuncti milites.'

[59] For mockery of knights who did not fight, see the twelfth-century satirist Nigel Longchamp's *Tractatus contra curiales et officiales clericos*, ed. André Boutemy (Paris, 1959), 204. On lay warriors' views of monks as weak and effeminate, see Thomas, *Vassals, Heiresses, Crusaders, and Thugs*, 142.

[60] For example: Gilbert Crispin, *Vita Herluini*, ed. Robinson, 87; Hugh Francigena, *Tractatus de conversione Pontii de Laracio*, ed. Kienzle, 288; *Vita S. Geraldi abbatis* [BHL 3417], c.23, AASS Apr. 1: 414–23 (at col. 420); *Vita Godefridi* [BHL 3575], c.1, ed. Jaffé, 515; Hariulf of Saint-Médard, *Vita S. Arnulfi (vita longior)* [BHL 703], c.4, PL 174: 1380.

[61] *Vita B. Simonis comitis Crespeiensis auctore synchrono* [BHL 7757], c.1, PL 156: 1211–24 (at col. 1211). For commentary on this *vita*, see H.E.J. Cowdrey, 'Count Simon of Crépy's Monastic Conversion,' in *The Crusades and Latin Monasticism, 11th-12th Centuries* (London, 1999), 253–66.

[62] *Vita Godefridi*, c.1, ed. Jaffé, 515: 'Fuit enim vir ... facundus eloquio, prudens in consilio, militiae quidem exercitio strenuus, sed regi supremo militare ... Christi ... inardescens quantocius.' Trans. Antry and Neel, *Early Norbertine Spirituality*, 93–4.

ties that could be the hallmarks of the ideal Christian *miles* or, alternately, the model monk. Such men did not abandon these virtues at the monastery gates, but strove to perfect them in their new lives. The *vita* of the reformer Gerald of Corbie (d.1095), for example, praised the cohort of ex-knights the holy man assembled at his new foundation of La Sauve Majeure as men who were virtuous (*probus*), prudent (*discretus*), pleasant (*amabilis*), and restrained (*temperatus*). At the same time, the anonymous hagiographer stressed that these men had been, without exception, highly successful in their former calling because of their martial prowess, physical strength, and fearlessness.[63] Such 'knightly' qualities were not presented as incompatible with the converts' more 'monastic' virtues, however; the author made it clear that these men's physical skills and endurance made them great assets to the fledgling community deep in the forest of the Gironde. As adult conversion to the religious life became the rule rather than the exception, and ever-larger numbers of repentant fighting men flocked to the new orders founded in the eleventh and twelfth centuries, hagiographers emphasized the worthiness of former *milites* to serve as full partners in reform.[64] Speaking of the well-known Cistercian fondness for tales of knightly converts, Martha Newman has suggested that such stories 'recognized that the companionship of friends and the love of adventure helped these men survive, but they suggested that such qualities would be even more beneficial if used in a spiritual battle for salvation.'[65] In other words, such *exempla* showed that good warriors could make good monks.

A knight's entrance into monastic life did not complete his conversion, but only marked the beginning of its most difficult stage. As Anselm of Canterbury wrote, after the initial joy that a convert experienced in giving himself to God came bitter, interminable 'battles of temptation (*certamina temptationis*)' which must be won if he hoped to attain the final phase, *perfectio*, and again taste the sweetness of divine love.[66] The notion that former *milites* might be particularly well-suited to fight these spiritual battles dated back at least to the ninth century, when Paschasius Radbertus observed that 'some men, whom the beginnings of virtue have nourished in military affairs, have afterward come to Christ's soldiery (*militia Christi*) tougher and sharper than if they had not previously been tested.'[67] In later centuries, it became commonplace for the *vitae* of saintly warriors to describe their monastic conversion in terms of the renuncia-

---

[63] *Vita S. Geraldi abbatis*, c.22–3, 420. For commentary on the depiction of *milites* in Gerald's *vita*, see Bull, *Knightly Piety*, 128–33.
[64] Joachim Wollasch ('Parenté noble,' 5–6) emphasizes the attraction new reformed orders held for adult men from military backgrounds.
[65] Newman, *Boundaries of Charity*, 24–5.
[66] 'Miscellanea Anselmiana,' c.10, in *Memorials of St. Anselm*, ed. Southern and Schmitt, 307.
[67] Paschasius Radbertus, *Epitaphium Arsenii* (*Vita Walae*), 1.7.8, ed. Ernst Dümmler, in *Philosophische und historische Abhandlungen der königlichen. Akademie der Wissenschaften zu Berlin, phil.-hist. Kl.* 2 (1900), 1–98 (quoting 31): 'At vero nonnulli, quos tirocinia virtutum enutrirunt in militaribus rebus, postmodum ad Christi militiam pueriores ac perspicatiores veniunt, quam si essent inexperti.' Trans. based on Allen Cabaniss, 'Life of

tion of worldly military service in favor of spiritual combats. Perhaps because such comments recur so frequently, modern readers have paid them little attention. Resituated within the context of the martial rhetoric characteristic of contemporary monastic sermons and letters, these descriptions can be read as commentaries on the relationship between knightly and monastic identity and as affirmations of the monk's status as the true *miles Christi*.

Martial allegories function in hagiography as a way of linking the pre- and post-conversion lives of saintly warriors, proclaiming the superiority of spiritual to worldly warfare, and defining the former as the rightful province of monks. Offered the choice between '[wearing] the belt of knighthood in the world or [performing] the military service of a monk in a monastery,' the monastic founder Benedict of Selby scorned to become a knight 'who disgraces himself by performing military service in name only (*solo nomine militare*),' and 'serves vice and idleness under worldly arms.' Instead, he vowed, 'I will take myself off to the spiritual castles (*spiritualia castra*) where virtue does not go unrewarded,' to 'fight for the Lord, who strengthens [monks] with virtue, gladdens them with calm, and crowns them with glory and honor.'[68] If earthly military service was merely a profession, the *militia Christi* demanded that soldiers devote themselves body and soul to the practice of spiritual warfare. Although the contemporary rhetoric of ecclesiastical reform insistently described monks as men of peace, hagiographers stressed that knightly converts did not cease to fight upon taking religious vows. Such was said to be the case for Ralph Haget, a *miles* who joined the Cistercians of Fountains in the twelfth century and later became the house's abbot. 'Once a soldier in the world,' the monk Hugh of Kirkstall wrote, Ralph 'did not loose the sword-belt of his military service, but changed it for a better one, joining himself to the camp of the Hebrews, afterward to be a prince among the people of God.'[69]

Vitae also juxtapose converts' pre-conversion military exploits with their post-conversion spiritual victories. Pons of Léras, who before his conversion had

---

Wala,' in *Charlemagne's Cousins: Contemporary Lives of Adalard and Wala* (Syracuse, NY, 1967), 102.

[68] *Selebeiensis Monasterii Historia*, c.4, in *The Coucher Book of Selby*, 2 vols, ed. J.T. Fowler, Yorkshire Archaeological Association Record Series 10, 13 (Durham, 1891–3), 2: 6: 'Infinita est in saeculo militantium multitudo, verum quod pudor est dicere, uitiis potius quam uirtutibus seruientium: infamis est militia solo nomine militare, et dedecus indecens vitiis et inertiae seruire sub armis, ad haec spiritualia castra me confero, ubi nec virtus praemio, nec honestas reuerentiae carebit honore: Illi Domino militabo, qui suos milites virtute corroborat, quiete laetificat, Gloria et honore coronat.' On this anonymous text, which describes the eleventh-century foundation of the abbey of Selby (Yorkshire) from the vantage point of 1164, see Janet E. Burton, *The Monastic Order in Yorkshire, 1069–1215* (Cambridge, 1999), 23–8.

[69] Hugh of Kirkstall, *Narratio de fundatione Fontanis monasterii*, in *Memorials of the Abbey of St. Mary of Fountains*, 3 vols, ed. John R. Walbran, Surtees Society Publications 42, 67, 130 (Durham, 1863–1918), 1: 117–20 (quoting 117); trans. A.W. Oxford, *The Ruins of Fountains Abbey* (London, 1910), 217. On the composition and dating of the *Narratio* (begun c.1204), see Elizabeth Freeman, *Narratives of a New Order: Cistercian Historical Writing in England, 1150–1220*, Medieval Church Studies 2 (Turnhout, 2002), chapter 5.

been 'mighty in strength and agile with arms,' showed equal fortitude when his monastery at Silvanès faced its first crisis in the form of a desperate food shortage. When his brothers proposed to abandon the new foundation Pons bravely exhorted them to spiritual battle, saying,

> Those who hasten to flee show that they have been conquered. Disgrace awaits the conquered, but glory the conquerors. Now we have come not for flight but to fight (*ad pugnam*). It is therefore fitting for us to stand, not escape, and to contend bravely (*viriliter decertare*) because no one will be crowned unless he has legitimately done battle (2 Tim. 2:5).[70]

Renowned for his feats of strength and bravery on the battlefield while he lived in the world, as a monk Herluin of Bec rapidly mastered the rudiments of spiritual combat and proved himself a worthy adversary of the devil. Whenever the evil one approached, day or night, 'he found [the holy man] keeping watch on the ramparts' of his cell, spiritual arms at the ready: 'Herluin kept his sword (*gladium*) aimed at the joints and marrows of the enemy,' and 'was defended by the strong shield (*forte clypeum*) of patience and forbearance.' 'What could be more glorious,' his biographer Gilbert Crispin asked, 'than the vanquished enemy succumbing to Herluin everywhere, under a conquering God?'[71] As great as his reputation had been before his conversion, it paled in comparison to the glory Herluin won for himself as a *miles Christi* in the monastery.

It is clear from the hagiographical evidence that monks themselves understood warriors' entrance into the cloister as an initiation into a new, better sort of warfare. But the *vitae* also hint that churchmen presented conversion to lay arms-bearers in martial terms. Take, for instance, Marbod of Rennes' account of how the canon Robert of Turlande (who founded La Chaise-Dieu in 1043), when asked by 'a certain repentant knight' how he might best atone for his numerous sins, counseled the man 'to abandon everything he had in order to transfer into the military service of Christ (*militia Christi*).'[72] The Life of Amedeus of Hauterive describes how the castellan was warned by John, the Cistercian abbot of Bonnevaux, that his new life in the cloister would require far greater endurance than the one he was leaving behind:

> Neither rampart, nor wall, nor iron gate, nor high towers can defend [monks] from [the devil's] attacks. For he cannot be kept out of any place, nor can he be wounded by a well-aimed lance, nor struck down by any material stone. He never grows weary, nor does he sleep; hunger does not bother him, nor thirst exhaust

---

[70] Hugh Francigena, *Tractatus de conversione Pontii*, ed. Kienzle, 296: 'Denique qui ad fugam properant, victos se esse demonstrant. Et victos ignominia, victores vero gloria manet. Nos autem non fugam venimus sed ad pugnam. Stare ergo nos oportet non fugere, et viriliter decertare quia non coronabitur nisi qui legitime certaverit (2 Tim. 2:5).' Trans. Kienzle, 'Conversion,' 501, 507.

[71] Gilbert Crispin, *Vita Herluini*, ed. Robinson, 87–8, 92–3; trans. Vaughn, *Abbey of Bec*, 68–9, 72.

[72] Marbod of Rennes, *Vita S. Roberti Casae Dei Abbatis* [BHL 7262], 1.8, PL 171: 1505–32 (at cols. 1508–9).

him.... I speak not out of ignorance, but as one already experienced in this type of single combat (*duellum*).[73]

As a monk, Abbot John counseled the would-be convert, Amedeus would not simply put aside his identity as a warrior to become a man of peace; rather, he would become a *miles Christi*, and dedicate himself to a different kind of military service, one which would require every ounce of his strength and courage.

The knightly converts of hagiography are hybrid figures, who frustrate attempts to classify them as either holy warriors or monastic saints, or as spiritual exemplars for either lay warriors or professed religious. It seems likely that lay arms-bearers, who could have heard these *vitae* in sermons or during visits to shrines, might have identified with these figures in a way they could not with most clerical saints. As a man who had won praise for his military prowess and other 'knightly' qualities, the figure of the warrior-convert would have appealed to the order-specific values of worldly *milites*; as a monk, such a saint would have reassured lay warriors that it was never too late to transfer into the *militia Christi*, and, most importantly, that men like themselves had made some of the best monks. We might see this hagiographical genre as offering a counterpoint to the contemporary *moniages*, which held out little hope that men steeped in battle could become warriors of the spirit. But, like most contemporary Latin *vitae*, these narratives were composed for mainly monastic audiences, which would have included converted warriors as well as many others whose kinsmen still served in the *militia saecularis*. Monks who had successfully made the transition to lives of spiritual warfare could certainly have related to the stories of other knightly converts, finding in these texts reassurance that they had made worthy sacrifices. Undoubtedly, the *vitae*'s most meaningful lessons for monastic audiences, regardless of their personal background, were that the religious life required greater courage and fortitude than the profession of arms, and that monks were the true *milites Christi*.

Holy weapons

Among the various miracles of Saint Benedict, his abbey's patron, Aimo of Fleury (d.c.1010) included the tale of a *miles* who mistook his sword for a holy relic during a visit to the cathedral of Reims.[74] Impelled by all the worst qualities clerics traditionally ascribed to members of his class – pride, vanity, and lack of restraint – the man laid his weapon upon the altar housing Benedict's relics and,

---

[73] *Vita Amedaei Altae Ripae*, c.6, ed. Dimier, 289: 'Non agger, non murus, non ferrea porta, nec altae turres ab ejus incursibus nos possunt defendere. Nam non arcetur loco, non telorum jactu confrigitur, nec cassatur percussus lapide materiali. Lassatur numquam, somno comprimitur numquam, fame non affligitur, ardore sitis non fatigatur.... Non loquor ignaro, sed duelli jam certamen experto ....' Compare the abbot's speech with contemporary monastic writings on the theme of the 'interior castle' discussed in Chapter 4.

[74] *Miracles de saint Benoît*, 2.6, ed. Certain, 106–7.

turning to his companions, joked that the sword was just as holy as the saint's bones within. Almost immediately, the warrior was struck dead, the victim of divine vengeance. Although Aimo left no room for doubt that the man had been justly punished, behind this anecdote lies a whole body of liturgical prayers, ritual gestures, and miraculous transformations that suggests there was more to the unfortunate *miles*' joke than the casual reader might imagine. While modern readers are accustomed to regard weapons as purely secular objects, medieval Christians – arms-bearers as well as clerics – were conditioned to see them as existing somewhere between the realms of secular and sacred, endowed with the potential to move back and forth between the two. Weapons were costly markers of social identity, badges of *ordo* that marked their possessors' free adult status as well as their professional association with bloodshed. But they were also potentially holy objects which could be inscribed with powerful prayers, blessed in special liturgical rites, and sanctified by their bearers' pious actions. Just as relics could function as weapons with the power to maim or even kill, weapons could attain the status of relics. Perhaps, then, Aimo's knight might be forgiven for insisting that his sword was as good as a relic; after all, he was hardly the first or the last to make such a bold claim.

In the Central Middle Ages highly specialized martial skills – namely, the ability to wield a sword, lance, and shield while mounted in full armor – came to identify men as members of a warrior elite: knights, if not actually nobles. Such skills were cultivated from childhood through adolescence, when youths trained in the use of arms alongside comrades of similar ages and backgrounds.[75] The ceremonies in which arms were bestowed on young men who had completed their training marked their entrance into the responsibilities and privileges of adulthood.[76] Of particular significance in these rites was the girding on of the sword in its sword-belt or baldric (*cingulum militiae* or *balteus militiae*), which, arguably more than any other component of the warrior's equipment, was synonymous with martial prowess, faithful service, elite social standing, and, in the latter part of our period, the values of Christian knighthood and chivalry.[77] The

---

[75] Régine Le Jan, 'Apprentissages militaires, rites de passage, et remises d'armes au haut Moyen Âge,' in *Initiation, apprentissages, éducation au Moyen Âge*, ed. P.-A. Sigal (Montpellier, 1993), 281–309; eadem, 'Frankish Giving of Arms and Rituals of Power: Continuity and Change in the Carolingian Period,' in *Rituals of Power from Late Antiquity to the Early Middle Ages*, ed. F. Theuws and Janet L. Nelson (Leiden, 2000), 281–309 (esp. 283–4); and Matthew Bennett, 'Military Masculinity in England and Northern France, c.1050-c.1225,' in *Masculinity in Medieval Europe*, ed. D.M. Hadley (London, 1999), 71–88 (esp. 73f.).

[76] Such rites seem to have originated among royalty and the high nobility in the Carolingian period, but by the twelfth century they had come to be applied to humbler *milites*, as we see from the rise of the term *miles accinctus* to designate a knight who had been 'girded' with the sword-belt. The rites ranged from simple, purely secular affairs (especially pre-1200) to highly elaborate ceremonials, in which members of a cohort were often given their arms together by a single adult man of high status. See Flori, *L'essor de la chevalerie*, chapters 1–5; Keen, *Chivalry*, 64–82; Barthélemy, *The Serf, the Knight, and the Historian*, 208–13; and David Crouch, *The Image of the Aristocracy in Britain, 1000–1300* (London, 1992), 103–5.

[77] On the significance of the baldric, see Le Jan, 'Apprentissages militaires,' 286–7; Karl Ferdinand Werner, *Naissance de la noblesse: l'essor des élites politiques en Europe* (Paris,

sword itself was the most valuable – and most mythologized – piece of the warrior's kit. Swords were handed down in families and were highly prized as gifts signifying the bestowal of authority or the creation of a special bond between the giver and recipient.[78] Their cost was such that some *milites* relied on their lords' generosity to equip them and, when arms-bearers put aside their arms in order to enter the monastic life, lords and kin sometimes sought to have these valuable objects returned.[79]

The traditional importance of the sword-belt as a marker of status is reflected in penitential sentences requiring men guilty of grave sins to divest themselves of the *cingulum militiae* and lay aside the calling of arms for years or even for life.[80] This practice was already current in the Carolingian era, when elites guilty of particularly heinous crimes (e.g., parricide or the murder of a priest) were excluded from holy places, denied the sacraments, separated from their wives, and deprived of civic office, all in addition to being stripped of the sword-belt that signified their public authority and free warrior status.[81] In 999 Pope Sylvester II meted out such a penitential sentence to the Italian prince Arduin of Ivrea, who had been implicated in the murder of the bishop of Vercelli. The pope offered Arduin a choice between living as a penitent, banned from all

---

1998), 210–25; Jean Flori, 'Les origines de l'adoubement chevaleresque: étude des remises d'armes et du le vocabulaire qui les exprime dans les sources historiques latines jusqu'au début du XIIIe siècle,' *Traditio* 35 (1979), 209–72 (esp. 216–17); and Johanna Maria van Winter, '*Cingulum militiae*: Schwertleite en miles-terminologie als Spiegel van veranderend menselijk gedrag,' *Tijdschrift voor rechtsgeschiedenis* 44 (1976), 1–92.

[78] Olivier Bouzy, 'Les armes symboles d'un pouvoir politique: l'épée du sacre, la Sainte Lance, l'Oriflamme, aux VIIIe–XIIe siècles,' *Francia* 22 (1995), 45–57; Emma Mason, 'The Hero's Invincible Weapon: An Aspect of Angevin Propaganda,' in *The Ideals and Practice of Medieval Knighthood III: Proceedings of the Fourth Strawberry Hill Conference, 1988*, ed. Christopher Harper-Bill and Ruth Harvey (Woodbridge, 1990), 121–37 (esp. 122–3).

[79] For weapons supplied by lords, see the *Liber miraculorum sanctae Fidis*, 4.10, ed. A. Bouillet (Paris, 1897). For examples of kin and lords seeking the return of weapons, see *Recueil des actes des ducs de Normandie de 911 à 1066*, ed. Marie Fauroux (Caen, 1961), 275 (no. 113); and *Cartulaire de l'abbaye de Noyers*, Mémoires de la Société archéologique de Touraine 22, ed. Casimir Chevalier (Tours, 1872), 68–9 (no. 59). As Charles de Miramon has shown (*Les 'donnés' au Moyen Âge*, 89), warriors also bequeathed their arms to houses of Templars or Teutonic Knights in lieu of joining one of these orders during their lifetimes.

[80] Canon law collections of the eleventh and twelfth centuries placed special emphasis on the renunciation of the sword-belt (*cingulum militiae*), the pre-eminent badge of knightly status. See Burchard of Worms, *Decretum*, 19.57, PL 140: 997; Ivo of Chartres, *Decretum*, 15.71, PL 161: 879; and Robert of Flamborough, *Liber poenitentialis*, 5.10, ed. J.J. Francis Firth (Toronto, 1971), 271.

[81] Leyser, 'Beginnings of Knighthood,' 57–9. For examples of Carolingian legislation to this effect, see the Council of Mainz (847), ed. W. Hartmann, MGH Conc. 3: 182 (no. 14, c.24); and Mansi, 17/2: 934 (c. 72). The most famous example of such a penance imposed in practice, of course, involved Louis the Pious, whose penitential sentences in 813 and 833 deprived him of the right to bear arms (and thus to lead troops into battle); see Mayke de Jong, *The Penitential State: Authority and Atonement in the Age of Louis the Pious, 814–40* (Cambridge, 2009), chapter 6. The importance of the *cingulum militiae* as a sign of public authority in the earlier Middle Ages is emphasized by Werner, *Naissance de la noblesse*, 211–12.

physical contact, eating no meat, and laying aside his arms (*arma deponere*), or becoming a monk.[82] As Rosa Maria Dessì has observed, the former option amounted to a 'monasticization' for an elite layman.[83] Significantly, church councils of the late tenth and eleventh centuries accorded the same protection to unarmed warriors as to monks and clerics.[84] Forbidden the accoutrements and behaviors that identified them as men of standing in the world, penitents like Arduin became unmoored from their social identity and were left floating helplessly between lay and monastic status.

If the Church claimed the right to deprive sinners of their arms, churchmen also possessed the power to enhance the strength of weapons. While there is little evidence for direct clerical participation in the 'dubbing' ceremonies in which warriors received their arms until the end of our period,[85] liturgical rituals designed to protect lay warriors proliferated from the tenth century onwards, as part of the Church's larger project of harnessing and redirecting the violence of arms-bearers.[86] Among these were formulae for the blessing of specialized military equipment, including war banners, swords, spears, helmets, and armor.[87] The language of such rituals evokes the rhetoric of ecclesiastical reform as well

---

[82] For the Roman synod of 999 which passed judgment on Arduin, see MGH Leges 4, ed. L. Wieland (Hanover, 1893), 53.

[83] Rosa Maria Dessì, 'La double conversion d'Arduin d'Ivrée: pénitence et conversion autour de l'An Mil,' in *Guerriers et moines*, 317–48 (esp. 317–18, 324–6). In the event, Arduin did become a monk, but this was a decision taken in 1014, when he entered the abbey of Fruttuaria (a community founded a decade before by his kinsman William of Volpiano with material support from Arduin himself). He died as a monk of the house just a year later, suggesting the decision may have been an *ad succurrendum* conversion prompted by declining health. Penitential disarmaments like Arduin's persisted through at least the twelfth century, as evidenced by the case of Thomas de Marle, condemned *in absentia* as an enemy of the Church by an episcopal council at Beauvais in 1115 and ordered to lay down his arms; see Suger of Saint-Denis, *Vita Ludovici grossi regis*, c.24, ed. and trans. Henri Waquet, Classiques de l'histoire de France au Moyen Age 11 (Paris, 1964), 174–6.

[84] Hans Werner-Goetz, 'La Paix de Dieu en France autour de l'An Mil: fondements et objectifs, diffusion et participants,' in *Le roi de France et son royaume*, ed. Parisse and Barral i Altet, 132–43 (at 133).

[85] For the chronology of clerical involvement in these ceremonies, see Jean Flori, 'Chevalerie et liturgie: remise des armes et vocabulaire "chevaleresque" dans les sources liturgiques du IXe au XIVe siècle,' *Moyen âge* 84 (1978), 247–78 and 409–42; and Keen, *Chivalry*, 64–6, 71–7.

[86] Jean Flori has undertaken an exhaustive study of these rituals, which seem to have grown out of early medieval blessings of the ceremonial arms of rulers and benedictions of specially designated defenders of churches; see his 'Chevalerie et liturgie,' and *L'essor de la chevalerie*, chapters 4–5. For the earliest known example of the blessing of weapons, see Janet L. Nelson, 'Ninth-Century Knighthood: The Evidence of Nithard,' in *Studies in Medieval History Presented to R. Allen Brown*, ed. Christopher Harper-Bill, Christopher Holdsworth, and Janet L. Nelson (Woodbridge, 1989), 255–66 (at 259 and n.26).

[87] Keen, *Chivalry*, 46–7, 71–2; Erdmann, *Idea of Crusade*, 83–7; for the original texts, see Flori, 'Chevalerie et liturgie,' 434–42, and idem, *L'essor de la chevalerie*, 377–86. War banners (*vexilli*) were often holy objects associated with the cults of particular saints and stored in churches when not in use; for a study of one well-documented example, see Claude Gaier, 'Le rôle militaire des reliques et de l'étendard de saint Lambert dans la principauté de Liège,' *Moyen âge* 72 (1966), 235–49 (esp. 240–9). On the other hand, the arms and even

as the traditionally monastic discourse of spiritual warfare. Receiving back his consecrated weapons, a *miles* was enjoined by the officiating priest to put the defense of the Church against its enemies above all his other duties, and reminded of the obligation of arms-bearers, as servants of God in the tradition of the warrior-king David, to protect the unarmed.[88] A warrior who vowed to fulfill these obligations was promised heavenly rewards as well as earthly victories, and his weapons were 'glossed' as partaking of a dual physical–spiritual nature.

> Remember [says the priest to the *miles* in one twelfth-century text] the words of the Holy Spirit: 'Gird your sword upon your thigh, O most mighty one (Ps. 44:4).' For the sword is the Holy Spirit, that is, the word of God (cf. Eph. 6:17). In this shape, then, you hold truth: defend the church, orphans, widows, the clergy, and laborers, and scatter the enemies of the holy Church, that you may be worthy of being armed with the sword of truth and crowned with justice in the sight of Christ.[89]

By the mid twelfth century the blessing of the sword had become an extension of the bestowal of arms. 'On the day a man is girded with the sword-belt (*militari cingulo decoratur*),' John of Salisbury wrote, 'he goes solemnly to church, and, placing his sword upon the altar like a sacrificial offering (*gladioque super altare posito et oblato* – shades of the *miles* at Reims!), and making as it were a public profession, he dedicates himself to the service of the altar and vows to God the constant obedience of his sword.'[90] Such rituals suggest a blurring of the distinction between temporal and spiritual arms, a blurring that coincided with (and perhaps resulted from) the rise of new groups of hybrid spiritual–temporal warriors in the eleventh and twelfth centuries.

But the blessing of arms should not be read as a sign that physical weapons had shed their negative connotations in the eyes of clerics. Contemporary sermons explicitly identified expensive, showy arms as symbols of the pride and vanity of lay arms-bearers,[91] and preachers told stories of dead knights condemned to the gruesomely fitting eternal torments of bearing red-hot arms, or having their

---

the horses of warriors who opposed churchmen's interests might be anathematized, as the canons of the 1031 Council of Limoges demonstrate; see Mansi, 19: 530.

[88] Flori, *L'essor de la chevalerie*, 369–84 (texts S.24–9), and 84–96 (commentary).

[89] Flori, *L'essor de la chevalerie*, 382 (text S.27.4): 'Tu, cum sis futurus miles, memor esto verbi spiritus sancti: Accingere gladio suo super femur tuum potentissime (Ps. 44:4). Gladius enim spiritus sancti est, quod est verbum dei (cf. Eph. 6:17). In hac ergo forma veritatem tene, ecclesiam defende, pupillos et viduas et oratores et laboratores, contra impugnatores sancte ecclesie promptus perge, ut possis coram Christo gladio veritatis et iusticie armatus coronatus apparere.'

[90] John of Salisbury, *Policraticus sive nugis curialium et vestigiis philosophorum*, 6.10, in PL 199: 602; trans. based on John Dickinson, *The Statesman's Book of John of Salisbury* (New York, 1927), 202–3. Compare the near-contemporary description of a similar rite by Peter of Blois, Letter 94, PL 207: 294: 'Sed et hodie tirones enses suos recipiunt de altari, ut profiteantur se filios Ecclesiae, atque ad honorem sacerdotii, ad tuitionem pauperum, ad vindictam malefactorum et patriae liberationem gladium accepisse.'

[91] For 'showy' arms as indicators of pride, see Peter of Celle, Sermon 16, PL 202: 683–5. On the sword-belt more specifically, see Baldric of Dol's version of Urban II's address to

armor nailed to their bodies by demons.⁹² Although a narrow route to salvation had been opened for *milites* who wielded their arms in the service of the Church, such men could hardly be compared with their comrades who rejected arms and worldly warfare altogether.

Accounts of the conversion from arms-bearer to monk in *vitae* and charters underscore the symbolic value of arms, consistently identifying the laying-down of weaponry as a pivotal moment in a convert's transfer from the worldly *militia* to the spiritual one. These rites, in which men seeking to become monks deposited their sword-belt (and sometimes other military equipment) upon the altar of their new community's church, closely resembled penitential disarming rituals,⁹³ underscoring the medieval understanding of monastic life as a lifelong state of penance.

The deposition of arms, first recorded in the eighth century, became an integral part of monastic profession ceremonies for elite converts in the Central Middle Ages. During the Carolingian period, men who offered up their sword-belts and locks of their newly tonsured hair on the altar of a monastic church were as likely to be political exiles as voluntary converts.⁹⁴ Later this was less often the case, and the proliferation of accounts of the *depositio cinguli* in charters and hagiography from the tenth century on has been linked to the increasingly common practice of adult conversion to the religious life.⁹⁵ By 1000 the phrase '*deponere cingulum militiae*' had become monastic shorthand for such conversions.⁹⁶ Converts' experience of such rites (and, no doubt, some monastic witnesses' perception of them) would likely have been shaped by personal memories of the *depositio*'s ritual double, the girding on of the sword-belt which had traditionally marked the transition to adulthood and which became a central element in the creation of a distinct knightly identity.⁹⁷

Frankish warriors at Clermont in 1095: 'Vos accincti cingulo militiae magno superbitis supercilio....' *Historia Hierosolimitana* 1.4, in RHC Occ. 4: 14.

92 As in the *Visio Gunthelmi* (cited in Chapter 2, n.76), and the story cited by Kaeuper, *Holy Warriors*, 67–8.

93 For example, the description of how in 833 Louis the Pious 'cingulum militiae deposuit et super altare collocavit' (MGH Capit. 2, ed. A. Boretius and V. Krause [Hanover, 1897], 55) closely resembles many of the accounts of monastic conversion considered below.

94 For early examples of the *depositio armarum*, see Le Jan, 'Frankish Giving of Arms,' 298–9; and van Winter, '*Cingulum militiae*,' 50–1. Mayke De Jong has highlighted the difficulty of distinguishing between political prisoners and voluntary converts on the basis of surviving evidence; see 'Monastic Prisoners or Opting Out: Political Coercion and Honour in the Frankish Kingdoms,' in *Topographies of Power in the Early Middle Ages*, ed. Frans Theuws, Mayke De Jong, and Carine van Rhijn (Leiden, 2001), 291–328.

95 Miramon, 'Embracer l'état monastique,' 841–5.

96 As in the miracles of Saint Maximinus composed by the Benedictine monk Letald of Micy (*Liber miraculorum S. Maximini Micianensis abbatis*, 3.15, PL 137: 803), who describes a contemporary wave of noble conversions this way: 'multi nobiles et saeculo expectabiles viri cingula deponentes militiae veteremque cum suis actibus hominem exuti, in eodem ipso loco Domino se mancipari gaudebant.'

97 For this argument, see van Winter, '*Cingulum militiae*.' For two descriptions of how rituals of arming were seen to instruct new *milites* in the obligations of Christian knighthood, see *ibid.*, docs. 131 (Peter of Blois) and 176 (Alan of Lille).

Monastic fascination with the ritual of *depositio* is revealed by hagiographers' tendency to linger over these moments in their conversionary narratives. The highly influential Latin *vita* of Saint Alexis (c.1000), as well as its Old French redactions, recounted how the newlywed nobleman had renounced his baldric (*balteus*), or alternately, his sword (*spede* or *espée*), together with his wealth and his new bride.[98] The Alexis narrative, which echoes contemporary penitential practices, has been credited with inspiring many nobles to embrace the *vita apostolica* in the eleventh and twelfth centuries.[99] Later works of hagiography depicted noble converts offering their swords or baldrics to the religious communities they entered. In the mid eleventh century Odo of Saint-Maur described one such donation in his Life of Count Burchard of Vendôme.[100] Long a generous patron of the house, Burchard marked his profession at Saint-Maur-des-Fossés with rich gifts, including his golden sword and sword-belt (*aureus ensis cum cingulo aureo*).[101] As Michel Lauwers has noted, the hagiographer positioned the description of Burchard's arms in the middle of a lengthy list of donated altar furnishings and sacramental vessels, thereby presenting them to the reader as holy, quasi-liturgical objects rather than as ordinary weapons.[102]

The Benedictine Hariulf of Saint-Médard, writing c.1114, similarly equated the conversion of his noble subject, Arnulf of Soissons, with his rejection of the sword-belt.[103] Although as a young man Arnulf had reluctantly let himself

[98] *Vita de S. Alexii* [BHL 286], c.2, AASS Jul. 4: 251–4 (at col. 252); *Vie de saint Alexis: poème du XIe siècle*, ed. Gaston Paris (Paris, 1885), 4 (stanza 15); *The Vie de Saint Alexis in the Twelfth and Thirteenth Centuries: An Edition and Commentary*, ed. Alison Goddard Elliott (Chapel Hill, 1983), 98 (stanza 17). For the composition and dissemination of these texts, see Tony Hunt, 'The Life of St. Alexis, 475–1125,' in *Christina of Markyate*, ed. Henrietta Leyser and Samuel Fanous (London, 2005), 217–28. The renunciation of the sword-belt and one's wife – probably the two most important markers of adult male status among elites – also appears in the description of the conversion of the Italian nobleman Heldric, who entered Cluny as a disciple of Maieul; Syrus, *Vita sancti Maioli*, 2.24, in *Agni immaculati*, ed. Iogna-Prat, 242.

[99] Brenda Bolton, 'Old Wealth and New Poverty in the Twelfth Century,' in *Renaissance and Renewal in Christian History*, Studies in Church History 14, ed. Derek Baker (Oxford, 1977), 95–103 (at 98); and Charles de Miramon, 'Guerre des récits,' 612–15.

[100] Odo of Saint-Maur, *Vita domni Burcardi* [BHL 1482], ed. Charles Bourel de la Roncière as *Vie de Bouchard le Vénérable* (Paris, 1892). For commentary on Odo's work, see Flori, *L'essor de la chevalerie*, 152–8. On the historical Burchard, see Barthélemy, 'Sur les traces du comte Bouchard'; and for Burchard's role in the Cluniac reform of Saint-Maur, Dominique Iogna-Prat, *Order and Exclusion: Cluny and Christendom Face Heresy, Judaism, and Islam (1000–1150)*, trans. Graham Robert Edwards (Ithaca, NY, 2002), 56–7.

[101] Odo of Saint-Maur, *Vita Burcardi*, c.11, ed. de la Roncière, 28. Burchard's arms recall descriptions of ceremonial weapons of the sort worn by royalty and the upper aristocracy, as well as descriptions of golden, gem-encrusted arms in the *chansons*.

[102] Michel Lauwers, 'La 'vie du seigneur Bouchard, comte vénérable': Conflits d'avouerie, traditions carolingiennes et modèles de sainteté à l'abbaye des Fossés au XIe siècle,' in *Guerriers et moines*, ed. Lauwers, 371–418 (at 404–5).

[103] For Arnulf's cult and hagiography, see Renée Nip, 'Life and Afterlife: Arnulf of Oudenbourg, Bishop of Soissons, and Godelieve of Ghistel: Their Function as Intercessors in Medieval Flanders,' in *The Invention of Saintliness*, ed. Anneke B. Mulder-Bakker (London, 2002), 58–76 (esp. 59–66).

be girded with the belt of secular knighthood (*secularis militiae cingulum*), he was destined to wield spiritual arms (*spiritualia arma*), and even while living in the world devoted himself to holy reading and attended the offices as assiduously as any monk.[104] Having made the decision to take monastic vows, Arnulf presented himself at Saint-Médard along with two squires (*armigeri*) whose help he had enlisted to transport the huge collection of military equipment he wished to present as an offering to Abbot Reynald.[105] His gifts and his plea for admittance having been accepted, the brethren were then summoned to witness Arnulf's profession in the abbey church, where the nobleman stripped off his sword-belt and fine clothing, and was tonsured and clothed in the monastic habit.[106] Divested of the arms and rich clothing of a worldly warrior, Arnulf was reborn as a *miles Christi*.[107] A century after Hariulf wrote, the Cistercian prior Caesarius of Heisterbach recounted an equally dramatic tale of transformation from knight to *miles Christi*. A German knight named Walewan arrived at the abbey of Hemmenrode, so the story went, seeking to join the community, and made his wishes known by entering the church in full panoply of arms and armor. Reaching the altar of the Virgin, 'with all the convent looking on, he laid down his arms and took up the monk's dress.' Walewan had thought it 'fitting and proper,' Caesarius continued, 'that he should lay down the warlike trappings of the world there where he proposed to assume the garments of a soldier of Christ (*miles Christi*).'[108] While here we see the same sort of insistence on continuity found in the conversion narratives described earlier in this chapter – Walewan was not ceasing to be a soldier, but exchanging worldly military service for membership in the soldiery of Christ – the *depositio* ritual is once again identified with the convert's rebirth as a spiritual warrior.

A comparison of the above descriptions of warriors' conversions with charter evidence strongly suggests these hagiographers based their narratives on contemporary ceremonies that they had themselves witnessed. According to a tenth-century charter of Cluny the loosening of the sword-belt, along with the shaving of the crown of the head and beard, removed the outward markers of knightly status and prepared the convert to be clothed with the monastic habit.[109] In charters, as in *vitae*, the offering of the sword or *cingulum militiae* upon the altar

---

[104] Hariulf, *Vita Arnulfi*, c.4, PL 174: 1378–9.
[105] Hariulf, *Vita Arnulfi*, c.5, PL 174: 1380.
[106] Hariulf, *Vita Arnulfi*, c.5, PL 174: 1381: 'excipiunt, atque militiae cingulum respuentem armaque cum vestibus cultissimus quas attulerat ad ecclesiam conferentem attondent, ac tonsoratum in habitu regulari crucis Christi mortificationem amiciunt.'
[107] Though Hariulf emphasized the loyalty, humility, and love of justice Arnulf displayed while living in the world, it is significant that he described Arnulf as a *miles Christi* only after the latter's conversion; see *Vita Arnulfi*, c.7, 24, PL 174: 1382, 1419.
[108] Caesarius of Heisterbach, *Dialogus miraculorum*, 1.37, ed. Strange, 1: 45–6; trans. Scott and Bland, *Dialogue on Miracles*, 1: 49. For commentary, see Murray, 'Masculinizing Religious Life,' 29.
[109] For example, see the charter commemorating the entrance of the *miles* Leutbald into Cluny in 951; *Recueil des chartres de l'abbaye de Cluny*, 5 vols, ed. Auguste Bernard and Alexandre Bruel (Paris, 1876–1903), 1: 756 (no. 802). The text reads: 'Ego denique predictus Leotbaldus cingulum militiae solvens et comam capitis barbamque pro divino

might be accompanied by donations of valuable movables or landed property that the new monk had formerly defended with worldly arms.[110] Hagiographers' insistence that the *depositio cinguli* marked the transition from a life of worldly warfare to membership in the spiritual militia is paralleled in contemporary charters. In the early eleventh century, for example, a *miles* named William was said to have joined the abbey of Lérins because he hoped to avoid the eternal damnation that awaited most men of his rank, and desired to 'fight' for a higher cause. A monastic scribe recorded William's profession in the house's cartulary as follows:

> And so I, William, in obedience to God's command, am leaving behind all that I possess in the world, and, in order to fight for God alone and to triumph according to the *Rule* of Saint Benedict, I am laying aside my sword-belt (*militiae deponens cingulum*) and taking up the monastic order, with God's approval, at the monastery of Lérins under Abbot Garnier.[111]

William was hardly alone; many of his contemporaries were said to have offered up their sword-belts in token of their willingness to fight for Christ.[112]

Customaries describe how, having put off his sword-belt, a converted warrior would be clothed in the monastic habit by his new superior and girded with the cincture (*cingulum*) which, like every item of the monk's clothing, was regarded as highly symbolic.[113] In the early twelfth century Stephen of Autun wrote that the cincture signified vigilance, and was meant to recall to wearers' minds Christ's admonition that the faithful should gird their thighs in preparation for the Lord's return (Luke 12:37).[114] Just as a secular warrior rarely removed his

---

amore detundens, monasticum ... habitum in predicto monasterio recipere dispono.' Cited by Barthélemy, *The Serf, the Knight, and the Historian*, 216n.

[110] An example is the story of Thomas Muschamps' admittance to the Benedictine community at Durham in c.1130, at which time the knight invested the community's patron Cuthbert with property by offering up his sword on the saint's altar. For the text, see J. Raine, *History and Antiquities of North Durham* (London, 1852), 141 (appendix); and for commentary, Clanchy, *Memory to Written Record*, 39–40.

[111] *Cartulaire de l'abbaye de Lérins*, ed. Henri Moris and Edmond Blanc (Paris, 1905), 2–3 (no. 3); cited in Dessì, 'Pénitence et conversion,' 342–3, n.108: 'At superna medicina, nolens in eternum perire quod fecerat, misericorditer omnibus clamat.... Quam ego Guilelmus jussionis vocem adimplere cupiens, relictis omnibus que seculi sunt, Deo soli amodo militaturus ac secundum regulam sancti Benedicti jam victurus, apud Lirinense monasterium sub abbate Guarnerio militiae deponens cingulum, ordinem assummo, Deo favente, monasticum.'

[112] For more examples, see van Winter, '*Cingulum militiae*'; Miramon, 'Embracer l'état monastique'; Dessì, 'Pénitence et conversion'; Le Jan, 'Frankish Giving of Arms.'

[113] For the importance of clothing in profession rites, see Constable, 'Ceremonies and Symbolism,' 808–16; and idem, 'Entrance into Cluny,' 337–8.

[114] Stephen of Autun, *Tractatus de sacramento altaris*, c.10: PL 172: 1282. Here Stephen is speaking of the belt worn by a priest over the alb. Compare the similar explanations of the cincture's significance offered by Hrabanus Maurus (*De institutione clericorum*, c.17, PL 107: 306); Sicard of Cremona (*Mitrale*, 2.5, PL 213: 74); and Guillaume Durand (*Rationale divinorum officiorum I–IV*, 3.4.1, 3.19.9, ed. A. Davril and T.M. Thibodeau, CCCM 140 [Turnholt, 1995], 188, 233).

sword-belt from the time he received his arms, a monk would wear his cincture almost constantly for the rest of his life, sleeping in it and eventually being buried in it.[115] As we saw in Chapter 3, Cassian had earlier identified the monk's 'double belt (*cingulum duplicis*)' as both an ascetic tool and a piece of spiritual armor; the monk girded his loins to subdue his flesh, but also to do spiritual battle with the devil.[116] Benedict's *Rule* specified that the brothers should sleep 'clothed, and girded with belts or cords (*cincti cingellis aut funibus*),' and later customaries upheld this practice, which simplified preparations for the night office and, most importantly, safeguarded wearers' modesty.[117] The monastic belt was thus a reminder of the monk's vow of chastity and of his status as a spiritual combatant pledged to lifelong battle against lust. On this basis, later monastic writers explicitly compared the cincture to the warrior's sword-belt. Just as worldly arms-bearers signaled their standing by the wearing of the baldric, Abbo of Fleury explained, 'We [clerics] have a belt of our own military service (*militiae nostrae cingulum*), with which we bind fast our inner purity.'[118] A century later, when Baldwin of Ford joined the Cistercians, he was said to have girded himself with the belt of the military service of Cîteaux (*cingulo militie Cisterciensis*).'[119]

The logic of spiritual warfare allowed for the monk's cincture and the knight's sword-belt to undergo surprisingly analogous transformations. Sanctified through their owners' renunciations, weapons traversed the boundary between the secular and the sacred, becoming physical embodiments of the spiritual arms of the *miles Christi*. Some discarded arms were preserved by religious houses as reminders of their former owners' sacrifices, even attaining the status of relics by virtue of their association with warriors venerated as saints. In the late tenth century the monks of Luxeuil proudly displayed the arms of Waldebert, a nobleman who had joined their community some three centuries earlier, 'as a testament to his spiritual warfare.'[120] At Brioude in the twelfth century the abbey of Saint-Julien possessed a 'most beautiful and striking shield' reputed to have belonged to the

---

[115] On the near-constant wearing of the *cingulum militiae*, see Le Jan, 'Frankish Giving of Arms,' 286–7.

[116] Cassian, *Institutiones*, 1.1.1–5 and 1.11.1–3, ed. and trans. Guy, 36–8, 52–4.

[117] RB, c.22, p. 218. For discussions of this injunction, see *Die consuetudines des Augustiner-Chorherrenstiftes Marbach im Elsass (12 Jahrhundert)*, c.55.123, ed. Josef Siegwart (Freiburg, 1965), 161.

[118] Abbo of Fleury, *Canones*, c.51–2, PL 139: 506: 'Non enim tantum de his militantibus Scriptura loquitur, qui armata militia detinentur, sed quisque militiae suae cingulo utitur, dignitatis suae miles ascribitur.... Haec sententia, quae ad milites loquitur, potest etiam ad clericos retorqueri, quia, etiamsi non militare videantur saeculo, tamen Deo militant.... Videmur, inquam, non militare remissis ac fluentibus tunicis: sed habemus militiae nostrae cingulum, quo castimoniae interiora constringamus.' Cited by Van Winter, 55–6 (doc. 27).

[119] Peter of Blois, Letter 10, in *The Later Letters of Peter of Blois*, Auctores Britannici Medii Aevi 13, ed. Elizabeth Revell (Oxford, 1993), 53.

[120] Adso of Montiérender, *Miracula SS. Waldeberti et Eustasii auctore Adsone abbate dervensi* [BHL 8775], c.1, ed. O. Holder-Egger (Hanover, 1888), MGH SS 15/2: 1172: 'praediis, armisque depositis, quae usque hodie in testimonium sacrae miliciae eius in eo loco habentur, servorum Dei numero addicitur sociandus....'

Carolingian nobleman William of Gellone before he entered religious life and offered his arms, most fittingly, to the abbey's patron, the Roman soldier-martyr Julian.[121] Their owners' metamorphoses into spiritual warriors had not erased the past histories of these instruments of bloodshed; on the contrary, the memory of their original function was crucial to any understanding of these weapons as relics. Such objects lent themselves to a number of ideological uses: they evoked the acts of rejection which had transformed their owners into *milites Christi*; and they proclaimed more generally the spiritual superiority of the monastic life to the worldly profession of war (and that of the monk's spiritual weapons to the physical arms of the knight).[122] Faith in the divine power of such relic-weapons was a feature of both monastic and lay spirituality. So well, in fact, did religious communities promote the miracle-working abilities of these objects that lay warriors were occasionally moved to steal them![123]

Like the conversion of arms-bearers to the monastic life, or the remaking of battle sites into strongholds of monastic prayer, the transformation of weapons forged for killing into holy relics highlights the thin line which separated the martial and the sacred in medieval Christendom. What were under ordinary circumstances instruments of pollution which stained their bearers' hands with blood and their souls with sin could become repositories of holy memory and conduits for celestial power. Through a process Philippe Buc has labeled 'object conversion,' a sword-belt laid upon an altar to mark its owner's transition from worldly *miles* to *miles Christi* acquired a new identity, but one which incorporated, rather than erased, its original nature. The greater the disparity between its original and its new function, the more important it was that 'the converted object should display its itinerary,' even while asserting the superiority of its present meaning.[124] Though relic-weapons retained their original form (the better to tell their origin stories), the conversion of their former owners extended to them as well, lending them a dual physical–spiritual status. For those initiated into their

---

[121] *Vita Willelmi Gellonensis*, 2.20, AASS May 6: 816.

[122] The relic-weapons of converted warriors form a subset of a larger group of holy weapons displayed at shrines in this period. Among the better-known examples are the arms and armor of Gangulf (a ninth-century nobleman 'martyred' by his wife's lover) at Varennes; the sword and shield of the archangel Michael at Mont-Saint-Michel; Roland's sword, Durendal, at Rocamadour; and the sword of Odo of Canterbury at Ramsey Abbey. For these objects, see, respectively, the *Vita Gangulfi martyris Varennensis* [BHL 3328], c.3, ed. W. Levison, MGH SS RerMerov 7/1: 159; Baldric of Dol, *Relatio de scuto et gladio sancti Michaeli*, ed. Jean Huynes in *Histoire générale de l'abbaye du Mont-Saint-Michel au péril de la mer*, 2 vols, ed. Eugène de Robillard de Beaurepaire (Rouen, 1872–3), 1: 137–46; Mason, 'The Hero's Invincible Weapon,' 126–7; and the *Chronicon abbatiae Rameseiensis*, ed. W.D. Macray, Rolls Series 83 (London, 1886), 16.

[123] The arms and armor of the 'martyr' Gangulf were the subject of two pious thefts in the eleventh century, on which see Michel Lauwers, 'À propos de l'usage seigneurial des reliques: Note sur les 'miracles de Saint Gengoul (1034 ou 1045),' in *Guerriers et moines*, ed. Lauwers, 285–8. The sword displayed as Durendal at Rocamadour was stolen multiple times, most famously by Henry II's eldest son Henry in 1183; see Mason, 'Hero's Invincible Weapon,' 126.

[124] Buc, 'Conversion of Objects,' 100, 104–7.

histories, such weapons were both material reminders of bearers' previous sins and proofs of their rebirth, physical weapons that had shed blood but now bore witness that their owners had exchanged physical instruments of war for the spiritual arms of the monk.

Martial asceticism

In his *vita* of the twelfth-century hermit Wulfric of Haselbury, the Cistercian John of Ford told of an unusual problem that confronted the holy man at the height of his ascetic career. After successfully overcoming his carnal impulses, training himself to sleep on a wicker hurdle, and surviving a direct attack by the devil disguised as a huge snake, Wulfric's ascetic regime was almost derailed for want of a good armorer. According to his biographer, the length of Wulfric's mail-shirt (*lorica*) interfered with his constant genuflections, and the hermit accordingly consulted William Fitzwalter, the local nobleman who had given it to him as a gift. Over William's protests that Wulfric ought to have his armor professionally altered, the hermit insisted they try cutting off several rows of rings with an ordinary pair of shears! Thanks to Wulfric's earnest prayers for divine intervention the impromptu alteration was a success, and the discarded links were distributed to the people of the neighborhood, who prized them as holy relics for many years afterwards. Most importantly, Wulfric was able to resume wearing 'the mail shirt with which he had armed himself to do battle in God's cause.'[125]

It is hardly surprising that Wulfric's monastic biographer would employ martial language to describe his subject's heroic spiritual accomplishments, but John's insistence that Wulfric not only engaged in spiritual combat but wore an actual coat of mail while doing so seems to call for additional explanation. In Wulfric's day, as we have seen, armor was a highly charged symbol synonymous with arms-bearers, whose identities were bound up in the costly and highly specialized tools of their trade: the powerful warhorse, double-edged sword, and hauberk, or long-sleeved shirt forged of small, interconnected metal links, which (as Wulfric discovered) was ideally custom-fitted to individual wearers.[126] But in the hands of an unusual group of holy men, the hauberks worn by contemporary knights became ascetic props designed to punish, rather than protect, wearers' bodies.[127] Extolled by monastic hagiographers as simultaneously *bellatores* and

---

[125] John of Ford, *Vita Wulfrici*, c.9, ed. Bell, 22–3. A slightly abridged translation by Pauline Matarasso may be found in *The Cistercian World: Monastic Writings of the Twelfth Century* (New York, 1993), 235–73 (here 241–2).

[126] In an assize of 1181 Henry II of England required all knights to come to fight for the king equipped with a hauberk, helmet, shield, lance, and warhorse; see John France, *Western Warfare in the Age of the Crusades* (Ithaca, NY, 1999), 32–3.

[127] I have defined *lorica* as a hauberk or mail shirt, its most common meaning after 1000, rather than as a breastplate, its usual meaning in classical Latin, except where the texts plainly refer to a breastplate. I also have limited my consideration to figures clearly stated to have worn armor, rather than iron chains or other metal penitential devices (although

oratores, these holy men, or *loricati* ('mailed ones'), were virtuoso practitioners of spiritual warfare who fought the devil in physical armor. Though their greatest admirers were monks, few armored ascetics were raised in traditional monastic settings; many had been soldiers before renouncing the world (but continuing to wear their rusting hauberks against their bare flesh), and most shunned formal religious vows in favor of a less structured solitary life. Their *vitae* show a reluctance to categorize these holy figures as members of either the monastic or the knightly 'orders,' though they insist on their suitability as spiritual exemplars for both monks (who were, after all, fellow spiritual warriors) and lay arms-bearers (who actively sought the *loricati*'s prayers and even made them gifts of armor). If lay warriors who fought in the service of the Church could rise to the status of spiritual warriors, and the weapons of *milites*-turned-monks be transformed into powerful relics, ascetics might in turn appropriate knightly equipment, further blurring the boundaries between the secular and the holy.

For arms-bearers, armor was not only a vital necessity from a military point of view but a key marker of identity, so much so that by the eleventh century the terms *lorica* and *loricatus* might designate not merely a warrior's coat of mail but the warrior himself.[128] So closely tied was the coat of mail to the calling of the *miles* that a warrior who owed knight's service was said to hold his lands *per loricam*.[129] Clerical views of armor, on the other hand, were conditioned by the clear differentiation in Scripture between its spiritual and temporal varieties. In the Hebrew Bible and New Testament alike, temporal armor is associated with some of the most formidable warriors sent by God to test or punish His people; the sixth plague of Revelation consists of twenty thousand warriors wearing 'breastplates of fire and of hyacinth and of brimstone' (Rev. 9:17), while the fearsomeness of the Philistine giant Goliath is emphasized by the heavy armor covering him from head to toe (1 Sam. 17:5). Some theologians went further, employing the *lorica* as a metaphor for all the worst traits of arms-bearers. A Lenten sermon by the Cluniac Peter of Celle offered the following gloss on Psalms 19:8 ('Some trust in chariots, and some in horses: but we will call upon the name of the Lord, our God'):

> 'Dearest brethren, the princes of darkness in their mail shirts and helmets, carried on horses and in chariots and bearing warlike arms, are rushing on the wind,

---

some of the *loricati* wore these in addition to mail shirts), since the latter items lack a clear association with combat, spiritual or otherwise.

[128] See the entries for '*lorica*' in Du Cange, *Glossarium*, 4: 142; Niermeyer, *Mediae Latinitatis Lexicon minus*, 621; and Albert Blaise, *Lexicon Latinitatis medii aevi* (Turnhout, 1975), 545. For examples of such usage see Regino of Prüm, *Chronica*, PL 132: 64; Sigebert of Gembloux, *Chronica*, PL 160: 490; and Thietmar of Merseburg, *Chronica*, PL 139: 1230, 1266, 1311, 1338. As the ideology of crusading developed, crusaders, too, came to be identified by their armor, as in the accounts of the First Crusade by Fulcher of Chartres (*Historia Hierosolymitana* 1.4, ed. Hagenmeyer, 140) and William of Tyre (*Historia* 16.9, ed. Huygens, 2: 727).

[129] For example, the charter of liberties issued by Henry I (August 1100), which refers to 'qui per loricas terras suas deserviunt.' See William Stubbs, *Select Charters: From the Beginning to 1307*, 5th edn, ed. H.W.C. Davies (Oxford, 1921), 119 and 519 (glossary).

coming from all parts of the heavens to conquer the people of Christendom, and especially religious communities.'[130]

Though Peter's clerical audience could have had no doubt as to the identity of those fearsome 'princes of darkness,' the preacher went on to explain that 'he who rides furious horses, whose hauberk (*lorica*) is impenetrable ... he is Pride, if he be not worthy of damnation.'[131]

While temporal armor was freighted with negative associations, a parallel tradition associated spiritual armor with righteousness. This symbolism is found in the Hebrew Bible (Isa. 59:17 and Wisd. 5:18–19),[132] and the metaphor of spiritual armor is picked up in Ephesians 6:13–17, where believers are encouraged to protect themselves with 'the armor of God (*armatura Dei*)' in anticipation of imminent judgment, and Thessalonians 5:8, which further describes the virtuous Christian as bearing 'the breastplate of faith and charity, and for a helmet the hope of salvation.' In the Central Middle Ages, as we saw in Chapter 4, the girding on of spiritual armor became a common form of monastic meditation, a way of reaffirming the monk's identity as a soldier of Christ. Likewise, the *loricati*'s wearing of material armor, a literal fulfillment of the biblical injunction to wear the 'armor of God,' was understood by admiring hagiographers as a sign of these men's humility and desire to do penance.

Of the twenty-eight *loricati* I have located in medieval sources, a full twenty-one lived between 1050 and 1250,[133] a period when, as we have seen, the

---

[130] Peter of Celle, Sermon 16, PL 202: 683: 'Attendite ergo, fratres charissimi, principes tenebrarum loricatos et galeatos, in equis et curribus gestatos; gestantes arma bellica, ab omni vento coeli venientes et concurrentes ad debellandum populum Christianorum; et praecipue congregationes religiosorum: Hi in curribus, et hi in equis; nos autem in nomine Domini Dei nostri invocabimus (Ps. 19:8).' The description is reminiscent of a vision of an aerial battle between horsemen seen by the people of Jerusalem that presaged a terrible massacre of the city's inhabitants (2 Macc. 5:1–3).

[131] Peter of Celle, Sermon 16, PL 202: 685: 'Jam vero dictum est de illa, quae ambulat in equis, sed et equis vehementibus, superbia; cujus lorica impenetrabilis, cujus hasta penetrabilis; cujus sella variabilis; cujus equus valde mobilis; cujus scutum mirabiliter depictum; cujus totus apparatus satis appetibilis, si non esset damnabilis.'

[132] Isa. 59:17: 'He put on justice as a breastplate (*lorica*), and a helmet of salvation upon his head'; Wisd. 5:18–19: 'And his zeal will take armor, and he will arm the creature for the revenge of his enemies. He will put on justice as a breastplate, and will take true judgment instead of a helmet.'

[133] For the twenty-one figures from this period who are my focus here, see the list of *loricati* in the Appendix. I have been able to discover three examples of armor-clad ascetics from the Carolingian era: Bishop Hubert of Liège (AASS Nov. 5: 834); the hermit Vitalis of Noirmoutier (AASS Oct. 7: 1096); and Abbot Tato of Saint Vincent in Vulterno (AASS Oct. 5: 660). Four later figures – Richard of Chichester (d.1253), Thomas Cantilupe (d.1282), Peter Morrone (Pope Celestine V, d.1296), and the Franciscan friar John of Alverna (d.1322) – were said to have worn *loricae* as a form of penance. On Richard, see *Saint Richard of Chichester: The Sources for His Life*, ed. David Jones, Sussex Record Society 79 (Lewes, 1995), 137, 155; I am grateful to Joe Creamer for this reference. On Thomas, see *Processus de vita et miraculis factus anno 1307*, c.5, in AASS, Oct. 1: 541–68 (at col. 556); on Peter, see Peter of Aliaco, *Vita et miracula S. Petri Caelestini*, c.1, AASS May 4: 484–97 (at col. 490); and for John see *The Little Flowers of St. Francis*, c. 49, trans.

conceptual relationship of monks and arms-bearers was thoroughly renegotiated in the wake of ecclesiastical reform movements. Monastic hagiographers of the eleventh and twelfth centuries also began to celebrate armored holy men in greater numbers than ever before. The *loricati* were a diverse group; their *vitae* locate them all over France, England, Italy, and the Empire, and describe a similarly wide range of personal backgrounds and institutional affiliations. Some were of noble birth, and lived as warriors before converting to the religious life, while others came from quite modest backgrounds. The entire spectrum of ecclesiastical offices is represented in their *vitae*, as priests, monks, and high-ranking prelates were associated with this ascetic practice, but many *loricati* lived on the fringes of the institutional Church as hermits only loosely affiliated with particular orders or communities. The one hagiographical constant is that the *loricati* were men; though holy women wore hairshirts and even iron chains, the wearing of armor appears to have been an almost exclusively male (and emphatically masculine) form of ascetic discipline.[134] The records of their spiritual battles, written by admiring monks across the Latin West, hint at the existence of a martial ascetic subculture and offer valuable evidence of monastic concern with the relationship between warfare and holiness.

Though there is some debate about the origins of penitential armor-wearing,[135] the earliest example of an armor-clad ascetic after the year 1000 is generally agreed to be the Italian Dominic *Loricatus*, a hermit of Fonte Avellana whose *vita* was written by his ardent admirer and self-proclaimed student Peter Damian.[136] Dominic had been destined for the priesthood by his parents, who had purchased his ordination while he was still a child. It was in order to expiate this act of simony that the adult Dominic abandoned his family and embarked on a life of great austerity, first as a monk and later as a hermit at Fonte Avellana, an eremitic community founded by the great tenth-century ascetic Romuald of Ravenna and renowned for its discipline. Until his death around 1060, Dominic

Raphael Brown (New York, 1991), 155. For the Latin text of John's *Life* see *Actus beati Francisci et sociorum ejus*, c.54, ed. Paul Sabatier (Paris, 1902), 164–70. While I have endeavored to find as many examples as possible, there are surely additional *loricati* to be discovered.

[134] The only holy woman I am aware of who was said to have used a *lorica* is Mabilia, the mother of the archbishop Edmund of Abingdon (d.1240). In his *vita* of Edmund, Matthew Paris wrote that when the future saint was a young man, his mother 'reliquerat ei loricam qua, dum viveret, utebatur.' See *Vita B. Edmundi Cantuariensis archiepiscopi*, c.1, ed. C.H. Lawrence in *St. Edmund of Abington: A Study in Hagiography and History* (Oxford, 1960), 223. I thank Joe Creamer for bringing this passage to my attention.

[135] It is tempting to link the *loricati* to the early medieval practice of wearing iron chains, bands, or rings as a form of penance for serious crimes, especially parricide; for that practice, which was repeatedly attacked by church reformers, including Charlemagne, see Henri Platelle, 'Pratiques pénitentielles et mentalités religieuses au moyen âge: La pénitence des parricides et l'esprit de l'ordalie,' *Mélanges de science religieuse* 40 (1983), 129–55. I am grateful to Sandy Evans for this reference.

[136] Peter Damian, *Vita S. Rodulphi episcopi Eugubini et S. Dominici Loricati* [BHL 7282], PL 144: 1007–24. On Dominic's asceticism as a form of *imitatio Christi* see Constable, *Three Studies*, 202–3.

adhered to a program of near-constant prayer and flagellation.¹³⁷ As his name suggests, Dominic mortified his flesh for fifteen years by wearing not one but two *loricae*, in which, in his biographer's words, 'he joined honorable battle with evil spirits and was always prepared for the fight.' Thus 'fortified, not only in his heart but in his body, the passionate warrior (*fervidus bellator*) marched against the battle lines of his enemies.'¹³⁸ In his *vita*, Peter celebrated Dominic as simultaneously *orator* and *bellator*, a holy man who not only armed himself with the spiritual weapons of prayer but wore temporal armor as well.

Dominic is representative of a new breed of spiritual athlete who appeared on the fringes of the Church in the eleventh century and whose feats of endurance reminded contemporaries of the Desert Fathers.¹³⁹ Many later *loricati* were also celebrated ascetics who wore armor as part of regimes of discipline and self-deprivation that could be extremely elaborate. Wulfric of Haselbury recited the Psalter each night while immersed in an icy pool, and another celebrated English hermit and *loricatus*, Godric of Finchale, subsisted on a diet of barley bread mixed with ashes, slept on a rock, and kept almost perpetual silence.¹⁴⁰ Nearly all of the *loricati* wore coarse hairshirts above or below their armor, and some, like the twelfth-century French hermit Geoffrey of Chalard, added heavy chains or iron plates in order to heighten their discomfort.¹⁴¹ The thirteenth-century Italian nobleman-turned-hermit Lawrence of Subiaco, who retired to a life of penance after accidentally killing a man, made himself an elaborate suit of penitential gear that reads like a parody of a knight's armor:

> Over his bare flesh he wore a net of knotty woven cord and above this a curved iron breastplate (*lorica*), which covered his threadbare and torn clothing; he had two plates of iron on his arms, four others on his legs, and he bore as many on his hips. He also carried another plate upon his stomach and another on his neck; he used iron chains around his loins.... On his head he bore a heavy iron crown, topped with two thin crosspieces of metal in the shape of a cross, one of which extended from the back of his head to his forehead and hung down to the middle of his nose like a soldier's helmet. The other piece extended from one ear to the other; from these, two smaller pieces of metal hung down, each touching his jaw. On each of these five spikes were affixed, pointed inwards, with which he was

---

137 Edward Gibbon heaped scorn on Dominic – and his biographer – for believing he could obtain the remission of purgatorial punishment for himself and others by such self-inflicted punishment; see *The Decline and Fall of the Roman Empire* 5.58, 12 vols (New York, 1845), 10: 204.

138 *Vita S. Rodulphi* 8, PL 144: 1015: 'Longo jam annorum elabente curriculo, ferrea ad carnem lorica praecinctus, infoederabilem pugnam cum iniquis spiritibus conserit, semperque paratus ad praelium, non solum corde, sed et corpore praemunito adversus hostiles acies fervidus bellator incedit.'

139 For the eleventh-century revivals of heroic asceticism and eremitism, see Jestice, *Wayward Monks*; and Leyser, *Hermits and the New Monasticism*.

140 Reginald of Durham, *Vita et miracula S. Godrici*, c.27 and 33, ed. Joseph Stevenson, *Libellus de vita et miraculis S. Godrici heremitae de Finchale*, Surtees Society 20 (London, 1847), 76 and 85–6.

141 *Vita Gaufridi Castaliensis*, c.8, ed. A. Bosieux, *Mémoires de la Société des sciences naturelles et archéologiques de la Creuse* 3 (1862), 75–119 (at 107).

pricked on both sides, so that he could bend his head neither back nor forward without its being punctured.[142]

As this passage demonstrates, hagiographers went to great lengths to evoke for their readers the physical pain inflicted by penitential armor, and emphasized the spiritual merit of such suffering. Another contemporary *vita* described how, in order to do penance for arranging the murder of his pious wife Godelieve, the knight Bertulf of Ghistelle retired to a monastery, where he secretly wore a coat of mail 'so tight that it constricted his entire body, so that no greater austerity could have been devised.'[143]

Wearing his *lorica* under his clothing in the heat of summer and the cold of winter 'dried out' the body of Stephen of Muret (d.1124), founder of Grandmont, prompting his biographer to speculate that Stephen 'seemed to exceed the faculties of the rest of humanity' in his endurance.[144] The weight of the penitential armor worn by another twelfth-century holy man, Stephen of Obazine, was such that it 'not only burdened his flesh but cut it in many places,' while the Italian abbot Peter of Policastro's *lorica* caused his skin to decay and peel away.[145] The pain Hugh of Cluny endured from wearing a mail-shirt next to his skin was such that it 'destroyed his youth,' but the holy man bore his suffering patiently in the hopes that he might thereby atone for the sins of his father Dalmatius, a

---

[142] *Vita B. Laurentii eremitae Sublaci*, c.1, AASS Aug. 3: 304–5: 'Induebatur super nudam carnem retiaculo ex funiculis contexto et nodoso: et desuper lorica hamata ferrea, quam depilata laceraque cooperiebat vestis: duos ferreos circulos in quolibet habebat brachio; quatuor alios in cruribus, totidemque in coxis portabat: ad ventrem quoque alterum gestabat circulum, & similiter in collo: circa lumbos catena utebatur ferrea ... in capite gestabat coronam ferream crassam, habentem in superiori parte duas laminas transversas in modum crucis, quarum una protendebatur ab occipite usque ad frontem, ex qua nasile dependebat usque ad medium nasi, adinstar galeae militaris. Altera vero lamina ab altera usque ad alteram extendebatur aurem: ab iis duabus aliae duae dependebant laminae, minae, utramque tangentes maxillam. In earum qualibet quinque affigebantur clavi, interius aculeati, quibus pungebatur utrimque; ita quod nec ante nec retro caput declinare poterat, quin ab iis pungeretur.'

[143] *Vita S. Godelevae virginis et martyris Ghistellae*, c.16, AASS Jul. 2: 402: 'Præcipuum vero poenitudinis instrumentum fuit lorica ferrea, artus omnes ita constringens, ut ejus asperitas nonnisi post fata potuerit ab ascetis ipsis excogitari.'

[144] *Vita S. Stephani fundatori Ordinis Grandimontensis*, c.3, AASS Feb. 1: 207: 'etiam lorica ferrea contra carnis insidias et mentis lasciuiam tamdiu incessit armatus, quousque toto exsiccato corpore, plenam de seipso obtinuit victriam? Ad cuius eximiæ perfectionis cumulum tanta parcitas vestium lectique accessit durities, quae cunctis humanae conditionis facultates cernentibus, vires hominum videatur excedere.'

[145] *Vita S. Stephani Obazinensis*, ed. and trans. Aubrun, *Vie de Saint Étienne*, 52: 'loricam sibi pater Stephanus coaptavit, quam multis annis occulte ad carnem gestavit, donec vetustate consumpta, paulatim scissa est.' *Vita S. Petri episcopi Policastrensis*, c.2, AASS Mar. 1: 331: 'Loricam subtus ad carnem occultam induit, quousque putresceret, et ab eius corpore rupta cecidisset.' Ian Peirce notes that a hauberk of this period weighed about twenty-five pounds; see 'The Knight, His Arms and Armour in the Eleventh and Twelfth Centuries,' in *The Ideals and Practice of Medieval Knighthood: Papers from the First and Second Strawberry Hill Conferences*, ed. Christopher Harper-Bill and Ruth Harvey (Woodbridge, 1986), 152–64 (at 158).

nobleman who had died violently with a heavy burden of sin upon his soul.[146] In the hands of these *loricati*, the normal function of armor in medieval culture was reversed: instead of protecting its wearers from harm, it became an instrument of bodily mortification; worn over a coarse, ragged hairshirt, the coat of mail was transformed from a badge of knightly pride into a mark of the wearer's abject humility.

The *loricati* were often said to have donned armor not only for penitential purposes but as a means of quelling their carnal desires. Similar practices are documented as far back as the earliest Christian centuries; Cassian, for instance, had advised monks struggling with the problem of nocturnal emissions to fast, limit their sleep, and cover their genitals with heavy lead plates at night, and the wearing of chain mail against the skin was credited with helping later holy men overcome lust.[147] When Stephen of Muret donned his coat of mail as a guard 'against the ambushes of his flesh and, so armed, assailed the licentiousness of his mind,' or Godric of Finchale used his armor as an effective protection against carnal 'fires,'[148] they were carrying on the age-old 'battle for chastity' which had been central to monastic spirituality since the time of Saint Antony.[149]

For some, wearing a *lorica* was intended to be a temporary penance; the French hermit William *Firmatus* donned one for a pilgrimage to the Holy Land, while the reformer Robert of Arbrissel gave up wearing his coat of mail after two years.[150] Other holy men wore their armor for many years before vanquishing their flesh, an accomplishment signaled in their *vitae* by the spontaneous breakage of their *loricae*. One day as he was walking on the road with some companions, Stephen of Obazine's coat of mail 'suddenly tore down the middle, and the lower part immediately fell to the ground, as if someone had cut [around] it in a circle.' In spite of efforts by Stephen and a companion to salvage it, the armor was found to be beyond repair, and the holy man finally accepted that 'it was not God's will that he bear it any longer.'[151] When Wulfric of Haselbury had reached a ripe old

---

146 Two of Hugh's *vitae* mention his wearing of a *lorica* as penance for his father's sins: Gilo, Vita S. Hugonis, c.51, ed. Cowdrey, *Two Studies*, 88; and Raynald of Vézelay, Vita S. Hugonis, c.6, *Vizeliacensia II: Textes relatifs à l'histoire de l'abbaye de Vézelay*, ed. R.B.C. Huygens, CCCM 42 Suppl. (Turnhout, 1980), 41.
147 Conrad Leyser, 'Masculinity in Flux: Nocturnal Emission and the Limits of Celibacy in the Early Middle Ages,' in *Masculinity in Medieval Europe*, ed. Hadley, 103–20 (at 105).
148 Stephen of Lissac, Vita Stephani de Mureto 17, PL 204: 1017: 'etiam lorica ferrea contra carnis insidias et mentis lasciviam tandiu incessit armatus.' See also Reginald of Durham, Vita et miracula S. Godrici, c.28, ed. Stevenson, 77–8.
149 The phrase 'battle for chastity' comes from Murray, 'Masculinizing Religious Life,' who adopted it from Michel Foucault's 1982 essay of the same name (see Chapter 3 n.69).
150 Stephen Fulgerius (?), Vita Guilielmi Firmati 3, AASS Apr. 3: 339; Baldric of Dol, Vita B. Roberti de Abrissello, c.10, PL 162: 1049: 'Destinans itaque carnis illecebris austerius dominari, subtus ad carnem indutus est loricam: qua veste duobus usus est annis, antequam ad eremum processerit.'
151 Vita S. Stephani Obazinensis, c.24, ed. Aubrun, 80: 'Gestabat etiam tunc loricam.... Que dum quadam die solus et ultimus pergeret, repente per medium est abrupta, ac si ab aliquo esset in rotundum precisa, inferiori parte ad terram protinus decidente. Unde

age, after having worn his *lorica* for many years, one day 'its rings miraculously parted and it slipped suddenly from his shoulders down to his knees,' prompting him to conclude that 'his service in Christ's army was coming to its end.'[152]

The *lorica* was a potent and multifaceted symbol in the thought world of these holy men, and a close reading of their *vitae* suggests that its longstanding associations with spiritual warfare were never far from the minds of their hagiographers. Some monastic writers sought to resolve the centuries-old tension between temporal and spiritual armor in the lives of *loricati* who had formerly lived as knights in the world and who continued to wear their battle-tested mail-shirts for ascetic purposes. The twelfth-century Flemish nobleman Gerlach of Houthem renounced the world after the death of his wife, ultimately settling as a hermit in a hollow oak tree, where he slept on a boulder and wore his old armor as a penance. His *lorica* served him well against the assaults of demons: 'covered with this protection, the strongest athlete fought in the difficult contest against the aerial troops and, in the name of Jesus, he gloriously triumphed.'[153] Another *bellator* who became a renowned ascetic was the Norman knight William of Llanthony, who settled at the future site of Llanthony Priory in Wales around 1100. As a hermit, William continued to wear 'the coat of mail with which he had been accustomed to guard his body against the arrows of enemies,' but, like other ascetics, he cinched it so tightly around his body that it became a tool of mortification rather than protection.[154] Ingebrand of Rurke, a soldier who joined the Hospitallers at Cologne in the early thirteenth century, 'wore the iron hauberk which he had used in the exercise of arms when he had served as a knight in the world (*miles saeculi*)' as a sign of his new status 'as a soldier of Christ (*miles Christi*) who, clothed in the same mail-shirt day and night, chastised his flesh in the service of God.'[155] Their hagiographers heralded these men as conversionary models, offering their Lives as proof that even those who had once lived by the sword might put their strength, endurance, and even their well-worn armor to good use in a higher calling.

---

mestus effectus, quemdam e sociis sibi conscium clam vocavit, ejusque auxilio quibusdam ligaminibus loricam ut potuit univit et sibi denuo coaptavit. Cumque paululum processissent, iterum dirupta cecidit.... Sed cum jam tertio rumperetur, intellexit vir sanctus, admonente etiam fratre, non esse voluntatis Dei ut eam ulterius ferret.'

[152] *Vita beati Wulfrici Haselbergiae*, c.99, ed. Bell, 124; trans. Matarasso, 268.

[153] *Vita Gerlaci eremitae in Belgio*, c.14, AASS Jan. 1:308: 'vir beatus loricam ferream, membra corporis castigans, et spiritui seruire cogens, assidue gestauit, qua deliciis et voluptatibus vitae huius insultauit; cuius munimine tectus, aduersus aereas cateruas athleta fortissimus certamine forti dimicauit, et in nomine Iesu gloriose triumphauit.'

[154] William's story is told as part of the foundation legend of Llanthony edited in William Dugdale, *Monasticon Anglicanum*, 3 vols (London, 1661–82), 2: 59–61 (at 59): 'nam loricam qua corpus muniri contra inimicorum jacula solebat, sibi strictissimi circumdedit....'

[155] Ingebrand's asceticism is described in the *Life* of Cordula, the legendary companion of Saint Ursula, whose relics were discovered at Cologne after the holy Hospitaller had a vision of the long-dead virgin. *Vita S. Cordulae virginis et martyris, S. Ursulæ sodali*, c.2, AASS Oct. 9: 580: 'sed lorica ferrea, qua olim cum miles esset saeculi, in armorum exercitio usus fuerat, nunc autem miles Christi, eadem super nudo indutus, nocte et die corpus castigans in Dei redegit servitutem.'

In a twist on the usual model of lay elites' patronage of the Church, some holy men obtained their penitential armor from knights still living in the world. When the twelfth-century Italian hermit William of Vercelli made a special trip from his mountaintop retreat to the city of Salerno with the object of obtaining a *lorica*, he was overjoyed to meet a knight who offered him his choice of several pieces of armor. After carefully selecting the heaviest of the lot, William returned home joyfully, where he commissioned a local blacksmith to make him a helmet to complete the penitential suit of armor necessary for a 'soldier of God (*miles Domini*).'[156] After Wulfric of Haselbury began to 'aspire to a coat of mail' to add to the hairshirt he already wore, the local knight William Fitzwalter heard of his wish and, in the 'anxious hope that he might share in the warrior's triumph by furnishing arms' to him, gave his own hauberk 'as though to a mightier knight than he, and dedicated this piece of his military equipment to the use of heaven's recruit.' Wulfric accordingly 'turned the arms of the world into the arms of justice' by employing them in spiritual rather than temporal battles.[157]

Like the prayers of monastic soldiers who fought for the souls of their lay patrons in monasteries all over Christendom, the martial exertions of armor-clad holy men like Wulfric were believed to benefit others as well as themselves. A knight who gave his armor to be transformed into a spiritual 'hauberk of justice' surely saw such an act as an investment in his own salvation. Furthermore, by allowing for the possibility of such transformations, these monastic hagiographers suggested that, as with the discarded swords of monastic converts, an instrument normally employed for the shedding of blood could become a powerful symbol of holiness. Such a conviction is further demonstrated by the elevation of the *loricati*'s armor to the status of relics; pilgrims to the cathedral of Osnabrück were proudly shown the mail shirt and iron chains worn by the thirteenth-century anchorite Raynerius, while the armor of Geoffrey of Chalard was similarly preserved.[158] As spiritual warriors in temporal armor, the *loricati* occupied a middle ground between the *bellatores* and the *oratores*, an intermediate space that was no longer supposed to exist in the neatly ordered society envisioned by medieval reformers.

---

156 *Vita Guilielmi abbatis fundatoris eremitarum Montis Virginis*, c.2, AASS Jun. 5:117.
157 *Vita beati Wulfrici Haselbergiae*, c.5, ed. Bell, 18–19: 'Proinde vestitu simplici cilicio interius inhaerere contentus erat. Ad cujus usum cum ex consuetudine duruisset intra paucos dies loricam coepit affectare. Cujus desiderii praefatus miles conscius effectus beati viri audacibus votis reverenter occurrit, sperans se tantae militiae futurum participem qui militanti arma ministrasset. Suam igitur loricam velut potiori militi cessit et vas bellicum caelesti tirocinio consecravit. Procedit itaque miles loricatus ad spirituale certamen terribilis nimirum futurus hostibus suis qui arma carnalia convertisset in arma justitiae; et haec armatura militiae diurnae.' Trans. Matarasso, 239.
158 *Vita B. Raynerii solitarii Osnaburgi in Westphalia*, c.2, AASS Apr. 2: 61; *Vita Gaufridi Castaliensis*, c.9, ed. Bosieux, 107.

Conclusion

The affinity of monastic writers for holy warriors might at first seem to be a yearning for a sort of life denied them, a life filled with adventure, danger, glory, and even romantic love. The hagiographical evidence surveyed in this chapter certainly shows that monks were hardly squeamish when it came to reading and writing about warriors' bloody exploits. But in the eleventh and twelfth centuries the vast majority of warrior-saints celebrated by monastic writers were men who had laid aside their arms and devoted themselves to God. Promoting the cults of these holy warriors, then, was actually a way of reaffirming the superiority of the monastic (or eremitic) life to service in the *militia saecularis*. Even the satirical *moniages* of failed converts implicitly recognized the spiritual inferiority of the fighting life (including the crusading mission) to the life of prayer. By composing the *vitae* of converts, proudly claiming them as patrons and founders, and even preserving their discarded arms and armor, monks commemorated these men's sacrifices and ensured the preservation of their memory, but above all reaffirmed the superiority of the *militia Christi* to worldly military service.

The great popularity of hagiographical narratives focused on conversion in this period also reflects the reality that the centuries-old practice of oblation was giving way to adult entrance into religious life. The *vitae* of knightly converts and even the *moniages* demonstrate a sympathetic awareness of the very real difficulties facing adult warriors who chose to become monks. Such sympathy indicates that while monks may have regarded particular arms-bearers with distrust and even fear, there was by no means a universal monastic hostility towards lay warriors. Even as contemporary reform movements created ever-sharper ideological and behavioral divisions between clerics and arms-bearers, conversion remained a strong bridge between the two groups. In the stories of worldly *milites* who successfully made the transition to religious life, monastic hagiographers and their audiences would have seen fellow monks, kinsmen, perhaps even themselves.

Converts to the religious life, whether that life was lived under the *Rule* in a monastery or as a hermit in the 'desert,' laid aside their secular arms and vowed they would never again raise violent hands against other men. But in doing so they did not simply cease to be soldiers, but rather became soldiers of a different, better sort. The persistent identification of the monk or hermit as *miles Christi* in hagiography parallels the concern with spiritual warfare as a meditative practice in monastic culture, a subject explored in detail in Chapter 4. Read in conjunction with contemporary homiletic and exegetical texts, as well as the evidence of monastic profession rites, the *vitae* of epic heroes, knightly converts, and armored ascetics offer evidence that monastic identity and the *miles Christi* ideal were more closely intertwined than ever in the eleventh and twelfth centuries. Even as the evolution of Christian knighthood extended the practice of spiritual warfare to lay arms-bearers, monastic hagiographers continued to insist that one could only join the true soldiery of Christ by abandoning the battlefields of the world.

Conclusion

Within the history of Christianity's long, vexed relationship with war, monastic communities have been assumed to have had little to do with warfare either conceptually or in practice. The main contention of this study, that monastic identity was negotiated through direct, constant confrontations with war and warriors, has challenged the traditional exclusion of professed religious from this historical narrative. In so doing, it has aimed to undermine one of the central divisions historians have traditionally emphasized in their reconstruction of the medieval past: the ideological separation of peace-loving religious communities from bloodthirsty knights, of 'those who prayed' from 'those who fought.' To be sure, recent scholarship focused on the piety and patronage of medieval elites has forced a re-evaluation of the first of these stereotypes, while studies of churchmen's role in defining and mediating just and unjust wars has challenged the second. But if it has been accepted that, at least to some degree, clerics taught warriors how to think and act as Christians, the possibility that churchmen in turn learned from lay warriors ought also to be considered. Arms-bearers' conceptions of sin, penance, and salvation were mediated by their relationships with religious institutions, and these contacts left their imprint on those living within the monastery as well. Monastic identity was constructed not simply in opposition to, but in dialogue with warriors, especially during the eleventh and twelfth centuries, against the backdrop of monastic reform and the early crusading movement.

This book has traced medieval monastic ideas about war to two main sources: a body of sacred texts, especially the Bible, liturgy, and works of hagiography, which treated warfare in historical and allegorical terms; and interactions with lay warriors, which might be of a friendly or hostile nature. A survey of the Scriptures and their commentary traditions has shown that many of the activities customarily associated with the peace of the medieval cloister – such as private *lectio*, biblical exegesis, and liturgical prayer – actually brought war to the forefront of the monastic experience. Over the course of the first millennium, monastic exegetes made spiritual (or spiritualized) warfare central to the historical narrative of Christianity. Their work also ensured that the concept of spiritual battle informed the daily lives of individual monks, who, in the guise of *milites Christi*, fashioned the Psalms into missiles to hurl at demons and wrested the souls of lay benefactors away from the devil.

But actual contact with arms-bearers was arguably an equally important source of medieval monastic knowledge about warfare. Contemporary spiritual renewal, together with changing recruitment practices among many religious orders, encouraged repentant warriors to enter the cloister in unprecedented numbers from the eleventh century onwards. Those who abandoned military careers to enter the religious life did not so much give up being soldiers, however, as learn to channel their martial energies into another, better sort of combat which was the ancient specialty of monks. For such men, learning to live as monks entailed the acquisition of specialized skills and the cultivation of new virtues, but it also involved becoming *tirones*, soldiers-in-training, all over again. For training in the combat of the spirit, converts naturally looked to their new brethren, some of whom were themselves former arms-bearers, others lifelong monks with no personal experience of war.

Defining themselves as spiritual warriors in the tradition of the ancient Israelites and Roman martyrs, monastic writers of the eleventh and twelfth centuries applied military metaphors to every aspect of life in the cloister, and spoke to one another in a distinctive martial language which resonated with the Scriptures and patristic hagiography, even as it borrowed imagery and terminology from contemporary military culture. Until now, this martial rhetoric has mostly managed to hide in plain sight; when they have noticed it at all, medievalists have tended to dismiss it as empty rhetoric, a collection of tropes rendered meaningless by their omnipresence. But, as revealed by a close examination of their sermons, letters, and *vitae*, monastic writers consistently associated specific martial themes – single combat, pitched battle, the siege of a castle – with particular challenges, virtues, and stages of spiritual development central to the monastic experience. When monks referred to themselves as *milites Christi* this was no mere rhetorical flourish, but rather the expression of a fundamental truth: in their self-appointed roles as opponents of the devil and defenders of the spiritual well-being of Christendom, monks *were* soldiers of Christ.

After the turn of the first millennium the concept of the *miles Christi* was dramatically expanded as spiritual warfare became intertwined with the emerging ethos of holy war and monks' long-held dominance of the spiritual battlefield was challenged by crusaders, members of the military orders, and pious arms-bearers more generally. This threat to monks' traditional dominance of spiritual combat may help to explain the explosion of martial rhetoric in monastic texts composed after c.1000. By drawing attention to their status as *milites Christi*, monastic writers sought to affirm the superiority of the religious life (be it coenobitic, eremitic, or somewhere between the two) to military service in the world, including participation in wars fought by or at the instigation of the reforming Church. This concern strongly impressed monks' letters and sermons, and took center stage in the hagiography of holy warriors produced in monastic scriptoria. In the *vitae* of legendary and historical arms-bearers who had renounced the world monastic hagiographers found abundant opportunities to celebrate spiritual combat and explore the implications of the transition from worldly military service to the *militia Christi*. Converts to the religious life, they affirmed, laid aside their weapons and vowed they would never again shed other men's blood, but in doing so they did not simply cease to be soldiers, but rather embraced a soldiery of a better sort.

In focusing primarily on north-western Europe from c.1000–c.1200, and on male members of religious communities, this book has inevitably shone light down some historical pathways while leaving others in relative darkness. It is my hope that future scholars will be sufficiently interested in the questions left unanswered here to take them up. One promising avenue for future research concerns the conceptual importance of war for medieval religious women. How did nuns, canonesses, and anchoresses fit the concept of spiritual warfare into their spirituality, in which their status as *sponsae Christi* loomed large? How might religious women's perception of themselves as 'soldiers of Christ' have reflected their generally more limited contacts with the world of lay arms-bearers? Furthermore, as readers will no doubt have recognized, this study has presented 'monastic writers' as a broad category encompassing a variety of orders and visions of the religious life. Explorations of how members of particular orders, clusters of communities, or even individual writers used military metaphors would add a desirable degree of nuance to the more general trends discerned here. Finally, following the history of spiritual warfare forward in time would undoubtedly reveal fascinating changes in this discourse reflecting broader developments in Christian spirituality, changing models of monastic life, the decline of the crusading movement, and even the late medieval military revolution that rendered obsolete many of the technologies and strategies that so fascinated earlier monastic thinkers.

In the meantime, this study has offered one new route by which to approach the history of monastic mentalities in the Central Middle Ages. The role of medieval religious communities in the promotion of peace and settlement of disputes has long been recognized, but scholars have overlooked evidence that war was as powerful an agent as peace in the making of monastic culture. For medieval monks, war was not simply a worldly evil but a path to self-knowledge and even a form of *imitatio Christi*; encountered at every turn in the texts and rituals that shaped life in the monastery, war was among the most useful tools in the monk's meditative arsenal, and its language and symbolism were intimately woven into the fabric of his identity. Looking long and hard at these images of war on their own terms, as this study has tried to do, allows us to see the medieval world in a way that approximates how these writers saw it, and affords us glimpses, however fleeting, of how medieval monks saw themselves. Collectively, these images also provide a salutary reminder that divisions modern historians draw between the sacred and secular in the premodern world are more likely to reflect their own outlooks than those of their subjects, and that too neatly compartmentalizing the study of the past into categories such as 'military history' and the 'history of religion' can prevent us from appreciating the complexity of earlier worldviews.

Appendix: The *Loricati*, c.1050–1250[1]

Note: Where multiple *vitae* exist, I have included references only to those texts which identify the subject as a *loricatus*. BHL numbers refer to the Bollandists' *Bibliotheca hagiographica Latina antiquae et mediae aetatis*, Subsida Hagiographica 6, 2 vols (Brussels, 1898–1901), with supplement, Subsidia Hagiographica 70 (Brussels, 1986).

1. Dominic *Loricatus* (d.1060), Italy. *Vita*: Peter Damian, *Vita S. Rodulphi episcopi Eugubini et S. Dominici Loricati*, PL 144: 1007–24. BHL 2239.

2. Bertulf of Ghistelle (d. after 1070), Flanders. *Vita*: Anonymous, *Vita S. Godelevae virginis et martyrae Ghistellae*, AASS Jul. 2: 401–36. BHL 3593.

3. Simon of Crépy (d.1081/82), France. *Vita*: Anonymous, *Vita B. Simonis comitis Crespeiensis auctore synchrono*, PL 156: 1211–24. BHL 7757.

4. William *Firmatus* (d.1103), France. *Vita*: Stephen Fulgerius (?), *Vita Guilielmi Firmati*, AASS April 3: 334–41. BHL 8914.

5. William of Llanthony (d. after 1108), Wales. *Vita*: Anonymous, 'Foundation Legend of Llanthony Priory,' in *Monasticon Anglicanum*, ed. William Dugdale, 3 vols (London, 1661–82), 2: 59–61. No BHL entry.

6. Hugh of Cluny (d.1109), France. *Vita*: Gilo of Cluny, *Vita S. Hugonis abbatis*, ed. H.E.J. Cowdrey in *Two Studies in Cluniac History, 1049–1126*, Studi Gregoriani per la storia della 'Libertas Ecclesiae' 11 (Rome, 1978), 45–109. BHL 4007. Raynald of Vézelay, *Vita S. Hugonis*, in *Vizeliacensia II: Textes relatifs à l'histoire de l'abbaye de Vézelay*, ed. R.B.C. Huygens, CCCM 42 Suppl. (Turnhout, 1980), 39–60. BHL 4008.

7. Robert of Arbrissel (d.1116), France. *Vita*: Baldric of Dol, *Vita B. Roberti di Arbrissello*, PL 162: 1043–58. BHL 7259.

8. Peter of Policastro (d.1123), Italy. *Vita*: Anonymous monk of Venusino, *Vita S. Petri episcopi Policastrensis*, AASS Mar. 1: 330–5. BHL 6767.

---

[1] In addition to the figures listed here, two other possible *loricati* deserve mention. The first is the father of Saint Hugh of Avalon, bishop of Lincoln (d.1200), who entered the Augustinians at Villarbenoît as a widower. He is described in the *The Metrical Life of Saint Hugh of Lincoln* (ed. and trans. Charles Garton [Lincoln, 1986], 15, lines 109-13) as having 'worn armor against his flesh (*induit arma / adversus carnem*).' The second is a hermit, Gilbert, who is said in the Life of the French recluse Alpaide of Cudot (d.1211) to have 'worn an iron hauberk (*lorica ferrea*) over his hair-shirt day and night' (*Vita B. Alpaide* (AASS Nov. 2, pt. 1: 196).

9. Stephen of Muret (d.1124), France. *Vita*: Stephen of Lissac, *Vita et miracula S. Stephani de Mureto*, PL 204: 1071–86. BHL 7907.

10. Geoffrey of Chalard (d.1125), France. *Vita*: Anonymous, *Vita Gaufridi Castaliensis*, ed. A. Bosieux, *Mémoires de la Société des sciences naturelles et archéologiques de la Creuse* 3 (1862): 75–119. BHL 3283.

11. William of Vercelli (d.1142), Italy. *Vita*: John of Nusco, *Vita Guilielmi abbatis, fundatoris eremitarum Montis Virginis*, AASS Jun. 5: 114–31. BHL 8924.

12. Wulfric of Haselbury (d.1154), England. *Vita*: John of Ford, *Vita Wulfrici Haselbergiae*, ed. Maurice Bell, *Wulfric of Haselbury by John, Abbot of Ford*, Somerset Record Society 47 (London, 1933). BHL 8743.

13. Stephen of Obazine (d.1159), France. *Vita*: Anonymous, *Vita S. Stephani Obazinensis*, ed. Michel Aubrun, *Vie de Saint Étienne d'Obazine*, Publications de l'Institut d'études du Massif Central 6 (Clermont-Ferrand, 1970). BHL 7916.

14. Godric of Finchale (d.1170), England. *Vita*: Reginald of Durham, *Libellus de vita et miraculis S. Godrici heremitae de Finchale*, ed. Joseph Stevenson, Publications of the Surtees Society 20 (London, 1847). BHL 3596.

15. Gerlach of Houthem (d.1177), Flanders. *Vita*: Anonymous, *Vita Gerlaci eremitae in Belgio*, AASS Jan. 1: 306–20. BHL 3449.

16. Arnulf of Braband (d.1228), Flanders. *Vita*: Goswin of Bussuto, *Vita Arnulfi monachi Villariensis in Belgio*, AASS Jun. 5: 608–31. BHL 713.

17. Dodo of Hascha (d.1231), Germany. *Vita*: Anonymous, *Vita B. Dodonis de Hascha Ordinis Praemonstratensis in Frisia*, AASS Mar. 3: 851–8. BHL 2206.

18. Raynerius of Osnabrück (d.1233), Germany. *Vita*: Anonymous, *Vita B. Raynerii solitarii Osnaburgi in Westphalia*, AASS Apr. 2: 61–2. BHL 7083.

19. Ingebrand of Rurke (d.after 1238), Germany. *Vita*: mentioned in *Vita S. Cordulae virginis et martyris, S. Ursulæ sodali*. AASS Oct. 9: 580–6. BHL 1951.

20. Edmund of Abington (d.1240), England. *Vita*: Matthew Paris, *Vita beati Edmundi Cantuariensis archiepiscopi*, ed. C.H. Lawrence, *St. Edmund of Abingdon: A Study in Hagiography and History* (Oxford, 1960), 222–89. BHL 2405.

21. Lawrence of Subiaco (d.1243), Italy. *Vita*: Anonymous, *Vita B. Laurentii eremitae confessoris Sublaci in Latio*, AASS Aug. 3: 304–7. BHL 4793.

Bibliography

Primary sources

Abbo of Fleury. *Canones.* PL 139: 473–508.
The Acts of the Christian Martyrs. Ed. and trans. Herbert Musurillo. Oxford, 1972.
Actus beati Francisci et sociorum ejus. Ed. Paul Sabatier. Paris, 1902.
Adalbéron of Laon. *Carmen ad Rotbertum francorum regem.* Ed. and trans. Claude Carozzi as *Poème au roi Robert.* Paris, 1979.
Adam of Eynsham. *The Life of St Hugh of Lincoln.* 2 vols. Ed. and trans. Decima Douie and Hugh Farmer. London, 1961.
Additamentum de reliquiis S. Austremonii. AASS Nov. 1: 80–82.
Adso of Montiérender. *Miracula SS. Waldeberti et Eustasii auctore Adsone abbate dervensi* [BHL 8775]. Ed. O. Holder-Egger in MGH SS 15/2: 1171–6. Hanover, 1888.
Aelred of Rievaulx. *De institutione inclusarum.* Ed. C.H. Talbot in *Aelredi Rievallensis Opera omnia, Vol. 1: Opera ascetica,* ed. Anselm Hoste et al., 635–82. CCCM 1. Turnhout, 1971.
———. *Relatio de Standardo.* In *Chronicles of the reigns of Stephen, Henry II, and Richard I,* 4 vols, ed. R. Howlett, 2: 181–99. London, 1884–92. Trans. Jane Patricia Freeland and ed. Marsha L. Dutton as *The Battle of the Standard,* in *Aelred of Rievaulx: The Historical Works.* CF 56. Kalamazoo, MI, 2005.
———. *Sermones de tempore et de sanctis.* PL 195: 209–360.
Aimo of Fleury. *Vita et martyrio S. Abbonis abbatis Floriaci.* PL 139: 387–414.
Amalarius of Metz. *De ecclesiasticis officiis libri quatuor.* PL 105: 985–1242.
Ambrose Autpert. *Expositio in Apocalypsin Libri IX.* 2 vols. Ed. Robert Weber. CCCM 27–27A. Turnhout, 1975.
Ambrose of Milan. *De officiis.* 2 vols. Ed. and trans. Ivor J. Davidson. Oxford, 2001.
Analecta hymnica medii aevi. 55 vols. Ed. Clemens Blume and Guido Maria Dreves. Leipzig, 1886–1922.
Andreas of Strumi. *Vita S. Arialdi.* Ed. F. Baethgen. MGH SS 30/2: 1047–75.
Anselm of Canterbury. *Epistolae.* PL 158: 1059–208; 159: 9–272. Trans. Walter Fröhlich as *The Letters of St. Anselm.* 3 vols. CS 96, 97, 142. Kalamazoo, MI, 1990–94.
Anselm. *Homiliae.* PL 158: 585–674.
The Apostolic Fathers. 2 vols. Ed. and trans. Bart Ehrman. Loeb Classical Library 24–5. Cambridge, MA, 2003.
Ardon Smaragdus. *Vita Benedicti Abbatis Anianensis et Indensis auctore Ardone.* Ed. George Waitz. MGH SS 15/1: 200–220.
Athanasius. *Vita Antonii* (Latin trans. by Evagrius of Antioch) [BHL 609]. PL 73: 125–70. Trans. Caroline White in *Early Christian Lives.* London, 1998.
Atto of Vercelii. *Expositio Epistolarum Beati Pauli.* PL 134: 125–834.
Augustine of Hippo. *De agone christiano.* PL 40: 284–310. Trans. Robert P. Russell in *Saint Augustine: Christian Instruction…,* FC 2. Washington D.C., 1947.
———. *De opere monachorum.* PL 40: 57–82.
———. *Enarrationes in Psalmos.* Ed. E. Dekkers, CCSL 38–40. Turnholt, 1956. Trans. Maria Boulding as *Expositions of the Psalms.* 6 vols. Park, NY, 2000–2004.

———. *Praeceptum*. Trans. George Lawless as 'Rule for Monks', in *Augustine of Hippo and His Monastic Rule*. Oxford, 1987.
———. *Sermones*. PL 38–39.
Baldric of Dol. *Historia Hierosolimitana*. RHC Occ. 4: 1–111.
———. *Relatio de scuto et gladio S. Michaeli*. Ed. Jean Huynes, in *Histoire générale de l'abbaye du Mont-Saint-Michel au péril de la mer*. 2 vols. Ed. Eugène de Robillard de Beaurepaire, 1: 137–46. Rouen, 1872.
———. *Vita B. Roberti de Abrissello* [BHL 7259]. PL 162: 1043–58.
Bede. *The Ecclesiastical History of the English People*. Trans. Leo Sherley-Price and R.E. Latham. Harmondsworth, 1990.
———. *Excerpts from the Works of Saint Augustine on the Letters of the Blessed Apostle Paul*. Trans. David Hurst. CS 183. Kalamazoo, MI, 1999.
Benedict of Aniane. *Codex regularum monasticarum et canonicarum*. PL 103: 423–700.
———. *Benedicti Anianensis Concordia regularum*. Ed. Pierre Bonnerue. CCCM 168. Turnhout: Brepols, 1999.
Bernard of Clairvaux. *In Praise of the New Knighthood*. Trans. M. Conrad Greenia. Kalamazoo, MI, 2000.
———. *On the Song of Songs*. 4 vols. Trans. Kilian J. Walsh and Irene M. Edmonds. CF 2, 4, 31, 40. Kalamazoo, MI, 1971–80.
Bruno of Asti. *Commentarium in Lucam, pars 1*. PL 165: 333–452.
———. *Expositio in Job commentarius*. PL 164: 551–696.
———. *Expositio in Pentateuchum*. PL 164: 551–696.
———. *Expositio in Psalmos*. PL 164: 695–1228.
Bruno of Chartreuse. *Expositio in Epistolas S. Pauli*. PL 153: 11–568.
———. *Expositio in Psalmos*. PL 152: 637–1419.
Burchard of Worms. *Decretum*. PL 140: 537–1057.
Caesarius of Heisterbach. *Dialogus miraculorum*. 2 vols. Ed. Joseph Strange. Cologne, 1851. Trans. H. von E. Scott and C.C. Swinton Bland as *The Dialogue on Miracles*. 2 vols. New York, 1929.
Cartulaire de l'abbaye cardinale de la Trinité de Vendôme. 5 vols. Ed. Charles Métais. Paris, 1893–1904.
Cartulaire de l'abbaye de Lérins. Ed. Henri Moris and Edmond Blanc. Paris, 1905.
Cartulaire de l'abbaye de Notre-Dame de Beaugency. Ed. G. Vignat. Mémoires de la Société archéologique et historique de l'Orléanais 16. Orléans, 1887.
Cartulaire de l'abbaye de Noyers. Ed. Casimir Chevalier. Mémoires de la Société archéologique de Touraine 22. Tours, 1872.
Cartulaire de l'abbaye de Redon en Bretagne. Ed. Aurélien de Courson. Paris, 1863.
Cartulaire de l'abbaye de Saint-Martin de Pontoise. 5 vols. Ed. J. Depoin. Pontoise, 1895–1909.
Cartularium abbathiae de Whiteby ordinis S. Benedicti. 2 vols. Ed. J.C. Atkinson. Surtees Society Publications 69, 72. Durham, 1879–81.
Cassian. *Collationes*, 3 vols. Ed. Eugène Pichery as *Conférences*. Paris, 1955–9. Trans. Colm Luibheid as *Conferences*. New York, 1985.
———. *Institutiones*. Ed. Jean-Claude Guy as *Institutions cénobitiques*. SC 109. Paris, 1965. Trans. Boniface Ramsey. Ancient Christian Writers 58. New York, 2000.
Cassiodorus. *Expositio Psalmorum*. Ed. M. Adriaen. CCSL 97–8. Turnholt, 1958. Trans. P.G. Walsh as *Explanation of the Psalms*. 3 vols. New York, 1990–91.
The Chronicle of the Abbey of Morigny, France, c. 1100–1150. Trans. Richard Cusimano. Lewiston, NY, 2003.
The Chronicle of Battle Abbey. Ed. and trans. Eleanor Searle. Oxford, 1980.

Chronicon abbatiae Rameseiensis. Ed. W.D. Macray. London, 1886.
Chronicon Novaliciense. Ed. George Pertz. Hanover, 1846.
Chroniques des églises d'Anjou. Ed. P. Marchegay and E. Mabille. Paris, 1869.
Collection des principaux cartulaires du diocèse de Troyes, t. IV. Ed. Charles Lalore. Paris, 1878.
The Commentaries of Origen and Jerome on St Paul's Epistle to the Ephesians. Ed. and trans. Ronald E. Heine. Oxford, 2002.
Commodian. *Instructiones adversus gentium deos pro christiana disciplina.* PL 5: 201–62.
Conciliorum Oecumenicorum Decreta. 3rd ed. Ed. Giuseppe Alberigo. Bologna, 1973.
Die consuetudines des Augustiner-Chorherrenstiftes Marbach im Elsass (12 Jahrhundert). Ed. Josef Siegwart. Freiburg, 1965.
Consuetudines Floriacenses antiquiores. Ed. Anselm Davril and Lin Donnat. Sources d'histoire médiévale 32. Paris, 2004.
The Coucher Book of Selby. 2 vols. Ed. J.T. Fowler. Yorkshire Archaeological Association Record Series 10, 12. Durham, 1891–3.
The Councils of Urban II, Vol. 1: Decreta Claromontensia. Ed. Robert Somerville. Amsterdam, 1972.
Cyprian. *De lapsis.* Ed. and trans. M. Bévenot. Oxford, 1971.
———. *Letters 1–81.* Trans. Rose Bernard Donna. FC 52. Washington D.C., 1965.
———. *Liber de zelo et livore.* PL 4: 637–52.
———. *De mortalitate.* PL 4: 603–24. Trans. Roy J. Deferrari as 'Mortality', in *Saint Cyprian: Treatises.* FC 36. Washington D.C., 1958.
De novitiis instruendis: Text und Kontext eines anonymen Traktates vom Ende des 12. Jahrhunderts. Ed. Mirko Breitenstein. Münster, 2004.
Les deux rédactions en vers du 'Moniage Guillaume.' 2 vols. Ed. Wilhelm Cloetta. Paris, 1906–11. Partial trans. Joan Ferrante in *Guillaume d'Orange: Four Twelfth-Century Epics.* New York, 1974.
De vera ac falsa poenitentia ad Christum devotam. PL 40: 113–30.
'Un document sur les débuts des Templiers.' Ed. Jean Leclercq in *Revue de l'histoire ecclesiastique* 52 (1957), 81–91.
Eigil of Fulda. *Die Vita Sturmi des Eigil von Fulda*, ed. Pius Engelbert. Marburg, 1968.
The Epistolae Vagantes of Pope Gregory VII. Ed. and trans. H.E.J. Cowdrey. Oxford, 1972.
Eucherius of Lyons, *Passio Acaunensium martyrum.* Ed. C.B. Krusch. MGH SS RerMerov 3: 20–41.
Eusebius of Caesarea. *The History of the Church.* 2nd edn. Trans. G.A. Williamson and A. Louth. London, 1989.
Expositiones Pauli Epistolarum ad Romanos, Galathas et Ephesios e codice S. Michaelis in periculo Maris (Avranches, Bibl. mun. 79). Ed. Gérard de Martel. Turnholt, 1995.
Fulbert of Chartres. *The Letters and Poems of Fulbert of Chartres.* Ed. and trans. Frederick Behrends. Oxford, 1976.
Fulcher of Chartres. *Fulcherius Carnotensis Historia Hierosolymitana.* Ed. Heinrich Hagenmeyer. Heidelberg, 1913. Trans. Edward Peters in *The First Crusade: The Chronicle of Fulcher of Chartres and Other Source Materials.* 2nd edn. Philadelphia, PA, 1998.
Galand of Regny. *Parabolaire.* Ed. and trans. Colette Friedlander, Jean Leclercq and Gaetano Raciti. SC 378. Paris, 1992.
———. *Petit livre de proverbes.* Ed. and trans. Jean Châtillon, Maurice Dumontier and Alexis Grelois. SC 436. Paris, 1998.
Geoffrey of Admont. *Homiliae festivales.* PL 174: 633–1060.
Geoffrey of Auxerre. *Sermo in anniversario obitus S. Bernardi.* PL 185: 575–88.
Geoffrey of Breteuil. *Epistolae.* PL 205: 827–88.

Geoffrey Grossus. *Vita b. Bernardi fundatoris congregationis de Tironio*. PL 172: 1363–446.
Gerhoh of Reichersberg. *Commentarius Aureus in Psalmos et Cantica Ferialia*. PL 193: 619–1814.
——. *Expositionis in Psalmos continuatio*. PL 194: 9–998.
Gerald of Wales. *Gemma animae*. Ed. and trans. John Hagen as *The Jewel of the Church*. Leiden, 1979.
Gesta Marcuardi abbatis Fuldensis. Ed. J.F. Böhmer. Stuttgart, 1853.
Gilbert Crispin. *Vita domni Herluini abbatis Beccensis*. In *Gilbert Crispin, Abbot of Westminster*, ed. J. Armitage Robinson, 87–110. Cambridge, 1911. Trans. Sally Vaughn as 'The Life of Lord Herluin, Abbot of Bec.' In *The Abbey of Bec and the Anglo-Norman State, 1034–1136*. Woodbridge, 1981.
Gilbert Foliot. *The Charters and Letters of Gilbert Foliot*. Ed. A. Morey and C.N.L. Brooke. Cambridge, 1967.
Gilbert of Hoyland. *Sermones in Cantica Canticorum*. PL 184: 11–252.
Gilo of Cluny. *Vita S. Hugonis abbatis* [BHL 4007]. Ed. H.E.J. Cowdrey in *Two Studies in Cluniac History, 1049–1126*. Studi Gregoriani per la storia della 'Libertas Ecclesiae' 11. Rome, 1978.
Gilo of Paris. *Historia vie Hierosolimitane*. Ed. and trans. C.W. Grocock and J.E. Siberry. Oxford, 1997.
Goscelin of Saint-Bertin. *Historia translationis Sancti Augustini* [BHL 777]. PL 80:13–46.
Goscelin of Saint-Bertin. *Liber Confortatorius*. Ed. C.H. Talbot as 'The *Liber Confortatorius* of Goscelin of Saint Bertin, *Studia Anselmiana* 37, Analecta Monastica, 3rd ser. (1955), 2–117. Trans. Monika Otter as *Goscelin of St Bertin, The Book of Encouragement and Consolation*. Cambridge, 2004.
Gregory the Great. *Dialogues*. 2 vols. Ed. Adalbert de Vogüé and trans. Paul Antin. SC 251, 260 and 265. Paris, 1978–9. Trans. Odo J. Zimmerman as *Gregory the Great: Dialogues*. FC 39. Washington D.C., 1959.
——. *Homiliarum in Evangelia libri duo*. PL 76: 1075–312.
——. *Homiliarum in Ezechielem prophetam libri duo*. PL 76: 785–1072.
——. *Moralia in Job*. 3 vols. Ed. Marcus Adriaen. CCSL 143–143B. Turnhout, 1979–85.
——. *Regula pastoralis*. 2 vols. Ed. Floribert Rommel and trans. Charles Morel as *Règle pastorale*. CS 381–2. Paris, 1992.
Grimlaicus. *Regula solitariorum*. PL 103: 573–664.
Guerric of Igny. *Sermones*. 2 vols. Ed. John Morson and Hilary Costello. SC 166, 202. Paris, 1970–73. Trans. Monks of Mount Saint Bernard Abbey as *Guerric of Igny: Liturgical Sermons*. CF 8. Spencer, MA, 1970–72.
Guibert of Gembloux. *Guiberti Gemblacensis epistolae*. 2 vols. Ed. Albert Derolez. CCCM 66–66A. Turnhout, 1989.
Guibert of Nogent. *De vita sua*. Ed. and trans. E.R. Labande as *Autobiographie*. Paris, 1981. Trans. John F. Benton as *Self and Society in Medieval France*. Toronto, 1984.
——. *Gesta Dei per Francos*. CCCM 127A. Ed. R.B.C. Huygens. Turnhout, 1996. Trans. Robert Levine as *The Deeds of God through the Franks*. Woodbridge, 1997.
Guillaume Durand. *Rationale divinorum officiorum*. 3 vols. Ed. Anselme Davril, T.M. Thibodeau, and Bertrand G. Guyot. CCCM 140, 140A, 140B. Turnhout, 1995–2000.
Guillaume le Clerc. *Le Besant de Dieu*. Ed. Pierre Ruelle. Brussels, 1973.
Guy of Amiens. *Carmen de Hastingae Proelio*. 2nd edn. Ed. and trans. Frank Barlow. Oxford, 1999.
Haimo of Auxerre. *Expositio in Apocalypsin*. PL 117: 937–1220.
Hariulf of Saint-Médard. *Vita S. Arnulfi* [BHL 703]. PL 174: 1367–438.

Herbert of Losinga. *Epistolae Herberti de Losinga, primi episcopi norwicensis*. Ed. Robert Anstruther. London, 1846.
Hervé of Déols. *Commentaria In Epistolas Divi Pauli*. PL 181: 591–1692.
Hildebert of Lavardin. *Sermones de diversis*. PL 171: 339–964.
Hildemar of Corbie. *Commentarium in regulam S. Benedicti*. Ed. Rupert Mittermüller. Regensburg, 1880.
Historia de expeditione Friderici imperatoris. Ed. A. Chroust. MGH SRG n.s. 5. Berlin, 1928.
Honorius Augustodunensis. *Gemma animae*. PL 172: 541–738.
——. *Speculum ecclesiae*. PL 172: 807–1107.
Honorius Augustodunensis. *Summa gloria*. PL 172: 1257–70.
Hortus Deliciarum of Herrad of Hohenbourg. 2 vols. Ed. Rosalie Green, Michael Evans, Christine Bischoff, and Michael Curschmann. Landsberg, 1979.
Hrabanus Maurus. *De rerum naturis*. PL 111: 9–614.
——. *Enarrationum in Epistolas Beati Pauli*. PL 112: 9–834.
Hugh of Amiens. *Vita S. Adjutoris monachi Tironensis*. PL 192: 1345–52.
Hugh Francigena. *Tractatus de conversione Pontii de Laracio et exordii Salvaniensis monasterii vera narratio*. Ed. Beverley Mayne Kienzle. *Sacris erudiri* 34 (1993), 273–311. Trans. Kienzle as 'The Tract of the Conversion of Pons of Léras and the True Account of the Beginning of the Monastery at Silvanes', in *Medieval Hagiography: An Anthology*, ed. Thomas Head, 495–513. New York and London, 2001.
Hugh of Saint-Victor. *De sacramentis christianae fidei*. PL 176: 172–618. Trans. Roy J. Deferrari as *On the Sacraments of the Christian Faith*. Cambridge, MA, 1951.
Ivo of Chartres. *Decretum*. PL 161: 59–1022.
——. *Epistolae*. Ed. Jean Leclercq as *Yves de Chartres: Corréspondance*. Paris, 1949.
Jerome. *Select Letters of St. Jerome*. Loeb Classical Library 262. Ed. and trans. F.A. Wright. London, 1933.
——. *Vita S. Hilarionis*. PL 23: 29–54.
——. *Vita S. Pauli eremitae*. PL 23: 17–28.
John Beleth. *Summa de ecclesiasticis officiis*. 2 vols. Ed. Herbert Douteil. CCCM 41–41A. Turnholt, 1976.
John of Fécamp. *Epistolae*. PL 147: 463–76.
John of Ford. *Super extremam partem Cantici Canticorum sermones CXX*. Ed. Edmund Mikkers and Hilary Costello. CCCM 17–18. Turnhout, 1970. Trans. Wendy Beckett as *John of Ford: Sermons on the Final Verses of the Song of Songs*. 6 vols. CF 29, 39, 43–47. Kalamazoo, MI, 1977–84.
——. *Vita beati Wulfrici Haselbergiae* [BHL 8743]. Ed. Maurice Bell. Somerset Record Society 47. London, 1933. Partial trans. Pauline Matarasso in *The Cistercian World: Monastic Writings of the Twelfth Century*. New York, 1993.
John of Fruttuaria. *Liber de ordine vitae et morum institutione*. PL 184: 559–84.
John of Salerno. *Vita S. Odonis*. PL 133: 43–86. Trans. Gerard Sitwell in *St. Odo of Cluny: Being the Life of St. Odo of Cluny by John of Salerno and Life of St. Gerald of Aurillac by St. Odo*. London, 1958.
John of Salisbury. *Policraticus sive nugis curialium et vestigiis philosophorum*. PL 199: 379–822. Trans. John Dickinson as *The Statesman's Book of John of Salisbury*. New York, 1927.
Julian of Vézelay. *Sermones*. 2 vols. Ed. and trans. Damian Vorreux. CS 192–3. Paris, 1972.
Lambert of Ardres. *The History of the Counts of Guines and Lords of Ardres*. Ed. and trans. Leah Shopkow. Philadelphia, PA, 2001.

Letald of Micy. *Liber miraculorum S. Maximini Micianensis abbatis.* PL 137: 795–824.
The Letters of Saint Bernard of Clairvaux. Trans. Bruno Scott James. New York, 1980.
Lettres des premiers chartreux. 2 vols. Ed. and trans. 'a Carthusian.' SC 88, 274. Paris, 1980–88.
Liber miraculorum Sanctae Fides. Ed. A. Bouillet. Paris, 1897. Trans. Pamela Sheingorn as *The Book of Sainte Foy.* Philadelphia, PA, 1995.
Liber de poenitentia et tentationibus religiosorum. PL 213: 863–904.
The Little Flowers of St. Francis. Trans. Raphael Brown. New York, 1991.
Marbod of Rennes. *Vita S. Roberti Casae Dei Abbatis* [BHL 7262]. PL 171: 1505–32.
Matthew Paris. *Vita B. Edmundi Cantuariensis archiepiscopi.* Ed. C.H. Lawrence in *St. Edmund of Abington: A Study in Hagiography and History.* Oxford, 1960.
Memorials of St. Anselm. Ed. R.W. Southern and F.S. Schmitt. London, 1969.
Memorials of the Abbey of St. Mary of Fountains. 3 vols. Ed. John R. Walbran, James Raine and J.T. Fowler. Surtees Society Publications 42, 67, 130. Durham, 1863–1918.
Les miracles de Saint Benoît écrits par les Adrevald, Aimon, André, Raoul Tortaire et Hugues de Sainte Marie, moines de Fleury. Ed. Eugène de Certain. Paris, 1958.
Nicholas of Clairvaux. *Epistolae.* PL 196: 1593–1654.
Nigel Longchamp. *Tractatus contra curiales et officiales clericos.* Ed. André Boutemy. Paris, 1959.
Odo of Cluny. *Collationum libri tres.* PL 133: 517–638.
———. *Epitome moralium in Job libri XXXV.* PL 133: 107–512.
———. *Sermones quinque.* PL 133: 709–52.
———. *Vita sancti Geraldi Auriliacensis (vita prolixior).* Ed. Anne-Marie Bultot-Verleysen. Subsidia hagiographica 89. Brussels, 2009. Trans. Gerard Sitwell in *St. Odo of Cluny: Being the Life of St. Odo of Cluny by John of Salerno and Life of St. Gerald of Aurillac by St. Odo.* London, 1958.
Odo of Saint-Maur. *Vita domni Burcardi* [BHL 1482]. Ed. Charles Bourel de la Roncière as *Vie de Bouchard le Vénérable.* Paris, 1892.
Orderic Vitalis. *The Ecclesiastical History.* 6 vols. Ed. and trans. Marjorie Chibnall. Oxford, 1969–80.
Origen. *Homélies sur les Nombres.* 3 vols. Ed. W.A. Baehrens et al. SC 415, 442, 461. Paris, 1996–2001.
Origen. *Opera omnia.* 25 vols. Ed. C.H.E. Lommatzsch. Berlin, 1831–48.
'Papsturkunden in Florenz.' In *Nachrichten von der Gesellschaft der Wissenschaften zu Gottingen,* ed. W. Wiederhold, 306–25. Gottingen, 1901.
The Papal Reform of the Eleventh Century: Lives of Pope Leo IX and Gregory VII. Ed. and trans. Ian S. Robinson. Manchester, 2004.
Paschasius Radbertus. *Epitaphium Arsenii (Vita Walae).* Ed. Ernst Dümmler, in *Philosophische und historische Abhandlungen der königlichen. Akademie der Wissenschaften zu Berlin,* phil.-hist. Kl., 2 (1900): 1–98. Trans. Allen Cabaniss as 'The Life of Wala,' in *Charlemagne's Cousins: Contemporary Lives of Adalard and Wala.* Syracuse, NY, 1967.
———. *Expositio in evangelium Matthaei libri XII.* CCCM 56. Ed. Beda Paulus. Turnhout, 1984.
Paul the Deacon. *Historia Langobardorum.* Ed. L. Bethmann and G. Waitz. MGH SSRerLang 1: 12–187.
Peter of Aliaco. *Vita et miracula S. Petri Caelestini.* AASS May 4: 484–97.
Peter of Blois. *The Later Letters of Peter of Blois.* Auctores Britannici Medii Aevi 13. Ed. Elizabeth Revell. Oxford, 1993.
Peter of Celle. *Adhortatio ad claustrales.* PL 202: 1097–146.
———. *De afflictione et lectione.* In *La spiritualité de Pierre de Celle,* ed. J. Leclercq, 231–9.

Paris: J. Vrin, 1946. Trans. Hugh Feiss as 'On Affliction and Reading' in *Peter of Celle: Selected Works*. CS 100. Kalamazoo, MI, 1987.
Peter Damian. *Die Briefe des Petrus Damiani*, 4 vols. Ed. Kurt Reindel. Munich, 1983–93. Trans. Owen J. Blum, Irven Resnick and Thomas Halton as *The Letters of Peter Damian*, 6 vols. Washington D.C., 1989–2005.
——. *Sermones*. Ed. Giovanni Lucchesi. CCCM 57. Turnhout, 1983.
——. *Vita S. Rodulphi episcopi Eugubini et S. Dominici Loricati* [BHL 7282]. PL 144: 1007–24.
——. *Vita S. Romualdis abbatis*. PL 144: 953–1008.
Peter of Dives. *Gesta septem abbatum Beccensium*. PL 181: 1709–18.
Peter Tudebode. *Historia de Hierosolymitano Itinere*. RHC Occ. 3: 9–117. Trans. John Hugh Hill and Laurita L. Hill. Philadelphia, PA, 1974.
Peter the Venerable. *The Letters of Peter the Venerable*. 2 vols. Ed. Giles Constable. Cambridge, MA, 1967.
——. *De miraculis*. Ed. Denise Bouthillier. CCCM 83. Turnholt, 1988.
Philip of Harvengt. *De institutione clericorum*. PL 203: 665–1206.
Philip of Navarre. *Les quatres ages de l'homme*. Ed. Marcel de Fréville. Paris, 1888.
Planctus de transitu Odilonis abbatis. PL 142: 1043–6.
A Pre-Conquest English Prayer Book. Ed. B.J. Muir. Henry Bradshaw Society 103. Woodbridge, 1988.
Processus de vita et miraculis factus anno 1307 (Canonization proceedings of Thomas de Cantilupe). AASS Oct. 1: 585–696.
Prudentius. *Works*. 2 vols. Ed. and trans. H.J. Thomson. Loeb Classical Library 387, 398. Cambridge, MA, 1949–53.
Pseudo-Basil of Caesarea. *Admonitio ad filium spiritualium*. PL 103: 685–6.
Ralph Glaber. *Opera*. Ed. Neithard Bulst, trans. John France and Paul Reynolds. Oxford, 1989.
Ralph of La Chaise-Dieu. *Vita Adelelmi Casae Dei* [BHL 71]. In *La España Sagrada*, 51 vols, ed. H. Florez, 27: 425–34. Madrid, 1743–1886.
Ranger of Lucca. *Vita Anselmi Lucensis*. Ed. Ernest Sackur, Gerhard Schwartz and Bernhard Schmeidler. MGH SS 30/2: 1152–307.
Raymond of Aguilers. *Historia Francorum qui ceperunt Iherusalem*. RHC Occ. 3: 235–309. Trans. John Hugh Hill and Laurita L. Hill. Philadelphia, PA, 1968.
Recueil des actes des ducs de Normandie de 911 à 1066. Ed. Marie Fauroux. Caen, 1961.
Recueil des chartres de l'abbaye de Cluny. 5 vols. Ed. Auguste Bernard and Alexandre Bruel. Paris, 1876–1903.
Reginald of Durham. *Vita et miracula S. Godrici*. Ed. Joseph Stevenson in *Libellus de vita et miraculis S. Godrici heremitae de Finchale*, Publications of the Surtees Society 20. London, 1847.
Regino of Prüm. *Chronica*. PL 132: 13–1332.
Das Register Gregors VII. 2 vols. Ed. Erich Caspar. MGH Epistolae selectae 2. Berlin, 1920–23.
Regula Magistri. Ed. and trans. Adalbert de Vogüé as *La Règle du maître*. 3 vols. SC 105–7. Paris, 1964–5.
Remigius of Auxerre. *Enarrationum in psalmos liber unus*. PL 131: 133–844.
Robert of Flamborough. *Liber poenitentialis*. Ed. J. Firth. Toronto, 1971.
Robert of Reims. *Historia Iherosolimitana*. RHC Occ. 3: 717–882. Trans. Carole Sweetenham as *Robert the Monk's History of the First Crusade: Historia Iherosolimitana*. Aldershot, 2005.
Rouleaux des morts du IXe au XVe siècle. Ed. Léopold Delisle. Paris, 1866.

Rupert of Deutz. *Commentaria in Apocalypsim*. PL 169: 825–1214.
Saint Richard of Chichester: The Sources for his Life. Ed. David Jones. Sussex Record Society 79. Lewes, 1995.
Sermo in Assumptione B. Mariae Virginis. PL 184: 1001–10.
Sicard of Cremona. *Mitrale, seu de officiis ecclesiasticis summa*. PL 213: 13–436.
Sigebert of Gembloux. *Chronica*. PL 160: 57–546.
Smaragdus of Saint-Mihiel. *Diadema monachorum*. PL 102: 593–690.
——. *Expositio in Regulam S. Benedicti*. Ed. A Spannagel and P. Engelbert. Corpus Consuetudinem Monasticarum. Siegburg, 1974. Trans. David Barry as *Smaragdus of Saint-Mihiel: Commentary on the Rule of Saint Benedict*. CS 212. Kalamazoo, MI, 2007.
S. Petri episcopi Policastrensis [BHL 6767]. AASS March 1: 330–5.
Stephen of Autun. *Tractatus de sacramento altaris*. PL 172: 1273–308.
Stephen Fulgerius (?). *Vita Guilielmi Firmati* [BHL 8914]. AASS Apr. 3: 334–41.
Stephen Harding. *Sermo in obitu praedecessoris sui*. PL 166: 1375–6.
Stephen of Lissac. *Vita Stephani de Mureto* ... [BHL 7907]. PL 204: 1071–86.
Stephen of Sawley. *Treatises*. Ed. Bede K. Lackner and trans. Jeremiah F. O'Sullivan. CF 36. Kalamazoo, MI, 1984.
Suger of Saint-Denis. *Vita Ludovici grossi regis*. Ed. and trans. Henri Waquet. Classiques de l'histoire de France au Moyen Age 11. Paris, 1964.
Sulpicius Severus. *Vita S. Martini*. Ed. Jacques Fontaine as *Vie de saint Martin: Introduction, texte, traduction, et commentaire*, 3 vols. SC 133–5. Paris, 1967–9. Trans. F.R. Hoare as 'The Life of Saint Martin of Tours', in *Soldiers of Christ: Saints and Saints' Lives from Late Antiquity and the Early Middle Ages*, ed. Thomas F.X. Noble and Thomas Head, 1–29. University Park, PA, 1995.
Tertullian. *Ad martyras*. In *Quinti Septimi Florentis Tertulliani Opera*. 2 vols. Ed. E. Dekkers, 1: 1–18. CCSL 1–2. Turnhout, 1954. Trans. Rudolph Arbesmann, Emily Joseph Daly and Edwin A. Quain as *To the Martyrs*, in *Tertullian: Disciplinary, Moral, and Ascetical Works*. FC 40. Washington D.C., 1959.
Thietmar of Merseburg. *Chronica*. PL 139: 1183–954.
Thomas of Perseigne. *Cantica Canticorum*. PL 206: 15–861.
Translatio S. Germani Parisiensis anno 846. Ed. Carolus de Smedt. *Analecta Bollandiana* 2 (1883), 69–98.
Translatio S. Sebastiani martyris. AASS Jan. 2: 278–93.
Vie de saint Alexis: poème du XIe siècle. Ed. Gaston Paris. Paris, 1885.
The Vie de Saint Alexis in the Twelfth and Thirteenth Centuries: An Edition and Commentary. Ed. Alison Goddard Elliott. Chapel Hill, NC, 1983.
'La vie de S. Gaucher, fondateur des chanoines réguliers d'Aureil en Limousin.' Ed. Jean Becquet. *Revue Mabillon* 54 (1964), 25–55.
Visio Gunthelmi. Ed. Giles Constable, in 'The Vision of Gunthelm and Other Visions Attributed to Peter the Venerable.' *Revue Bénédictine* 66 (1956), 92–114.
Vita altera (Petri Venerabilis abbatis). PL 189: 27–42.
Vita B. Johannis de Monte-Mirabili [BHL 4415]. AASS Sept 8: 218–35.
Vita B. Laurentii eremitae Sublaci [BHL 4793]. AASS Aug. 3: 304–7.
Vita B. Raynerii solitarii Osnaburgi in Westphalia [BHL 7083]. AASS Apr. 2: 61–2.
Vita S. Roberti abbatis Molesmensis [BHL 7265]. PL 157: 1269–94.
Vita B. Simonis comitis Crespeiensis auctore synchrono [BHL 7757]. PL 156: 1211–24.
Vita Gangulfi martyris Varennensis [BHL 3328]. Ed. W. Levinson. MGH SS RerMerov 7: 142–74.
Vita Gaucherii Aurelii. Ed. Jean Becquet as 'La vie de saint Gaucher, fondateur des chanoines réguliers d'Aureil en Limousin.' *Revue Mabillon* 54 (1964): 25–55.

Vita Gaufridi Castaliensis [BHL 3283]. Ed. A. Bosieux in *Mémoires de la Société des sciences naturelles et archéologiques de la Creuse* 3 (1862), 75–119.

Vita Gerlaci eremitae in Belgio [BHL 3449]. AASS Jan. 1: 306–20.

Vita Godefridi comitis Cappenbergensis [BHL 3578]. Ed. Philippe Jaffé. MGH SS 12: 513–30. Trans. Theodore J. Antry and Carol Neel in *Norbert and Early Norbertine Spirituality*. New York, 2007.

Vita Guilielmi abbatis fundatoris eremitarum Montis Virginis [BHL 8924]. AASS Jun. 5: 114–31.

Vita Leonis IX. In *Pontificum romanorum vitae*. 2 vols. Ed. I. M. Watterich, 1:127–70. Leipzig, 1862.

Vita de S. Alexii [BHL 286]. AASS Jul. 4: 251–4.

Vita S. Ansegisi abbatis Fontanellensis et Luxoviensis. PL 105: 735–50.

Vita S. Avito eremita in Sarlatensi apud Petracoricos diocesi [BHL 884]. AASS Jun. 3: 360–65.

Vita S. Bobonis [BHL 1383]. AASS May 5: 184–91.

Vita S. Cordulae virginis et martyris, S. Ursulæ sodali [BHL 1951]. AASS Oct. 9: 580–86.

Vita S. Geraldi abbatis [BHL 3417]. AASS Apr. 1: 414–23.

Vita S. Godelevae virginis et martyris Ghistellae [BHL 3593]. AASS Jul. 2: 401–36.

Vita S. Stephani Obazinensis [BHL 7916]. Ed. and trans. Michel Aubrun as *Vie de Saint Étienne d'Obazine*. Publications de L'Institut du Massif Centrale 6. Clermont-Ferrand, 1970.

Vita S. Teobaldi [BHL 8032]. AASS June 5: 592–5.

Vita venerabilis Amedaei Altae Ripae († c.1150). Ed. Anselme Dimier in *Studia monastica* 5 (1963), 265–304.

Vita Willelmi Gellonensis [BHL 8916]. AASS May 6: 811–20.

Vizeliacensia II: Textes relatifs à l'histoire de l'abbaye de Vézelay. Ed. R.B.C. Huygens. CCCM 42 Suppl. Turnhout, 1980.

Walafrid Strabo. *Expositio in viginti primos psalmos*. PL 114: 751–94.

Walter of Aquitaine: Materials for the Study of His Legend. Ed. Francis Peabody Magoun and H.M. Smyser. New London, CT, 1950.

Walter Daniel. *Vita Ailredi abbatis Rievall'* [BHL 2644]. Ed. and trans. F.M. Powicke. Oxford, 1950.

William Dandina of Saint-Savin. *Vita Hugonis de Lacerta* [BHL 4017]. In *Vetera scriptorum ... amplissima collectio*, 9 vols, ed. Edmond Martène and Ursin Durand, 6: 1143–86. Paris, 1724–33.

William of Poitiers. *Gesta Guillelmi*. Ed. R.H.C. Davis and Marjorie Chibnall. Oxford, 1998.

William of Saint-Thierry. *Expositio in epistolam ad Romanos*. PL 180: 547–694. Ed. John D. Anderson and trans. John Baptist Hasbrouck as *Exposition on the Epistle to the Romans*. CF 27. Kalamazoo, MI, 1980.

William of Saint-Thierry et al. *Vita prima S. Bernardi*. PL 185: 225–368.

William of Tocco. *Ystoria sancti Tome de Aquino*. Ed. Claire Le Brun-Gouanvic. Toronto, 1996.

William of Tyre. *Historia rerum in partibus transmarinis gestarum*. Ed. R.B.C. Huygens. 2 vols. CCCM 63–63A. Turnhout, 1986. Trans. Emily Atwater Babcok and Augustus C. Krey as *History of Deeds Done Beyond the Sea*. 2 vols. New York, 1943.

Secondary works

Airlie, Stuart. 'The Anxiety of Sanctity: St. Gerald of Aurillac and His Maker.' *Journal of Ecclesiastical History* 43 (1992), 372–95.

Alberi, Mary. '"The Sword Which You Hold in Your Hand": Alcuin's Exegesis of the Two Swords and the Lay *Miles Christi*.' In *The Study of the Bible in the Carolingian Era*, ed. Celia Chazelle and Burton Van Name Edwards, 117–31. Medieval Church Studies 3. Turnholt, 2003.

Alexander, J.J.G. 'Ideological Representation of Military Combat in Anglo-Norman Art.' *Anglo-Norman Studies* 15 (1992), 1–24.

Alphandéry, P. *La chrétienté et l'idée de croisade*. Paris, 1954.

Ambrose, Kirk. *The Nave Sculpture of Vézelay: The Art of Monastic Viewing*. Toronto, 2006.

Ashley, Kathleen and Pamela Sheingorn. *Writing Faith: Text, Sign, and History in the Miracles of Sainte Foy*. Chicago, MI, 1999.

Auer, Johann. 'Militia Christi.' In *Dictionnaire de spiritualité ascétique et mystique*, 17 vols, ed. Marcel Villers et al., 10: 1210–23. Paris, 1937–94.

Bachrach, Bernard S. 'The Combat Sculptures at Fulk Nerra's "Battle Abbey" (c. 1005–1012).' *Haskins Society Journal* 3 (1991), 63–80.

——. 'The Feigned Retreat at Hastings.' *Mediaeval Studies* 33 (1971): 344–7.

Bachrach, David S. *Religion and the Conduct of War, c.300–1215*. Woodbridge, 2003.

Bainton, Roland H. *Christian Attitudes Toward War and Peace: A Historical Survey and Critical Re-evaluation*. New York, 1960.

Barber, Richard. 'When is a Knight not a Knight?' In *The Ideals and Practice of Medieval Knighthood V: Papers from the Sixth Strawberry Hill Conference*, ed. Stephen Church and Ruth Harvey, 1–17. Woodbridge, 1995.

Barber, Malcolm. *The New Knighthood: A History of the Order of the Temple*. Cambridge, 1994.

Barratt, Alexandra. 'The *De institutione inclusarum* of Aelred of Rievaulx and the Carthusian Order.' *The Journal of Theological Studies* 28 (1977): 528–36.

Barthélemy, Dominique. *Chevaliers et miracles: la violence et le sacré dans la société féodale*. Paris, 2004.

——. *The Serf, the Knight, and the Historian*. Trans. Graham Robert Edwards. Ithaca, NY, 2009.

——. 'Qu'est-ce que la chevalerie en France aux Xe et XIe siècles?' *Revue Historique* 290 (1993), 15–74.

——. 'Sur les traces du comte Bouchard: Dominations châtelaines a Vendôme et en Francia vers l'an Mil.' In *Le roi de France et son royaume autour de l'an Mil*, ed. Michel Parisse and Xavier Barral i Altet, 99–109. Paris, 1992.

Bédier, Joseph. *Les légendes épiques: Recherches sur la formation des chansons de geste*. 4 vols. Paris, 1908–13.

Bennett, Matthew. 'Military Masculinity in England and Northern France, c.1050-c.1225.' In *Masculinity in Medieval Europe*, ed. D.M. Hadley, 71–88. London, 1999.

Berman, Constance H. *The Cistercian Evolution: The Invention of a Religious Order in Twelfth-Century Europe*. Philadelphia, PA, 2000.

Bernards, Matthäus. *Speculum virginum: Geistigkeit und Seelenleben der Frau in Hochmittelalter*. Cologne, 1982.

The Bishop Reformed: Studies of Episcopal Power and Culture in the Central Middle Ages. Ed. John Ott and Anna Trumbore Jones. Burlington, VT, 2007.

Blaise, Albert. *Lexicon Latinitatis medii aevi*. Turnhout, 1975.
Blowers, Paul M. 'Interpreting Scripture.' In *The Cambridge History of Christianity, Vol. 2: Constantine to c.600*, ed. Augustine Casiday and Frederick W. Norris, 618–36. Cambridge, 2007.
Bolton, Brenda. 'Old Wealth and New Poverty in the Twelfth Century.' In *Renaissance and Renewal in Christian History*, Studies in Church History 14, ed. Derek Baker, 95–103. Oxford, 1977.
Bostock, John K., Kenneth C. King and D.R. McLintock. *A Handbook of Old High German Literature*. Oxford, 1976.
Boswell, John. *The Kindness of Strangers: The Abandonment of Children in Western Europe from Late Antiquity to the Renaissance*. Chicago, MI, 1988.
Bouchard, Constance Brittain. *'Every Valley Shall Be Exalted': The Discourse of Opposites in Twelfth-Century Thought*. Ithaca, NY, 2003.
———. *Strong of Body, Brave and Noble: Chivalry and Society in Medieval France*. Ithaca, NY, 1998.
———. *Sword, Miter, and Cloister: Nobility and the Church in Burgundy, 980–1198*. Ithaca, NY, 1987.
———. 'Noble Piety and Reformed Monasticism: The Dukes of Burgundy in the Twelfth Century.' In *Noble Piety and Reformed Monasticism: Sudies in Medieval Cistercian History VII*, ed. E. Rozanne Elder, 1–9. Kalamazoo, MI, 1981.
Bouzy, Olivier. 'Les armes symboles d'un pouvoir politique: l'épée du sacre, la Sainte Lance, l'Oriflamme, aux VIIIe–XIIe siècles.' *Francia* 22 (1995), 45–57.
Bowman, Jeffrey Alan. *Shifting Landmarks: Property, Proof, and Dispute in Catalonia Around the Year 1000*. Ithaca, NY, 2004.
Boynton, Susan. *Shaping a Monastic Identity: Liturgy and History at the Imperial Abbey of Farfa, 1000–1125*. Ithaca, NY, 2006.
———. 'Performative Exegesis in the Fleury *Interfectio puerorum*.' *Viator* 29 (1998), 39–64.
Brakke, David. *Demons and the Making of the Monk: Spiritual Combat in Early Christianity*. Cambridge, MA, 2006.
Bredero, Adriaan H. *Bernard of Clairvaux: Between Cult and History*. Grand Rapids, MI, 1996.
Brennan, Peter. 'Military Images in Hagiography.' In *Reading the Past in Late Antiquity*, ed. Graeme Clark et al., 323–45. Rushcutters Bay, 1990.
Brooke, Christopher. *Age of the Cloister*. Mahwah, NJ, 2003.
Brown, Elizabeth A.R. 'George Duby and the Three Orders.' *Viator* 17 (1986), 51–64.
Brown, Elizabeth A.R. and Michael W. Cothren. 'The Twelfth-Century Crusading Window of the Abbey of Saint-Denis: *praeteritorum enim recordatio futurorum est exhibitio*.' *Journal of the Warburg and Courtauld Institutes* 49 (1986), 1–40.
Brundage, James A. 'Adhemar of Puy: The Bishop and His Critics.' *Speculum* 34 (1959), 201–12.
———. 'Crusades, Clerics, and Violence: Reflections on a Canonical Theme.' In *The Experience of Crusading, 1: Western Approaches*, ed. Marcus Bull and Norman Housley, 147–56. Cambridge, 2003.
———. 'Holy War and the Medieval Lawyers.' In *The Holy War*, ed. Thomas Patrick Murphy, 99–140. Columbus, OH, 1976.
———. 'The Limits of War-Making Power: The Contributions of Medieval Canonists.' In *Peace in a Nuclear Age: The Bishops' Pastoral Letter in Perspective*, ed. Charles J. Reid, 69–86. Washington D.C., 1986. Repr. in *The Crusades, Holy War, and Canon Law*, 69–86. Aldershot, 1991.
———. 'St. Anselm, Ivo of Chartres, and the Ideology of the First Crusade.' In *Les muta-*

tions socio-culturelles au tournant des XI–XII siècles, ed. Raymond Foreville, 175–87. Paris, 1984. Repr. in *The Crusades, Holy War, and Canon Law*.

———. 'A Transformed Angel (X 3.31.18): The Problem of the Crusading Monk. In *Studies in Medieval Cistercian History Presented to Jeremiah F. O'Sullivan*, CS 13, ed. J.F. O'Callaghan and J.S. Donnelly, 55–62. Shannon, 1971.

Buc, Philippe. 'Conversion of Objects.' *Viator* 28 (1997), 99–143.

Bugge, John. *Monastic and Religious Orders in Britain*. Cambridge, 1994.

———. *Virginitas: An Essay in the History of a Medieval Ideal*. The Hague, 1975.

Bull, Marcus. *Knightly Piety and the Lay Response to the First Crusade: The Limousin and Gascony, c. 970–1130*. Oxford, 1993.

———. 'The Pilgrimage Origins of the First Crusade.' *History Today* 47 (1997), 10–15.

———. 'The Roots of Lay Enthusiasm for the First Crusade.' *History* 78 (1992), 353–72.

Bulst-Thiele, M.L. 'The Influence of St. Bernard of Clairvaux on the Formation of the Order of the Knights Templar.' In *The Second Crusade and the Cistercians*, ed. Michael Gervers, 57–65. New York, 1992.

Burrow, J.A. *The Ages of Man: A Study in Medieval Writing and Thought*. Princeton, 1986.

Burrus, Virginia. 'Hybrid Desire: Empire, Sadism, and the Soldier Saint.' In *The Sex Lives of Saints: An Erotics of Ancient Hagiography*, 91–127. Philadelphia, PA, 2004.

———. 'Queer Lives of Saints: Jerome's Hagiography.' *Journal of the History of Sexuality* 10 (2001), 442–79.

Burton, Janet E. *Monastic and Religious Orders in England, 1000–1300*. Cambridge, 1994.

———. *The Monastic Order in Yorkshire, 1069–1215*. Cambridge, 1999.

Bynum, Caroline Walker. *Docere verbo et exemplo: An Aspect of Twelfth-Century Spirituality*. Missoula, MT, 1979.

———. *Jesus as Mother: Studies in the Spirituality of the High Middle Ages*. Berkeley, 1982.

Cain, Andrew. '*Vox clamantis in deserto*: Rhetoric, Reproach, and the Forging of Ascetic Authority in Jerome's Letters from the Syrian Desert.' *Journal of Theological Studies* 57 (2006), 500–525.

Callahan, Daniel F. 'William the Great and the Monasteries of Aquitaine.' *Studia Monastica* 19 (1977), 321–42.

Carruthers, Mary. *The Craft of Thought: Meditation, Rhetoric, and the Making of Images, 400–1200*. New York, 1998.

Caspary, Gerard E. *Politics and Exegesis: Origen and the Two Swords*. Berkeley, 1979.

Chastang, Pierre. 'Fabrication d'un saint: la *Vita Guillelmi* dans la production textuelle de l'abbaye de Gellone au début du XIIe siècle.' In *Guerriers et moines*, ed. Lauwers, 429–47.

Chenu, M.-D. *Nature, Man and Society in the Twelfth Century: Essays on New Theological Perspectives in the Latin West*. Ed. and trans. Jerome Taylor and Lester Little. Chicago, MI, 1968.

Cherf, John Frank. 'The Latin Manuscript Tradition of the *Vita Sancti Pauli*.' In *Studies in the Text Tradition of St. Jerome's Vitae Patrum*, ed. William Abbott Oldfather, 65–142. Urbana, IL, 1943.

Chibnall, Marjorie. *The World of Orderic Vitalis: Norman Monks and Norman Knights*. Oxford, 1984.

The Church and War: Papers Read at the 21st Summer Meeting and the 22nd Winter Meeting of the Ecclesiastical History Society. Ed. W.J. Sheils. Oxford, 1983.

Clanchy, Michael T. *From Memory to Written Record: England, 1066–1307*. 2nd edn. Oxford, 1993.

Cochelin, Isabelle. 'Peut-on parler de novitiat à Cluny pour les Xe-XIe siècles?' *Revue Mabillon* n.s. 9 (1998): 17–52.

Cole, Penny J. *The Preaching of Crusades to the Holy Land, 1095–1270.* Cambridge, MA, 1991.
Colish, Marcia L. 'Cicero, Ambrose, and Stoic Ethics: Transmission or Transformation?' In *The Classics in the Middle Ages, Papers of the 20th Annual Conference of the Center for Medieval and Early Renaissance Studies,* ed. Aldo S. Bernardo and Saul Levin, 95–112. Binghamton, NY, 1990.
Constable, Giles. *Crusaders and Crusading in the Twelfth Century.* Burlington, VT, 2008.
——. *Letters and Letter Collections.* Typologie des sources du Moyen Âge occidental 17. Turnhout, 1976.
——. *Three Studies in Medieval Religious and Social Thought.* Cambridge, 1998.
——. 'The Ceremonies and Symbolism of Entering the Religious Life and Taking the Monastic Habit from the Fourth to the Twelfth Century.' In *Segni e riti nella chiesa altomedievale occidentale,* 2 vols, 2: 771–834. Spoleto, 1987.
——. 'Entrance into Cluny in the Eleventh and Twelfth Centuries According to the Cluniac Customaries and Statutes.' In *Mediaevalia Christiana, XIe-XIIIe siècle: Hommage à Raymond Foreville,* ed. Coloman Étienne Viola, 334–54. Paris, 1989.
——. '"*Famuli*" and "*Conversi*" at Cluny: A Note on Statute 24 of Peter the Venerable.' *Revue Bénédictine* 83 (1973), 326–50.
——. 'Medieval Charters as a Source for the History of the Crusades.' In *Crusade and Settlement,* ed. Peter W. Edbury, 73–89. Cardiff, 1985.
——. 'Medieval Latin Metaphors.' *Viator* 38 (2007), 1–20.
——. 'Metaphors for Religious Life in the Middle Ages.' *Revue Mabillon* 19 (2008), 231–42.
——. 'Moderation and Restraint in Ascetic Practices in the Middle Ages.' In *From Athens to Chartres: Neoplatonism and Medieval Thought,* ed. Haijo Jan Westra, 315–27. Leiden, 1992.
——. 'The Place of the Crusader in Medieval Society.' *Viator* 29 (1998), 377–403.
——. *The Reformation of the Twelfth Century.* Cambridge, 1996.
——. 'The Three Lives of Odo Arpinus: Viscount of Bourges, Crusader, Monk of Cluny.' In *Religion, Text, and Society in Medieval Spain and Northern Europe: Essays in Honor of J.N. Hillgarth,* ed. Thomas E. Burman, Mark D. Meyerson and Leah Shopkow, 183–99. Toronto, 2002.
Contamine, Philippe. *War in the Middle Ages.* Trans. Michael Jones. Oxford, 1984.
Cornelius, Roberta D. 'The Figurative Castle: A Study in the Mediaeval Allegory of the Edifice with Especial Reference to Religious Writings.' Unpub. PhD thesis, Bryn Mawr, 1930.
Cousin, P. 'Les débuts de l'Ordre des Templiers et Saint Bernard.' In *Mélanges S. Bernard,* 41–52. Dijon, 1953.
Cowdrey, H.E.J. *Pope Gregory VII, 1073–1085.* Oxford, 1998.
——. 'Bishop Ermenfried of Sion and the Penitential Ordinance Following the Battle of Hastings.' *Journal of Ecclesiastical History* 20 (1969), 225–42.
——. 'Cluny and the First Crusade.' *Revue Bénédictine* 83 (1975), 285–311.
——. 'Count Simon of Crépy's Monastic Conversion.' In his *The Crusades and Latin Monasticism, 11th–12th Centuries,* 253–66. London, 1999.
——. *The Crusades and Latin Monasticism, 11th–12th Centuries.* Aldershot, 1999.
——. 'The Genesis of the Crusades: The Springs of Western Ideas of Holy War.' In *The Holy War,* ed. Patrick T. Murphy, 9–32. Columbus, OH, 1976.
——. 'The Gregorian Papacy, Byzantium, and the First Crusade.' In *Byzantium and the West, c.850–1200,* ed. J. Howard-Johnston, 145–69. Amsterdam, 1988.
——. 'Gregory VII and the Bearing of Arms.' In *Montjoie: Studies in Crusade History in*

Honor of Hans Eberhard Mayer, ed. Benjamin Z. Kedar, Jonathan Riley-Smith and Rudolf Hiestand, 23–35. Aldershot, 1997.

———. 'The Mahdia Campaign of 1087.' *English Historical Review* 92 (1977), 1–29.

———. 'Martyrdom and the First Crusade.' In *Crusade and Settlement*, ed. Edbury, 46–56.

———. 'Pope Urban's Preaching of the First Crusade.' *History* 55 (1970), 177–88.

Crouch, David. *The Image of the Aristocracy in Britain, 1000–1300*. London, 1992.

———. *William Marshal: Knighthood, War and Chivalry, 1147–1219*. 2nd edn. London, 2002.

Cullum, Patricia H. 'Clergy, Masculinity and Transgression in Late Medieval England.' In *Masculinity in Medieval Europe*, ed. D.M. Hadley, 178–96. New York, 1999.

Cushing, Kathleen G. *Reform and the Papacy in the Eleventh Century: Spirituality and Social Change*. Manchester, 2005.

Dagens, Claude. *Saint Grégoire le Grand: culture et expérience chrétienne*. Paris, 1977.

Dahan, Gilbert. *L'Exégèse chrétienne de la Bible en Occident médiéval, XIIe-XIVe siècle*. Paris, 1999.

Damon, John Edward. *Soldier Saints and Holy Warriors: Warfare and Sanctity in the Literature of Early England*. Aldershot, 2003.

Daniel, Norman. *Heroes and Saracens: An Interpretation of the chansons de geste*. Edinburgh, 1984.

Daniélou, Jean. *The Bible and the Liturgy*. Notre Dame, IN, 1956.

Delaruelle, Étienne. *L'Idée de la croisade au moyen âge*. Turin, 1980.

———. 'L'Idée de croisade chez Saint Bernard.' In *Mélanges S. Bernard*, 53–67.

Delehaye, Hippolyte. *Les Légendes grecques des saints militaires*. Paris, 1909.

Deschamps, Paul. 'Combats de cavalerie et épisodes des Croisades dans les peintures murales du XIIe et du XIIIe siècle.' *Orientalia Christiana periodica* 13 (1947), 454–74.

Dessì, Rosa Maria. 'La double conversion d'Arduin d'Ivrée: pénitence et conversion autour de l'an Mil .' In *Guerriers et moines*, ed. Lauwers, 317–48.

de Vogüé, Adalbert. *Community and Abbot in the Rule of St Benedict*. Trans. Charles Philippi. CS 5/1. Kalamazoo, MI, 1979.

———. 'The Master and St Benedict: A Reply to Marilyn Dunn.' *English Historical Review* 107 (1992): 95–103.

Dimier, Anselm. 'Saint Bernard et le recrutement de Clairvaux.' *Revue Mabillon* 42 (1952), 17–30, 56–68 and 69–78.

Dolle, Réné. '"Fraterna ex acie": À propos du chapitre 1 (5) de la Règle Bénédictine.' *Studia Anselmiana* fasc. 44 (1959), 126–8.

Doubleday, J.F. 'The Allegory of the Soul as Fortress in Old English Poetry.' *Anglia* 88 (1970), 503–8.

Dubois, Jacques. 'Comment les moines du Moyen Âge chantaient et goutaient les Saintes Écritures.' In *Le Moyen Âge et la Bible*, ed. Pierre Riché and Guy Lobrichon, 261–98. Paris, 1984.

Duby, Georges. *The Chivalrous Society*. Trans. Cynthia Postan. Berkeley, 1977.

———. *The Three Orders: Feudal Society Imagined*. Trans. Arthur Goldhammer. Chicago, MI, 1980.

Du Cange, Charles et al. *Glossarium mediae et infimae Latinitatis*. 2nd edn. 10 vols. Niort, 1883–7.

Dugdale, William. *Monasticon Anglicanum*. 3 vols. London, 1661–82.

Dunbabin, Jean. 'From Clerk to Knight: Changing Orders.' In *The Ideals and Practice of Medieval Knighthood II: Papers from the Third Strawberry Hill Conference*. Ed. Christopher Harper-Bill and Ruth Harvey, 26–39. Woodbridge, 1987.

———. 'The Maccabees as Exemplars in the Tenth and Eleventh Centuries.' In *The Bible*

in the Medieval World: Essays in Memory of Beryl Smalley, ed. Katherine Walsh and Diana Wood, 31–41. Oxford, 1985.
Dunn, Marilyn. 'Mastering Benedict: Monastic Rules and their Authors in the Early Medieval West.' *English Historical Review* 105 (1990), 567–94.
Dyer, Joseph. 'The Psalms in Monastic Prayer.' In *The Place of the Psalms in the Intellectual Culture of the Middle Ages*, ed. Nancy van Deusen, 59–89. Albany, NY, 1999.
Eliade, Mircea. *The Sacred and the Profane*. Trans. Willard Trask. New York, 1968.
Elliott, Dyan. 'The Priest's Wife: Female Erasure and the Gregorian Reform.' In *Medieval Religion: New Approaches*, ed. Constance Hoffman Berman, 123–55. New York, 2005.
Erdmann, Carl. *The Origins of the Idea of Crusade*, Trans. Marshall W. Baldwin and Walter Goffart. Princeton, 1977.
Evans, Gillian R. *The Language and Logic of the Bible: The Earlier Middle Ages*. Cambridge, 1984.
——. *The Thought of Gregory the Great*. Cambridge, 1986.
Evans, Michael. 'An Illustrated Fragment of Peraldus' *Summa* of Vice: Harleian MS 3244', *Journal of the Warburg and Courtauld Institutes* 45 (1982), 14–68.
Evergates, Theodore. 'Historiography and Sociology in Early Feudal Society: The Case of Hariulf and the "*Milites*" of Saint-Riquier.' *Viator* 6 (1975), 35–49.
Fichtenau, Heinrich. *Living in the Tenth Century: Mentalities and Social Orders*. Trans. Patrick J. Geary. Chicago, 1993.
Flahiff, G.B. 'Deus non vult: A Critic of the Third Crusade.' *Mediaeval Studies* 9 (1947), 162–88.
Flanigan, C. Clifford, Kathleen Ashley and Pamela Sheingorn. 'Liturgy as Social Performance: Expanding the Definitions.' In *The Liturgy of the Medieval Church*, ed. Thomas J. Heffernan and E. Ann Matter, 674–714. Kalamazoo, MI, 2001.
Flori, Jean. *La Guerre sainte: La formation de l'idée de croisade dans l'Occident chrétien*. Paris, 2001.
——. *L'essor de la chevalerie: X^e et XIe siècles*. Geneva, 1986.
——. 'Chevalerie et liturgie: remise des armes et vocabulaire "chevaleresque" dans les sources liturgiques du IXe au XIVe siècle.' *Moyen âge* 84 (1978), 247–78 and 409–42.
——. 'Mort et martyre des guerriers vers 1100: L'exemple de la Première Croisade.' *Cahiers de civilisation médiévale* 34 (1991), 121–39.
——. 'Les origines de l'adoubement chevaleresque: étude des remises d'armes et du le vocabulaire qui les exprime dans les sources historiques latines jusqu'au debut du XIIIe siècle.' *Traditio* 35 (1979), 209–72.
Fontaine, Jacques. 'Le culte des martyrs militaires et son expression poétique au IVe siècle: l'idéal évangélique de la non-violence dans le christianisme théodosien.' *Augustinianum* 20 (1980), 141–71.
——. 'Sulpice Sévère a-t-il travesti Saint Martin de Tours en martyr militaire?' *Analecta Bollandiana* 81 (1963), 31–58.
Foucault, Michel. 'La combat de la chasteté.' *Communications* 35 (1982): 15–25.
France, John. *Western Warfare in the Age of the Crusades*. Ithaca, NY, 1999.
Fransen, P.-I. 'D'Eugippius à Bède le Venerable: à propos de leurs florilèges Augustiniens.' *Revue Bénédictine* 97 (1987), 187–94.
Frassetto, Michael, ed. *Medieval Purity and Piety: Essays on Medieval Clerical Celibacy and Religious Reform*. Garland Medieval Casebooks 19. New York, 1998.
Freeman, Elizabeth. *Narratives of a New Order: Cistercian Historical Writing in England, 1150–1220*. Medieval Church Studies 2. Turnhout, 2002.
Fulton, Rachel. *From Judgment to Passion: Devotion to Christ and the Virgin Mary, 800–1200*. New York, 2002.

Gaborit-Chopin, Danielle. 'Les dessins d'Adémar de Chabannes.' *Bulletin du comité des travaux historiques et scientifiques*, n.s. 3 (1967): 163–225.
Gaier, Claude. 'Le rôle militaire des reliques et de l'étendard de saint Lambert dans la principauté de Liège.' *Moyen âge* 72 (1966), 235–49.
Gamble, Harry Y. 'Marcion and the "Canon".' In *The Cambridge History of Christianity, Vol. 1: Origins to Constantine*, ed. Margaret M. Mitchell and Frances M. Young, 487–528. Cambridge, 2006.
Geary, Patrick J. *Living with the Dead in the Middle Ages*. Ithaca, NY, 1994.
——. 'Vivre en conflit dans une France sans état: Typologie des méchanismes de règlement des conflits, 1050–1200.' *Annales ESC* 41 (1986), 1107–33.
Gehl, Paul. 'Mystic Language Models in Monastic Educational Psychology.' *Journal of Medieval and Renaissance Studies* 14 (1982), 219–43.
Gibbon, Edward. *The Decline and Fall of the Roman Empire*. 12 vols. New York, 1845.
Gibson, Margaret T. 'Carolingian Glossed Psalters.' In *The Early Medieval Bible: Its Production, Decoration, and Use*, ed. Richard Gameson, 78–100. Cambridge, 1994.
Green, D.H. *The Millstätter Exodus: A Crusading Epic*. Cambridge, 1966.
Grégoire, Réginald. 'Esegesi biblica e "militia christi"' In *Militia christi e crociata*, 21–48.
Griffiths, Fiona J. *The Garden of Delights: Reform and Renaissance for Women in the Twelfth Century*. Philadelphia, PA, 2007.
——. 'Siblings and the Sexes within the Medieval Religious Life.' *Church History* 77 (2008), 26–53.
Grundmann, Herbert. 'Adelsbekehrungen im Hochmittelalter: *Conversi* und *Nutriti* im Kloster.' In *Adel und Kirche: Gerd Tellenbach zum 65. Geburtstag dargebracht von Freunden un Schulern*, ed. Joseph Fleckenstein and Karl Schmid, 325–44. Frieburg, 1968.
Guevin, Benedict. 'Benedict's "Military" Vocabulary Reconsidered.' *American Benedictine Review* 49 (1998), 138–47.
Hallam, Elizabeth M. 'Monasteries as "War Memorials": Battle Abbey and La Victoire.' In *The Church and War*, ed. Sheils, 47–57.
Hamel, Christopher de. *The Book: A History of the Bible*. London, 2001.
Hamilton, Bernard. 'Ideals of Holiness: Crusaders, Contemplatives, and Mendicants.' *International History Review* 17 (1995), 693–712.
Hamilton, Sarah. *The Practice of Penance, 900–1050*. Woodbridge, 2001.
Hanley, Catherine. *War and Combat, 1150–1270: The Evidence from Old French Literature*. Woodbridge, 2003.
Hare, Kent G. 'Clerics, War, and Weapons in Anglo-Saxon England.' In *The Final Argument: The Imprint of Violence on Society in Medieval and Early Modern Europe*, ed. Donald J. Kagay and L.J. Andrew Villalon, 3–12. Woodbridge, 1998.
Harnack, Adolf. *Marcion: The Gospel of the Alien God*. Trans. John E. Steely and Lyle D. Bierma. Durham, NC, 1990.
——. *Militia Christi: Die christliche Religion und der Soldatenstand in den ersten drei Jahrhunderten*. Tübingen, 1905. Trans. David McInnes Grace as *Militia Christi: The Christian Religion and the Military in the First Three Centuries*. Philadelphia, PA, 1981.
Harper-Bill, Christopher. 'Herluin, Abbot of Bec and His Biographer.' In *Religious Motivation: Biographical and Sociological Problems for the Church Historian. Papers Read at the 16th Summer Meeting and the 17th Winter Meeting of the Ecclesiastical History Society*, ed. Derek Baker, 15–25. Oxford, 1978.
——. 'The Piety of the Anglo-Norman Knightly Class.' In *Proceedings of the Battle Conference on Anglo-Norman Studies* 2, ed. R. Allen Brown, 63–77. Woodbridge, 1979.

Harper, John. *Forms and Orders of the Western Liturgy from the Tenth to the Eighteenth Century*. Oxford, 1991.
Harpham, Geoffrey Galt. *The Ascetic Imperative in Culture and Criticism*. Chicago, 1987.
Head, Thomas F. *Hagiography and the Cult of Saints: The Diocese of Orléans, 800–1200*. Cambridge Studies in Medieval Life and Thought, 4th ser., 14. Cambridge, 1991.
——. 'The Development of the Peace of God in Aquitaine (970–1005).' *Speculum* 74 (1999), 656–86.
——. 'The Judgment of God: Andrew of Fleury on the Peace League of Bourges.' In *The Peace of God*, ed. Head and Landes, 219–38.
—— and Richard Landes, ed. *The Peace of God: Social Violence and Religious Response in France Around the Year 1000*. Ithaca, NY, 1992.
Hebron, Malcolm. *The Medieval Siege: Theme and Image in Middle English Romance*. Oxford, 1997.
Hehl, Ernst-Dieter. 'War, Peace, and the Christian Order.' In *The New Cambridge Medieval History, Vol. IV/1: c.1024–1198*, ed. David Luscombe and Jonathan Riley-Smith, 185–228. Cambridge, 1995.
Helgeland, John. *Christians and the Military: The Early Experience*. Philadelphia, PA, 1985.
Helsinger, Howard. 'Images on the 'Beatus' Page of Some Medieval Psalters.' *Art Bulletin* 53 (1971): 161–76.
Hobbs, Raymond. 'The Language of Warfare in the New Testament.' In *Modelling Early Christianity: Social–Scientific Studies of the New Testament in its Context*, ed. Philip F. Esler, 259–62. London, 1995.
Holdsworth, Christopher J. 'An Airier Aristocracy: The Saints at War.' *Transactions of the Royal Historical Society* 6th ser., 6 (1996), 103–22.
——. 'Ideas and Reality: Some Attempts to Control and Defuse War in the Twelfth Century.' In *The Church and War*, ed. Sheils, 59–78.
——. 'Were the Sermons of St Bernard on the Song of Songs Ever Preached?' In *Medieval Monastic Preaching*, ed. Carolyn Muessig, 295–318. Leiden, 1998.
Hollis, Stephanie and W.R. Barnes. *Writing the Wilton Women: Goscelin's Legend of Edith and Liber confortatorius*. Medieval Women 9. Turnhout, 2004.
Holmes, Robert L. 'St. Augustine and the Just War Theory.' In *The Augustinian Tradition*, ed. Gareth B. Matthews, 323–44. Berkeley, CA, 1999.
Hornus, Jean-Michel. *It is not lawful for me to fight: Early Christian Attitudes toward War, Violence, and the State*. Trans. Alan Kreider. Scottdale, PA, 1980.
Howe, John. *Church Reform and Social Change in Eleventh-Century Italy: Dominic of Sora and His Patrons*. Philadelphia, PA, 1997.
——. 'Greek Influence on the Eleventh-Century Revival of Hermitism.' 2 vols. Unpub. PhD thesis, UCLA, 1979.
——. 'The Nobility's Reform of the Medieval Church.' *American Historical Review* 93 (1988), 317–39.
——. 'St Benedict the Hermit as a Model for Italian Sanctity: Some Hagiographical Examples.' *American Benedictine Review* 55 (2004), 42–54.
Hunt, Tony. 'The Life of St. Alexis, 475–1125.' In *Christina of Markyate*, ed. Henrietta Leyser and Samuel Fanous, 217–28. London, 2005.
Iogna-Prat, Dominique. *Agni immaculati: Recherches sur les sources hagiographiques relatives à saint Maieul de Cluny (954–99)*. Paris, 1988.
——. 'Éverard de Breteuil et son double: Morphologie de la conversion en conversion en milieu aristocratique (v.1070–v.1120).' In *Guerriers et moines*, ed. Lauwers, 537–57.

———. *Order and Exclusion: Cluny and Christendom Face Heresy, Judaism, and Islam (1000–1150)*. Trans. Graham Robert Edwards. Ithaca, NY, 2002.
Jackson, Peter. 'The Vitas Patrum in Eleventh-Century Worcester.' In *England in the Eleventh Century: Proceedings of the 1990 Harlaxton Symposium*, ed. Carola Hicks, 119–34. Stamford, 1992.
Jean-Nesmy, Claude. *La Tradition médite le psautier chrétien*, 2 vols. Paris 1973–74.
Jestice, Phyllis. *Wayward Monks and the Religious Revolution of the Eleventh Century*. Leiden, 1997.
Johnson, Penelope D. *Equal in Monastic Profession: Religious Women in Medieval France*. Chicago, MI, 1990.
———. *Prayer, Patronage, and Power: The Abbey of la Trinité, Vendôme*. New York, 1981.
Jong, Mayke de. *The Penitential State: Authority and Atonement in the Age of Louis the Pious, 814–40*. Cambridge, 2009.
———. *In Samuel's Image: Child Oblation in the Early Medieval West*. Leiden, 1996.
———. 'Monastic Prisoners or Opting Out: Political Coercion and Honour in the Frankish Kingdoms.' In *Topographies of Power in the Early Middle Ages*, ed. Frans Theuws, Mayke De Jong and Carine van Rhijn, 291–328. Leiden, 2001.
———. 'Power and Humility in Carolingian Society: The Public Penance of Louis the Pious.' *Early Medieval Europe* 1 (1992), 29–52.
Jordan, William C. 'The Representation of the Crusades in the Songs Attributed to Thibaud, Count Palatine of Champagne.' *The Journal of Medieval History* 25 (1999), 27–34.
Kaeuper, Richard W. *Chivalry and Violence*. Oxford, 1999.
———. *Holy Warriors: The Religious Ideology of Chivalry*. Philadelphia, PA, 2009.
Karkov, Catherine E. 'Broken Bodies and Singing Tongues: Gender and Voice in the Cambridge, Corpus Christi College 23 Psychomachia.' *Anglo-Saxon England* 30 (2002): 115–36.
Karras, Ruth Mazo. 'Thomas Aquinas's Chastity Belt: Clerical Masculinity in Medieval Europe.' In *Gender and Christianity in Medieval Europe*, ed. Lisa M. Bitel and Felice Lifshitz, 52–67. Philadelphia, PA, 2008.
Katzenellenbogen, Adolf. 'The Central Tympanum at Vézelay: Its Encyclopedic Meaning and Its Relation to the First Crusade.' *Art Bulletin* 26 (1944), 141–51.
Keen, Maurice. *Chivalry*. New Haven, CT, 1984.
Kelly, Joseph F. *The World of the Early Christians: Message of the Fathers of the Church*. Collegeville, MN, 1997.
Kerr, Bernice. *Religious Life for Women, c.1100–1350: Fontevraud in England*. Oxford, 1999.
Kienzle, Beverly Mayne, ed. *The Sermon*. Typologie des sources du Moyen Âge occidental 81–83. Turnhout, 2000.
Kitchen, John. *Saints' Lives and the Rhetoric of Gender: Male and Female in Merovingian Hagiography*. Oxford, 1998.
Krey, Augustus C. 'Urban's Crusade: Success or Failure?' *American Historical Review* 53 (1948), 235–50.
Kuefler, Mathew. *The Manly Eunuch: Masculinity, Gender Ambiguity, and Christian Ideology in Late Antiquity*. Chicago, MI, 2001.
———. 'Dating and Authorship of the *Vitae* of Saint Gerald of Aurillac' (forthcoming).
Lackner, Bede K. *Eleventh-Century Background of Cîteaux*. CS 8. Washington D.C., 1972.
La Corte, Daniel Marcel. 'Abbot as *Magister* and *Pater* in the Thought of Bernard of Clairvaux and Aelred of Rievaulx.' In *Truth as Gift: Studies in Cistercian History in*

Honor of John R. Sommerfeldt, ed. Marsha Dutton, 389–406. CS 204. Kalamazoo, MI, 2004.

——. 'Smaragdus of Saint-Mihiel: Ninth-Century Sources for Twelfth-Century Reformers.' *Cistercian Studies Quarterly* 41 (2006), 273–90.

Lakoff, George. 'The Contemporary Theory of Metaphor.' In *Metaphor and Thought*, 2nd edn, ed. Andrew Ortony, 202–52. Cambridge, 1993.

Lampe, G. 'The Exposition and Exegesis of Scripture, I: To Gregory the Great.' In *Cambridge History of the Bible*, 3 vols, ed. Peter Ackroyd et al., 2: 155–83. Cambridge, 1963.

Landes, Richard A. *Relics, Apocalypse, and the Deceits of History: Ademar of Chabannes, 989–1034*. Cambridge, MA, 1995.

——. 'Popular Participation in the Peace of God.' In *The Peace of God*, ed. Head and Landes, 184–218.

Lauwers, Michel, ed. 'La 'vie du seigneur Bouchard, comte vénérable:' Conflits d'avouerie, traditions carolingiennes et modèles de sainteté à l'abbaye des Fossés au XIe siècle.' In *Guerriers et moines*, ed. Lauwers, 371–418.

——. *Guerriers et moines. Conversion et sainteté aristocratiques dans l'Occident médiéval*. CNRS Collection d'études médiévales 4. Antibes, 2002.

Lawrence, Clifford. *Medieval Monasticism: Forms of Religious Life in Western Europe in the Middle Ages*. New York, 1984.

Learned, Marion Dexter. 'The Saga of Walther of Aquitaine.' *Proceedings of the Modern Language Association* 7 (1892), 1–129 and 207–8.

Leclercq, Jean. *The Love of Learning and Desire for God: A Study of Monastic Culture*. Trans. Catharine Misrahi. New York, 1982.

——. *Monks and Love in Twelfth-Century France*. Oxford, 1979.

——. 'Écrits monastiques sur la Bible aux XIe-XIIIe siècles.' *Mediaeval Studies* 15 (1953), 95–106.

——. 'The Exposition and Exegesis of Scripture: From Gregory the Great to Saint Bernard.' In *The Cambridge History of the Bible, Vol. 2: The West from the Fathers to the Reformation*. Ed. Peter R. Ackroyd, Geoffrey W.H. Lampe and Stanley L. Greenslade, 183–97. Cambridge, 1969.

——. 'Lettres de vocation à la vie monastique.' *Studia Anselmiana* 37, Analecta monastica, 3rd ser., fasc. 27 (1955), 169–97.

——. 'Origène au XIIe siècle.' *Irénikon* 24 (1951), 425–39.

——. 'S. Antoine dans la tradition monastique médiévale.' In *Antonius Magnus Eremita, 356–1956*, ed. Basilius Steidle, 229–47. Studia Anselmiana 38. Rome, 1956.

——. 'Le thème de la jonglerie chez S. Bernard et ses contemporains.' *Revue d'histoire de la spiritualité* 48 (1972), 385–99.

——. 'La vêture ad succurrendum.' *Studia Anselmiana* 3rd ser., 37 (1955), 158–68.

Le Jan, Régine. 'Apprentissages militaires, rites de passage, et remises d'armes au haut Moyen Âge.' In *Initiation, apprentissages, éducation au Moyen Âge*, ed. P.-A. Sigal, 213–32. Montpellier, 1993.

——. 'Frankish Giving of Arms and Rituals of Power: Continuity and Change in the Carolingian Period.' In *Rituals of Power: From Late Antiquity to the Early Middle Ages*, ed. Frans Theuws and Janet L. Nelson, 281–309. Leiden, 2000.

Le Maître, Philippe. 'Les méthodes exégétiques de Raban Maur.' In *Haut Moyen-Age: culture, éducation et societé*, ed. Michel Sot, 343–52. La Garenne Colombes, 1990.

LePree, James. 'Two recently discovered passages of the Pseudo-Basil's *Admonition to a Spiritual Son* (*De admonitio ad filium spiritualem*) in Smaragdus' *Commentary on the Rule of St. Benedict* (*Expositio in regulam s. Benedicti*) and the *Letters* (*Epistolae*) of Alcuin.'

The Heroic Age 11 (2008), online at http://www.mun.ca/mst/heroicage/issues/11/lepree.php.

Leyser, Conrad. 'Masculinity in Flux: Nocturnal Emission and the Limits of Celibacy in the Early Middle Ages.' In *Masculinity in Medieval Europe*, ed. D.M. Hadley, 103–20. New York, 1999.

Leyser, Henrietta. *Hermits and the New Monasticism: A Study of Religious Community in Western Europe, 1000–1150*. New York, 1984.

Leyser, Karl. 'Early Medieval Canon Law and the Beginnings of Knighthood.' In *Communications and Power in Medieval Europe: The Carolingian and Ottonian Centuries*, ed. Timothy Reuter, 51–71. London, 1994.

——. 'Warfare in the Western European Middle Ages: The Moral Debate.' In *Communications and Power in Medieval Europe: The Gregorian Revolution and Beyond*, ed. Timothy Reuter, 189–203. London, 1994.

Little, Lester K. *Benedictine Maledictions: Monastic Cursing in Romanesque France*. Ithaca, NY, 1993.

——. 'Pride Goes before Avarice: Social Change and the Vices in Latin Christendom.' *American Historical Review* 76 (1971), 16–49.

Livingstone, Amy. 'Brother Monk: Monks and Their Family in the Chartrain, 1000–1200AD.' In *Medieval Monks and Their World: Ideas and Realities*, ed. David Blanks, Michael Frassetto and Amy Livingstone, 93–115. Leiden, 2006.

Longère, Jean. 'La prédication sur saint Benoît du Xe au XIIIe siècle.' In *Sous la Règle de saint Benoît: Structures monastique et sociétés en France au Moyen Âge à l'époque moderne*, 433–60. Geneva, 1982.

Lot, Ferdinand. *Études sur les légendes épiques françaises*. Paris, 1958.

Lubac, Henri de. *Histoire et esprit: l'intelligence de l'Écriture d'après Origène*. Paris, 1950.

——. *Medieval Exegesis: The Four Senses of Scripture*. Trans. Mark Sebanc. Grand Rapids, MI, 1998.

Lumsden, Douglas W. *And Then the End Will Come: Early Latin Christian Interpretations of the Opening of the Seven Seals*. London, 2001.

Lynch, Joseph H. *Simoniacal Entry into Religious Life from 1000 to 1260*. Columbus, OH, 1976.

——. 'The Cistercians and Underage Novices.' *Cîteaux* 24 (1973), 283–97.

McCormick, Michael. *Eternal Victory: Triumphal Rulership in Late Antiquity, Byzantium, and the Early Medieval West*. Cambridge, 1986.

——. 'The Liturgy of War from Antiquity to the Crusades.' In *The Sword of the Lord: Military Chaplains from the First to the Twenty-First Century*, ed. Doris L. Bergen, 45–67. Notre Dame, IN, 2004.

——. 'The Liturgy of War in the Early Middle Ages: Crisis, Litanies, and the Carolingian Monarchy.' *Viator* 15 (1984), 1–23.

McGinn, Bernard. 'Iter Sancti Sepulchri: The Piety of the First Crusaders.' In *Essays on Medieval Civilization: The Walter Prescott Webb Memorial Lectures*, ed. Bede Karl Lackner and Kenneth Roy Philip, 33–70. Austin, 1978.

MacGregor, James B. 'The Ministry of Gerold d'Avranches: Warrior-Saints and Knightly Piety on the Eve of the First Crusade.' *Journal of Medieval History* 29 (2003), 219–37.

——. 'Negotiating Knightly Piety: The Cult of the Warrior-Saints in the West, ca.1070–ca.1200.' *Church History* 73 (2004), 317–45.

McHugh, M.P. 'Satan and St. Ambrose.' *Classical Folia* 26 (1972), 94–106.

McLaughlin, Megan. *Consorting with Saints: Prayer for the Dead in Early Medieval France*. Ithaca, NY, 1994.

McNally, Robert E. *The Bible in the Early Middle Ages*. Westminster, MD, 1986.

McNamara, Jo Ann. 'The *Herrenfrage*: The Restructuring of the Gender System, 1050–1150.' In *Medieval Masculinities*, ed. Clare A. Lees, 3–29. Minneapolis, 1994.
Maier, Christoph T. 'Crisis, Liturgy, and the Crusade in the Twelfth and Thirteenth Centuries.' *Journal of Ecclesiastical History* 48 (1997), 628–57.
Malone, Edward E. *The Monk and the Martyr: The Monk as Successor of the Martyr*. Washington D.C., 1950.
——. 'Monk and the Martyr.' In *Antonius Magnus Eremita*, ed. Steidle, 201–28.
Mann, C. Griffith. 'Picturing the Bible in the Thirteenth Century.' In *The Book of Kings: Art, War, and the Morgan Library's Medieval Picture Bible*, ed. William Noel and Daniel Weiss, 39–59. London, 2002.
Mann, Jill. 'Allegorical Buildings in Medieval Literature.' *Medium Ævum* 63 (1994), 191–210.
Manning, Eugène. 'La signification de *militare-militia-miles* dans la Règle de S. Benoît.' *Revue Bénédictine* 72 (1962), 135–8.
Martindale, Jane. 'Monasteries and Castles: The Priories of St-Florent de Saumur in England after 1066.' In *England in the Eleventh Century: Proceedings of the 1990 Harlaxton Symposium*, ed. Carola Hicks, 135–56. Stamford, 1992.
Mason, Emma. 'The Hero's Invincible Weapon: An Aspect of Angevin Propaganda.' In *The Ideals and Practice of Medieval Knighthood III: Proceedings of the Fourth Strawberry Hill Conference, 1988*, ed. Christopher Harper-Bill and Ruth Harvey, 121–37. Woodbridge, 1990.
Matthew, Donald. 'The Incongruities of the St Albans Psalter.' *Journal of Medieval History* 34 (2008): 396–416.
McCormick, Michael. 'Liturgie et guerre des Carolingiens à la Première Croisade.' In *Militia christi e crociata*, 209–40.
Militia Christi et crociata nei secoli XI–XIII. Atti della undecima settimana internazionale di studio. Miscellanea del Centre di studi medioevali. Milan, 1974.
Miller, Maureen C. *Power and the Holy in the Age of the Investiture Conflict: A Brief History with Documents*. Boston, 2005.
——. 'Masculinity, Reform, and Clerical Culture: Narratives of Episcopal Holiness in the Gregorian Era.' *Church History* 72 (2003), 25–52.
——. 'Why the Bishop of Florence Had to Get Married.' *Speculum* 81 (2006), 1055–91.
Miramon, Charles de. *Les 'Donnés' au moyen âge: Une forme de vie religieuse laïque (v.1180–v.1500)*. Paris, 1999.
——. 'Embracer l'état monastique à l'âge adulte (1050–1200): Étude sur la conversion tardive.' *Annales HSS* 56 (1999), 825–49.
——. 'Guerre de récits: autour des moniages du XIIe siècle.' In *Guerriers et moines*, ed. Lauwers, 589–636.
Mohrmann, Christine. 'Encore une fois "paganus".' *Vigiliae Christianae* 6 (1952), 109–21.
——. 'La langue de Saint Benoît.' In *Sancti Benedicti Regula Monachorum*, ed. Philibert Schmitz, 9–39. Maredsous, 1955.
——. '*Sacramentum* dans les plus anciens textes chrétiens.' *Harvard Theological Review* 47 (1954), 141–52.
——. 'Statio.' *Vigiliae Christianae* 7 (1953), 221–45.
Moore, R.I. *The First European Revolution, c. 975–1215*. London, 2000.
Morris, Colin. 'Martyrs on the Field of Battle Before and During the First Crusade.' In *Martyrs and Martyrologies*, Studies in Church History 30, ed. Diana Wood, 93–104. London, 1993.
Morrison, Karl F. *Conversion and Text: The Cases of Augustine of Hippo, Herman-Judah, and Constantine Tsatsos*. Charlottesville, VA, 1992.

———. *Understanding Conversion*. Charlottesville, VA, 1992.
Mostert, Marco. *The Political Theory of Abbo of Fleury*. Hilversum, 1987.
Le Moyen Âge et la Bible. Ed. Pierre Riché and Guy Lobrichon. Paris, 1995.
Murray, Alexander. *Reason and Society in the Middle Ages*. Oxford, 1978.
Murray, Jacqueline. 'Masculinizing Religious Life: Sexual Prowess, the Battle for Chastity and Monastic Identity.' In *Holiness and Masculinity in the Middle Ages*, ed. P.H. Cullum and Katherine J. Lewis, 24–42. Toronto, 2004.
Nelson, Janet L. *Kirkham Priory from Foundation to Dissolution*. Borthwick Papers 86. York, 1995.
———. 'Ninth-Century Knighthood: The Evidence of Nithard.' In *Studies in Medieval History Presented to R. Allen Brown*, ed. Christopher Harper-Bill, Christopher Holdsworth and Janet L. Nelson, 255–66. Woodbridge, 1989.
———. 'Violence in the Carolingian World and the Ritualization of Ninth-Century Warfare.' In *Violence and Society in the Early Medieval West*, ed. Guy Halsall, 90–107. Woodbridge, 1998.
Newman, Martha G. *The Boundaries of Charity: Cistercian Culture and Ecclesiastical Reform, 1098–1180*. Stanford, CA, 1996.
Nicholson, Helen. *Templars, Hospitallers and Teutonic Knights: Images of the Military Orders, 1128–1291*. Leicester, 1993.
Niditch, Susan. *War in the Hebrew Bible: A Study in the Ethics of Violence*. New York, 1993.
Niemeyer, Gerlinde. 'Die Vita Godefridi Cappenbergensis.' *Deutsches Archiv für Erforschung des Mittelalters* 23 (1967), 405–67.
Niermeyer, J.F. *Mediae Latinitatis lexicon minus*. Leiden, 1976.
Nip, Renée. 'Life and Afterlife: Arnulf of Oudenbourg, Bishop of Soissons, and Godelieve of Ghistel: Their Function as Intercessors in Medieval Flanders.' In *The Invention of Saintliness*, ed. Anneke B. Mulder-Bakker, 58–76. London, 2002.
Openshaw, Kathleen. 'Weapons in the Daily Battle: Images of the Conquest of Evil in the Early Medieval Psalter.' *Art Bulletin* 75 (1993), 17–38.
Ortigues, E. 'Haymon d'Auxerre, théoricien des trois ordres.' In *L'Ecole carolingienne d'Auxerre de Murethach à Rémi, 830–908*, ed. Dominique Iogna-Prat, C. Jeudy, and Guy Lobrichon, 181–227. Paris, 1991.
Ortony, Anthony. *Metaphor and Thought*. 2nd edn. Cambridge, 1993.
Osborn, Eric. *Tertullian: First Theologian of the West*. Cambridge, 1997.
O'Sullivan, Sinéad. *Early Medieval Glosses on Prudentius' Psychomachia: The Weitz Tradition*. Leiden, 2004.
Oxford, A.W. *The Ruins of Fountains Abbey*. London, 1910.
Pächt, Otto, C.R. Dodwell and Francis Wormald. *The St. Albans Psalter*. London, 1960.
Palazzo, Éric. *Liturgie et société au Moyen Âge*. Paris, 2002.
Parisse, Michel. 'La conscience chrétienne des nobles aux XIe et XIIIe siècles.' In *La cristianità dei secoli XI e XII in occidente, coscienza e strutturre di una società. Atti della ottava settimana internazionale di studi, Mendola, 30 giugno-5 iuglio 1980*. Miscellanea del Centro di studi medievali 10, 259–280. Milan, 1983.
Peirce, Ian. 'The Knight, His Arms and Armour in the Eleventh and Twelfth Centuries.' In *The Ideals and Practice of Medieval Knighthood: Papers from the First and Second Strawberry Hill Conferences*, ed. Christopher Harper-Bill and Ruth Harvey, 152–64. Woodbridge, 1986.
Penco, Gregorio. 'Il concetto di monaco e di vita monastica in occidente nel secolo VI.' *Studia monastica* 1 (1959), 7–50.
Petersen, Joan M. *The Dialogues of Gregory the Great in their Late Antique Cultural Context*. Toronto, 1984.

Pfitzner, Victor C. *Paul and the Agon Motif: Traditional Athletic Imagery in the Pauline Literature*. Leiden, 1967.
Philips, Jonathan. *The Second Crusade: Extending the Frontiers of Christendom*. New Haven, CT, 2007.
Platelle, Henri. 'Pratiques pénitentielles et mentalités religieuses au moyen âge: La pénitence des parricides et l'esprit de l'ordalie.' *Mélanges de science religieuse* 40 (1983), 129–55.
Poggiaspalla, Ferminio. 'La chiesa e la partecipazione dei chierici alla guerra nella legislazione conciliare fino allo Decretali di Gregorio IX.' *Ephemerides iuris canonici* 15 (1959), 140–53.
Prinz, Friedrich. *Klerus und Krieg im früheren Mittelalter. Untersuchgen zur Rolle der Kirche beim Aufbau der Königsherrschaft*. Monographien zur Geschichte des Mittelalters 2. Stuttgart, 1971.
Purkis, William J. *Crusading Spirituality in the Holy Land and Iberia, c.1095–c.1187*. Woodbridge, 2008.
Raine, James. *The History and Antiquities of North Durham*. London, 1852.
Rebenich, Stefan. *Jerome*. New York, 2002.
——. 'Der Kirchenvater. Hieronymus als Hagiograph: Die *Vita S. Pauli primae eremitae*.' In *Beiträge zur Geschichte des Paulinerordens*, ed. Kaspar Elm, 23–40. Berlin, 2000.
Reid, Charles J. 'Clerical Participation in Warfare: A Canonical Survey from Pseudo-Isidore to Joannes Teutonicus.' Unpub. JCL thesis, Catholic University of America, 1985.
Remensnyder, Amy G. *Remembering Kings Past: Monastic Foundation Legends in Medieval Southern France*. Ithaca, NY, 1995.
——. 'Pollution, Purity, and Peace: An Aspect of Social Reform between the Late Tenth Century and 1076.' In *The Peace of God*, ed. Head and Landes, 280–307.
Reuter, Timothy. 'Episcopi cum sua militia: The Prelate as Warrior in the Early Staufer Era.' In *Warriors and Churchmen in the High Middle Ages: Essays Presented to Karl Leyser*, ed. Timothy Reuter, 79–93. London, 1992.
Riché, Pierre. 'Les Représentations du palais dans les textes littéraires du haut moyen âge.' *Francia* 4 (1976): 161–71.
Richter, Horst. '*Militia Dei*: A Central Concept for the Religious Ideas of the Early Crusades and the German *Rolandslied*.' In *Journeys Toward God: Pilgrimage and Crusade*, ed. Barbara N. Sargent-Baur, 107–26. Kalamazoo, MI, 1992.
Riley-Smith, Jonathan. *The First Crusade and the Idea of Crusading*. Philadelphia, PA, 1986.
——. 'Crusading as an Act of Love.' *History* 65 (1980), 177–92. Repr. in *The Crusades: The Essential Readings*, ed. Thomas F. Madden, 32–50. London, 2002.
——. 'Death on the First Crusade.' In *The End of Strife*, ed. D.M. Loades, 13–41. Edinburgh, 1984.
——. 'The First Crusade and St. Peter.' In *Outremer: Studies in the History of the Crusading Kingdom of Jerusalem*, ed. B.Z. Kedar, H.E. Mayer and R.C. Smail, 41–63. Jerusalem, 1982.
——. 'The State of Mind of Crusaders to the East, 1095–1300.' In *The Oxford History of the Crusades*, ed. Jonathan Riley-Smith, 68–89. Oxford, 2002.
Robinson, Ian S. *The Papacy, 1073–1198: Continuity and Innovation*. Cambridge, 1990.
——. 'Gregory VII and the Soldiers of Christ.' *History* 58 (1973), 169–92.
Le roi de France et son royaume autour de l'an Mil. Ed. Michel Parisse and Xavier Barral i Altet. Paris, 1992.

Rondeau, Marie-Josèphe. *Les Commentaires patristiques du Psautier (IIIe-Ve siècles)*. Orientalia Christiana Analecta 219. Rome, 1982.

Rosenwein, Barbara H. *To Be the Neighbor of Saint Peter: The Social Meaning of Cluny's Property, 909–1049*. Ithaca, NY, 1989.

——. 'Feudal War and Monastic Peace: Cluniac Liturgy as Ritual Aggression.' *Viator* 2 (1971), 127–57.

——. 'Perennial Prayer at Agaune.' In *Monks and Nuns, Saints and Outcasts*, ed. Sharon Farmer and Barbara H. Rosenwein, 37–56. Ithaca, NY, 2000.

——. 'St. Odo's St Martin: The Uses of a Model.' *Journal of Medieval History* 4 (1978), 317–31.

——, Thomas Head and Sharon Farmer. 'Monks and Their Enemies: A Comparative Approach.' *Speculum* 66 (1991), 764–96.

Rubenstein, Jay. *Guibert of Nogent: Portrait of a Medieval Mind*. London, 2003.

——. 'What is the *Gesta Francorum*, and Who was Peter Tudebode?' *Revue Mabillon* 16 (2005), 179–204.

Rudolph, Conrad. *Violence and Daily Life: Reading, Art, and Polemics in the Cîteaux Moralia in Job*. Princeton, 1997.

Russell, Frederick H. *The Just War in the Middle Ages*. Cambridge, 1975.

Salisbury, Joyce E. *The Blood of the Martyrs: Unintended Consequences of Ancient Violence*. New York, 2004.

Saxer, Victor. 'Le culte et la légende hagiographique de Saint Guillaume de Gellone.' In *La chanson de geste et le mythe carolingien: Mélanges Réné Louis*, 2 vols, 2: 565–89. Saint-Père-sous-Vézelay, 1982.

Sayers, Jane. 'Violence in the Medieval Cloister.' *Journal of Ecclesiastical History* 41 (1990), 533–42.

Schatkin, M.A. 'The Influence of Origen Upon St. Jerome's Commentary on Galatians.' *Vigiliae Christianae* 24 (1970): 49–58.

Schein, Sylvia. *Gateway to the Heavenly City: Crusader Jerusalem and the Catholic West (1099–1187)*. Burlington, VT, 2005.

Scourfield, J.H.D. *Consoling Heliodorus: A Commentary on Jerome, Letter 60*. Oxford, 1993.

Sears, Elizabeth. 'Louis the Pious as *Miles Christi*: The Dedicatory Image in Hrabanus Maurus's *De laudibus sanctae crucis*.' In *Charlemagne's Heir: New Perspectives on the Reign of Louis the Pious (814–40)*, ed. Peter Goodman and Roger Collin, 605–28. Oxford, 1990.

Seidel, Linda. *Songs of Glory: The Romanesque Façades of Aquitaine*. Chicago, MI, 1981.

Siberry, Elizabeth. *Criticism of Crusading, 1095–1274*. Oxford, 1985.

Smalley, Beryl. *The Study of the Bible in the Middle Ages*. Notre Dame, IN, 1964.

Smith, Gregory A. '*Sine rege, sine principe*: Peter the Venerable on Violence in Twelfth-Century Burgundy.' *Speculum* 77 (2002), 1–33.

Smith, Katherine Allen. 'Saints in Shining Armor: Martial Asceticism and Masculine Models of Sanctity, ca. 1050–1250.' *Speculum* 83 (2008), 572–602.

——. 'Spiritual Warriors in Citadels of Faith: Martial Rhetoric and Monastic Masculinity in the Long Twelfth Century.' In *Negotiating Clerical Identities: Priests, Monks, and Masculinity in the Middle Ages*, ed. Jennifer D. Thibodeaux, 86–110. London, 2010.

Souter, Alexander. *The Earliest Latin Commentaries on the Epistles of St. Paul*. Oxford, 1927.

Southern, R.W. *Western Society and the Church in the Middle Ages*. Harmondsworth, 1970.

Stancliffe, Claire. *Gregory the Great: Perfection in Imperfection*. Berkeley, 1988.

———. *St. Martin and his Hagiographer: History and Miracle in Sulpicius Severus.* Oxford, 1983.
Stewart, Columba. *Cassian the Monk.* Oxford, 1999.
Straw, Carole. 'Gregory, Cassian, and the Cardinal Vices.' In *In the Garden of Evil: The Vices and Culture in the Middle Ages,* ed. Richard Newhauser, 35–58. Toronto, 2005.
———. *Gregory the Great: Perfection in Imperfection.* Berkeley, 1988.
Strickland, Matthew. *War and Chivalry: The Conduct and Perception of War in England and Normandy, 1066–1217.* Cambridge, 1996.
Stubbs, William. *Select Charters: From the Beginning to 1307.* 5th edn. Ed. H.W.C. Davies. Oxford, 1921.
Stuckey, Jace. 'Charlemagne as Crusader? Memory, Propaganda, and the Many Uses of Charlemagne's Legendary Expedition to Spain.' In *The Legend of Charlemage in the Middle Ages: Power, Faith, Crusade,* ed. Matthew Gabriele and Jace Stuckey, 137–52. New York, 2008.
Swift, Louis J. *The Early Fathers on War and Military Service.* Wilmington, 1983.
Taylor, Andrew. 'A Second Ajax: Peter Abelard and the Violence of Dialectic.' In *The Tongue of the Fathers: Gender and Ideology in Medieval Latin,* ed. David Townsend and Andrew Taylor, 14–34. Philadelphia, PA, 1998.
Tellenbach, Gerd. *Church, State, and Christian Society at the Time of the Investiture Contest.* Trans. R.F. Bennett. Oxford, 1940; repr. ed. Toronto, 1991.
Thibodeaux, Jennifer D. *The English and the Normans: Ethnic Hostility, Assimilation, and Identity, 1066–c.1220.* Oxford, 2005.
———. 'Man of the Church, or Man of the Village? Gender and the Parish Clergy in Medieval Normandy.' *Gender and History* 18 (2006), 380–99.
Thomas, Hugh M. *Vassals, Heiresses, Crusaders, and Thugs: The Gentry of Angevin Yorkshire, 1154–1216.* Philadelphia, PA, 1993.
Thouzellier, Christine. 'Ecclesia militans.' In *Études d'histoire du droit canonique dédiées à Gabriel Le Bras,* 2 vols, 2: 1407–23. Paris, 1965.
Torchia, Joseph. 'De Agone Christiano.' In *Augustine through the Ages: An Encyclopedia,* ed. Joseph C. Cavadini, 15–16. Grand Rapids, MI, 1999.
Trotter, D.A. *Medieval French Literature and the Crusades (1100–1300).* Geneva, 1988.
Van Dam, Raymond. *Leadership and Community in Late Antique Gaul.* Berkeley, 1992.
———. 'Images of Saint Martin in Late Roman and Early Merovingian Gaul.' *Viator* 19 (1988), 1–27.
van der Horst, Koert. 'The Utrecht Bible: Picturing the Psalms of David.' In *The Utrecht Psalter in Medieval Art,* ed. Koert van der Horst, William Noel and Wilhelmina C.M. Wüstefeld, 22–84. Tuurdijk, 1996.
Van Engen, John. 'The Crisis of Coenobitism Reconsidered: Benedictine Monasticism in the Years 1050–1150.' *Speculum* 61 (1986): 269–304.
Van Loveren, A.E.D. 'Once Again: "The Monk and the Martyr" – Saint Anthony and Saint Macrina.' *Studia Patristica* 17 (1982), 528–38.
van Winter, Johanna Maria. '*Cingulum militiae*: Schwertleite en miles-terminologie als Spiegel van veranderend menselijk gedrag.' *Tijdschrift voor rechtsgeschiedenis* 44 (1976), 1–92.
Vergnolle, Eliane. 'La collégiale Notre-Dame de Beaugency: les campagnes romanes.' *Bulletin monumental* 165 (2007), 71–90, 131–3
Waddell, Chrysogonus. 'The Liturgical Dimensions of Twelfth-Century Cistercian Preaching.' In *Medieval Monastic Preaching,* ed. Muessig, 335–50.
———. 'Simplicity and Ordinariness: The Climate of Early Cistercian Hagiography.' In

Simplicity and Ordinariness, Studies in Medieval Cistercian History 4, ed. John R. Sommerfeldt, 14–25. Kalamazoo, MI, 1980.

Ward, Benedicta. 'The Desert Myth: Reflections on the Desert Ideal in Early Cistercian Monasticism.' In *One Yet Two: Monastic Tradition East and West*, ed. M. Basil Pennington, 183–99. Kalamazoo, MI, 1976.

Werner, Karl Ferdinand. *Naissance de la noblesse: l'essor des élites politiques en Europe*. Paris, 1998.

Werner-Goetz, Hans. 'La Paix de Dieu en France autour de l'An Mil: fondements et objectifs, diffusion et participants.' In *Le roi de France*, ed. Parisse and Barral i Altet, 132–43.

Wheatley, Abigail. *The Idea of the Castle in Medieval England*. York, 2004.

Whitby, Michael. 'Deus Nobiscum: Christianity, Warfare, and Morale in Late Antiquity.' In *Modus Operandi: Essays in Honour of Geoffrey Rickman*, ed. Michel Austin, Jill Harries, and Christopher John Smith, 191–208. London, 1998.

White, Stephen D. 'The Politics of Anger in Medieval France', in *Anger's Past: The Social Uses of an Emotion in the Middle Ages*, ed. Barbara H. Rosenwein, 127–52. Ithaca, NY, 1998.

Whitehead, Christiania. *Castles of the Mind: A Study of Medieval Architectural Allegory*. Cardiff, 2003.

——. 'Making a Cloister of the Soul in Medieval Religious Treatises.' *Medium Ævum* 67 (1998), 1–29.

Wiles, Maurice. *The Divine Apostle: The Interpretation of St Paul's Epistles in the Early Church*. Cambridge, 1967.

Wilken, Robert Louis. *The Spirit of Early Christian Thought*. New Haven, CT, 2003.

Williams, Michael Stuart. *Authorised Lives in Early Christian Biography: Between Eusebius and Augustine*. Cambridge, 2008.

Witters, Willibrord. 'Smaragde au Moyen Âge: la diffusion de ses écrits d'après la tradition manuscrite.' In *Études ligériennes d'histoire et d'archéologie médiévales*, 361–76. Auxerre, 1975.

Wolf, Kenneth Baxter. 'Crusade and Narrative: Bohemond and the *Gesta Francorum*.' *Journal of Medieval History* 17 (1991), 207–16.

Wollasch, Joachim. 'Das Schisma des Abtes Pontius von Cluny.' *Francia* 23 (1996), 31–52.

——. 'Parenté noble et monachisme réformateur: Observations sur les 'conversions' à la vie monastique aux XIe et XIIe siècles.' *Revue historique* 264 (1980), 3–24.

Woods, David. 'The Origin of the Legend of Maurice and the Theban Legion.' *Journal of Ecclesiastical History* 45 (1994), 385–95.

Zaluska, Yolande. *L'Enluminure et le scriptorium de Cîteaux*. Cîteaux, 1989.

Index

abbesses 124
　as spiritual warriors 96, 141
Abbo of Fleury, abbot 44, 50, 185
abbots 100, 113, 114, 116, 122–3, 132, 140–2, 147, 149, 153, 161, 165, 185
　as commanders of monastic armies 93, 96, 140–2
　as stand-ins for Christ 93, 140–1, 142
Abraham 12
acedia 79
Adalbert of Laon, bishop 123
Adam of Eynsham, monk 123
Adelelme of La Chaise-Dieu, abbot 168
Ademar of Chabannes, monk 124
Adhemar of Monteil, bishop of Le Puy 14, 46
Adjutor of Tiron, St 171
adolescence 117
Aelred of Rievaulx, St and abbot 67–8, 112, 135, 145, 150, 150
Æthelfrith, king of Northumbria 29
Agaune, abbey 32, 158
Aimo of Fleury, monk 44, 88, 176–7
Aimon of Bourges, bishop 100
Alcuin of York, scholar 97
Alexander II, pope 101
Alexis, St 182
Amalarius of Metz, liturgist 32–3
Amalek, Amalekites 14, 29
Ambrose of Milan, St and bishop 12, 74–5
Amedeus of Hauterive, monk 128–9, 170, 175–6
Andreas of Strumi, abbot 15
anger 60–1, 79, 92, 134
Angers, canons of 55
Aniane, abbey 165
Anselm of Canterbury, St and archbishop 58–9, 70, 110, 117, 118, 120, 173
Antioch, siege of 15, 105, 105
Antony, St 12–13, 79, 80–3, 85, 87, 88, 92, 130, 193
　as model for later monks 79, 88
apostasy 54, 77, 83
apostles 16, 17, 18, 37, 123; *see also*: Paul; Peter
Arduin, margrave of Ivrea 178–9
armor 156, 179, 187–95, 196
　in Scripture 188–9; *see also*: hauberk; *loricati*
arms; *see* weapons
arms-bearers, lay:
　as patrons of Church 1–4, 29, 31, 35–7, 57, 162, 182
　as spiritual warriors 99–111
　conversion to religious life; *see* conversion to religious life, of arms-bearers
　depiction in hagiography 15, 57, 77–9, 97–9, 156–87, 194, 196
　duties of, as defined by churchmen 50–1, 96–111, 180
　military training of 52, 168, 187
　penance of 3, 31, 62–5, 160–6, 168–70, 178–9, 181, 182, 194
　violence of 31, 50, 161–2, 165, 166, 169–71
　vices of 4, 77, 85, 87, 108, 176
　virtues of 4, 77, 154, 167, 172–3
Arnulf of Soissons, bishop 182–3
Ascalon, battle of 124–5
asceticism 22, 79, 80–8, 89, 92, 93, 96, 110, 113, 128, 135, 153, 156, 160, 164, 166, 185, 187–95
　excessive 58, 135
　involving armor; *see loricati*
　see also: fasting; flagellation; hairshirts; plates, metal
Athanasius of Alexandria, bishop 12–13, 79, 80–1, 83, 87, 92, 130
athletic imagery 18, 21, 22, 75, 76, 99, 105, 194
Atto of Vercelli, monk and bishop 22
Augurius, martyr 76
Augustine of Hippo, St and bishop 12, 16, 20, 21, 24, 25–7, 32, 71, 74, 89
　Enarrationes in Psalmos 25–7
avarice 134, 165, 169
Avitus of Sarlat, St 159

Babylon 143
baldric; *see* sword-belt
Baldric of Dol, bishop 103, 104
Baldwin II, king of Jerusalem 124
Baldwin of Ford, abbot 185
banners, military 51, 142–3, 146, 179

baptism 19, 83, 85
Basil of Caesarea, St and bishop 90
Battle, abbey 64
battle, pitched, allegory of 124–5
beard, shaving of 61, 183
Beaulieu-lès-Loches, abbey 65
Bec, abbey 53, 117, 118, 142, 170
Bede, the Venerable 20, 29
bellatores; see arms-bearers, lay
belt, of monk 91, 95, 104, 184–5; see also: sword-belt
Benedict of Modena, bishop 14
Benedict of Nursia, St and abbot 30, 54, 66, 79, 87–9, 92–5, 115, 116, 121, 131, 132, 139, 140–1, 142, 176–7
  Rule; see Rule of Benedict
Benedict of Selby, abbot 174
Bernard *Grossus*, monk 48
Bernard of Clairvaux, St and abbot 13, 48–9, 54, 57, 82, 100, 119, 124, 127–8, 137, 142, 144, 147, 149, 151
  De laude novae militiae 100, 107–8
Bernard of Morlaix, prior of Cluny 141
Bernard of Portes, monk and bishop of Belley 135
Bertulf of Ghistelle, knight and monk 192
bishops 44, 45–6, 100
Bohemond of Taranto, crusader 107
Bonnevaux, abbey 128–9, 170, 175; see also: Amedeus of Hauterive
Boso of Bec, abbot 142
Bruno of Chartreuse, St and abbot 22, 27
Burchard of Vendôme, count 172, 182

Cadalan Schism 101
Caesarius of Heisterbach, prior 45, 54, 61, 183
Canaanites 14
caritas, monastic virtue 119, 122–3, 139, 150
Carthusians 23, 52, 53, 109, 115, 118, 130, 135
  see also: Bernard of Portes; Bruno of Chartreuse; Guigo of La Grande Chartreuse; Stephen of Chalmet
Cassian, St and monk 10, 11–12, 2,4, 90–2, 93, 95, 115, 140, 185, 193
Cassiodorus, monk and theologian 25–6
castles 66–9, 70, 127, 147–53; see also: monasteries, allegorized as castles
celibacy, clerical; see chastity
cell, of monk or hermit 115, 120, 133, 135, 149, 175
Cerne, abbey 47
Chanson de Roland 160, 161
chansons de geste 143, 160

  see also: *moniages*; *Chanson de Roland*
Charlemagne, emperor 29, 30, 160, 161, 163
Charles the Bald, emperor 30
Charroux, council of 47
charters 35–6, 52, 62, 99, 181, 183–4
  conversion described in 52, 62, 183–4
chastity 22, 40–1, 43, 44, 79, 81, 83–4, 88, 91, 98, 115, 149, 150, 185, 193
Chester, battle of 29
Christ:
  as commander of heavenly armies 21, 37, 74, 93, 104, 142–4, 172, 174
  as spiritual warrior 17, 37, 80–1, 150, 151, 152, 163
  see also: *Christus victor*
Christina of Markyate, recluse 138–9
Christopher, St 134
Christus victor 17, 140
Cistercians 22, 32, 52, 53, 54, 59, 61, 63, 68, 94, 112, 115, 116, 119, 123, 127–9, 130, 136, 138, 145, 149, 151, 154, 169, 170, 173, 185, 187
  see also: Aelred of Rievaulx; Bernard of Clairvaux; Galand of Reigny; Guerric of Igny; Henry of Waverley; John of Ford; Thomas of Perseigne
Cîteaux, abbey 57, 136, 138, 141, 185
Civitate, battle of 101
Clairvaux, abbey 127
Clermont, council of 103–5; see also: Urban II, pope
Cluniacs 98, 106, 108, 115, 117, 123, 126, 127–8, 129, 154
  see also: Bernard of Morlaix; Odilo of Cluny; Odo of Cluny; Gilo of Cluny; Hugh Francigena; Peter of Celle; Peter the Venerable; Pons of Cluny
Cluny, abbey 22, 35, 47–8, 53, 59, 97, 126, 127, 183
commilito, *commilitones*, monks as 126–7, 128–9, 141
Commodian, poet 73–4
confraternity, bonds of 54–5
Conquereuil, battle of 65
conversion to religious life:
  ad succurrendum 55, 58, 172
  conceptual models of 166–8, 173
  discouraged 102
  false 58, 61, 164–5
  of adults 4–5, 52–63, 113, 121, 154, 159, 173, 197
  of arms-bearers 15, 41, 51, 52–63, 69–70, 156–87, 194, 196
  rituals associated with 61–2, 181–7; see also: tonsure

courage, as monastic virtue 82, 87, 96, 153, 167, 173
cowardice 83, 127–8, 142, 172
crossbow 135
crusades:
    chronicles of 14–15, 103–7
        see also: Baldric of Dol; Fulcher of Chartres; Gilo of Paris; Guibert of Nogent; Peter Tudebode; Raymond of Aguilers; Robert of Reims
    clerical participation in 48–9
    First Crusade 2, 14–15, 32, 46, 48, 51, 53, 100, 102–6, 109, 111
    referenced in sermons 154–5
    Second Crusade 48, 53, 54
    see also: crusading; military orders
crusading:
    and martyrdom 105–6
    as spiritual combat 71, 103–7, 111, 155, 163, 198
    compared to monastic conversion 51, 53–4, 104, 109, 164, 171
curses 9, 29, 31
Cuthbert, St 184
Cyprian of Carthage, St and bishop 73, 76, 110, 148

Dalmatius of Semur, nobleman 192–3
David 1–3, 12, 14, 28, 29, 34, 102, 137–8, 147, 149, 180
Demetrius, St 158
demons 4, 49, 71, 73, 79, 81, 88, 90, 92, 95, 112, 115, 121, 129, 145, 147, 148, 151, 152, 194, 197; see also: devil, the
desert 79–83, 110, 130, 132, 196
devil, the 13, 17, 19, 23, 26, 33, 34, 35, 36, 49, 80, 95, 96, 97, 108, 110, 117, 119, 122, 128, 130, 135, 139, 140, 142, 143, 144, 148, 150, 151, 175–6, 185, 188, 197; see also: demons
Dominic *Loricatus* 190–1
dragon 136–7, 138
Drogo of Fleury, monk 88–9

Ekkehard of Saint Gall, monk 161
envy 134, 136
eremitism; see solitary life
Erlembald, leader of Pataria 15, 102
Eucherius of Lyon, bishop 78
Eugippius, monk 20
Eulogius, martyr 76
Eusebius of Caesarea, bishop 77
Eustace, St 158
Eustochium, virgin 83–4
Eva of Wilton, nun and recluse 133, 145–6

Evagrius of Antioch, bishop 80–1
Everard of Barres, Grand Master of Templars 109
Everard of Berg, nobleman 53
Everard of Breteuil, viscount of Chartres 168–9
excommunication 31, 178
exegesis:
    Carolingian 26–7, 140
    monastic 21–3, 27–8, 37–8, 124
    of Epistles 18–23, 27, 33, 37, 75, 76–7, 79, 81, 82, 95, 105, 144, 149, 175, 189
    of Gospels 16–18, 49, 90–1, 145, 150, 184
    of Job 12–13, 95, 117, 138
    of Old Testament 10–16, 37, 38, 121, 147, 149, 152, 188–9
    of Psalms 23–8, 140, 147, 151, 188–9
    of Revelation 140, 143, 145, 145, 188
    of Song of Songs 121, 122, 127, 141, 147, 148, 149, 151
    patristic 10–13, 19–20, 25–6, 49, 115, 140, 154
    see also: Aelred of Rievaulx; Amalarius of Metz; Andreas of Strumi; Atto of Vercelli; Augustine of Hippo; Bede; Bernard of Clairvaux; Bruno of Asti; Bruno of Chartreuse; Cassian; Florus of Lyon; Fulcher of Chartres; Gregory the Great; Guerric of Igny; Guibert of Nogent; Guy de Pin; Hervé de Déols; Hildebert of Lavardin; Honorius Augustodunensis; Hrabanus Maurus; Hugh of Saint-Victor; Jerome; John Beleth; Odo of Cluny; Origen; Paschasius Radbertus; Peter Damian; Ranger of Lucca; Remigius of Auxerre; Sicard of Cremona; Thomas of Perseigne; Walafrid Strabo; William of Saint-Thierry

fasting 79, 81, 115, 135, 191
feasts; see liturgy
Florus of Lyon, deacon 20
Fonte Avellana, hermitage 190; see also: Dominic *Loricatus*; Peter Damian
Fountains, abbey 174
Fructuosus, martyr 76
Fruttuaria, abbey 57
Fulbert of Chartres, bishop 49
Fulcher of Chartres, chaplain 14, 103–4, 105
Fulk Nerra, count of Anjou 65

Galand of Reigny, monk 143–4, 149
Gangulf of Varenne, nobleman 98

Gellone, abbey   162, 163, 165
Geoffrey *Festucam*, knight   55
Geoffrey of Auxerre, monk   142
Geoffrey of Breteuil, canon   115
Geoffrey of Cappenberg, count   68, 172
Geoffrey of Chalard, recluse   191, 195
George, St   105–6, 157, 158
Gerald of Aurillac, St   97–99
Gerald of Avranches, preacher   15, 158
Gerald of Corbie   173; *see also*: La Sauve Majeure
Germanus, St   158
Gerlach of Houthem, recluse   194
Gilbert Crispin, monk   170, 171–2, 175
Gilbert of Brionne, count   170–1
Gilbert of Senlis, recluse   126
Gilo of Cluny, monk   168
Gilo of Paris, monk   106
Gimon of Conques, monk   47
Gisors, battle of   46
Glastonbury, abbey   47
gluttony   92
Godelieve, St; *see* Bertolf of Ghistelle
Godric of Finchale, recluse   191, 193
Goliath   1–3, 14, 34, 137, 188
Goscelin of Saint-Bertin, monk   133, 143, 145–6
Grandmontines   130, 192; *see also*: Hugh of Lacerta; Stephen of Lissac; Stephen of Muret
Great Persecution   80
Gregory VII, pope   58, 100, 101–2
Gregory the Great, pope   13, 18, 29, 58, 79, 87–8, 90, 93–4, 131, 148
Grimlaicus, recluse   132
Guerric of Igny, abbot   116, 118, 136, 146
Guibert of Nogent, abbot   14, 15, 51, 103, 104, 107
Guigo of La Grande Chartreuse, prior   109
Guillaume d'Orange; *see* William of Gellone
Guillaume le Clerc   69
Gunthelm, novice; *see Vision of Gunthelm*
Guy de Pin, prior   23

hagiography   15, 30–1, 43–4, 57, 63, 76–89, 90, 96, 97–9, 100, 107, 112, 115, 140, 153, 156–96, 198; *see also*: arms-bearers, depiction in hagiography
hairshirts   190, 191, 193
Hariulf of Saint-Médard, abbot   182–3
Hastings, battle of   32, 46, 50, 64
hauberk   108, 120, 144, 187–95
    used for ascetic purposes: *see loricati*
Heliodorus, monk   83
hell   54, 61, 95, 170, 180–1

Hemmenrode, abbey   183
Henry I, king of England   67, 68
Henry IV, Holy Roman Emperor   45
Henry of Waverley, abbot   169–70
Herbert of Losinga, bishop   117, 119
heresy   22, 81
Herluin of Bec, abbot   170–1, 172, 175
hermitage; *see* cell, of monk or hermit
hermits; *see* solitary life
Herrad of Hohenbourg, abbess   124
Hervé of Déols, monk   22
Hervé of Saint-Martin, monk   42
Hilarion, St   82
Hildebert of Lavardin, bishop   28
Hildegard of Bingen, abbess   141
Hildemar of Corbie, abbot   62
Hilduin of Saint-Médard, abbot   159
Honorius II, anti-pope   101
Honorius Augustodunensis, theologian   33–4, 151
horses   61, 120, 123, 140, 145
Hospitallers   194; *see also*: military orders; Ingebrand of Rurke
Hrabanus Maurus, abbot   12, 20, 21–2, 97
Hugh I, duke of Burgundy   34
Hugh Francigena, monk   169
Hugh of Avranches, earl of Chester   158
Hugh of Besançon, bishop   34
Hugh of Cluny, St and abbot   58, 168, 192–3
Hugh of Kirkstall, monk   174
Hugh of Lacerta, monk   171
Hugh of Lincoln, St and bishop   135–6
Hugh of Payns, Grand Master of Templars   109
Hugh of Saint-Victor, canon   37
humility, monastic virtue   30, 60, 85, 98, 119, 135, 136, 137, 150, 154, 157, 158, 164, 165, 166, 169, 172, 193

Ignatius of Antioch, bishop   75
imitatio Christi   53, 84, 101, 110, 147, 153, 170, 199
imprisonment, allegory of   143, 151
Ingebrand of Rurke, Hospitaller   194
Israelites   13–16, 24–5, 26, 29, 30, 89, 104, 174, 188
    allegorized as spiritual warriors   13–16, 89, 96, 107, 156, 157
Ivo of Chartres, bishop   58, 131–2

Jebusites   104
Jerome, St   11, 19–20, 21, 79, 81–4, 87, 92, 115, 130, 150
Jerusalem   15, 48, 54, 65, 104, 105, 110, 111, 143, 148, 152

Job   12–13; *see also*: exegesis, of Job
John Beleth, liturgist   33
John of Fécamp, abbot   132
John of Ford, abbot   142, 144, 151, 187
John of Fruttuaria, monk   117, 136
John of Montmirail, nobleman and monk   63
John of Salerno, monk   43
John of Salisbury, bishop   180
John the Baptist   145, 146
Joshua   12, 14, 17, 29
Judah Maccabee   14;   *see also*: Maccabees
Julian, martyr   158, 163, 186
Julian of Vézelay, monk   119, 124–5, 144–5, 152, 154–5
Julian, Roman emperor   86
Julius the Veteran, martyr   78

kinship ties:
   continued importance to converts   56–7
   within religious communities   55–6
Kirkham, priory   68
knighthood, Christian   7, 15, 40, 41, 44, 50, 100, 143, 157, 171, 177, 196

La Chaise-Dieu, abbey   175
La Grande Chartreuse, priory   135
Lambert of Ardres, priest   65
Lancelin II, lord of Beaugency   2
La Réole, priory   44
La Sauve Majeure, abbey   173
La Trinité, Caen, abbey   141
Lawrence of Subiaco, hermit   191–2
lay brothers and sisters   39, 48
lectio divina   12, 38, 197; *see also*: monks, as readers
Leo IX, pope   101, 102
Lérins, abbey   184
literacy, monastic standards of   59–60, 166
liturgy   23–37, 59–60, 128, 153, 166
   as spiritual warfare   23–37, 121
   see also: Psalms
Longpont, abbey   63
loricati:
   admired by monks   156, 187–95
   admired by arms-bearers   188, 195
   see also: Arnulf of Soissons; Bertulf of Ghistelle; Dominic *Loricatus*; Geoffrey of Chalard; Gerlach of Houthem; Godric of Finchale; Hugh of Cluny; Ingebrand of Rurke; Lawrence of Subiaco; Peter of Policastro; Raynerius of Osnabrück; Robert of Arbrissel; Simon of Crépy; Stephen of Muret; Stephen of Obazine; William *Firmatus*;

William of Llanthony; William of Vercelli; Wulfric of Haselbury
Louis the German, king of the East Franks   30
Louis the Pious, emperor   97
lust   88, 91, 185
Luxeuil, abbey   185

Macarius, *Rule* of   89
Maccabees   14, 104
mailshirt; *see* hauberk
Marbod of Rennes, bishop   175
Marcionites   10
Markwald of Fulda, abbot   66–7
Marmoutier, abbey of   85, 168–9
Martin, St   42–3, 78, 79, 85–7, 88, 99, 110, 169
   influence on later monks   42–3, 79
   renunciation of soldiering   42, 78
   see also: Sulpicius Severus
martyrs   71, 73, 75–9, 93, 98, 101, 102, 107, 110, 123, 133, 144, 153, 157–9
   as models for monks   79–81, 82, 133, 134
   as spiritual warriors   71–9, 81, 158
   passiones of   76–9, 90, 110, 158
   soldiers as   77–8, 86, 105, 157–9, 186
masculinity   43, 113, 139, 146, 190
mass, as a battle   33–4
Mathathias   15
Matilda, abbess of La Trinité, Caen   141
Maurice, St   31, 78, 96, 157, 158; *see also*: Theban Legion
Maximilian, martyr   77
Maximilianus, Roman emperor   78
Michael, archangel   49
miles Christi; *see* warfare, spiritual
military martyrs; *see* warrior-saints
military orders   39, 71, 72, 100, 107–9, 111, 156, 198
   see also: Hospitallers; Templars
militia Christi; *see* warfare, spiritual
Millstätter Exodus   15
monasteries:
   allegorized as castles   35–7, 51, 69, 112, 115, 147, 148–50, 174
   as war-memorials   64–5
   built on places associated with bloodshed   41, 63–9, 186
   transformed into castles   66–7
   violence in   47–8, 165
moniages   160–6, 176, 196
   see also: Ogier the Dane; Rainoart; Walter of Aquitaine; William of Gellone
monks:
   as former arms-bearers   4–5, 15, 41, 51, 52–63, 69–70, 156–87, 194, 196

as readers   12, 92, 93, 115, 116
as spiritual warriors   12, 22–3, 57, 70, 71, 79–96, 97, 99, 103, 106–11, 112–55, 156–96
clothing of   61–62; *see also*: belt, of monk
meditative practices of   120–1, 124, 134, 136–9, 146–53, 189, 196
profession rites of   61–2, 182–7
spiritual development of   114–21, 130, 154
violence by   42–5, 46–9, 50
virtues of; *see* humility; obedience; patience
Montecassino, abbey   66, 88
Montiérender, abbey   55
Morimond, abbey   53
Moses   12, 14, 15, 29
Muslims   16–17, 30, 103, 105, 106, 125, 161, 162, 163

New Minster, Winchester   35–6
Nicholas of Clairvaux, monk   126–7
Norbert of Xanten, St   68
Novalesa, abbey   161–2
novices   54, 58, 62, 113, 114–15
nuns and canonesses   4–5, 39, 46, 124, 199

obedience, monastic virtue   60, 87, 93, 119, 129, 147, 157, 158, 165, 166, 172
oblates   35, 52, 57, 58–9, 154, 170
Odelerius of Orleans, priest   36
Odilo of Cluny, abbot   141
Odo Arpinus, viscount of Bourges   53
Odo of Cluny, St and abbot   13, 23, 43, 62, 97, 116, 123
Odo of Saint-Maur, monk   172, 182
Ogier the Dane, epic hero   161
Oilard of Wimille, hermit   66
Old Testament; *see* exegesis, of Old Testament
Orderic Vitalis, monk   15, 32, 36–7, 60–1, 158, 159–60
orders of society, idea of   39–51, 69–70, 188, 195, 197
warfare and the definition of   40–51
Origen, theologian   10–11, 17–18, 19–20, 21, 79

pagans   73, 79, 86, 88, 96, 110, 123, 159
papacy, use of armies by   50–1, 100–5; *see also*: Leo IX, pope; Urban II, pope
parables; *see* Bernard of Clairvaux; Galand of Reigny
Pascal II, pope   53
Paschasius Radbertus, abbot   17, 173
passiones; *see* martyrs, *passiones* of
Pataria   15, 102

patience, monastic virtue   85, 98, 119, 149
Paul, St   16, 17, 18, 23, 81, 88, 89, 110, 115–16
Paul the Hermit, St   79, 82, 85, 88, 130; *see also*: Jerome, St
peace councils   44–5, 46–7, 100
penance; *see* arms-bearers, penance of
Perpetua, St   133
Peter Damian, St   23, 34–5, 47, 115–16, 117, 118, 132, 134, 137, 142, 144, 149, 190, 191
Peter of Celle, abbot   115, 121–2, 145
Peter of Dives, monk   142
Peter of Policastro, bishop   192
Peter, St   16, 17, 101, 116
Peter the Venerable, abbot   47–8, 54, 67, 109, 126, 141
Peter Tudebode, priest   106
Philip Augustus   63
Philip of Harvengt, canon   39
Philip of Navarre   52
picturae   114, 119, 121, 124, 136, 138, 143, 147–9
plates, metal   22, 191, 193
Polycarp of Smyrna, bishop   75
Pons of Cluny, abbot   47–8
Pons of Léras, abbot   169, 174–5
prayer   28–37, 79, 81, 86, 88, 108, 113, 121, 135, 147, 153, 154, 160, 162, 188, 191, 196, 197
for victory   28–31, 49
preaching, monastic   116, 119–20, 124–5, 134, 136, 141, 142–3, 144–5, 147, 149–52
Premonstratensians   52, 68, 172
see also: Geoffrey of Cappenberg; Norbert of Xanten; Philip of Harvengt; Simon of Crépy
pride   79, 82, 98, 134, 135, 136, 137, 164, 165, 169, 180
priests   33–4, 46, 59, 190
as spiritual warriors   33–34
Prudentius; see *Psychomachia*
Psalms:
exegesis of; *see* exegesis, of Psalms
martial imagery in   9–10, 38, 144
memorization of   24, 60
place in monastic liturgies   9–10, 37, 135, 191, 197
Psychomachia   75, 123–4
purity, reformers' concern with   40–1, 44–5, 46–7

Rainoart, epic hero   161
Ralph Glaber, monk   42, 65
Ralph Haget, abbot   174
Ralph of Beaugency, nobleman   2

Raphael, archangel   54
Raymond of Aguilers, priest   15, 32, 105, 106
Raynerius of Osnabrück, recluse   195
Redon, abbey   62
Reims, cathedral   176
Reinfrid, re-founder of Whitby   169
relics   176–7, 187, 188, 195
    weapons venerated as   185–7
Remigius of Auxerre, monk   27
Reynald, recluse   135
Richard of Heudicourt, monk   56
Robert I, count of Flanders   65
Robert of Arbrissel, hermit and preacher   131, 193
Robert of Châtillon, monk   127
Robert of Grandmesnil, abbot and bishop   60–1
Robert of Molesme, abbot   136, 141, 169
Robert of Moncontour, monk   56
Robert of Reims, monk   14, 105, 106
Robert of Saint-Pierre-sur-Dives, abbot   67
Robert of Turlande, abbot   175
Roger Montgomery, earl of Shrewsbury   36
Romuald of Ravenna, hermit   118, 190
Rule of Benedict   10, 12, 88, 90, 92–6, 104, 116, 121, 122–3, 129, 130–1, 132, 162, 184, 185, 196
    commentaries on   94–6
        see also: Hildemar of Corbie; Smaragdus of Saint-Mihiel
rules, monastic   89–96

Saint Albans Psalter   138–9
Saint-Avit-Sénieur, priory   159; *see also*: Avitus of Sarlat
Saint-Benoît, Fleury, abbey   30, 43, 88–9, 121, 158
Saint-Denis, abbey   30
Saint-Évroul, abbey   56, 60; *see also*: Orderic Vitalis
Sainte-Foy, Conques, abbey   47
Saint-Florent, abbey   67
Saint-Gall, abbey   158
Saint-Germain-des-Prés, abbey   30–1
Saint-Julien, Brioude, abbey   158, 163, 185
Saint-Martial, Limoges, abbey   124
Saint-Martin, Tours, abbey   42
Saint-Maur-des-Fossés, abbey   172, 182
Saint-Médard, Soissons, abbey   158–9, 182–3
Saint-Sulpice, priory   119
Saint-Yvione, abbey   67
saints:
    as protectors of religious communities   30–1

miracles of   30–1, 176–7
Satan; *see* devil, the
Scriptures; *see* exegesis; *lectio divina*
Sebastian, St   157, 158–9
Selby, abbey   174
sermons, monastic; *see* preaching, monastic
Sicard of Cremona, bishop   33
siege, allegory of   128, 132–3, 147–53; *see* monasteries, allegorized as castles
Silvanès, abbey   169, 175
Simon of Crépy, count   172
simony   40–1, 44, 190
single combat, allegory of   96, 130–9, 143–4, 176; *see also*: solitary life, and spiritual warfare
Smaragdus of Saint-Mihiel, abbot   94–5, 96
solitary life   79–83, 126, 129, 130–5, 139, 165, 169, 188, 190, 196, 199
    and spiritual warfare   93, 95, 96, 130–5, 139
    see also: Christina of Markyate; Dominic Loricatus; Eva of Wilton; Gilbert of Senlis; Godric of Finchale; Grimlaicus; Reynald; Robert of Arbrissel; Wulfric of Haselbury
Solomon   127
soul, as fortress   147, 148, 150–2
spiritual warfare; *see* warfare, spiritual
spiritual weapons; *see* weapons, spiritual
Stephen Harding, St and abbot   136, 141
Stephen of Autun, monk   184
Stephen of Chalmet, monk   118
Stephen of Monceaux, nobleman   68–9
Stephen of Muret, St and hermit   171, 192, 193
Stephen of Obazine, St and hermit   68, 192, 193
Stoicism   19
Sulpicius Severus, hagiographer   77–8, 79, 85–7, 89, 99; *see also*: Martin, St
sword-belts   78, 91, 104, 174, 177, 178, 181, 182, 183–5, 186
    see also: weapons, renunciation of
swords   177–8, 79, 182, 187
Sylvester II, pope   178

Templars   107–9, 111
    see also: Bernard of Clairvaux, *De laude novae militiae*; Everard of Barres; Hugh de Payns
Tertullian, theologian   76
Theban Legion   31, 78, 157, 158; *see also*: Maurice, St
Theodore, St   158
Thibaud of Provins, hermit   168

Thomas Aquinas, St 91
Thomas of Perseigne, monk 32, 151
Thundering Legion, legend of 77
tiro, tirones, monks as 70, 114, 115–21, 126, 142, 170, 198
tonsure 43, 62, 181, 183; *see also*: monks, profession rites of
Turks; *see* Muslims

Urban II, pope 14, 48, 102–5; *see also*: Clermont, council of

Vallombrosans 103, 130
Venantius Fortunatus, bishop 17
Vikings 14, 30, 31, 169
Virgin Mary 150, 183
virtues and vices 4, 60, 81, 82, 90, 92, 93, 123–4, 134, 148, 152, 154, 156, 157, 165, 166, 172–3, 174
    see also: acedia, anger, avarice, envy, chastity, gluttony, humility, lust, obedience, pride, *Psychomachia*, vainglory
Vision of Gunthelm 54, 61

Walafrid Strabo, monk 26–7
Waldebert of Luxeuil, abbot 185
Walewan, knight 183
Walter Espec, nobleman 67–8
Walter of Aquitaine, epic hero 161–2, 165
Waltherius; see Walter of Aquitaine
warfare, secular:
    as a divine ordeal 64–5
    as *malitia* 41, 49, 50, 51, 104, 155, 168, 171
    churchmen's attempts to regulate 49–51, 97–102
    clerical participation in 45–50
    penances associated with 50, 64–5; *see also*: arms-bearers, penance of
warfare, spiritual 6, 9, 71–111, 112–55, 156–99
    as meditative practice 112–55
    compared to worldly warfare 92, 94–5, 99–100, 113, 119–20, 124–5, 155, 162, 163, 166, 167, 173–6, 183, 186, 198
    depicted in manuscripts 137–9
    development of concept of 71–111
    training in 114–21
    vocabulary of 73, 112–55, 197

    see also: weapons, spiritual; specific allegories: pitched battle; siege; single combat
warrior-saints 156, 157–66, 176
    see also: Demetrius; Eustace; George; Maurice; Sebastian; Theodore
warriors, lay; *see* arms-bearers
Watten, priory 65
weapons 62–3, 176–87
    as markers of status 177–9, 181
    blessing of 177, 179, 180
    clerics forbidden to carry 43–8, 120
    renunciation of 62–3, 69, 163, 169–70, 178–9, 181–7
    venerated as relics 177, 185–6
    see also: armor; sword-belts; swords
weapons, spiritual
    compared to weapons of lay warriors 18, 19, 22, 26, 33, 82, 92, 97, 106, 108, 115, 118–21, 135, 136, 144, 149, 151, 158, 163, 185, 189
    liturgical vestments as 33–4
    Pauline model of 18, 33, 76, 82, 119, 124, 136, 149, 189
    see also: warfare, spiritual
Whitby, abbey 169
William I, king of England 32, 50, 64, 169
William *Firmatus*, hermit 193
William Fitzwalter, nobleman 195
William Giroie, monk 53
William of Gellone, nobleman 98, 159–60, 162–5, 185–6
William of Llanthony, hermit 194
William of Nevers, count 53
William of Pavia, bishop 102
William of Poitiers, priest 32
William of Saint-Thierry, abbot 2
William of Tocco, friar 91
William of Vercelli, hermit 195
William of Volpiano, abbot 57
women:
    as recluses 133–5, 138–9
    as spiritual warriors 76, 84, 133, 135, 138–9, 145–6, 199
wrath; *see* anger
Wulfric of Haselbury, recluse 187, 193–4, 195

Other Volumes in
Studies in the History of Medieval Religion

I: Dedications of Monastic Houses in England and Wales 1066–1216
Alison Binns

II: The Early Charters of the Augustinian Canons of
Waltham Abbey, Essex, 1062–1230
Edited by Rosalind Ransford

III: Religious Belief and Ecclesiastical Careers in Late Medieval England
Edited by Christopher Harper-Bill

IV: The Rule of the Templars: the French text of the Rule of
the Order of the Knights Templar
Translated and introduced by J. M. Upton-Ward

V: The Collegiate Church of Wimborne Minster
Patricia H. Coulstock

VI: William Waynflete: Bishop and Educationalist
Virginia Davis

VII: Medieval Ecclesiastical Studies in honour of Dorothy M. Owen
Edited by M. J. Franklin and Christopher Harper-Bill

VIII: A Brotherhood of Canons Serving God: English Secular
Cathedrals in the Later Middle Ages
David Lepine

IX: Westminster Abbey and its People c.1050–c.1216
Emma Mason

X: Gilds in the Medieval Countryside: Social and
Religious Change in Cambridgeshire c.1350–1558
Virginia R. Bainbridge

XI: Monastic Revival and Regional Identity in Early Normandy
Cassandra Potts

XII: The Convent and the Community in Late Medieval England:
Female Monasteries in the Diocese of Norwich 1350–1540
Marilyn Oliva

XIII: Pilgrimage to Rome in the Middle Ages: Continuity and Change
Debra J. Birch

XIV: St Cuthbert and the Normans: the Church of Durham 1071–1153
William M. Aird

XV: The Last Generation of English Catholic Clergy:
Parish Priests in the Diocese of Coventry and Lichfield in
the Early Sixteenth Century
Tim Cooper

XVI: The Premonstratensian Order in Late Medieval England
Joseph A. Gribbin

XVII: Inward Purity and Outward Splendour:
Death and Remembrance in the Deanery of Dunwich, Suffolk, 1370–1547
Judith Middleton-Stewart

XVIII: The Religious Orders in Pre-Reformation England
Edited by James G. Clark

XIX: The Catalan Rule of the Templars:
A Critical Edition and English Translation from Barcelona,
Archito de la Corona de Aragón, 'Cartes Reales', MS 3344
Edited and translated by Judi Upton-Ward

XX: Leper Knights:
The Order of St Lazarus of Jerusalem in England, c.1150–1544
David Marcombe

XXI: The Secular Jurisdiction of Monasteries
in Anglo-Norman and Angevin England
Kevin L. Shirley

XXII: The Dependent Priories of Medieval English Monasteries
Martin Heale

XXIII: The Cartulary of St Mary's Collegiate Church, Warwick
Edited by Charles Fonge

XXIV: Leadership in Medieval English Nunneries
Valerie G. Spear

XXV: The Art and Architecture of English Benedictine Monasteries, 1300–1540:
A Patronage History
Julian M. Luxford

XXVI: Norwich Cathedral Close: The Evolution of the
English Cathedral Landscape
Roberta Gilchrist

XXVII: The Foundations of Medieval English Ecclesiastical History
Edited by Philippa Hoskin, Christopher Brooks and Barrie Dobson

XXVIII: Thomas Becket and his Biographers
Michael Staunton

XXIX: Late Medieval Monasteries and their Patrons:
England and Wales, c.1300–1540
Karen Stöber

XXX: The Culture of Medieval English Monasticism
Edited by James G. Clark

XXXI: A History of the Abbey of Bury St Edmunds, 1182–1256:
Samson of Tottington to Edmund of Walpole
Antonia Gransden

XXXII: Monastic Hospitality:
the Benedictines in England, c.1070–c.1250
Julie Kerr

XXXIII: Religious Life in Normandy, 1050–1300:
Space, Gender and Social Pressure
Leonie V. Hicks

XXXIV: The Medieval Chantry Chapel: An Archaeology
Simon Roffey

XXXV: Monasteries and Society in the British Isles
in the Later Middle Ages
Edited by Janet Burton and Karen Stöber

XXXVI: Jocelin of Wells: Bishop, Builder, Courtier
Edited by Robert Dunning

XXXVII: War and the Making of Medieval Monastic Culture
Katherine Allen Smith

XXXVIII: Cathedrals, Communities and Conflict in the
Anglo-Norman World
Edited by Paul Dalton, Charles Insley and Louise J. Wilkinson

XXXIX: English Nuns and the Law in the Middle Ages:
Cloistered Nuns and Their Lawyers, 1293–1540
Elizabeth Makowski

XIV: The Nobility and Ecclesiastical Patronage in
Thirteenth-Century England
Elizabeth Gemmill

www.ingramcontent.com/pod-product-compliance
Lightning Source LLC
Chambersburg PA
CBHW070342240426
43665CB00046B/2427